Supervision

Supervision
THE ART OF MANAGEMENT

George L. Frunzi, Ed.D.
Wilmington College

Jack Halloran

THIRD EDITION

Prentice Hall
Englewood Cliffs, New Jersey 07632

Library of Congress Cataloging-in-Publication Data

Frunzi, George L.
    Supervision : the art of management / George L. Frunzi, Jack
Halloran.
        p.   cm.
    Includes bibliographical references and index.
    ISBN 0-13-876947-8
    1. Supervision of employees.   2. Personnel management.
I. Halloran, Jack   II. Title.
HF5549.H276   1991
658.3'02—dc20   90-38240
                                                                      CIP

Acquisitions editor: Maureen Hull
Editorial/production supervision: Mary McDonald
Interior design: Karen Buck
Cover design: Singer Design
Prepress buyer: Ilene Levy
Manufacturing buyer: Ed O'Dougherty

© 1991, 1986, 1981 by Prentice-Hall, Inc.
A Division of Simon & Schuster
Englewood Cliffs, New Jersey 07632

Printed in the United States of America
10 9 8 7 6 5 4 3 2

ISBN   0-13-876947-8

Prentice-Hall International (UK) Limited, *London*
Prentice-Hall of Australia Pty. Limited, *Sydney*
Prentice-Hall Canada Inc., *Toronto*
Prentice-Hall Hispanoamericana, S.A., *Mexico*
Prentice-Hall of India Private Limited, *New Delhi*
Prentice-Hall of Japan, Inc., *Tokyo*
Simon & Schuster Asia Pte. Ltd., *Singapore*
Editora Prentice-Hall do Brasil, Ltda., *Rio de Janeiro*

To the Memory of

Jack Halloran

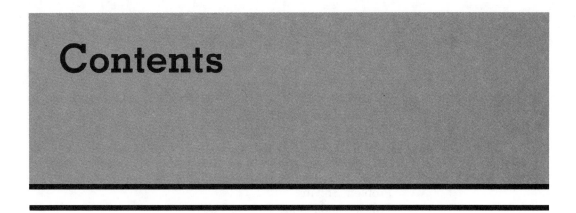

Contents

PART II: The Organization

PART IV: Special Concerns

Preface

The field of supervision has changed significantly during the past two decades. Not only have new approaches and concepts been developed, but interest in supervision has increased and has moved into every conceivable type of institution. Today, supervisory seminars are held in all types of organizations—public agencies, educational institutions, hospitals, military installations, service companies, and manufacturing organizations. Some organizations send their supervisors and supervisors-to-be to training sessions and seminars conducted by independent managerial consultants to sharpen the employees' skills and/or to prepare them for the exciting challenge of supervision.

This book was written to meet the ever-expanding need for a practical resource that can be used as a text for supervision courses offered at community and junior colleges, adult schools, extension programs, and internal supervisory training and development seminars and workshops. The direct, straightforward language emphasizes the person in the organization rather than traditional theories of management and supervisory philosophy. Effort has been made to relate actual examples to each situation.

The book represents an attempt to integrate basic supervisory research and present it in a practical, down-to-earth manner. In effect, it is the ability to practice effective supervision that makes the difference in the long run.

ORGANIZATION

The text is divided into four parts, each focusing on a major topic within the scope of supervision and management. Part I presents concepts and practices that describe the challenge of supervision. Subjects discussed include attitudes, morale, individual behavior, group behavior, and motivation. Part II discusses the role of the supervisor within the organization. Included are chapters on supervisory functions, goal setting, management by objectives, structure, delegation, responsibility, and organizational development. Part III examines the role of the supervisor and the employee. Recruiting, selecting, training, appraisals, counseling, leadership, and communication are covered in this section. Part IV explores the supervisor and special interests. Decision making, problem solving, conflict, change, special groups, unions, and stress and burnout are examined here.

A standard format is used throughout the book. Each chapter begins with a list of objectives and ends with a chapter summary. Following the summary, brief case studies are included for discussion and application purposes. Also, a checklist of terms and concepts is presented for reinforcement; practical discussion questions are provided to stimulate additional thought; and a selected reading list is offered to encourage the student to explore the topics for more ideas.

ACKNOWLEDGMENTS

My students over the past 20 years deserve a special note of thanks. Their questions, discussions, and general thirst for knowledge helped to formulate and reinforce my understanding of the supervisory process. I wish to express my appreciation to Wilmington College, Wesley College, the University of Delaware, and Delaware Technical and Community College for opportunities to teach and learn. Also, I wish to extend my thanks to the many companies and organizations that provided me with the chance to offer seminars, workshops, and developmental sessions over the years.

As this book enters the third edition, it is only fitting that all reviewers be recognized for their special contributions. My appreciation for these efforts is extended to Richard H. Barnett, Purdue University, West Lafayette, Indiana; Maurice H. Boutelle (retired), Brevard Community College, Brevard County, Florida; William Davenport, Broome County Community College, Binghamton, New York; Norman Ellis, Tarrent County Community College, Hurst, Texas; Charles F. Falk, Northern Illinois University, De Kalb; Charles Freedman, Dutchess Community College, Poughkeepsie, New York; Ed. A. Giermak, College of DuPage, Green Ellyn, Illinois; Eugene E. Holeman, Baltimore, Maryland; Steven Levy, California State University, San Bernardino; Dorothy Maass, Delaware County Community College, Delaware County, Pennsylvania; Eugene E. Mielke, Normandale Community College, Bloomington, Minnesota; Joan D. Minch, Cabrillo College, Aptos, California; Michelle L. Slagle, George Washington University, Washington, DC; and George H. Sutcliffe, Central Piedmont Community College, Charlotte, North Carolina. Their ideas, suggestions, and guidance helped to improve the content and accuracy of this edition.

Ralph Lopez and Winifred (Fred) Way enriched the quality of the chapters with their drawings and illustrations.

Special thanks are extended to Sally DeLoy, Michele Perry, Dianne C. Ayrey, and Dana Abbott-Painter for their unique ability to decipher rough drafts and convert them into smooth and accurate manuscript copy.

A special note of acknowledgment is due to Brenda Kaiser for her grammatical and editorial expertise. Her willingness to help was exceeded only by her generosity. Also, words cannot express the contribution made by Pat Savini—my friend, associate, and partner. In so many ways, the text reflects our thinking and beliefs about supervision.

The Prentice Hall staff is responsible for making the project possible. To Read Wickham—Thank you for the opportunity! To Esther S. Koehn—Thank you for all your help. To Whitney Blake—Thank you for making the third edition a reality.

George L. Frunzi

What Is Supervision?

"The man who knows **how** *will always have a job. The man who knows* **why** *will always be his boss." (Ralph Waldo Emerson)*

LEARNING OBJECTIVES

When you complete this chapter, you should be able to:
1. Identify and discuss the trends that affect supervision.
2. Understand the difference between technical skills, human skills, and administrative skills, and their role in the management and supervisory process.
3. Identify the five functions of supervision and management, and explain the major characteristics of each function.
4. Indicate the logical sequence of the supervisory and managerial functions.
5. Realize that people are the key ingredient of each function.

"The success of others is often generated by the confidence we have in them."

Here are some questions to contemplate while reading this chapter. Some answers are given in the chapter, while others are only a matter of opinion. A discussion among your colleagues may draw forth feelings that are quite different from yours—and worth considering.

To be a good supervisor, is it important to be "one of the team"?

What is one of the hardest roles of a supervisor?

Which is better: specific or general supervision?

What are the five major aspects of supervision?

THE CHALLENGE OF SUPERVISION

As the world changes, so does the role of the supervisor. The American labor force is becoming both larger and more educated. When 1970 started, approximately 75 percent of the labor force had completed high school, as compared with 60 percent in the decade before. In 1980 some ten million potential workers were enrolled in colleges. Both the amount and the variety of education being offered have increased tremendously. As these trends continue, think of the supervisory challenge of the 1990s—and beyond.

More women in the work force

The work force has become dramatically more diverse in the last decade, and disadvantaged groups are making strong gains. As a result, the role of the supervisor has become correspondingly more complex and challenging. Many men have not worked for a woman manager before or had the experience of supervising a multicultural work force. Since forced retirement at age 65 can no longer be part of company policy, the age range of the work force will be even greater in the near future. A work force of adults from 18 to 80 could be possible. The differences in values of such a divergent work force places unique demands on today's supervisor.

No more forced retirement at 65

OSHA

Government regulations, unions, and the use of computers will add more pressure and scope to the role called "boss." The government will be looking out for the employees' health and safety through OSHA (Occupational Safety and Health Administration), but it may be costly to the company and frustrating to supervisors. Providing women workers with pregnancy benefits in terms of time off with pay will be part of the controversy that many supervisors will have to handle in the future, along with concerns about air and water standards in the work place.

Unions challenge supervisors

The unions have shop stewards in many work places to challenge the supervisor's authority. Understanding the goals and motives of union officials is a necessary part of the supervisor's job. The third-generation computers and minicomputers also will have a profound effect in every place of business. Supervisors need to know something about them, and to use them to their benefit and their employees' benefit as well. As people meet the challenges of the 1990s and prepare for the turn of the century, some are finding a reduction in work or even the cessation of work attractive. Unemployment payments and welfare budgets may take a toll. Financial rewards will be insufficient motivation for many workers. Leisure time may increase. The straight 8-hour day and 40-hour week may give way to modified schedules, or flex time. The 4-40—a 4-day, 10-hour-a-day work week—has entered the work environment. Some people now only work 30 hours a week, and the program of two people teaming up to fill a 40-hour work week is becoming more common.

More leisure time

Intrinsic motivation

Important in the new attitudes of some workers is the need for intrinsic motivation, which springs from an internal desire to do a meaningful job. Accomplishment and job growth are part of this meaningfulness. Real recognition for a job well done, as well as real decision-making power for an employee on how his or her job is done, will be among the foremost management concepts of the present decade.

The self-administered test in this chapter will help you evaluate your position today and your potential direction for the future.

TEST YOURSELF

Sᴏ Yᴏᴜ Aʀᴇ ᴀ Sᴜᴘᴇʀᴠɪsᴏʀ

1. So you are a supervisor or hope to become one. What was or will probably be the single most important item in your selection as a supervisor?
   a. Your managerial ability _____
   b. Your technical competence _____
2. What do you imagine was or is the most important item in the selection of your superior?
   a. The managerial ability _____
   b. The technical competence _____
3. How many people do you or will you supervise? _____
4. Although the workers you supervise obviously have or will have different feelings about you, in general what do they expect most from you as a supervisor?
   a. _____
   b. _____
   c. _____

5. Do the expectations you have listed seem to be more related to
   a. Managerial ability? _____
   b. Technical competence? _____
6. When you became or become a supervisor, you suddenly discovered or will discover that you were or are a "person in the middle." You were or are caught between the employees you supervise and your own superior. Part of the reason you are "caught" between the two is they expect different things from you. What would you say your supervisor expects of you?
   a. _____
   b. _____
   c. _____
7. Do the expectations you have listed seem to be more related to
   a. Managerial ability? _____
   b. Technical competence? _____
8. When an opportunity for your promotion comes along, what do you think will be the most important item?
   a. Managerial ability _____
   b. Technical competence _____
9. You have a certain amount of technical competence in your field and have gained more since you have worked in your department. Do you feel you can learn to develop better managerial ability?
   Yes _____ No _____
10. How have you developed managerial talent in the past? How could you better do it in the future?
11. You have probably been thinking about supervision for some time. What are some of the important aspects of managing?
   a. _____
   b. _____
   c. _____
   d. _____
   e. _____
12. This textbook lists some other functions that are basic to managing. According to Chapter 1 these are
   a. _____
   b. _____
   c. _____
   d. _____
   e. _____

THE ROLE OF THE SUPERVISOR

Supervisors are responsible for directing the work of subordinates. Their jobs may vary widely, depending on the structure of the organization and their level within the firm. Certainly the personalities of the manager and of his or her subordinates and the kind of job to be done all influence the role of the supervisor.

Emphasis on the first-line supervisor

This text will be devoted primarily to the first-level supervisor, who is the link between the rank-and-file employees and middle management. First, this supervisor must have a certain general knowledge of the company and its product as well as the technical competence to accomplish many of the assigned jobs. Second, the supervisor must be able to manage people in an efficient manner that is acceptable to them as well as to the supervisor's superior. Perhaps the ability to handle people is the more important of these requirements. As a person moves up the supervisory ladder, he or she will spend less time performing physical tasks and more time planning and coordinating. The managerial qualifications for the supervisor's position are too often neglected, and a person is made a supervisor without having been prepared. A new manager without training may, instead of running the department, be run *by* it.

It is believed that when people develop certain leadership qualities, they can be transferred from one situation to another. This theory of the transferability of supervisory skills from one department to another or from one situation to another was developed by Henri Fayol, who called it the *principle of universal management.* Do you feel his theory is applicable today?

Principle of universal management

For easier understanding, we may break down the duties of the supervisor into the various general areas, which are usually planning, organizing, staffing, directing, and controlling.

1. *Planning* represents the logical first step in the process. By definition, planning is *determining the goals to be accomplished and developing a scheme for achieving them.*
2. *Organizing* emerges from planning. It involves arranging a unity and sequence in order to accomplish predetermined tasks. By definition, organizing is *determining how work is to be segmented and coordinated.*
3. *Staffing* involves securing a qualified work force to perform desired tasks. By definition, staffing is *selecting, orienting, training, and compensating people according to organizational purpose and objective.*
4. *Directing* involves encouraging and inspiring employees to perform assigned tasks. By definition, directing is *leading and motivating people toward successful goal accomplishment.*
5. *Controlling,* the final stage of the process, involves objectively evaluating performance. By definition, controlling is *measuring performance against standards and taking corrective action if necessary.*

In summary, the five functions represent a sequential process. They are uniquely related yet distinctly independent (see Figure 1–1). As the process in action is reviewed, *planning* represents a "road map" that clearly identifies the point of destination. It sketches the path leading toward goal accomplishment. *Organizing* provides a breakdown of the tasks that must be accomplished for goals to be attained. While planning describes *what* is to be accomplished, organizing indicates *how* it will be accomplished. *Staffing* determines *who* will do the jobs. Proper organizing permits the formulation of job descriptions based on needed skills and

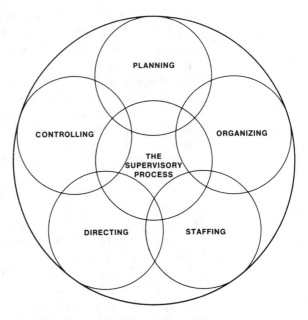

FIGURE 1–1 The five basic functions of supervision

talents. Staffing matches people to the appropriate jobs. *Directing* is the enthusiastic conveyance of *why* the job needs to be done and the ability to inspire its timely accomplishment. It involves daily communication with and motivation of the workers. *Controlling* objectively decides *if* the job has been done by ensuring that standards have been met. Controlling enables the organization to assess the relationship between expectations and reality. While planning determines expectations, controlling determines reality. In effect, the supervisor on the lowest or operative level of management ("the boss") probably will spend more time directing and controlling, while the executive near the top of the organizational ladder will spend more time planning and organizing, as shown in Figure 1–2.

PLANNING

Now that we have noted the five primary functions of a supervisor, let us study each in greater detail. We have seen that planning means determining in advance what should be done. It involves deciding the goals, policies, and procedures needed to achieve the objectives of the organization. It includes collecting and sorting out information from numerous sources to make decisions. As the su-

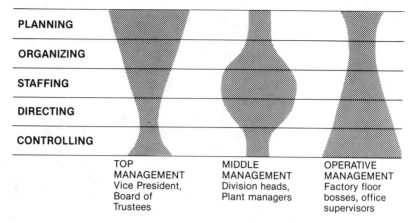

FIGURE 1–2   Division of duties by various levels of management

pervisor proceeds to act on his or her plans, he or she continues to revise them and choose different alternatives as necessary. This is particularly true as the supervisor evaluates the results of previous plans and adjusts his or her future plans accordingly.

Goal must be defined in detailed terms

Often the job is related to the supervisor by his or her superiors in very abstract terms, which the supervisor must translate into more concrete and detailed terms for subordinates. When you detail the parts of the job for your employees, you must take into account both the off-the-job factors and company factors. For example, as a mill supervisor in a machine factory you are responsible for turning out 500 parts a day. The task sounds simple, because you alone could turn out 150 parts a day. Now you have five people working for you, so they only have to average 100 parts per person. On your second day on the job, however, Henry becomes ill and Peter loses his father, and thus both of them will be out for the rest of the week. The next week a machine breaks down, so one person will be idle unless you can come up with a solution. Thus planning is interwoven with the duties of a floor supervisor.

The operative supervisor must be concerned with planning as it relates to tools, equipment, space, supplies, and available personnel. Top management must be concerned with setting long-range objectives, standard procedures, budgets, and forecasts.

Prepare to handle potential problems before they happen

Preparing to handle potential problems before they happen is another task of the supervisor. How well can you spot incidents that are symptomatic of a larger or growing problem? If deliveries of a product are slow, are you looking for another source? If a machine continually breaks down, are you suggesting buying a new one in the budget, anticipating that funds will not become available for about six months or a year?

ORGANIZING

At one time the supervisor was the "be-all and end-all" of the working group. He or she hired and fired, and was the fountain of all knowledge of the operations. The supervisor apportioned the work, decided how much someone was paid, fixed production rates, and in general had an authority that could hardly be questioned. The growing complexity of industry has changed this picture, however, and today's supervisor is surrounded by specialists of all kinds—work study experts, accountants, engineers, and personnel workers—some of whom he or she understands and is glad to rely on, and some of whom he or she distrusts thoroughly. The distrust develops because the specialists appear to take away some authority but leave the supervisor with the responsibility for all that goes wrong in the department. The relationship with staff advisors is more nebulous than that with subordinates or superiors. It is therefore important to understand the management structure and how supervisors operate within it.

Relationship with staff advisors

Supervision and Organizational Structure

Organizational structure may create difficulties

The way in which a supervisor carries out his or her job is defined and limited by the structure of organizations in general and of the supervisor's own organization in particular. This limitation makes supervision a difficult job, for at the first level of management relatively little flexibility may be allowed, and yet flexibility is the key to good human relations, because people vary so much. Structure by definition limits flexibility.

Other problems involving structure may arise also. The structure of an organization develops from its goals. A goal may be questionable, however, or it may conflict with larger goals. Workers will tend not to accept an organization's structure if they do not accept its objectives. If an organization establishes an inflexible structure of rules and regulations, it may thwart its own purposes. A social welfare organization that makes people afraid to apply for help, or makes conditions for securing help difficult, illustrates this point.

Structure serves purposeful activity

Nevertheless, there is hardly any purposeful human activity that does not benefit from *some* form of structure. A college student with five final exams in three days usually develops an informal structure for studying. When more than one person is involved in an activity, structure is usually essential for reasons of communication, division of labor, assignment of authority, and apportionment of rewards or losses from the activity. Modern business organizations may employ thousands of people, whose efforts must be coordinated toward certain common goals.

It is important for a supervisor to understand the structure of the organization. This understanding will make the job easier, more pleasant, and more productive.

STAFFING

Division of staffing tasks

Staffing includes recruiting, hiring, appraising, orienting, training, promoting, and compensating. These areas more directly affect all subordinates than any other form of supervision. As a company grows, some aspects of staffing may be performed by the human resource department. For example, the human resource department may recruit applicants through newspaper or magazine ads, using job descriptions provided by the supervisor. After an initial screening of applicants by a selection committee, the supervisor may make the final decision. The human resource department may organize the company training program, with certain phases being handled by an individual supervisor. Consideration of a promotion may involve interviews, reviews of personnel records, and conferences with several peers. The supervisor may have considerable influence in establishing or rewriting job descriptions, yet the total compensation package, including the wage and bonus system, may be established and implemented by the salary and negotiation staff in the human resource department with little or no input from the supervisor. As the separate staffing tasks in an organization become more scientific in approach, more coordination is needed to perform them all effectively.

DIRECTING

Directing includes the difficult tasks of leading, guiding, motivating, and teaching as well as supervising employees. It requires a special talent to encourage employees to work a little harder while enjoying their work more. This task also means helping people to accept more responsibility and to develop their potential to a greater degree.

The amount of direction a supervisor gives may vary. He or she is accountable to the company for the time, quantity, and quality of the work. The effects of these controllable factors can clearly be measured in cost accounting. If, as a supervisor, you were working only with machines, you might decide to monitor them continuously, but since you are working with people, you must understand how people respond to close supervision. In most cases, a supervisor who controls or supervises very closely reduces the

Close supervision is a threat

workers' effectiveness. Very close supervision is a threat to the workers. Most workers want enough supervision to be sure that they are doing their work correctly, and they may even ask for direction so that they can be sure of performing well enough to keep their jobs or to advance. Systems that allow workers to self-check their performance help ease the strain of direction and control.

The supervisor must devise systems that take into account various factors that affect the amount of control needed. Studies also show that cultural differences may affect the amount of control necessary for optimal productivity. American workers appear to want less supervision than do workers in other lands, a fact that may or may not be correlated with our democratic social patterns.

New workers need close supervision

The supervisor must also know when direction is a necessity. New workers usually need closer supervision than experienced workers. Projects that require a very high level of quality, such as missile programs, require a correspondingly complex and tight control system, as do jobs that are planned on a very tight schedule, as in the typing of government proposals.

Authority and Power

The supervisor's job is greatly influenced by power and authority. These terms are often confused, and some people think they are the same. Actually, in practice the terms, although related, are quite different. The supervisor must understand this difference as well as how the effective practice of each plays a significant role in the achievement of job objectives:

- *Authority* is the right or privilege of directing or requesting workers to do or to refrain from doing something. It includes the right to take disciplinary action if a subordinate refuses to do as he or she is told.
- *Power* is the ability to achieve the expected outcomes that emerge from supervisory directives. In effect, *authority* is the right to *tell* a subordinate what to do; *power* is the ability to *get* the subordinate to do it.

Formal authority is appointed

Informal authority is conferred

Authority can originate in two ways: (1) *formal authority* is given by the organization in appointing the first-line supervisor; and (2) *informal authority* is conferred upon the supervisor by his subordinates. Some humanists say that authority is given from above and that leadership is granted from below. A new supervisor should consider both aspects of his or her authority, since each weighs heavily in the practice of supervision.

Ambivalence Toward Authority

The manager's job is complicated by the ambivalence that most people feel toward authority. As Eric Fromm has suggested, most of us have complicated, mixed feelings toward independence and dependence. We value freedom, but sometimes we feel lost and anchorless when we have too much. We like protection, but we don't like interference. In other words, we are generally willing to tolerate and may even crave some aspects of our lives that are unpredictable and exciting, but we insist that most events occur as expected.

A research scientist, for example, may relish the novelty and uncertainty of laboratory work but insist that his or her secretary always be on call, that his or her technician give predictable responses, and that his or her car start with complete regularity. So it is with supervision. Employees want a certain amount of the freedom and excitement that come from self-determination, but they also want a dependable supervisor who gives security and the correct answers at the right time.

Employees want both freedom and security

Advantages to General Supervision

General supervision saves time

There are significant advantages to a general approach to supervision, which means giving overall information on how to perform a task without specifying how to execute every detail. If the manager oversees in general broad terms, he or she will have more time to handle his or her own job as a supervisor. In addition, a supervisor's detailed decisions are not likely to be as good as those of his or her employees, since they are usually closest to the problems. The broad approach gives employees a chance to develop their talents. It is difficult to teach employees how to make decisions without letting them make some. Finally, general supervision motivates employees to take more pride in results of their own decisions.

Earning Employee Approval

The supervisor can earn approval from subordinates in many ways, such as taking an active interest in workers, listening to their problems, giving praise when justified, and showing tolerance when mistakes are made. In fact, the existence of employee approval determines how the supervisor's acts are interpreted. If such a feeling exists, employees may tend to excuse their boss's mistakes rather than exaggerate them.

Two-way loyalty

Praise for good work is not enough; all people have bad days as well as good. The supervisor must demonstrate a consistent, personal loyalty to his or her subordinates. Until he or she has done so, the supervisor cannot expect loyalty to flow the other way: "One thing about Christianson, he does some things I don't care about, but I feel he'd stand behind us if we really needed him when things got rough; I can't say that about the other supervisors. That's why I am going to support him now that he is getting all that flak from the head office.''

Coping with Contingencies or the Unexpected

When plans go wrong, machines develop defects, materials turn out to be faulty, or operators have accidents, the supervisor is the person who has to cope with the problem. Dealing with the unforeseen is a major part of every supervisory job.

Technical, human relations, and conceptual aspects

Coping with contingencies has three broad aspects: technical, human relations, and conceptual. The technical aspect is the easiest to understand. Most people obtain their job because of their ability to do certain tasks. Their first promotion may be based on how much they know about the department and the technical aspects related to their particular positions. However, as a person is promoted up the ranks, the technical aspect becomes less important, and the abilities to work with people and to handle abstract ideas become more important. Figure 1–3 illustrates the varying mix of these three types of abilities.

The human relations aspect, or the ability to work well with people, will be important at any level, regardless of how many promotions one receives. More important at the upper levels is the conceptual skill, or the ability to put many unrelated ideas together to form new approaches to operating a department or a company.

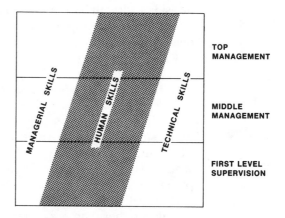

FIGURE 1–3 The three skills necessary in management leadership. Technical skill is most important to the first-line supervisor, and conceptual skill is the most important to the company president.

A company president spends time studying not only the firm's problems but also new laws, lobbying groups, community relations, and of course the competition. The president then uses the information on all these outside groups as well as on actions taking place inside the firm to decide the best path for the company to travel. The president's direction may seem intuitive, but it is actually based on information and feelings developed from a broad range of sources.

First-line bosses deal mostly with technical problems

Thus, in general, the most important type of problem to the line supervisor is the technical. A supervisor may deal with such contingencies as

1. Variations in the product or the raw materials
2. Shortage of raw materials
3. Breakdowns of machines
4. Shortages and variations of tools and equipment
5. Shortage of space

Top management, on the other hand, might have to deal with more broadly conceptual problems such as

1. Failure of a bank to grant a needed loan
2. Community objections to a new bank
3. Failure to receive a large sales contract that was expected
4. An unexpected strike

CONTROLLING

Deadlines require controls

As company goals are set into action through the organization, management sets objectives that include minimum standards and completion dates. The attempt to meet these goals entails meetings, reports, and feedback among peers, supervisors, and subordinates. If job deadlines are not met consistently, the manager must decide whether the workers are too slow, the deadlines are unrealistic, or external events are interfering. Management must remain flexible in redesigning company plans to adapt to problems as they are discovered.

Controlling means flexibility

Proper control means knowing how others operate

All aspects of an assembly line or of office work must be controlled so that work does not pile up in one area while workers are idle elsewhere. Systematic procedures must be established to move the initial sales order by the salesperson through the business office to the stock room to the transportation office. Control and coordination between departments are the responsibility of each manager. Too often the horizontal coordination, or the communication between managers, is forgotten by superiors.

It would not seem unreasonable that 20 percent or more of a supervisor's time is spent controlling the work of the employees in the department. Obviously, the responsibilities of the supervisor are more than just assuring that the employees are working. Besides controlling, the supervisor is responsible for planning, organizing, staffing, and directing. Often little time remains for the boss to be a working supervisor.

As a supervisor, however, don't expect your employees to understand completely your obligations and responsibilities. They see things through a different window.

REWARDS OF SUPERVISION

Obviously, you must believe that supervision has rewards, or you would not have considered holding such a position. A typical first-line or first-level supervisor should receive more income than subordinates. Other tangible rewards can include a title, a desk, or special privileges such as a company car. Additional benefits may be enhanced prestige, more flexible hours, and greater self-esteem.

However, most of us enter the ranks of supervisors for more intangible rewards. The satisfaction that one can do a better job in handling the position than one's peers is often a psychological reward in itself. We all enjoy accepting a challenge, and nothing can match the feeling that results from accepting one and doing an outstanding job. A job well done is soul satisfying.

SUMMARY

As the 1990s give way to the turn of the century, the role of supervision will be even more challenging. The work force will be even more educated, and workers may challenge arbitrary decisions made by the manager.

Differences in values from such a divergent work force place unique demands on today's supervisor. To meet these demands, the supervisor must depend on the efficient practice and application of the supervisory functions of planning, organizing, staffing, directing, and controlling. A supervisor will spend more time directing and coordinating, whereas the executive will spend more time planning and organizing.

Regardless of the level of management at which a supervisor performs, the human aspect commands approximately 50 percent of a supervisor's job. Interaction with people remains one of the most critically important elements of any supervisor's job. The remaining 50 percent is distributed between technical and managerial skills. *Power* and *authority* greatly influence the supervisor's job. These terms are often confused, but have different meanings in action and in operation.

The rewards of supervision are both tangible and intangible. Although a supervisor typically receives a higher salary than his or her subordinates, the intangible reward of accepting the challenge and doing a good job is a tremendous personal reward that is impossible to match.

CASE STUDY 1

Whom Would You Select?

A small company, Continental Celluloid, principally produces standard photography film for 35-millimeter cameras. John Thornley, the company's vice-president and production manager, was forced to retire because of illness. The company promoted Andy Oldham to fill his post. Andy was the only person within the company with the necessary qualifications to keep production rolling. That decision was easy, but now someone is needed to fill Andy's former job as head of research and development.

Andy's assistant, Tim Clarke, expects to be promoted into Andy's position. However, Andy is hesitant about having Tim promoted. He has been in research for only three or four years, and all his experience has been within the company. His performance has been adequate, but he has shown far from excellent ingenuity. It is likely that Tim will quit if he does not get the promotion.

Recently, Sam Guild, a skilled production technician from a competitor, applied for the position and stated that he required a higher salary than was listed. The new job opening would satisfy Sam's needs and challenges, and when he applied he did not hesitate to explain that he thoroughly understood the processes of Continental's competitors.

One of the newer workers, Ted Monroe, made the company's most important product improvement of the year. Although Ted has been with the company less than two years, he has more education than anyone on the research and development staff. His rapport with his peers seems excellent, and he has settled many disputes between the employees.

QUESTIONS

Whom should Andy Oldham select to head research and development?

1. Should he promote his assistant, Tim Clarke, rather than risk losing him?
2. Should he give Sam Guild the position in exchange for the knowledge of competitors he would provide?
3. Should he give Ted Monroe the position because of his education and his ability to get along with his peers?
4. What are the various possible ramifications of the selection of each candidate?
5. What factor seems to be most important in this case: technical competence or managerial ability?

(Refer to Figure 1–3 for ideas in solving the case.)

Terms and Concepts Supervisors Should Know

Authority; Close supervision; Controlling; Directing; First-line supervisor; General supervision; Managerial ability; Operative management; Organizing; OSHA; Planning; Power; Staffing; Technical competence.

Questions for Discussion

1. What are some of the trends in your locality that will affect supervision in the next few years?
2. Which is more important in the selection of a supervisor on your level: technical skill or managerial skill? Why?
3. How do you give instructions or orders? Be specific; give an example in writing or verbally.
4. What is the difference between authority and leadership?
5. What are the five functions of supervision? At which one do you spend the most time?

For Further Reading—And More Ideas

"Are You a Good Supervisor?" *Supervision* (March 1984).

Baker, H. Kent, and Steven R. Holmberg, "Stepping up to Supervision: Being Popular Isn't Enough," *Supervisory Management* (January 1982).

Baker, H. Kent, and Steven R. Holmberg, "Stepping Up to Supervision: Making the Transition," *Supervisory Management* (September 1981).

Bartolome, F., "Nobody Trusts the Boss Completely—Now What?" *Harvard Business Review* (March–April 1989).

Brodigan, J., "Pitch in to Win Workers," *Supervision* (February 1989).

Callarman, W. G., and McCartney, W. W., "The Supervisor's Place in Strategic Planning," *Supervisory Management* (May 1989).

Cole, D., "Do You Have What It Takes to Be Boss?" *Mademoiselle* (December 1983).

Denton, D. K., "Supervising the Younger Employee," *Supervisory Management* (March 1984).

Drake, R. T., "How Good a Supervisor Are You?" *Supervisory Management*, (March 1981).

Farrant, D., "Supervising Your Old Pals," *Supervisory Management* (March 1989).

Feuer, D., "Making the Leap (from Supervision to Management)," *Training* (December 1988).

Gerard, R., "Supervisor Apathy: How to Cure It," *Safety & Health* (January 1989).

Humphreys, L. W., and N. F. Humphreys, "Applying the Management Process to Your Work Day," *Supervisory Management* (March 1983).

Johnston, R. W., "What You Need to Know to Be a Supervisor," *Supervisory Management*, (March 1983).

Lippert, R. G., "Responsibilities of a Supervisor: On the Level?" *Supervision* (March 1983).

McClenahen, J. S., "Managing More People in the '90s," *Industry Week* (March 20, 1989).

McGarvey, R., "Taking Charge (Making the Transition from Worker to Manager)," *Executive Female* (November–December 1988).

Pulich, M. A., "The Supervisor's Relationship with Employees," *Supervisory Management* (March 1984).

Sharinger, Dale H., "Simplifying the Job of Supervision," *Supervisory Management* (January 1982).

Thornton, N. F., "What Is a Bad Supervisor?" *Supervision* (October 1983).

Weiss, W. H., "Supervise the Job—Don't Do It," *Supervision* (July 1982).

Woodruff, D. M., "Seven Steps to Better Employee Relations," *Supervisory Management* (January 1989).

Attitudes and Morale

2

"So that's what makes the employee happy?"

LEARNING OBJECTIVES

When you complete this chapter, you should be able to:

1. Give a working definition of morale.
2. Understand how individual attitudes affect the person's and the group's morale.
3. Identify the consequences of dissatisfaction on the job and how they affect the company.
4. Recognize the various life cycles in a person's career.
5. Understand the difference between the morale of the white-collar versus the blue-collar worker.
6. Discuss the philosophy behind the motto: "Self-confidence starts with the supervisor."

"Employees are more often released from their job because of their attitudes rather than their aptitudes."

This chapter will help you discover certain feelings about your work and how they relate to morale. Begin by considering the following questions.

Do you like your job, or do you find it boring?

How do you feel about the people you supervise?

Do you think you and your subordinates are paid enough?

What are your attitudes toward the company?

How do these attitudes affect your relations with your co-workers?

WHAT IS MORALE?

Morale is the attitude of each individual in a group toward the group's purposes and goals. It is always present in some form, although it may change from moment to moment. People are more apt to notice morale when it is conspicuously high or low. High morale develops over a long time, is difficult to maintain, and often is taken for granted. If morale is low, sometimes little else is noticed.

Like health, morale requires regular attention

In the same way that health is important, so is morale. Both require regular attention, diagnosis, and treatment.

Morale has been defined as a state of mind and emotions. Morale is a composite of the feelings of individuals and groups toward life, environment, and work. It affects our own attitude, which in turn affects the attitude of others. It can vary from positive to negative at any time, yet for all its evasiveness, good morale is vital to an organization.

People need recognition in work

Most would agree that people need personal recognition. Work, more than any other activity, is a source of such recognition. Recognition in work gives a sense of pride, a feeling of personal fulfillment, and an uplift in morale. Denying people this recognition causes them to become bored and frustrated.

Importance of the Employee's Attitude

Attitude is important to success

An employee's attitude is an important factor in determining his or her job success. Repeated studies reveal that an employee is more often released because of poor attitude than because of inefficiency. Similar studies show that when a supervisor fails to attain his or her objectives, the cause is closely related to attitude. Often it is not *what* supervisors do, but rather *how* they try to do it—not what they say, but rather how they say it—that determines their success in working effectively with people.

In modern industry, morale is closely related to productivity and the attainment of work objectives. The morale of everyone within the company—supervisors and employees alike—largely determines the company's success.

THE CHANGING ENVIRONMENT

The philosophies of management and supervision in organizations have undergone major changes during the last 50 years. Several changes in the composition of the work force require supervisors to pay more attention to human relations. In general, the manager must adapt to changing worker needs and job situations.

Educational levels continue to increase

The educational level of the working population has risen dramatically. The proportion of Americans between the ages of 25 and 34 with four years of high school has doubled since the 1940s. Currently, more than 80 percent of the work force fits in this category.

Additionally, the trend toward the increased participation of individuals and work groups requires supervisors to be technically proficient in people skills in order to practice leadership principles effectively.

These deal with motivating and controlling employee performance, participation, adjustment, and cooperation.

Stan Kossen outlined the following reasons for supervisors to show increased concern for human relations and what he called the "quality of worklife"[1]:

1. The significant increase in the education of today's workers, who as a result demand more from their jobs and their employers
2. The court protection of worker groups since the 1930s
3. More university-trained managers with greater understanding of human relations
4. Increased publicity about employment problems among special groups, such as minorities and women, that require a greater awareness and sensitivity by managers
5. Changing attitudes toward work and leisure, which demand that managers develop new attitudes toward work as a major pursuit
6. The changes in the work environment—for example, the greater

---

[1] Stan Kossen, *The Human Side of Organizations* (New York: Harper and Row, 1983), pp. 12–13.

specialization of work activities, the larger scope of operations, and the introduction of "steel-collar workers" (robots) to the production line—that require managers to work more effectively with and through existing organizational members

7. Greater managerial concern for increased product quality and productivity as a result of the intense competition from Japanese manufacturers

Effective management is vital to an organization's success, and a thorough understanding of human relations is vital to effective management.

Work and Leisure

Work is an important aspect of life because it gives us the income to satisfy our basic needs. It also gives us the feeling of being part of a larger society and of having a purpose in life. The success of the Peace Corps suggests that many seek meaning in their work as a way of finding meaning in their lives.

We seek meaning in work; it has to have importance

The importance of work in our society is reflected in our reaction to unemployment and retirement. We have all heard the comment, "After Dad retired, he just fell apart. He didn't know what to do with himself."

Today people in many occupations spend less time on the job than they did in the past. A half-century ago the six-day work week was the rule, and vacations were rare. Today few people work more than five days a week. In addition, our life span grows longer, and retirement can occur anytime between 55 and 72 years of age.

The four-day work week allows for three-day leisure weekends for many; for others, it provides a chance for "moonlighting." With the advent of flexible working hours or work weeks, some people have become "workaholics," while others have become "surf bums" or "free agents" who seek new self-expression away

Work may not be central to some people's lives

from work. Work is not central to the lives of the latter. Creative endeavors off the job are their personal paths to self-development. Such people frequently tell their supervisors that they are unable to work more than 30 or 40 hours. To force more work from them may lead them to leave their jobs suddenly. If supervisors allow such self-expressive people to determine their own schedules, they will often perform better.

Many argue that it is impossible to compartmentalize work and leisure activities, and that expanded leisure activities will never substitute for what is missing on the job. Some companies do their best to combine leisure and work by providing child care, bowling alleys, swimming pools, and gyms on the company grounds. If such programs are satisfactory to both the company and the employees, then the work and play do not occupy two separate spheres. It is when both spheres are very different that the employees must decide which is more important.

Dissatisfaction with the Job

According to Gerald Susman, author of *Autonomy at Work*, both society and individuals suffer when many workers are dissatisfied with their jobs. Approximately 15 to 20 percent of the work force, some 20 million persons, are dissatisfied. This dissatisfaction is found primarily in assembly-type work and in clerical work in large firms.

One such worker is Cal Shaw, who has been earning his living by pulling heavy cases from a moving belt and shoving them toward the loading docks. "You're on half an hour, you're off half an hour," Shaw says. "That's four hours of real physical labor. The other time you're looking for leakers." Sometimes Shaw and the other workers get violent headaches from these "leakers," which are fumes released by chlorine and muriatic acid, but the worst part of the job is the tedium. Echoing others, Shaw says, "This job is very monotonous." He has a typical small-cog-in-the-wheel feeling. "Being a peon, I don't have any say in the company," he complains. "The waste bothers me, but I'm not in a situation where I can say anything." He doesn't plan to make a career of his job, and like many others, he lives from day to day on vague goals.

In contrast to Shaw, some workers do not find boredom an everyday problem and have actually found reward in what would seem to be a dull task. One toll collector said, "It's just a type of job that you accept for what it is." When traffic slows up, he and other workers converse over the intercom. He often sings to himself and even whips out his harmonica. To some, boredom is in the person, not in the job.

Managers must nurture their people

Managers must cultivate an environment in which people can grow both personally and professionally. One management consultant feels very strongly that putting good people into the wrong job is like throwing good bricks and mortar into a vacant lot and expecting a building to materialize magically.

Consequences of Dissatisfaction

Underutilization of skills constitutes a loss to society. Dissatisfied workers have increased absenteeism as well as diminished productivity. Alcoholism and drug addiction resulting from dissat-

Longevity and job satisfaction are related

isfaction have economic consequences to society and unhealthy consequences for individuals. Research shows that longevity is correlated more highly with job satisfaction than with genetic or health factors.

THE MEANING OF WORK

Work is the mental and/or physical effort directed toward an individual or organizational goal. But whether people work as hard as they once did is a topic of debate. Some experts contend that the old American "work ethic" is alive and well in most organizations. Others contend that many workers just do enough to get by and point to recent quality problems as the proof. A strong case can be made for either argument, with both maintaining a degree of right and wrong.

Workaholics are a dying breed

Are workaholics as common today as they were 40 years ago? Times have changed, and so have attitudes about work. A workaholic sees work as the sole means of individual satisfaction. It is argued that the workaholic of yesterday is a dying breed, and that today's worker is more likely to adhere to the "leisure ethic."

The Work Ethic Versus the Leisure Ethic

A host of sociological and psychological forces have led to the shift away from the work ethic and toward the leisure ethic. Most successful people still believe in the work ethic, which includes the following characteristics:

1. Long days and hard work
2. Pride in one's work
3. High productivity
4. Loyalty to one's profession, work groups, and organization
5. Achievement orientation

Even though many individuals still identify with the work ethic, a new leisure ethic has emerged. Those workers subscribing to the leisure ethic display the following characteristics:

1. Work as a pathway to a desirable life style
2. Individual recognition
3. Minimum performance
4. Promotion as a means to make more money to pursue leisure activities
5. Self-loyalty

Whereas those who value the work ethic more highly "live to work," those who adhere to the leisure ethic "work to live." Those who emphasize the leisure ethic seek tangible job rewards to secure goals such as a boat, vacation house, or sports car. The work-oriented individual also seeks tangible rewards, but as a means of job security and organization betterment.

Ideally, supervisors can achieve unlimited goals with subordinates who subscribe to the work ethic. Unfortunately, a significant portion of the work force identifies with the leisure ethic, and this group is far more difficult to manage. Supervisors can attempt to make work more meaningful and challenging to them by implementing such techniques as job enrichment, job rotation, job design, quality circles, participative management, and equitable reward systems. But these are not easy tasks. Supervisors must handle such workers with extreme care and diligence.

Absenteeism: The High-Priced Headache

Every day from 3 to 7 percent of the work force is absent, representing a loss of $20 to $25 billion a year in wages. Absenteeism also incurs the significant expenses of training workers to fill in for absentees, disrupting production, and overstaffing to minimize the impact of absenteeism.

There appears to be a growing tendency among workers to shirk their job obligations. This is evidenced by failure to show up for work on a Monday or Friday before or after a holiday, or at such times as the opening of hunting season. The usual absentees are the dissatisfied worker, the alcoholic or drug user, the blue-collar worker, the assembly-line worker (especially in the auto industry), the laborer and the service industry worker. Companies most apt to have no-shows are those that offer sick-leave pay, and those that keep scanty records and are lax about absences.

In seven studies Victor H. Vroom, an industrial psychologist, found a consistent negative correlation between job satisfaction and turnover.[2] The higher the employee's satisfaction, the less likely it is that the employee will quit. Another negative relationship exists between job satisfaction and absenteeism; the happy employee is likely to be absent less frequently, particularly for unexcused reasons.

---

[2] Victor H. Vroom, *Work and Motivation* (New York: John Wiley and Sons, Inc., 1964).

Vroom also developed the "expectancy theory," which holds that human motivation is affected by anticipated rewards and costs. The employee will be motivated to work toward the company goal if he or she perceives that this will lead to the satisfaction of a personal goal and if the anticipated rewards outweigh the costs. As Figure 2–1 expresses in formula form, one's desire for a goal (valence) times what others expect of him or her and the ease of the path (expectancy) will equal a great deal of satisfaction and motivation.

To see Vroom's expectancy theory in action, suppose a worker desires to be promoted. This worker would thus ask the supervisor about what is required to be promoted. Suppose promotion results only from superior performance, which is defined as making at least 100 widgets per day with minimal absenteeism. The worker now understands the expectations required for promotion.

In effect, the most desired form of behavior to exhibit on the job would be superior performance, especially if *one opts for promotion*. Other behaviors fall short of expected outcomes, as demonstrated in Table 2–1. The worker must evaluate the importance of the promotion (valence), his or her ability to make 100 widgets (expectation), and management's ability to recognize and assess the above performance in proper evaluation (instrumentation).

INDIVIDUAL AND GROUP MORALE

Individual Morale

Our general outlook on life depends to a great extent on how we feel about ourselves. Our self-concept must be in a state of continuous renewal. As we pass through life, we accumulate habits and opinions that affect our general feeling. In simple terms, individual morale involves knowing one's own expectations and living up to them. If we recognize our needs and how to satisfy them, our morale will be high.

Valence (Strength of individual's desire for goal)	×	Expectancy (Ease of accomplishment and strength of others' expectations)	=	Motivation and job satisfaction

FIGURE 2–1   Vroom's expectancy theory

TABLE 2–1 Standards of worker performance

Standards of Performance	Absenteeism (Annually)	Instrumentation Result (Evaluation)
100 widgets per day (superior)	0–3 days	Promotion
75 widgets per day (above average)	4–7 days	Falls short
50 widgets per day (average)	8–11 days	Falls short
40 widgets per day (below average)	12–15 days	Falls short
Less than 40 widgets (undesirable)	15+ days	Falls short

Group Morale

Whereas individual morale is one person's attitude toward life, group morale is the general tone, or esprit de corps, of a group of personalities. Each person either heightens or lowers the concept of a cooperative effort. Group morale is everyone's business.

Workers may give extra effort to team success

To many workers, team work and team spirit are often more important than their individual achievement. This is especially true in groups of ten or less. Workers may also be more concerned with the team success than with the overall success of the company.

The final choice of a goal and of how hard to work to achieve it depends on two conflicting tendencies. One is a person's need for success; a person with strong success motives tends to choose challenging goals. The other is a person's fear of failure; a person with strong motives to avoid failure will choose goals that are either extremely easy or extremely hard. Groups operate in a similar manner. When members have a strong desire for their group to succeed, they tend to choose realistic goals and work hard for them. Members who strongly desire the group to avoid failure often choose very easy or very difficult goals, and they will not work very hard at either. It is understandable why groups select easy goals. Groups that choose unrealistic and difficult goals find scapegoats and cite outside forces as the reasons for not achieving them.

Working conditions that emphasize the negative consequences of failure actually reduce performance. Repeated failure gives group members a "Who cares?" attitude. Members of failure groups enjoy their jobs less, have less pride in their group, and tend to blame others for their failure. They feel their success is unimportant.

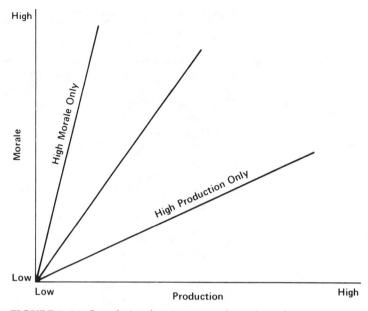

FIGURE 2–2   Correlation between morale and production

MORALE AND PRODUCTION

High morale doesn't mean high production

It is natural to believe that high morale will lead to high production. However, researcher Keith Davis points out that there is not always a positive correlation between the two.[3] A supervisor can push for high productivity by using scientific management, time studies, and close supervision. High production with low morale may result, but it is questionable whether this combination can last. The opposite—low production with high morale—can also occur. In this instance, the supervisor works so hard to please his or her subordinates that they are too happy to work hard for themselves. Relationships between morale and production are illustrated in Figure 2–2.

BLUE-COLLAR AND WHITE-COLLAR MORALE

Blue-Collar Blues

Today's jobs are not as likely to bring the same satisfaction earned by craftspeople such as the cabinetmaker or blacksmith of the last century. Work skills are now linked to machine operations,

---

[3]Keith Davis, *Human Behavior at Work: Organizational Behavior* (New York: McGraw Hill, 1977, 5th edition), pp. 75–76.

and what we make is mostly the product of other machines and other workers. The mechanized worker stands at a psychological distance from his or her work and is not identified with the end product. Often this type of employee is confined to a fixed work station and is expected to leave it only with permission. Such restrictions can affect one's attitude toward work.

Some blue-collar jobs are more meaningful

When work provides an opportunity for meaningful expression, as in the fields of carpentry, electricity, or plumbing, it becomes an end in itself, rather than simply a means to live. These blue-collar workers are engaged in a skill and can take pride in the end product.

A short job cycle can cause boredom

An important determinant of job satisfaction is the length of the job cycle—how long it takes to perform an operation before starting over. For a college professor the work cycle is often a semester. For a skilled craftsman it may be weeks, while for the worker on the assembly line it may last only a minute: "The job can get sickening, if it is only plugging in ignition wires. You get through with one motor, turn around, and there's another motor staring you in the face."

Most people like variety in their work rhythm; they may work fast for a while and then slow down gradually as the day wears on. Such change of pace helps to reduce both fatigue and job boredom. The assembly line offers few provisions for worker preference. The pace is set, and the worker may never be allowed to change it. Therefore, the machine may be a worse autocrat than any supervisor.

Variety helps break monotony

There are still many blue-collar jobs that are physically exhausting. Some workers must be on their feet a good deal of the time. For example, crane operators have to sit in one place for long, fatiguing hours, and some generator assemblers have to crouch. A change in body movement helps break the monotony.

The simpler the job, the less attention it needs. A doctor enjoys his or her work because it is constantly challenging and demands careful attention. Routine jobs are much like driving on a long, straight road with little traffic. Your mind is frequently hundreds of miles away, yet you are subconsciously still watching the road.

The opportunity for advancement in production plants is minimal, as there are few promotional steps. Because seniority is a common factor in manufacturing companies, promotions, layoffs, and "bumping" rights are based more on length of service than on merit. An eager worker can find little to satisfy motivational needs beyond pay and fringe benefits.

Employees invent games to add "spice" to the work place

To make work more enjoyable, many employees invent games that supply new goals. When job pressure is not tightly paced, the worker may experiment with various speeds and set various output goals. Social games frequently provide another form of diversion. Flipping coins to see who buys the coffee, World Series pools, number games, and other forms of gambling offer variety in the work place.

Many plants have depressing environments; they are old, poorly lighted, too hot or too cold, noisy, dirty, and smelly. All of these factors can contribute to low morale, which in turn affects job performance. Employees do appreciate clean, comfortable, cool, well-lighted, and airy work places and lounges where they can sit. Most supervisors know this, but some jobs are difficult to adapt to such universal desires.

Job Satisfaction in the White-Collar World

Banks, retail stores, hospitals, and service industries are providing more white-collar jobs than ever. Even in the factories the ratio of managers and engineers to production workers is growing. Research, design, marketing, and finance now offer more opportunities for white-collar people. Universally, white-collar work provides more prestige than blue-collar. The white-collar jobs are thought to give more individuality and are more likely to provide middle-class status. Industrial psychology has found that a job title such as "staff assistant" may provide an increased sense of advancement to an employee who was doing almost the same job when it was called "chief clerk."

A change in title can mean higher morale

White-collar jobs demand more intellectual than physical effort. Copywriters, programmers, and laboratory technicians all must display initiative and creativity. Such positions require a deep concentration of attention and a varied work pace, both of which tend to raise employees' morale.

When the assignment is going badly or deadlines are approaching, internal tensions are generated. Even the slightest inconvenience or friction can cause a blowup. Therefore, morale in the white-collar industry is likely to have wider variations. High morale occurs at the beginning of a project, low morale occurs as friction develops or the deadline comes closer, and either low exhaustive morale or high exhilaration can result upon completion of the task. The blue-collar industries are more likely to see a steady increase, decrease, or status quo in group morale.

There is a relationship between promotion and high morale

Several studies suggest that the higher someone is promoted, the higher his or her morale is likely to be. Perhaps those who are happy on the job are more likely to be promoted, and additional responsibilities seem to make promoted people happier. Top management people seem to enjoy work more than first-line employees. Consequently, you should not expect your subordinates to be as happy on the job as you are or to spend as much time on the job as you do.

There also seems to be some difference between the morale of men and women. Contrary to studies done ten and fifteen years ago, women are now less satisfied with their jobs, perhaps because of rising ambitions and expectations.

Professionals

A few concepts may help those who supervise professionals. Regardless of the location, professionals tend to be the most contented. However, you may find a real challenge in dealing with the individual teacher, engineer, physicist, psychologist, or doctor. The hospital administrator who deals with a doctor, for example, encounters delicate situations that will affect the administrator, the doctor, and the hospital. Almost every professional likes a challenging assignment and may even be a perfectionist, but you, as a supervisor, see the time constraints, the need for compromise, or the necessity of solving problems immediately. For example, rapid shifts in budgets may require engineers to abandon a favorite project even as completion is near.

Deal with professionals diplomatically

Professionals can be indifferent to rules and procedures. They may feel that an unorthodox method is better suited to their individuality and that more can be accomplished through their idiosyncrasies. The professional may also be more critical of management's decisions than of those of their fellow experts. The difference between the professional's wishes and the company's demands will require diplomacy in solving human relations problems and in maintaining maximum performance.

MAKING DULL JOBS MORE INTERESTING

Although the trend toward job enrichment is still experimental in many areas, industry is trying to inject interest and incentives into jobs that have become monotonous. Here are some ways to combat monotony:

1. Let the worker decide the pace of the line.
2. Let employees complete the whole assembly, not just one part.
3. Shift jobs on a rotating basis to provide variety.
4. Participate in the type of give-and-take sessions with management that medical team staffs have been using for years.
5. Utilize *quality circles.*

The whole job concept

With the *whole job concept*, the worker is responsible for assembling, finishing, and testing a complete unit, whereas with the

---

WOULD THESE FRINGE BENEFITS RAISE YOUR MORALE?

The Flick-Reedy Corporation in Bensenville, Illinois, which manufactures pistons and cylinders, gives high priority to employee happiness. Here are some company benefits:

The plant has its own coffee shop, cafeteria, swimming pool, auditorium/gym, chapel, tennis courts, and library.

A company-owned motel with showers and sauna is situated on the grounds. It is used by company salespeople and also by employees when the midwest blizzards make travel impossible. At the plant entrance are landscaped grounds and lagoons, which during the summer are stocked with fish. For those who do not fish, there is square dancing, swimming, bowling, tennis, volleyball, or target golf.

The factory workers are furnished with a set of six white shirts to wear at work, an indication of the surprisingly clean working environment. Long-time employees receive reserved parking spaces, and, while their parents work, children can stay on the premises in a special day-care program. The benefits are rooted in a company philosophy that places a high premium on both its workers and its products.

---

assembly-line approach, each worker is assigned one small, repetitive task. In one plant rejects dropped from 23 percent to 1 percent in the six months following the change from the assembly-line concept to whole-job concept. The company also found that absenteeism dropped from 8 to 1 percent and that productivity increased.

Another method of job enrichment is encouraging job participation by helping the hourly employees to realize that they are not part of a machine and challenging them to use their thinking abilities. The workers are involved in problem solving and planning instead of just routinely performing duties. Decision making leads to the expansion of responsibilities, and work teams hold regular discussion sessions to express complaints. A sense of pride and an achievement of increased efficiency are usually the outcomes of this method.

Job rotation   In job rotation, the work force is divided into three rotating teams for processing, shipping, and office duties. This method has reduced production costs to 10 to 48 percent below normal and pushed productivity up by 10 to 40 percent. Surprisingly, most team members were on the job 20 minutes early.

The new concept of office design dispenses with private executive offices, engraved nameplates, and impersonal rows of desks for secretaries and clerks. Employees are also allowed to decorate their work areas to suit themselves.

The trend is definitely toward making day-to-day chores more interesting and rewarding. Hopefully, by-products of this new concept will be happier employees and reductions in the high rate of turnover that has plagued many industries.

Quality Circle

In quality circles, the work force is divided into small groups with the objective of generating ideas that will improve job quality and job performance. This method has resulted in tremendous cost savings and job improvements. It provides employees with an opportunity for input and participation. Quality circles are used extensively in Japan and have become popular in the United States during the past few years. As they continue to grow in popularity, the pattern is to have employees explore day-to-day operations with the intent of improving aspects of the job to make it more challenging and satisfying. Ultimately, quality circles will produce strategies that result in higher productivity, lower costs, and greater profitability for the organization. Companies that have successfully used quality circles include General Electric, Ford, Rockwell International, American Airlines, General Motors, Westinghouse, and JC Penney.

Job enrichment

Job enrichment involves altering job tasks to make them more interesting and less confining. This is an excellent means of reducing monotony and making dull jobs interesting.

Supervisors must utilize job rotation, quality circles, and job enrichment with extreme caution. All these approaches are attempts to humanize the job, and make it more interesting and challenging. Research has proven that specialization has led to heightened productivity on one hand and monotony and boredom on the other hand. Supervisors must learn to create an effective balance by removing monotony and humanizing the job while still maintaining production goals and achieving objectives. Creating this balance is the challenge of supervision.

METHODS OF DETERMINING MORALE

Analysis of Records

Check company records first

What methods can industry use to ascertain employee morale? The first one is an analysis of the company's records. Heavy absenteeism, excessive tardiness, long lunch hours, early quitting, and poor safety records all could indicate low morale. Low production and high spoilage may be another indication. Finally, personnel records show the percentage of employee turnover, which in some industries can be expected to be 10 or even 20 percent.

Turnover can indicate morale

The human resource department should evaluate morale

The human resource department can certainly do much to evaluate the company's morale. Every employee who terminates his or her position should be given an exit interview in which he or she is encouraged to speak freely about the positive or negative aspects of the job.

The following records should give some indication of employee morale and should be reviewed before a company survey is attempted:

1. Labor turnover
2. Production records
3. Waste and spoilage
4. Absenteeism
5. Tardiness
6. Pilferage records
7. Grievance reports
8. Exit interviews
9. Safety records
10. Medical reports
11. Suggestion boxes
12. Production-quality records

Informal Questions and Answers

Another way to determine morale is to ask employees outright how they feel and what they want. Employees do not act on the basis of what management thinks or what management thinks they think; they act on their own opinions. One common mistake is for supervisors and management to assume that morale is high or low. They must instead take concrete measures to assess their employees' thoughts and feelings.

In many ways morale can be talked about informally. The larger the company, the more formal are the procedures needed to ensure channels of communication between employees and top management. Two time-honored methods of employee feedback are notes in a suggestion box and letters to management, with the latter sometimes finding a forum in the employee newspaper. Suggestions and letters do reflect individual satisfaction or discontentment, but they do not adequately represent the morale of an entire firm.

Personnel interviews discover personal feelings

Human resource specialists can hold confidential, informal interviews with employees. The success of this method depends on the impartiality of the interviewer and the degree of trust felt by the employee. Those who have complaints often prefer to remain anonymous for fear of reprisals.

Supervisors close to working groups can be asked to report periodically on employee morale. Often a supervisor may not be aware what employees are really thinking, especially when their morale is low *because* of the supervisor. Supervisors sometimes may be unwilling to reveal low employee morale because it reflects on their own professional competence.

Management executives can be encouraged to tour working areas and chat with employees to discover morale problems. But this kind of survey is spotty at best, and employees also may be more concerned with making a good showing than presenting complaints about their work situation.

Surveys

Employee surveys are the most comprehensive way to study morale. In a survey everyone is asked to respond to the same questions, thus giving management an accurate view of the general level of morale. Surveys can be conducted by impartial interviewers or through questionnaires. A combined survey approach would be to distribute a questionnaire to pinpoint problem areas and then to use the interview technique to discover details.

EMPLOYEE RESPONSES

Merely conducting a survey tends to boost morale by indicating that the company is interested in what employees think. Questionnaires that do not require employees to identify themselves add to the validity of the answers. One-page, concise questionnaires draw more response than multiple-page, wordy ones. Mail surveys are not as effective as those conducted personally.

If employees are to be interviewed, the best person for the task is a disinterested third party, such as a consultant. Employees are more likely to be honest with an outside source. Employees who are experienced in taking surveys and who are outside the direct chain of command also can be acceptable interviewers.

MANAGEMENT'S APPROACH TO A SURVEY

One reason a survey might fail is if management has no clear idea of the reason for conducting one. It is not enough to take an employee survey because a neighboring company is doing so; management must have definite purposes of its own. Management should also be wary of making assumptions about morale before a survey is taken, because preconceived notions can prejudice the results.

Define objectives; avoid preconceptions

The survey's basic approach has a great deal to do with its validity. Management's indifference, hostility, or fear is easily sensed by employees. The approach should always be, "What can be learned from the study?" rather than, "Whom can we find to blame?" If management is seriously interested in the results, employees will be likely to cooperate.

Once management has determined the questions, it must know how to ask them. Clear, direct questions elicit the most valid responses. If management wants to know whether employees are content with their working hours, it should ask, "Do you like your working hours? If not, what hours would you prefer?" If it wants to know how many employees are planning to leave the company and when, it should ask, "Are you planning to leave the company in the next three years?"

An example of a well-designed employee attitude questionnaire is given later in the chapter.

SELF-CONFIDENCE BEGINS WITH THE SUPERVISOR

Success and high morale in a department begin with the supervisor's self-confidence, which can be contagious. Psychologists claim that you need a large dose of confidence to succeed in business. Many leaders feel they are seriously lacking in this vital ingredient. Certainly, to be a successful supervisor, you must have a strong sense of self-confidence. You are the sole determiner of what you think about any circumstance; it's your choice. If you go into a situation with a negative and self-defeating attitude, you will destroy your self-confidence before you can act. Thus shift negative *You can shift to positive* thoughts such as "I'm not very good at this sort of thing," and *attitudes* "I've always been poor at speaking in front of groups" to affirmations such as "I'm going to work at this thing until I become good at it. I've been giving people too much power over me, and I'm going to stop worrying about it."

Self-expectations and self-confidence go hand in hand. If you expect that you will fail and that others will surpass you, it is unlikely that you will succeed. Start expecting to be effective, to succeed; see yourself as talented and do not worry about what others are thinking. You are deluding yourself if you blame others for your shortcomings. As a child, it may have been true that your self-confidence was affected by others, but you are now an adult, and you must assume the responsibility.

"Bag behaviors" are ways in which people enclose themselves and limit their development. Even their speech patterns, such as excessive use of "just," "if any," "perhaps," and "I'm not sure" prove their lack of self-confidence.

Bag behavior also can enclose others. That is, "baggers" bag people with sarcastic and belittling words. They tend to place their negative feelings and attitudes on others.

Assertive behavior helps overcome bag behaviors. Be direct

Being assertive helps overcome lack of confidence

and honest, and demonstrate your respect for others. People can choose either to stand by their issues or to jump back into the bag. We must recognize that we are not infallible and that we must take risks, knowing that some mistakes are inevitable. You must accept yourself and your limitations, and remember: "If you aren't number one with yourself, you won't be number one with anyone."

Give yourself rewards for mastering a new situation. When you have resolved an employee conflict or finished a project on time, take yourself out for a cup of coffee and a piece of pie. At times take a big risk. Muster your courage to tackle a big situation. Ask for the raise you want, or talk to your partner about your feelings of being cheated. Start changing your life to suit the person you choose to be.

How to Get More from Your Job

Judge your work by your company's goals

Judge your work by your employer's goals as well as by your own. Consider and work toward both. It is important to evaluate your work, ideas, and decisions in fundamental terms. How are you contributing to the profit-making potential of your company? Are you an asset to your employer? If you do not relate to your company's needs, your work may be found unsatisfactory for that reason. Never downplay your work or ideas in public; however, do your self-criticism in private.

Take your work seriously, but not too personally

Taking your work seriously is the only way to get ahead, but taking your work too personally can hurt your progress. Think of work as a competitive sport and of yourself as a team member. Viewing it from a group perspective enables you to think and act objectively.

More people get fired for not playing the rules of the game than for not doing the job well. If you are too involved in your work, you may unknowingly overstep your bounds. The closer your philosophy and personality are to your company's, the greater are your chances of success.

Try not to be defensive when under pressure

Avoid overreaction. It is natural to become defensive when under pressure, but try to phrase your reply in objective rather than personal language. If you cannot respond with control, remove yourself from the situation. Vent your emotional reactions elsewhere. If your colleagues and boss see that you are not oversensitive, they will be more apt to deal with you honestly.

EMPLOYEE ATTITUDE QUESTIONNAIRE

This questionnaire is designed to help you give us your opinions quickly and easily. There are no "right" or "wrong" answers; we only want your own, honest opinion. Please do not sign your name.

	Agree	Unsure	Disagree
1. The working hours here are alright.	____	____	____
2. Working conditions here are better than in other companies.	____	____	____
3. In my opinion, the pay here is better than in other companies.	____	____	____
4. I understand what benefits are provided for our employees.	____	____	____
5. The people I work with help each other when someone falls behind or gets in a tight spot.	____	____	____
6. My supervisor is too interested in his or her own success to care about the needs of others.	____	____	____
7. If I have a complaint to make, I feel free to talk to someone up the line.	____	____	____
8. There are plenty of good jobs in our firm for those who want to get ahead.	____	____	____
9. They expect too much work from us around here.	____	____	____
10. The company should provide more opportunities for employees to know each other.	____	____	____
11. For my kind of job, working conditions are satisfactory.	____	____	____
12. Compared with other companies, our benefits are better than average.	____	____	____
13. My supervisor gets everybody to work together as a team.	____	____	____
14. You can get fired around here without much cause.	____	____	____
15. I have plenty of freedom on the job as long as I do good work.	____	____	____
16. My job is often dull and monotonous.	____	____	____
17. There is too much pressure on my job.	____	____	____
18. I have the right equipment to do my work.	____	____	____
19. The people I work with are very friendly.	____	____	____

20. My supervisor welcomes our ideas even when they differ from his or hers. ___ ____ _____
21. My supervisor has the work well organized. ___ ____ _____
22. I do not get enough instruction on how to do a job. ___ ____ _____
23. I'm proud to work for our firm. ___ ____ _____
24. I received fair treatment in my last performance review. ___ ____ _____
25. I would recommend employment here to my friends. ___ ____ _____
26. Filling in this questionnaire is a good way to let management know what employees think. ___ ____ _____
27. Please check one term that most nearly describes the kind of work you do: ____ Clerical or office ____ Production ____ Technical ____ Maintenance ____ Manufacturing ____ R&D ____ Engineering ____ Other
28. ____ Hourly ____ Salaried
29. ____ Male ____ Female
30. Do you supervise three or more people? ____ Yes ____ No

SUMMARY

People notice morale, especially when it is conspicuously high or low. Morale consists of the feelings of individuals and groups toward life. It is always present, and can vary quickly from positive to negative and back to positive again. Attitude is one of the most important parts of one's morale and job success. Today, workers' attitudes often are related to a feeling of accomplishment that can come from finishing a task.

The consequences of job dissatisfaction can be seen in psychosomatic ills, high-priced absenteeism, and a dislike of workaholics.

Some research seems to indicate that team spirit is often more important than individual achievement. Groups with a strong sense of unity are consistently more realistic in choosing their goals. Therefore, the supervisor must develop a strong sense of team work.

The blue-collar worker can find meaningful expression in occupations such as carpentry, electricity, or plumbing, or jobs having work cycles of a day or several weeks. The work cycle for the assembly-line worker, however, may last for only a minute, which leads to monotony and job dissatisfaction.

Several studies suggest that the higher one is promoted, the higher his or her morale is likely to be. Top management people do seem to enjoy work more than first-line employees.

Analysis of records is one way to check the morale of employees. Looking at time sheets, safety records, and employee turnover can indicate employee morale. An objective survey can give additional indication and may even locate the source of problems.

Without a doubt, the morale of the department is influenced by the supervisor. A strong self-concept is important in successful supervision. Thinking "success" is a good beginning, and you should reward yourself for completed tasks.

CASE STUDY 2

Cable TV Has a Morale Problem

When Cable TV first came to our town, the employment opportunities seemed fairly good. Initially, working at the firm appeared to be the ideal situation. I was to work with three others addressing and stuffing envelopes from 6 P.M. to 10 P.M. Since I needed money, the job seemed perfect.

The first night we were introduced to the office manager, assistant manager, salespeople, and technicians. Then we were left alone in a large room full of envelopes, maps, and literature. We began by talking and learning about each other. Then came the work: We wrote and stuffed all evening, and it seemed adequate.

After a week, that room with one long table seemed very boring. Two of the women left. Our manager, assuming that two workers could handle as much as four had, refused to hire more help. This is where our problem began, and we quickly lost motivation. We felt that our boss was unreasonable to expect us to work until midnight or 1 A.M. to catch up. Our surroundings looked less and less pleasing.

When the other woman left, the assistant manager called for an office meeting to discuss the reasons for the loss of employees. After reviewing the problem, we decided that the lack of feeling important was possibly to blame.

QUESTIONS

1. As office manager, what would you do?
2. What physical changes could be made?

CASE STUDY **3**

A Morale Problem in the County Jail

One responsibility of the sheriff of a California county is to assign police officers to run the county jail. A number of problems have arisen, because the younger men assigned as custodial officers do not relish the job and would rather be outside enforcing the law. Only the older officers, who have had enough of the streets, are willing to work inside the jail for any length of time. The younger officers also are unhappy about being assigned to the jail for indefinite periods: "Even the prisoners know when they're getting out!" The problem is compounded by the officers' awareness that those who do a good job in the jail system spend more time there than those who fail to do their work properly.

All of this has led to not only a serious morale problem but also a performance problem among the younger officers. They no longer take pride in their work, and their laxness is posing actual physical dangers to their fellow workers.

QUESTIONS

1. What is the logical solution to dealing with the younger and the older officers?
2. Will this solution work in the long run as well as the short run? Explain.

Terms and Concepts Supervisors Should Know

Absenteeism; Bag behaviors; Expectancy theory; Group morale; Individual morale; Job cycle; Job enrichment; Job rotation; Morale; Objective surveys; Quality circles; Team spirit; Whole-job concept; Workaholism.

Questions for Discussion

1. Discuss the job cycle in your company, and how it influences you and other workers.
2. Is your company one of workaholics? Who sets the pace or attitude for this behavior? What specifically indicates such an attitude?
3. Who has the greater influence on an employee: the supervisor or the peers? Why?
4. Consider the expression: "A rotten apple can spoil the whole barrel." How would you handle a person who seems to have a negative effect upon the other employees?
5. Who tends to have higher morale: men or women? younger or older employees? blue-collar or white-collar workers? the supervisor or the subordinates?
6. Discuss ways of developing self-confidence. Which ways were discussed in the text? What additional ways could be tried?

For Further Reading—And More Ideas

Beck, A. C., and E. D. Hillmar, "What Managers Can Do to Turn Negative Attitudes Around in an Organization," *Management Review* (January 1984.)

Brown, B. I., "Baby Boom Generation Now Mirrors the Values and Attitudes of Its Elders," *Marketing News* (April 13, 1984).

Brown, M., "How to Create Success," *Management Today* (January 1984).

Chapman, Elwood N., *Your Attitude Is Showing*, Chicago: SRA, 1978.

Day, D., "New Supervisors and the Informal Group," *Supervisory Management* (May 1989).

Dewar, Donald L., *Quality Circles: Answers to 100 Frequently Asked Questions*, Red Bluff, CA: Quality Circle Institute, 1979.

Dreyer, R. S., "The Witless Workaholic," *Supervision* (January 1989).

Feinberg, M. R., "A Change in Work Attitudes," *Restaurant Business* (May 15, 1983).

"Getting Your People to Level with You," *Supervision* (March 1989).

Harmon, J. F., "The Supervisor and Quality Control Circles," *Supervisory Management* (February 1984).

Harrigan, B. L., "Job Frustration," *Working Women* (June 1983).

Herman, S. M., "Ready, Aim, Fire (Handling Poor Performers)," *Training and Development Journal* (March 1989).

"The Hidden Job Values Behind Employee Motivation," *Personnel* (March–April 1984).

List, Charles, "How to Make Q. C. Work for Your Organization," *Personnel Journal* (December 1983).

Mischlind, L. A., "No-Nonsense Surveys Improve Employee Morale," *Personnel Journal* (November 1983).

Mishra, J., and M. Delano, "How to Manage Problem Employees," *The Arbitration Journal* (December 1988).

Morris, S., and N. Charney, "Stop It! Workaholism: Thank God It's Monday," *Psychology Today* (June 1983).

Nave, J. L., and B. Thomas, "How Companies Boost Morale," *Supervisory Management* (October 1983).

Nelton, S., "Managing Morale," *Working Women* (May 1983).

Osgood, D., "How Your Personal Attitudes Can Make or Break You," *Supervisory Management* (February 1984).

Pesci, M. L., "Morale Management," *Personnel Administrator* (May 1983).

"Recession vs. Morale: A Matter of Strong Opinion," *Management Review* (May 1983).

Reinhardt, R. L., "Management Morale," *Nursing Homes and Senior Citizen Care* (May–June 1983).

Santonocito, P., "When an Employee Becomes Emotional," *Supervisory Management* (January 1989).

Tharp, V. K., "Winners and Losers: Attitude Makes the Difference," *Futures* (December 1983).

"Want to Know How People Feel About Their Jobs? Ask 'Em," *Training* (April 1984).

Zahra, S. A., "How to Be an Effective Q. C. Leader," *Supervisory Management* (February 1984).

Zuker, E., "Attitudes That Work Against You," *Supervisory Management* (August 1983).

The Individual

3

"What makes people tick?"

LEARNING OBJECTIVES

When you complete this chapter, you should be able to:
1. Appreciate the complexity of individual behavior.
2. Understand the components of human behavior.
3. Explain the mystery of the black box.
4. Describe transactional analysis and its on-the-job implications.
5. Realize why effective supervisors must consider individual behavior.

"I've gotta be me."

This chapter will help you develop questions for class discussion, while also helping you formulate an understanding of individual behavior. Some answers to the questions below may be found in the chapter, whereas others may require personal reflection.

> Why is individual behavior so difficult to understand?
>
> If I am confused about my own behavior, what makes me think I can understand someone else?
>
> Why do different people react differently to the same situation?
>
> As a supervisor, why do I need to be concerned about individual behavior?
>
> If each individual is unique, why do some supervisors try to get people to act the same?

THE INDIVIDUAL AND THE ORGANIZATION

An organization hires more than just a physical being with job skills and work experience. When the selection is made, the organization receives a complex person with individual values, attitudes, emotions, expectations, and more. As a matter of fact, the organization has hired an entity that is more complex than a computer, and potentially more productive than any machine or process. However, unless this vital and paramount resource is effectively supervised and understood, its productivity potential will not be realized. Even worse, it could serve as a negative factor, jeopardizing the accomplishment of organizational goals. Supervisors must thus understand the individual behavior of subordinates if they expect to achieve company goals.

THE COMPLEXITIES OF THE INDIVIDUAL

People react differently   No two people are exactly alike. For example, consider the opportunity to work overtime. Some individuals will jump at the chance to make more money, while others will view it as an infringement on personal time. Why do individuals react differently to the same stimulus? Figure 3–1 depicts "the reaction fraction," which is a starting point for understanding this complex phenomenon.

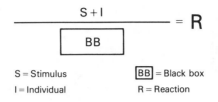

S = Stimulus $\boxed{BB}$ = Black box

I = Individual   R = Reaction

FIGURE 3–1   The reaction fraction

THE REACTION FRACTION

In the model shown in Figure 3–1, the components of an individual's "black box," which include values, attitudes, perception, learning ability, background, world view, personal needs, and societal influences, determine how that person mentally evaluates a stimulus and then reacts.

The reaction fraction clearly indicates how individual reactions can differ. For example, suppose that a subordinate reports to work 30 minutes late. Possible supervisory reactions to this stimulus could include any of the following scenarios:

- Supervisor A might overlook the situation completely.
- Supervisor B might lightly bring the matter to the subordinate's attention.
- Supervisor C might inquire as to the cause of the lateness.
- Supervisor D might give a verbal warning.
- Supervisor E might establish a formal counseling session to identify and solve the problem.
- Supervisor F might dock the worker's pay.
- Supervisor G might document the occurrence for future reference.
- Supervisor H might suspend the worker.
- Supervisor I might fire the worker.

The basis for the different reactions rests with supervisory values, emotions, and expectations.

The Black Box (BB)

The Black Box   The most mysterious element about an individual is the contents of the person's black box. Whereas the basic components of everyone's box are similar, their particular meaning and mix result in different reactions to stimuli. Obviously not everyone has the same values or perception of the world. Although solving the mystery of the black box is virtually impossible, recognizing its existence is the critical first step to understanding individual behavior. Some of the major components of the black box are as follows.

TABLE 3–1   Organizational implications of Maslow's needs hierarchy

Need	Explanation	Organizational Examples
Basic	Basic necessities of life	Rest periods, work breaks, lunch breaks, wages
Safety	Security	Seniority, pensions, hospitalization and life insurance
Social	Desire to be accepted by others	Work groups, team work, company softball team
Self-esteem	Self-image and ego	Status symbols, promotions, recognitions, awards
Self-actualization	Maximization of one's potential	Doing the job well for the sake of doing it well

VALUES

Values are a set of beliefs that influence behavior

Values are a system of beliefs determining what is important to the individual. It is easy to see how values influence human behavior. Conversely, different jobs or positions in life can create different values. For example, business executives place great importance on economic values, while artists emphasize aesthetic values and ministers stress high religious values. What is important to one person may not be important to another. Thus, what is important to a supervisor may not be of value to an employee.

NEEDS

Needs are inborn desires

A need is an inborn desire. The most widely accepted theory explaining individual needs is Abraham Maslow's needs hierarchy, which states that needs fall into five hierarchial categories: basic, safety, social, self-esteem, and self-actualization.[1] Table 3–1 shows the implications of Maslow's theory in an organizational setting. Individuals can reach different levels of satisfaction in the hierarchy at different points in life, for needs change over time.

---

[1] Abraham H. Maslow. *Motivation and Personality* (New York: Harper and Row, 1957).

GOALS

People need to achieve goals

Goals are the objectives set by an individual. When a goal is achieved, individuals experience a feeling of success. The assumption is that behavior is goal directed, meaning that people act with a purpose in mind.

When individuals feel their goals cannot be obtained in their present group, organization, or situation, they question their continued membership.

They may look for achievement elsewhere or modify their goals. If the goals are strong, the former will be the result. Individuals must recognize the importance of setting realistic goals that are neither too high nor too low, and determining the best method of goal achievement. Complexities occur when a supervisor has five subordinates with five different goals.

ATTITUDES

Attitudes are learned over time

An attitude is an individual's feeling or opinion about an abstract concept, a material element, or an individual. In effect, it is how a person feels about events, activities, and other people. Attitudes are learned over time and influenced by three sources:

1. Past experiences
2. Environmental stimuli
3. Present and future expectations

Past Experiences

The past is a good predictor of the future when analyzing individual attitudes. Our past experiences, whether good, bad, or indifferent, affect the way we interpret the present. If the last time you gave a suggestion the supervisor reprimanded you, your attitude about a newly announced company suggestion box will probably be negative.

Environmental Stimuli

The individual is influenced by external factors that are collectively called the environment. Specific environmental factors affecting attitudes are culture, demographics, groups, geography, and social trends. An individual's attitude about a company dress code, for example, may be influenced by upbringing, especially if the person is a product of an urban professional, white-collar family rather than a rural farm family.

Present and Future Expectations

An individual's goals and needs can affect that person's attitude about a particular situation. For example, someone who strongly desires promotion will see overtime as an opportunity to display commitment and loyalty. Conversely, an individual without promotional goals may view overtime as an infringement on personal leisure time.

ROLES

Roles provide structure for behavior

Roles are socially accepted patterns that structure individual behavior. Individuals in today's complex society may assume many roles simultaneously, such as teacher and student; parent, employee, and civic leader or business investor and politician. As a result, people may experience conflicting role demands, role conflict, role ambiguity, and role acceptance.

Conflicting Role Demands

In a 24-hour day, if 8 hours are spent resting and 8 hours are spent on the job, then 8 hours are left to pursue other interests. If one role, such as work, becomes too demanding, it will take more time away from other roles. The best advice is to seek a balance among the demands of one's various roles.

Role Conflict

Role conflict occurs when individuals envision their role differently than the organization does. For example, some organizations urge their supervisors to play a major role in political, civic, and other community groups. Supervisors in such organizations could experience role conflict if they envision their role strictly in a nine-to-five context.

Role Ambiguity

Role ambiguity arises when individuals possess an unclear understanding of their role. This situation can be extremely dangerous, because it permits individuals the option of interpreting their own job. The dangers of role ambiguity are obvious. Can you imagine the problems that emerge when an individual's interpretation differs from supervisory and/or organizational interpretations?

Role Acceptance

Role acceptance occurs when individuals assume their prescribed roles. From an organizational and supervisory point of view, this is the ideal situation. It is important that individuals understand their role in the organization and even more important that they accept the role.

NORMS

Norms indicate expected actions and behaviors

Norms are group standards for acceptable behavior. For many years, behavioral scientists have studied the influence of group behavior on the individual. Norms indicate how each group member is supposed to act. For example, a work group may decide that the quota is 100 units per day. Individuals who wish to remain in good standing with the group must follow this norm.

Supervisors and managers must be aware of group norms since they determine what a group will or will not do, and thereby establish what an individual must do.

PERCEPTION

Perception is our interpretation of reality

Perception is how an individual receives and interprets stimuli. In other words, it is how one views reality. It is a selective process enabling the individual to sort information based on its relative importance. Obviously, an individual's value system affects perception.

The company's desire to purchase a new computer system serves as an effective example. The individual may perceive the computer as a device that results in lost jobs and insecurity, whereas the organization might see it as a cost-saving device leading to increased productivity. Each side is correct in its assessment of the situation, based on selective perception.

LEARNING

Learning is influenced by six factors

Learning is the acquisition and application of new information. It leads to different behavior and/or the reinforcement of existing behavior. There are six factors that influence individual learning.

1. Reinforcing
2. Spacing
3. Positioning
4. Generalizing
5. Participating
6. Feedback

Reinforcing

Individuals tend to maintain behavior that is positively reinforced and eliminate behavior that is negatively reinforced. Positive reinforcement leads to habit.

Spacing

An individual learns more effectively if the stimuli are spaced, or repeated over several intervals, rather than concentrated. For example, an employee can better learn a new job if training occurs several hours each day over a period of days rather than during one concentrated, "crammed" session.

Positioning

An individual has a tendency to remember information based on its order or sequence. Research indicates that the first and last pieces of information received tend to be more easily remembered. A supervisor can capitalize on this finding to enhance learning by properly sequencing the order of information given to subordinates.

Generalizing

Individuals will group similar pieces of information and relate them to past experiences. Supervisors can thus maximize learning if they appeal to something familiar to an employee.

Participating

Learning is enhanced if the individual is an active participant in the process. Therefore, democratic management styles are more effective.

Feedback

Feedback is a learning monitor resulting in evaluation. Supervisors must develop suitable measures to assess employee learning effectively.

PERSONALITY

People are unique

Personality is the composite of behavioral and emotional factors that determine similarities and differences between people. Because people are different, no two individuals possess the same personality. Some are outgoing, while others are introverted. Some are passive, some are active. Some are hard to get along with, while others are easygoing. Some are a combination of all of the above, but no two people are the same. Personality is a composite of many factors, making it a difficult concept to understand. Figure 3–2 illustrates five major factors that directly affect the development of the individual personality:

1. Heredity
2. Internal environment
3. External environment
4. Culture and values
5. Life experiences

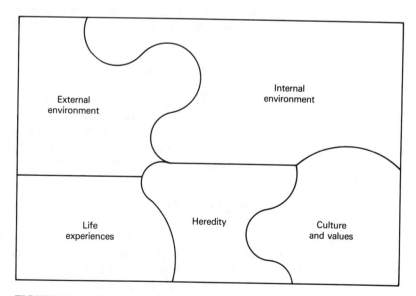

FIGURE 3–2 The personality puzzle

Heredity

Every individual is born with certain physical characteristics, including height, weight, intelligence, and appearance. A highly intelligent person might behave in a forceful, overbearing manner, while a less intelligent person may compensate by being passive.

Internal Environment

The internal environment is the family structure. Our upbringing, particularly in our early years, forms the basis for our personality. A liberal setting creates one type of personality, whereas a rigid one creates another.

External Environment

External environmental factors such as neighborhood and community life significantly affect our view of self as well as of others. A supervisor who desires to understand individual personalities should analyze the external environment of each subordinate.

Culture and Values

Culture and values also influence individual personality. If great value is placed on religious beliefs, for example, individuals will be expected to possess honesty, integrity, and ethics.

Life Experiences

Even though theorists agree that personality is largely shaped by age six, an individual's education and/or life experiences can alter basic personality. For example, experiencing a tragedy that causes someone to step back, reflect, and change directions in life may also alter the person's personality.

PROBLEM SOLVING

Problem solving is part of life

Life is a series of choices. Whether an individual is making a career choice or a supervisor is making a business decision, problem solving is an integral part of life.

As discussed, perception, values, attitudes, and other components of the personal black box influence how we view the world and, consequently, how we approach a problem. To maximize our

---

TEST YOURSELF

You Own Personality Puzzle

1. Describe those on-the-job values that are important to you.

   _____
   _____
   _____
   _____

2. Which social and self-esteem needs motivate you?

   _____
   _____
   _____
   _____

3. What are your life goals? job goals?

   _____
   _____
   _____
   _____

4. What are your attitudes about work?

   _____
   _____
   _____
   _____

5. Describe your personality. What factor of the personality puzzle most influences you?

   _____
   _____
   _____
   _____

---

problem-solving abilities, we must rise above the emotional quality of the situation and approach the dilemma in an objective, rational, and systematic fashion. Our attributes, including our values, attitudes, and perceptions, should be used to help clarify the problem, not cloud the issue.

TRANSACTIONAL ANALYSIS

Transactional analysis (TA), which has gained significant popularity in recent years, is one approach to understanding individual and interpersonal behavior. It uses the study of communication transactions between people to analyze what happens when two people interact. According to TA theory, all individuals have three typical patterns of behavior, or ego states.[2]

---

[2] Adapted from Eric Berne, *Games People Play* (New York: Grove Press, 1964); Berne, *Transactional Analysis in Psychotherapy* (New York: Grove Press, 1961); Thomas A. Harris, *I'm OK—You're OK* (New York: Avon Books, 1967); and Muriel James and Dorothy Jongeward, *Born to Win: Transactional Analysis with Gestalt Experiments* (Reading, MA: Addison-Wesley, 1971).

1. The parent ego state
2. The adult ego state
3. The child ego state

The Parent Ego State

When an individual communicates from the parent ego state, the source of the transaction is likely to be parental by nature. Statements from this state are ones of authority. The parent ego state is so named because major statements and actions of authority have usually come from people who cared for us in our early years, normally our parents. Typical parent statements can be categorized as either critical or supportive.

The Adult Ego State

When an individual communicates from the adult ego state, the source is likely to be an adult by nature. The adult ego state is that part of the individual that thinks and solves problems in a logical, rational manner. The basis of this state is linked to experience and education.

The Child Ego State

When an individual communicates from the child ego state, the source of the transaction is likely to be childlike in nature. There is a little bit of the child in each of us. The child ego state can be characterized by childlike expressions including pouting, sulking, and whining. Communication from this state tends to be carefree, spontaneous, and emotional.

Types of Transactions

The three ego states serve as a foundation for analyzing the nature of transactions. Two types of transactions are of interest: complementary and crossed. A *complementary transaction* represents the ideal and proceeds according to expectations (see Figures 3–3 and 3–4). A *crossed transaction* is not ideal and does not proceed according to expectations (see Figures 3–5 and 3–6).

It is imperative that supervisors choose the proper ego state when responding to subordinates' statements. Otherwise, the supervisor risks causing a crossed transaction, which results in poor interpersonal relationships. For this reason, supervisors must un-

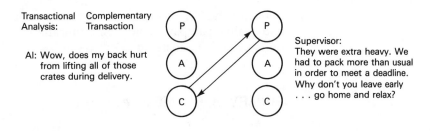

FIGURE 3–3   Transactional analysis: complementary transaction*

*P = Parent ego state
A = Adult ego state
C = Child ego state

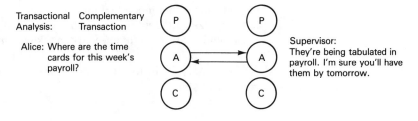

FIGURE 3–4   Transactional analysis: complementary transaction

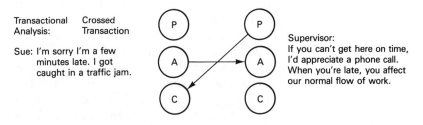

FIGURE 3–5   Transactional analysis: crossed transaction

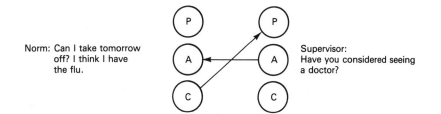

FIGURE 3–6   Transactional analysis: crossed transaction

derstand the TA process and take every opportunity to analyze and evaluate all patterns of communication, so that excellent relationships can be fostered.

SUPERVISORY IMPLICATIONS

Supervisors must be able to analyze individual behavior

Because of the complexities of individual behavior, a supervisor must guide and nurture the most valuable and intricate asset of all—the individual. When attempting to understand the individual, the supervisor must go beyond the surface of the situation and attempt to analyze the many aspects of behavior. Effective supervisors are those who are able to:

1. Understand that individual differences exist
2. Recognize and identify those differences
3. Account for those differences when taking supervisory action

In the final analysis, individual behavior speaks louder than words. Be ready to listen!

SUMMARY

An organization hires a total, complex individual comprised of many characteristics, which an effective supervisor must attempt to understand. This can be done by reviewing the reaction fraction and analyzing the mysterious composition of each individual's black box, which includes values, needs, goals, attitudes, roles, norms, perception, and learning. Along with the contents of the black box, the individual's personality must also be understood, for both significantly influence individual problem-solving ability. Supervisors can use transactional analysis (TA) as a device for probing both individual and interpersonal behavior. By considering all of these aspects, a supervisor will not be able to explain the intricacies of individual behavior, but at least they will be recognized.

CASE STUDY 4

Changing Roles

You are a personnel specialist in a large corporation. The majority of your time is spent dealing with employee grievances and counseling workers with job-related problems. Today, a newly hired secretary entered your office and expressed the following problem:

"When I was hired two months ago as the secretary for the director of marketing, everything was great. But over the past three weeks all the sales managers have been bringing me reports to be typed. I find myself constantly bogged down with their work and can't get my own work done. Since I've only been here two months, I don't know what to do. If I complain to my boss, it'll sound like I can't handle the job. If I don't type the sales managers reports, I'll offend them and they are above me on the organizational chart. But now I find myself taking work home and my family's getting short-changed. What should I do?"

QUESTIONS

1. How can this problem be expressed in terms of roles.
2. Is this problem common among employees?
3. What would you tell the secretary to do?

CASE STUDY 5

How Would You Answer?

A peer supervisor approaches you and states in confidence:

"There seems to be a vast difference in values and personality between me and my workers. We just don't consider the same things to be important. They say that the way I like to do things is old-fashioned. I understand I'm 20 years older than most of them and there's a generation gap, but it gets frustrating. Since we differ in personality and values, does that mean I can't supervise them?"

QUESTIONS

1. How would you answer your peer?
2. Is the supervisor correct? Why or why not?
3. Would you want to work for this supervisor?

Terms and Concepts Supervisors Should Know

Attitudes; Black box; Generalizing; Goals; Learning; Needs; Norms; Perception; Personality; Personality puzzle; Positioning; Reaction fraction; Reinforcing; Role; Role acceptance; Role ambiguity; Role conflict; Spacing; Transactional analysis; Values.

Questions for Discussion

1. How can transactional analysis benefit a supervisor? How can it contribute to positive interpersonal relations?
2. Compare and contrast role conflict and role ambiguity. Why are they of utmost concern with new employees?
3. How is an individual's problem-solving ability influenced by that person's black box?
4. Comment on the statement, "Our complete personality is formed at birth."
5. Have worker values and attitudes changed in the last ten years? Defend your position.

For Further Reading—And More Ideas

Bennett, Dudley, *Transactional Analysis and the Manager*, New York: AMACOM, 1976.

Berne, Eric, *Games People Play*, New York: Grove Press, 1964.

Berne, Eric, *Transactional Analysis in Psychotherapy*, New York: Grove Press, 1961.

Blotnick, S., "People Do Matter," *Forbes* (December 3, 1984).

Bolton, R., and D. G. Bolton, "Different People, Different Approaches to Management," *Supervisory Management* (August 1984).

Brass, D. J., "Being in the Right Place: A Structural Analysis of Individual Influence in an Organization," *Administrative Science Quarterly* (December 1984).

Buckwalter, N., "Bankers Manage Management," *U.S. Banker* (July 1983).

Comer, J. P., "What's Normal?" *Parents* (January 1989).

Connor, Patrick E., "A Critical Inquiry into Some Assumptions and Values Characterizing OD," *Academy of Management Review* (October 1977).

Diffie-Couch, P., "Building a Feeling of Trust in the Company," *Supervisory Management* (April 1984).

Evans, H., "Making Hostages of Our Values

(Corruption of Language Leads to Twisting of Social Values)," *U.S. News & World Report* (April 25, 1988).

Fox, N., "What Are Our Real Values?" *Newsweek* (February 13, 1989).

Howard, Jane, *Please Touch: A Guided Tour of the Human Potential Movement*, New York: McGraw-Hill, 1970.

Isaacs, S., "You Can Do It!" *Parents* (February 1989).

Jongeward, Dorothy, *Everybody Wins: Transactional Analysis Applied to Organizations*, Reading, MA: Addison-Wesley, 1973.

Kahn, Robert L., et al. *Organizational Stress: Studies in Role Conflict and Ambiguity*, New York: Wiley, 1964.

Mager, R. F., and P. Pipe, *Developing Attitude Toward Learning*, Palo Alto, CA: Fearon, 1968.

Maslow, Abraham, "A Theory of Human Motivation," *Psychological Review* (April, 1943).

Murray, H. A., *Explorations in Personality*, New York: Oxford University Press, 1938.

Pearce, J. L., and R. H. Peters, "A Contradictory Norms View of Employer-Employee Exchange," *Journal of Management* (Spring 1985).

Rosenbaum, Bernard L., *How to Motivate Today's*

Workers: Motivational Model for Managers and Supervisors, New York: McGraw-Hill, 1972.

Tyler, Leona E., *The Psychology of Human Differences,* New York: Appleton-Century-Crofts, 1956.

Varela, Jacobo A., "Solving Human Problems with Human Science," *Human Nature* (October 1978).

Vroom, Victor, *Work and Motivation,* New York: John Wiley & Sons, 1964.

Winninger, T. J., "What Type of People Are You Trying to Persuade?" *Supervision* (August 1983).

Yankelovich, Daniel. *New Rules: Searching for Self-Fulfillment in a World Turned Upside Down,* New York: Random House, 1981.

Group
Behavior

4

"Is there strength in numbers?"

LEARNING OBJECTIVES

When you complete this chapter, you should be able to:
1. Explain the concept of a group.
2. Discuss why individuals seek membership in groups.
3. Understand key group concepts such as leadership, status, norms, communication, cohesiveness, and competition.
4. Identify the various ways groups can be classified.
5. Recognize the impact groups can have on worker productivity and decision making.
6. Explain how supervisors can effectively deal with groups.

"No man is an island, entire of itself."

This chapter will help you develop questions for class discussion. It will also help you formulate an understanding of group behavior. Some answers to the questions below may be found in the chapter, whereas others may require personal reflection.

Why are some groups more productive than others?

What supervisory skills are essential to deal effectively with groups?

Is it easier for supervisors to work with groups or with individuals?

Do groups make better decisions than individuals? Why or why not?

Which are more important to the organization: individuals or groups? to the supervisor? Why?

THE INFLUENCE OF OTHERS

Individuals are hired to fill various roles in an organization because the majority of tasks are accomplished on an individual basis. Thus the cornerstone of supervision is individual behavior. However, not all behavior in an organization is based on the characteristics, behavior, and motivation of individuals. Many activities, outcomes, and interactions are instead the direct result of the interpersonal relationships that constitute group behavior.

People are influenced by others   Organizations hire individuals, but once people begin work, they interact, join, and are significantly influenced by others. Group behavior is therefore more than just the sum of individual behaviors; it is a complete entity in and of itself. Furthermore, it is the foundation of the personality of an organization. To be effective, supervisors must extend their knowledge of individual behavior, and accept that individual actions and behaviors will be influenced by group dynamics.

THE LINKING CONCEPT

The issue of individual versus group behavior is further complicated because individuals are members of many groups. This multigroup membership contributes to the linking concept, which is based on four major principles:

1. *An individual is strengthened by group membership.* A sharing of ideas, information, and opinions broadens an individual's scope and perspective.
2. *An individual seeks membership in more than one group.* Ideas, opinions, and information gained from one group can be brought to another. Other group members are engaged in the same process, thereby exploding the concept into a multiplier effect.
3. *Over time, group membership expands and contracts based on need.* As individual needs change, so do group associations. As people grow, they seek affiliations congruent with their changing wants and needs. As new groups are joined, influences from previous groups remain and serve as the basis of the new group. As this phase of the linking concept expands, so does the multiplier effect.
4. *In reciprocal fashion, all groups and all members benefit* from every group interaction, old or new. This contributes to the multiplier effect and enriches the linking concept. This process is ongoing and never ending.

The linking concept, while dynamic, is somewhat paradoxical. The process gives an individual a greater sense of reality and a better understanding of self, but constant interaction with many groups over time will change the individual. Being influenced by so many groups on so many issues is likely to complicate individual behavior from a supervisor's perspective (see Figure 4–1).

Supervisory Implications

The complexity of group behavior requires the supervisor to practice human relations techniques

Being a supervisor requires the ability to lead others. Knowing how to understand and shape behavior is essential for a leader. Unfortunately, because of its complexity, group behavior is far more difficult to comprehend and shape than individual behavior. As Figure 4–2 illustrates, individual behavior is a starting point, since supervisors interact with people on an individual basis. However, individuals' membership in groups modifies their behavior, and supervisors must understand such changes. The complexity of group behavior forces a supervisor to practice effective human relations techniques. The supervisor must think ahead and assess the consequences of every decision and action on both an individual and group basis. Each day a supervisor must think beyond individual implications to consider questions such as the following: How will the group react to a particular decision? Will the group's reaction influence the individual? Will that influence be positive or negative? How will the organization be affected?

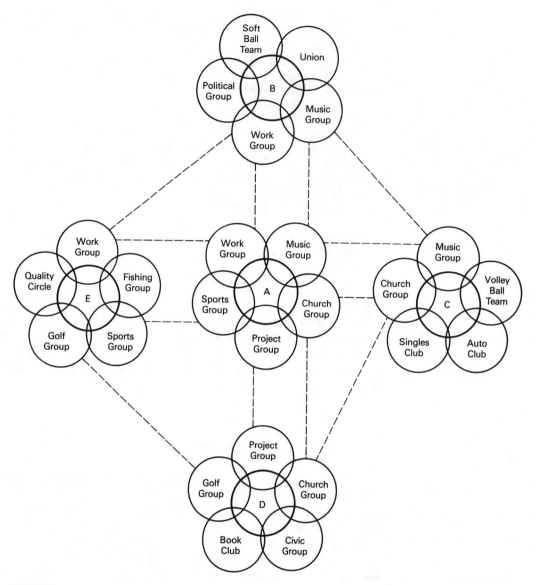

FIGURE 4–1 The linking concept

WHAT IS A GROUP?

A group is a collection of two or more individuals who are psychologically aware of one another, share a sense of collective identity, have a common interest, and work toward a shared goal. Groups are created whenever and wherever human interaction occurs. Take a minute and think of all the groups to which you belong:

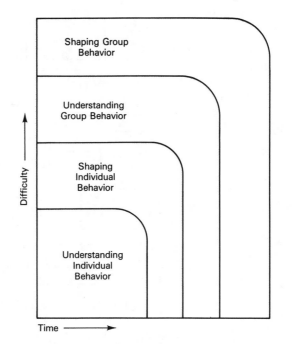

FIGURE 4-2 The complexity of group behavior

- Do you work in a department?
- Do you eat lunch with anyone?
- Are you a member of a professional society?
- Do you engage in recreational activities?
- Do you car pool to work or school?
- Are you active in civic and community organizations?
- Have you joined a union?

Whether inside or outside the formal structure of an organization, groups can greatly influence and modify your behavior. Very few of us can exist alone. We have a basic need to associate with and be accepted by others.

WHY JOIN A GROUP?

Individuals seek membership in groups for many reasons (see Figure 4–3).Some of the most frequently cited include:

1. Structural necessity
2. Reinforcement
3. Support
4. Information

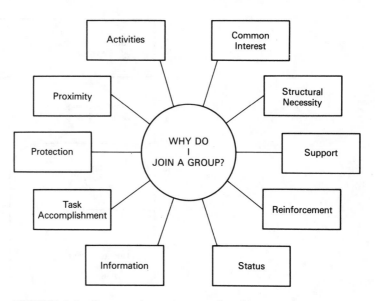

FIGURE 4–3   Reasons for group membership

5. Status
6. Protection
7. Task accomplishment
8. Proximity
9. Common interest
10. Activities

Structural Necessity

Structural requirements lead to group formation. For example, tennis, racquetball, bridge, softball, and football are difficult to play alone. Organizations are created out of necessity. Complex goals and objectives are accomplished more readily in a structured organizational setting in which individuals with specific skills and abilities are hired to perform required tasks. Somewhat automatically, individuals interact and form groups. The formal and informal formation of groups constitutes the structural anatomy of an organization within which organizational goals are attained.

Groups form through individual interaction

Reinforcement

Groups reinforce an individual's value system. Individuals have a common desire to have their thoughts and ideas supported, and groups enable them to be surrounded with like-minded people. Today, more than ever, the old adage holds true: Birds of a feather *do* flock together.

Support

Groups provide the individual with support

Groups provide emotional and physical support for members. Friendships are formed, thus providing encouragement, guidance, direction, and advice. Such support enables individuals to function with the confidence of knowing that others are behind them.

Information

Groups provide members with increased accessibility to relevant information. Communication networks form to facilitate the exchange of such information, the transfer and acquisition of which among group members heightens individual awareness while reducing feelings of uncertainty.

Status

Membership in a group can increase an individual's status by providing identification with a distinct entity. Consider the pride, esteem, and status associated with being a member of the Green Berets.

Protection

There is strength in numbers, and employees quickly discover the benefits of group membership. Organized efforts enhance their safety and security. For example, employee councils, unions, and other groups protect them from arbitrary treatment by management.

Task Accomplishment

The collective efforts of individuals enable the accomplishment of tasks that cannot be done alone. The specialization of labor exists in both informal and formal groups. Consider, for example, the many individuals whose joint efforts are necessary to assemble an automobile.

Proximity

Proximity leads to group formation

Frequently, people join groups because of their proximity to other members. As a child, you were most likely to interact with those in your neighborhood. In school, interactions frequently occurred among those who were in the same class or curriculum. So it is on the job. Informal groups are likely to emerge from work settings in which individuals constantly interact.

Common Interest

Individuals who share interests tend to socialize. Strong bonds are established when people's concerns are the same. For example, study groups emerge among students who want to succeed in a course or pass a difficult exam.

Activities

Certain activities force the formation of groups. For example, supervisors from different departments and divisions are frequently brought together to discuss ways and means to increase production, reduce absenteeism, or improve work methods.

GROUPS CONCEPTS

For supervisors to deal with groups effectively, six concepts must be understood:

1. Leadership
2. Status
3. Norms
4. Communication
5. Cohesiveness
6. Competition

Leadership

The primary function of any group leader is to direct and facilitate member behavior toward the accomplishment of group goals and objectives. Leaders achieve this goal by making decisions, resolving conflicts, and exerting power and authority.

Leadership roles vary
with the situation

Leadership positions within a group can vary with the situation and specific goal to be accomplished. For example, group members who possess organizational ability and attention to detail may emerge as leaders of the company picnic, while those with motivational ability may be asked to lead workers on important work tasks.

Successful leadership is based on the following characteristics:

1. Rigid adherence to norms
2. Perceived expertise or skill
3. Charisma
4. Communication skill
5. Perceived reward
6. Voluntary actions
7. Situational aspects
8. Family ties
9. Natural ability
10. Behavior
11. Manipulation

RIGID ADHERENCE TO NORMS

Generally, group leaders are those who closely follow the norms of the group. Because such individuals become the "guardians" of group norms, they generate respect and are often selected for leadership positions.

PERCEIVED EXPERTISE OR SKILL

Members of groups automatically look to the most expert member for leadership. Expertise can be based on education or training, achievements, experience, and seniority.

CHARISMA

Charisma is a special, inborn quality of some individuals to command respect and inspire others because of appearance, personality, or some other desirable characteristic. Many individuals achieve and are successful in leadership positions because of charisma.

COMMUNICATION SKILL

In leadership situations, an effective communicator can quickly gain control. It may be the person who talks the loudest or the most, or controls relevant information. Knowledge is power, and information is *the* source of knowledge. Additionally, the ability to convey knowledge is prerequisite to effective leadership.

PERCEIVED REWARD

Individuals may assume a leadership role based on the resources at their command. Whoever promises the best reward may gain member support.

VOLUNTARY ACTIONS

In some cases, individuals rise to a leadership position on the basis of their voluntary actions. Although this approach is not totally scientific, some people do volunteer for jobs that ultimately result in permanent leadership responsibilities.

SITUATIONAL ASPECTS

Sometimes, being in the right place at the right time pays off. Countless individuals have landed in leadership roles simply because they were the next in line or were the only available choice.

FAMILY TIES

Although it is not always fair, leadership roles are frequently filled by family members. It is not unusual for the owner of a business to appoint a son or daughter to an important leadership function.

NATURAL ABILITY

Often, individuals with natural ability, such as the proper personality, innate intelligence, and other qualities expected of a leader, are chosen for leadership. These gifted people tend to rise through the ranks swiftly.

BEHAVIOR

To be a leader, an individual must learn to act like one. A leader is expected to set a good example, dress appropriately, say the right thing, and act within the image of the group or organization. Many individuals attain leadership because they demonstrate these behavioral characteristics.

MANIPULATION

Although it has negative connotations, some individuals manipulate their way to the top, which is understandable since leadership positions carry status, power, financial rewards, control, and other privileges. This is not a recommended course of action. However, some people will resort to anything to get what they want (see Figure 4–4).

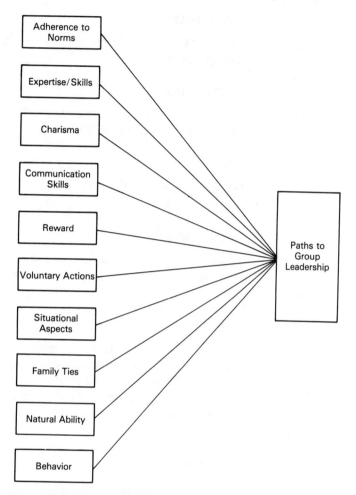

FIGURE 4-4   Paths to group leadership

Status

People can acquire status in groups

Status is the amount of esteem and prestige one receives. Various degrees of status can exist within a group. Some group members are held in higher regard by their peers than are others. Status differentiation is the result of one or more of the following factors:

1. Group roles
2. Contribution
3. Ability
4. Type of work
5. Seniority

GROUP ROLES

Higher status is usually granted to the member who serves as group leader.

CONTRIBUTION

Higher regard is given to members who contribute to the success of the group than to mere "followers."

ABILITY

Status increases with an individual's skill, ability, knowledge, education, or training.

TYPE OF WORK

Status grows with the perceived importance of the task performed. For example, the airline pilot has more status than the flight attendant.

SENIORITY

As length of service to and membership in a group increases, so does status. Newcomers must earn respect over time. Status can be a powerful motivator and is thus a major factor in understanding behavior within groups. If members do not achieve their desired status, they will seek membership in other groups.

Norms

Norms may be performance-oriented

Norms are the standards of thought and behavior expected of group members. They provide the order that controls the group. Group norms may be behavior- or performance-oriented. Behavior-oriented norms include attitudes, values, interests, language, and dress. Performance-oriented norms deal with productivity. The group has considerable power to reward and punish members who deviate from its norms. Since people wish to retain valued membership, they behave accordingly. Deviation may result in one or more of the following group sanctions:

1. Instruction on the "right way" to behave
2. Friendly joking about the situation
3. Verbal warnings
4. Arguments
5. The "cold shoulder" treatment
6. Verbal abuse and threats
7. Sabotaging of the individual's productivity

8. Physical violence
9. Social isolation

Even though formal organizations establish standards of behavior, they may be superseded by group norms.

Communication

Communication through informal groups is commonly called "the grapevine." This type of communication plays a vital role in any organization and is a frequent source of information for members. The grapevine rapidly passes along the facts and rumors that are of general interest to the group. However, as the messages travel, their accuracy is distorted.

Formal information reduces grapevine communication

The amount of information in "the grapevine" is directly related to the amount of communication shared through the formal system. As organizations and supervisors freely exchange information, the need for the grapevine decreases. The informal channels are most active when the formal mechanisms fail to provide timely, accurate information.

Cohesiveness

Some groups are highly cohesive

Cohesiveness is the strength, closeness, and solidarity of group members. In a highly cohesive group, members act as a single unit, interact frequently, and work well together. Performance- and behavior-oriented norms are usually well defined, with a high degree of conformity. Additionally, a highly cohesive group has a reduced amount of tension and internal conflict. Several factors determine group cohesiveness:

1. Goal achievement
2. Perceived dependency
3. Frequency of interaction
4. Group size
5. Isolation
6. Similarity
7. Communication
8. Status
9. Conflict

GOAL ACHIEVEMENT

As a group sets and achieves goals, cohesiveness increases. Success breeds togetherness, while failure leads to disunity.

PERCEIVED DEPENDENCY

If individual members believe that the group satisfies a need that no other vehicle can satisfy, cohesiveness increases.

FREQUENCY OF INTERACTION

If group members continually interact, cohesiveness will increase. The lack of interaction and contact weakens group bonds.

GROUP SIZE

Smaller groups can have more frequent and informal interactions. As group size increases, the resulting formality stymies interaction.

ISOLATION

Physical boundaries and environmental constraints can isolate a group, thereby clarifying membership and increasing cohesiveness.

SIMILARITY

If group members are alike in skills, opinions, attitudes, interests, and resources, cohesiveness will increase.

COMMUNICATION

As group members share thoughts and information, cohesiveness is increased.

STATUS

Higher-status groups have greater cohesiveness because membership in them is valued.

CONFLICT

Pressures, dangers, threats, and attacks by outside forces result in increased cohesiveness. Differences can be minimized through a united effort. Highly cohesive groups have a great impact upon member behavior and productivity. Since membership in such groups is valued, individuals are more responsive to group norms and expectations. If the group expects high productivity, individual output will increase. Conversely, if the group restricts output, individual members will be less productive.

Competition

Two types of group competition are possible:

1. *Intergroup competition,* or competition between groups
2. *Intragroup competition,* or competition within a group

The potential advantages and disadvantages of each are outlined below.

INTERGROUP COMPETITION

Advantages

- Increases the cohesiveness and morale of the "winning" group
- Increases group identity
- Unifies members
- Increases group loyalty
- Sets goals to be reached

Disadvantages

- Decreases the cohesiveness and morale of the "losing" group
- Increases tension and pressure
- May lead to sabotage
- Produces anger
- May be viewed as a management control device

INTRAGROUP COMPETITION

Advantages

- Maximizes individual productivity
- Increases individual motivation
- Increases individual goal orientation
- Rewards positive efforts and contributions
- Reduce waste and inefficiency

Disadvantages

- May lead to sabotage
- Decreases morale of the "losers"
- Increases tension and pressure
- Produces frustration
- May be viewed as a management control device

THE USE OF COMPETITION IN AN ORGANIZATIONAL SETTING

Competition may be good or bad

Each supervisor must closely assess the potential pros and cons of competition. If goal achievement and productivity greatly exceed the need for cooperation, competitive strategies should be considered. If cooperation is the ultimate goal, however, competition may not be the best method. Because all groups and organizations are different, it is very difficult to make universal statements. Supervisors must assess each circumstance and employ the strategy best meeting the needs of the organization.

CLASSIFICATION OF GROUPS IN THE ORGANIZATION

Informal groups spring up naturally in organizational settings. While formal groups are established by the organization, the informal groups are established by employees. Understanding and recognizing group classifications is essential for today's supervisor. Six helpful categories are listed below:

1. Sayles's classifications
2. Primary versus secondary groups
3. Formal versus informal groups
4. Permanent versus temporary groups
5. Task versus social groups
6. Reference groups

Sayles's Classifications

Leonard R. Sayles[1] identified four types of informal groups in work organizations:

1. Apathetic groups
2. Erratic groups
3. Strategic groups
4. Conservative groups

APATHETIC GROUPS

From an organizational standpoint, apathetic groups are viewed as trouble free. Such groups

- Are unlikely to develop grievances
- Are unlikely to put pressures on management
- Are uninterested in union involvement
- Have weak leadership
- Have low cohesiveness
- Include low-skilled and low-paid individuals
- Have little power and unity
- Suppress discontent

---

[1]Leonard R. Sayles, "Informal Work Groups and the Formal Organizations," Robert Dubin, ed., in *Human Relations in Administration*, 4th ed. (Englewood Cliffs, NJ: Prentice Hall, 1974), pp. 144–149.

- Suppress jealousy
- Are not fully cooperative
- Are not consistently high in productivity

ERRATIC GROUPS

From an organizational viewpoint, erratic groups are inconsistent and therefore are the most dangerous. Such groups

- Exhibit unpredictable behavior
- Show radical tendencies
- Have highly centralized leadership
- Are union activists
- Have undefined group roles
- React strongly to threats

STRATEGIC GROUPS

From an organizational standpoint, strategic groups demand constant attention but are predictable. Strategic groups

- Have a detailed plan of action
- Are highly organized
- Exhibit consistent and predictable behavior
- Are high in perceived power
- Have high cohesiveness
- Are involved in union affairs
- Contain skilled employees who perform specialized tasks
- Are perceived to perform important functions
- Are usually productive in the long run

CONSERVATIVE GROUPS

From an organizational viewpoint, conservative groups are highly stable and passive. Such groups

- Are perceived to perform critical tasks
- Feel secure in the organization
- Have substantial and highly recognized power
- Are low in union participation
- Have achieved seniority and special privileges
- Are high in perceived status
- Act only out of necessity
- Are self-policing
- Show no internal conflict

Primary Versus Secondary Groups

Primary group membership is perceived by the individual to be the most important. Typical primary groups are friendship groups, the family, and fraternal organizations. These groups receive the majority of an individual's time, effort, and thought. They are critical to the satisfaction of social needs.

Secondary groups only require minimum commitment

Secondary groups are perceived by the individual as requiring only a minor commitment of time and effort. Typical secondary groups include professional associations, organization-based groups, and committees. Membership in such groups may be secured for symbolic reasons or to satisfy ego needs.

Each group, whether primary or secondary, affects individual behavior. However, what may be a primary group to one person may be a secondary group to another.

Formal Versus Informal Groups

Formal groups exhibit all the characteristics of a formal organization. Typically, such have leaders, followers, and a clearly defined purpose, as well as specific goals, policies, procedures, and rules of operation. Formal groups are usually established by organizations and are rich in tradition.

Informal groups exist without formal structure

Informal groups, on the other hand, exist without formal structure. Within them roles, responsibilities, and goals are either loosely defined, nonexistent, or minimal. Membership is voluntarily sought on the basis of interest or friendship.

Permanent Versus Temporary Groups

Permanent groups meet continually and are perceived as enduring and stable. After such groups achieve one goal, they quickly move to the next task at hand.

Temporary groups, however, last for only a limited or specified period of time. After a task or goal is accomplished, they will disband.

Task Versus Social Groups

Task groups are goal-oriented, emphasizing work to be accomplished. They are often aligned with important causes and objectives.

By contrast, social groups are people-oriented, emphasizing companionship. Group activities are designed with this objective in mind.

Reference Groups

Reference groups are groups to which individuals belong or aspire to belong. Individuals who identify with reference groups will tend to imitate the attitudes, behavior, beliefs, ideas, values, dress, and actions they believe group norms demand in an attempt to gain membership.

Ideally, if supervisors create an exciting environment and clearly convey the mission and purpose of the organization, individuals will identify with the organization and allow it to serve as their reference group.

THE GROUP LIFE CYCLE CONCEPT

Groups develop and evolve

Groups develop and evolve over time. Formal and informal groups must adapt to environmental conditions and constantly meet societal challenges. Group evolution can thus be analyzed using the group life cycle concept, the stages of which are presented below (see Figure 4–5).

Stage 1: Formation

The formation stage of a group typically begins with a few members who have a goal or purpose in mind. These are the founders of the group, and initially determine rather sketchy goals,

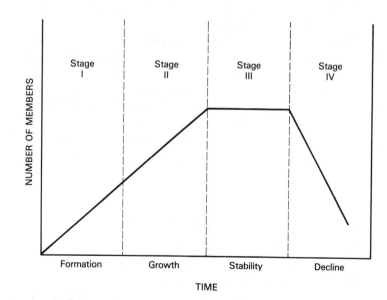

FIGURE 4–5 Group life cycle concept

policies, procedures, rules, structure, and membership criteria. In this stage, one of the founders usually emerges as the group leader.

Stage 2: Growth

During the growth stage, the group's objectives are modified, solidified, and possibly put in writing. At this point, the group makes critical decisions about seeking new members. The specialization of tasks and group roles also occurs at this stage.

Stage 3: Stability

Groups must adapt to survive

In the stability stage, the group's structure is fixed, its purpose becomes known, and its membership peaks. This is the critical time for its perpetual existence. Should a group refuse to make necessary changes, it may endanger its own future. On the other hand, if the group adapts to social and environmental factors, it increases its chance for survival.

Many theorists argue that today's union movement is at this stage. Since many of the initial goals of unionization, such as better pay, working conditions, and benefits, have been achieved, new objectives must be shaped to comply with current work problems, a changing work force, and new management styles. Some of the decline in union membership can be traced to the inability of union leaders to establish strategies that are consistent with the stability stage.

For example, the railroad industry is rich in tradition. However, social change combined with technological advances has increased the need for people to travel more expediently. The airline industry responded to this demand and subsequently attracted former railroad passengers. If the railroad unions had taken a broader perspective, they could have unionized *all* transportation employees and achieved greater stability. Instead, their limited view endangered their existence. Unions that have made the necessary changes continue to serve a needed and viable purpose.

Stage 4: Decline

For many groups, decline is inevitable

For many groups and organizations, decline is inevitable. The life span of group will be shortened or lengthened according to how the group responds to the third stage. Those groups with effective strategies prolong their existence, while those with limited strategies—or none at all—seriously accelerate the process of

decline. To state that *all* groups will decline is a matter of specu-
lation and debate. Adaptability will certainly extend group existence. For example, an educational institution cannot rely on funds
from just one graduating class, but establishing an alumni association broadens its perspectives and perpetuates the concept of class
giving as long as the institution exists. The legacy of the group thus
continues because of creative adaptability.

THE EFFECT OF GROUPS ON PRODUCTIVITY

The Productivity Payoff

Organizations and supervisors need to know the effect of the
formation of groups on the productivity of organizational members
(see Table 4–1). This "productivity payoff" can be either positive or
negative.

THE POSITIVE PAYOFF

Groups can have a positive impact on the productivity of its members for the reasons listed on page 82.

TABLE 4–1   Advantages and disadvantages of groups in an
organization

Advantages	Disadvantages
1. Members internally handle conflict.	1. The work environment can become unpleasant.
2. Norms and standards of behavior are established.	2. Group norms and standards may differ from those of the organization.
3. The predictability of member behavior is increased.	3. Groups tend to resist change and innovation.
4. Intraunit cooperation is increased.	4. Interunit cooperation is decreased.
5. Communication and feedback are enhanced.	5. Communication can be distorted.
6. Productivity is enhanced.	6. Groups may set lower productivity standards.
7. Groups can aid a supervisor in dealing with large numbers of employees.	7. Groups may obstruct organizational goals.
8. Groups provide strength and unity.	8. Some individuals may become isolated.

1. The formation of groups enables the specialization of tasks, which can increase productivity.
2. Working in groups improves morale.
3. Working in groups increases the time an employee spends on a task, which results in improved job satisfaction and a feeling of pride and commitment.
4. Groups become self-monitoring, enforcing rigid standards of behavior.
5. The formation of groups improves the cohesiveness of work units.
6. Working in groups results in the pooling of efforts and the sharing of ideas.
7. Groups enhance communication.

THE NEGATIVE PAYOFF

However, groups can negatively affect productivity for the following reasons:

1. Commitment to the group may supersede commitment to the organization.
2. Groups can set productivity limits and may ostracize individuals who exceed such limits.
3. Groups tend to resist innovation and change.
4. The formation of groups may increase organizational conflict.
5. The formation of groups may lead to isolation of units and/or members.
6. Groups, group leaders, and group members may engage in empire building.
7. Groups may resist organizational goals and supervisory policies.
8. Groups may restrict individual freedom and initiative.

GROUP DECISION MAKING

Supervisors are decision makers. If one task separates workers from managers, it is decision making, which remains the hallmark of supervisory responsibility.

While employees refer problems, supervisors must solve them. While quality decisions serve to benefit the organization, poor decisions may lead to its demise.

Individuals enjoy being included in the decision-making process

Supervisors must be constantly concerned with ways to improve the quality of their decision making. Recent trends suggest that a participative management style, which includes individuals and groups in the decision-making process, is most effective. Quality circles, committees, and task groups are examples of group decision making in action.

While group decision making has its advantages, it does have its drawbacks. A close review of the advantages and disadvantages of group decision making can aid a supervisor in determining when and if the process should be used:

Advantages of Group Decision Making

- Groups can generate more ideas: Two heads *are* better than one.
- Group decision making promotes increased understanding among participants.
- People feel more committed to decisions when they were part of the process that formed them. A sense of "ownership" is thus created.
- Group decision making provides individuals with increased feelings of freedom. Additionally, their inhibitions are lessened and their creativity is enhanced.
- Group participation increases the possibility of making a more informed decision, since the members possess a wide range of knowledge, experience, expertise, and information.
- Group involvement communicates the supervisor's trust in the workers. Employees try hard to live up to that trust.
- A team approach to decision making enhances the cohesiveness of a department.

Disadvantages of Group Decision Making

- Group decision making requires more time than individual decision making.
- Groups are more likely to take risks since no one person can be blamed, thereby creating a decreased sense of responsibility.
- One individual can overpower others in the group, and nonassertive people may tend to go along with bad decisions.
- To keep all members happy, groups may produce a nonoptimal decision.
- The group approach sacrifices the consistency and continuity of decisions.

Impact on the Supervisor

Supervisors must recognize the influence of groups

Groups have a major influence on individual behavior and performance. Supervisors cannot ignore the impact of co-workers, friends, and outside groups on their employees. Today's supervisor must respect, recognize, and understand the informal organization, or suffer possible negative consequences (see Table 4–2 to 4–4). Dealing with groups is not an easy task, but it is a vital supervisory skill. To be successful, supervisors must do the following:

1. *Understand why groups are created.* Supervisors should realize that the formation of groups does not represent a failure on the part of their supervisory skills. Groups are a social phenomenon and fulfill individual needs. In effect, they are a natural outcome of personal interaction.

TABLE 4–2   A supervisor's positive reactions to group formation

Action	Potential Outcome
Actively working with the group	A better understanding of groups, members, and individual behavior
Promote and stress a sense of teamwork	Loyalty to both the supervisor and the organization
Take an interest in individual members	Better decisions and more commitment to a selected course of action
Promote a communication network	Increased upward communication to the supervisor

TABLE 4–3   A supervisor's neutral reactions to group formation

Action	Potential Outcome
Ignore group activities	Alienation from group members
Deal with individuals	Failure to reap the benefits of group dynamics
Refuse to admit a group exists	Frustration and anxiety of group members
	Increased group cohesiveness and strength
	Underground group activities
	Expanded group membership

TABLE 4–4   A supervisor's negative reactions to group formation

Action	Potential Outcome
Attempt to break up the group	Morale and productivity problems
Add and enforce rigid controls	Less time for the supervisor to plan
Reduce the number of group interactions and activities	A lack of trust between workers and supervisor
Separate group members	Underground activities, including sabotage
	Increased group cohesiveness and strength
	Verbal wars, lack of cooperation, and attempts to undermine the supervisor
	Loss of control by the supervisor
	Expanded group membership

2. *Recognize the groups' existence.* They are a key to understanding individual behavior, and ignoring them results in animosity and loss of respect.
3. *Identify what type of group has been formed* (for example, task or social, primary or secondary).
4. *Recognize and work with the groups' leaders.* These individuals can aid the supervisor. It is easier to deal with one person than with fifteen.
5. *Communicate through informal as well as formal channels.* If handled properly, the grapevine is a fast and effective means of communicating with group members.

SUMMARY

Groups have a significant impact on the activities, outcomes, and interaction of individuals. Whether inside or outside the formal structure of an organization, groups will form and influence human behavior. The linking concept further reinforces this aspect. Individuals join groups for various reasons, including structural necessity, reinforcement, support, information, status, protection, task accomplishment, proximity, common interest, and activities.

For supervisors to cope with groups effectively, six concepts must be understood: leadership, status, norms, communication, cohesiveness, and competition. Supervisors must also assess the type of group that exists. The following categories may prove helpful: Sayle's classifications, primary versus secondary groups, formal versus informal groups, permanent versus temporary groups, task versus social groups, and reference groups.

Group development evolves through four stages: formation, growth, stability, and decline. Concerns are different at each stage.

From an organizational viewpoint, groups may have a positive or negative impact on productivity and should be included in the decision-making process. Supervisors cannot ignore the concept of groups. They must understand why they are created, recognize their existence, appropriately classify them, work with the group leader, and use grapevine communication. Group skills are a vital aspect of successful supervision.

CASE STUDY 6

Selecting Work Groups

You are a supervisor at an auto assembly plant. Your company has recently decided to change its method of production from an individual assembly-line operation to a team approach. You have been selected to be on a committee to determine how the work groups are to be selected. One proposal is for the company to establish units randomly. The other is for the employees to form their own units.

QUESTIONS

1. What are the advantages and disadvantages of each plan from a group behavior standpoint?
2. Should other alternatives be considered? If so, what are they? What are their advantages and disadvantages of these alternatives?
3. Which plan would you favor? Why?

CASE STUDY 7

The Incentive Plan

You are the supervisor of the sales force in a department store. Sales have been slowly declining over the past two years, and the store owner suggests implementing an employee incentive plan whereby each month the leading salesperson in each department will receive a $25 gift certificate. The manager asks your opinion of this plan.

QUESTIONS

1. What group concepts must be considered in the analysis of any incentive plan?
2. Would such a concept have a positive or a negative impact on productivity?
3. What advantages and disadvantages of this plan must be considered?
4. Would you favor such a plan? Discuss.

Terms and Concepts Supervisors Should Know

Apathetic groups; Cohesiveness; Conservative groups; Erratic groups; Formal groups; Grapevine; Group; Group life cycle concept; Informal groups; Intergroup competition; Intragroup competition; Linking concept; Norms; Paths to leadership; Permanent groups; Primary groups; Proximity; Reference groups; Secondary groups; Social groups; Status; Strategic groups; Structural necessity; Task groups; Temporary groups.

Questions for Discussion

1. What are the bases for status differentiation?
2. How are group norms determined? How are they enforced?
3. Give an example that distinguishes each of the following group classes:
   a. Primary versus secondary
   b. Formal versus informal
   c. Permanent versus temporary
   d. Task versus social
4. Why have *you* joined groups?
5. What are the advantages and disadvantages of forming groups in organizations?

For Further Reading—And More Ideas

Anderson, R. H., and K. J. Snyder, "Team Training," *Training and Development Journal* (February 1989).

Bassin, M., "Teamwork at General Foods," *Personnel Journal* (May 1988).

Bernstein, A., and W. Zellner, "Detroit vs. the UAW: At Odds over Teamwork," *Business Week* (August 24, 1987).

Bookman, R., "Teamwork Works When Leaders Lead," *Bureaucrat* (Winter 1987–88).

Brody, E. W., "Credibility and Productivity: The New Rules for Organizational Survival," *Public Relations Quarterly* (Fall 1988).

Buhler, W., "Group Management—The Group as a Change Agent," *Supervision* (May 1988).

Day, D., "New Supervisors and the Informal Group," *Supervisory Management* (May 1989).

Duffey, J., "Competitiveness and Human Resources," *California Management Review* (September 1988).

Farish, P., "Managing Teams (Metal Can Using Team System to Run New Plant in Windsor, Colo.)," *Personnel Administrator* (December 1988).

Farish, P., "Up from Kalmar (Volvo's Assembly Plant Using Team Concept)," *Personnel Administrator* (January 1989).

Fodor, G. M., "Teamwork Raises Margins (Florida Bolt Earns Quality Vendor Status with Florida Power & Light)," *Industrial Distribution (April 1989).*

Gabor, A., "GM's Bootstrap Battle: The Factory-Floor View (E. Schaefer Brings Team Management to Van Nuys Plant)," *U.S. News & World Report* (September 21, 1987).

Goddard, R. W., "Work Force 2000," *Personal Journal* (February 1989).

Greco, G., "Teams Score Victories at Work," *Nation's Business* (April 1988).

Herbert, W., "The Sources of Cooperation (Study by James Beggan and David Messick)", *Psychology Today* (January–February 1989).

Hoerr, J. P., "Is Teamwork a Management Plot? Mostly Not," *Business Week* (February 20, 1989).

Horton, T. R., "Competing Through Cooperation (Labor and Management)," *Management Review* (February 1988).

Kanter, R. M., "Increasing Competitiveness Without Restructuring," *Management Review* (June 1987).

McGee, J., and H. Thomas, "Strategic Groups: Theory, Research, and Taxonomy," *Strategic Management Journal* (January–February 1989).

McLaughlin, A., "Building a Quality Workforce," *Business Administration* (May 9, 1988).

Medvescek, C., "Everybody Wins! (Cooperative Games)," *Parents* (April 1988).

Nakao, Keiko, "Social Class in the Workplace: The United States Versus Japan," *Society* (January–February 1989).

Nickle, B. W., and R. C. Maddox, "Fortysomething: Helping Employees Through the Midlife Crisis," *Training and Development Journal* (December 1988).

Prince, G., "Recognizing Genuine Teamwork," *Supervisory Management* (April 1989).

Saxe, S., "Peer Influence and Learning," *Training and Development Journal* (June 1988).

Schweiger, D. M., "The Utilization of Individual Capabilities in Group Approaches to Strategic Decision-Making," *Strategic Management Journal* (January–February 1989).

Smith, D. G., "Participation: Team Players," *Training* (January 1989).

"Ten Tips for Team Leaders," *Training* (April 1988).

Vogt, J. F., and B. D. Hunt, "What Really Goes Wrong with Participative Work Groups? (Work Groups, Project Management Teams,

etc.)," *Training and Development Journal* (May 1988).

Wagel, W. H., "Opening the Channels to Interdepartmental Cooperation (Professional Education Systems, Inc.)," *Personnel* (April 1988).

Whyte, G., "Groupthink Reconsidered," *Management Review* (January 1989).

Zellner, W., "The UAW Rebels Teaming up Against Teamwork," *Business Week* (March 27, 1989).

Motivation on the Job

5

"How do I motivate my workers?"

LEARNING OBJECTIVES

When you complete this chapter, you should be able to:

1. Give a working definition of motivation, and describe how internal drive is related to an external goal.
2. Recognize Maslow's hierarchy of motivation and be able to identify its levels in real-life examples.
3. Understand the different motivational needs of different age groups and the ways in which a supervisor can satisfy each of these needs.
4. Determine which basic need tends to motivate you the most.
5. Determine the difference between intrinsic and extrinsic motivators, and decide which ones you as a supervisor can influence the most.
6. Understand how the following ideas can be applied to motivation in work situations: delegation, participation, flexibility, job rotation, job enrichment, and positive reinforcement.

"Attitude controls motivation, motivation controls performance, performance controls success." (Dick Vermeil, former head coach of the Philadelphia Eagles)

This chapter will help you develop some questions for class discussion. It will also help you formulate your own definition of motivation. Some answers to the questions below may be found in the chapter, whereas others may require personal reflection.

> Why do some methods motivate some people and not others?
>
> What methods have you used to motivate people? Can they be related to Maslow's basic needs?
>
> Which can a supervisor influence more: intrinsic or extrinsic motivators?
>
> How can someone be motivated in terms of power or affiliation?
>
> Are power and affiliation related, or are they opposites? Are they related to Maslow's basic needs?
>
> Of the managerial approaches to motivation mentioned in the text, which is the easiest to develop at the work place? Which seems to be the hardest to develop? Why?

WHAT IS MOTIVATION?

In Chapter 2 we saw that production, now more than ever, depends on management's understanding of human behavior and employee motivation. A key to the survival of many companies will be their answer to the question, "What motivates people?"

In motivating people we must learn to motivate individuals, for there are as many ways of motivating people as there are people to be motivated. What might suffice for Joe under a certain set of circumstances might prove a failure for Bob under the same set of circumstances. In exploring this subject, we must accept the possibility that motivational problems have more than one solution.

We must also accept the possibility that the needs of workers vary. An excellent starting point for a supervisor who wants to understand worker needs is to recognize worker differences. The last few decades have produced workers with varying views about the meaning of work, which have significantly changed their expectations concerning what they want out of their jobs. In general, research studies and surveys point to the following changes in employees' attitudes over the past decade:

- Unpopularity of menial or routine work
- Decrease in loyalty to the organization
- Less pride in quality of workmanship
- Work itself not as great a part of life as it once was
- Greater independence with multiple wage earners in the family
- More premium placed on leisure time
- Less desire for overtime
- More control and influence over job components
- Less responsive to authority
- More input desired
- Greater emphasis on communication
- More awareness of quality of life aspects as they relate to the job

When a psychologist uses the word *motivation*, he or she thinks of it as something from *within* a person—an internal control that depends upon the individual's perception of the world. We are moved or motivated by others only when we find personal meaning in what they suggest. Often this meaning revolves around the satisfaction of unconscious needs.

We are moved to satisfy internal needs

In its simplest form motivation can be understood as a three-step process (see Figure 5–1): There is a need, a behavioral action or direction to satisfy that need, and the accomplishment or the satisfaction of that need. Let us begin with a simple example. You feel a hunger pang, a need you want to satisfy. You have to select a way to satisfy that need, and until you satisfy it, the tension will build and become more important. Your behavior can take one of

STEP 1:
INTERNAL

STEP 2:
OBSERVED ACTION

STEP 3:
EXTERNAL SATISFACTION

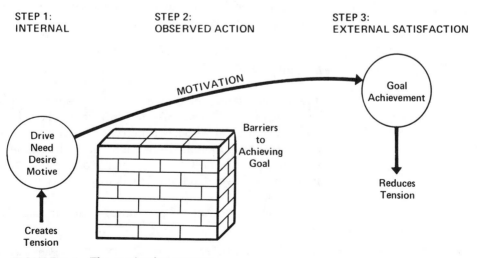

FIGURE 5–1 The motivation process

a number of directions. Sometimes the biggest problem may be that there are too many solutions available to satisfy your hunger need. Perhaps the ability to keep possible solutions to a minimum speeds our decisions and reduces tension and anxiety, thus making life easier.

Achievement is gratifying and releases tension—temporarily

The achievement of a goal is very satisfying and the tension release is gratifying, but the feeling of satisfaction is usually short-lived. The "glow" of achieving a goal lasts but a few minutes to an hour, and seldom more than a day.

Effects on the Job

What happens if workers are not motivated? One result is reduced productivity. This reduction should not happen, since employees should become more proficient at their jobs as time passes. Research involving the *learning curve* supports this statement. The learning curve indicates that our performance should improve as we continue on our job over time. A decrease in output suggests a lack of motivation, which in turn could have a drastic negative effect on the organization (see Figure 5–2).

PRIORITY OF NEEDS

Abraham Maslow's hierarchy of needs

A behavioral scientist, Abraham H. Maslow, has offered what he calls "A Dynamic Theory of Human Motivation"[1] based on a hierarchy of needs. He believes that people strive for higher needs after lower ones have been satisfied. People's basic needs are considered to be physical, followed by various safety, social, self-esteem, and self-actualization needs (see Figure 5–3).

Physical Needs

Physical needs take precedence

Little can motivate a person who has not reasonably satisfied his or her basic physical needs. As Maslow said, "For the man who is extremely and dangerously hungry, no other interest exists but food. He dreams of food, he thinks about food, he emotes only about food, he perceives only food and wants only food." Gandhi put it another way: "Even God cannot talk to a hungry man except in terms of bread."

Other basic physical needs are water, clean air, satisfactory

---

[1] Abraham H. Maslow. Motivation and Personality (New York: Harper and Row, 1957).

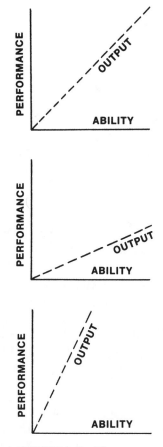

FIGURE 5–2 The learning curve

temperature, sex, and protection from the elements. Generally, most Americans feel that their physical needs are satisfied.

Adequate pay is necessary for motivation

No supervisor can motivate an employee beyond the physical needs if the pay is inadequate and not equivalent to that earned by others in the same field. Adequate pay, however, is merely the base upon which motivation can be developed.

Safety Needs

The need for safety and security is strong. It is expressed very early in life, and continues in one way or another through the retirement years. Those born to parents of modest means may find they have a greater personal need for security than those born to affluent parents.

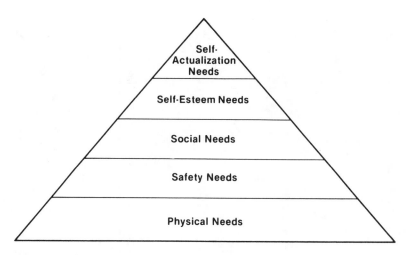

FIGURE 5–3   Maslow's hierarchy of needs

Some companies manipulate people's need for security

Today people are generally free from direct threats to their physical security, yet subtle, more sophisticated threats do exist. Some companies motivate people by manipulating their insecurities. The millions spent in emphasizing people's basic need for security are evidenced by life and car insurance programs, savings programs, and manufacturers of baby furniture, burglar alarms, and tires.

The supervisor provides security

We all need security. Some of us need it more strongly than others. The role of the supervisor is often that of a parent to employees. He or she provides the psychological security by letting them know, "I'm here when you need me."

Social Needs

People need a sense of belonging

Once people have relatively satisfied their physiological and safety needs, they feel an urge for acceptance, affection, and the feeling of belonging. This need expresses itself in a desire to be loved by someone and to have someone to love. It is important to remember that a person needs to *give* as well as *receive* affection. Supervisors can see how strong the social need is by observing the cliques during coffee breaks or the groups leaving work together. This need can be satisfied by providing employees with social activities, such as an annual picnic, bowling teams, chess clubs, investment meetings, or company committees.

The social need may more aptly be called the belonging need. Recent studies show that teamwork and team spirit are often more important than individual achievement, but many leaders and administrators underestimate their importance. Alvin Zander, a social psychologist, noted that all decisions about goals represent a compromise between a group's need for achievement and its fear of failure. A strong desire for group success means that the individuals within the group will feel satisfied if the group accomplishes its goal and embarrassed if it does not.

The desire for group success is not a permanent trait in individuals, but one that develops in certain situations. The following are factors in a group's ability to succeed:

1. A sense of unity
2. Increased responsibility for the success of one's group
3. Working conditions
4. The continual success or failure of a group

Research shows that managers often set unrealistically high goals for their workers. Such a condition may contribute to failure, because groups will tend to develop their own aspirations that they believe they will achieve. Further studies show that if there is a conflict between group and individual goals, the group goals will usually prevail.

Isolation is punishment

By contrast, complete physical or psychological isolation is one of the greatest and most feared punishments known to humans. Many people have been able to survive long terms of ordinary imprisonment without drastic deterioration of personality, but few can endure the agony of solitary confinement without profound personality changes. Isolation in milder or more subtle forms occurs in many ways on the job. For some workers it may be demoralizing. Others may be motivated to change their behavior in order to regain a sense of belonging.

Self-Esteem Needs

Every psychologically mature person needs to feel individually important. We all want self-respect and self-esteem, and we want others to think of us as important. Our attitude toward ourselves reflects a need to feel confident, adequate, and secure in meeting our day-to-day challenges. We seek a reaction from others that reflects our position as people of good reputation and prestige who deserve recognition and attention.

Status symbols satisfy the self-esteem need

Most supervisors recognize that individual needs often can be better satisfied with status symbols than with money. Although they may sneer at executive status symbols, blue-collar workers have many of their own. For example, the shop supervisor or union boss may rate the end locker or wear some distinctive symbol, such as a jacket or badge, to denote his or her position. A

stenographer may gain self-esteem by serving as a private secretary rather than as a member of the steno pool. A salesperson gains
status by driving a company car or by receiving a new car from the
company every three years.

Sometimes our needs are in conflict. The need to be an integrated, accepted member of a group may conflict with the need to
be a leader. A good worker who is selected as a supervisor may
become an ambivalent leader, because the need to be an accepted
member of the group proves stronger than the ego drive to be a
supervisor.

Self-Actualization Needs

Only after we have satisfied our lower needs are we able to
become as much as we can be. The drive within us for this satisfaction
becomes as strong as or stronger than the other needs we have
gratified. According to Maslow, "Even if all these needs are satisfied, we may often expect that a new discontent and restlessness
will soon develop, unless the individual is doing what he is fitted
to do." It is believed that the need for self-actualization and

All needs are never
totally satisfied
achievement is never really satisfied. We strive to do a better job at
work or attempt to revise our work schedule to accomplish more.

In recent years, ideas of success have begun to revolve around
various forms of self-fulfillment. Instead of wanting to "keep up
with the Joneses," people have expressed more independent sen-
timents: "I have my own life to live; let the Joneses keep up with
themselves."

Overview of Needs

When a person joins the work force, he or she brings along
certain needs. They are summarized in Table 5–1 together with
possible ways of satisfying them on the job.

PRIORITY OF MOTIVES

Motives are very
important in
understanding employees
Motivation can also be analyzed from a motive point of view. Some
psychologists maintain that learned needs (motives) are more important to the understanding of today's employee than unlearned
(physiological) needs. Considerable research has offered the following explanations of the more significant motives:

TABLE 5–1 How work can satisfy our various needs

Needs	Satisfaction	Work Element
1. Physical	Food, air, water, warmth, sex, sleep, shelter from the elements	Clean restrooms, safe working area, cafeteria, air conditioning
2. Safety	Safety, security, freedom from pain and worry, familiar things and ideas, stability	Tenure, retirement programs, seniority systems, helmets, credit union
3. Social	Love, rewarding personal relationships, secure friendships, families, parents, feeling of belonging, social approval, social acceptance	Bowling leagues, softball teams, million-dollar insurance club, uniforms, athletic teams, company newspaper, parties
4. Self-esteem, ego	Feeling of adequacy, self-respect, self-worth, prestige, confidence, recognition, appreciation, importance	Titles, promotions, desks, certificates of achievement, private office, private secretary
5. Self-actualization	Achievement, growth, realization of potential, full capability challenge, opportunity	Work itself

Power Motive: The Need for Control

Some individuals have an intense desire to be in charge, to be in a position of authority. A supervisor would normally have a high need for power.

Affiliation Motive: The Need to Be with Others or to Belong to a Group

Some individuals have an intense need to be part of and accepted by a group of co-workers. Whereas supervisors generally have a high power motive, their subordinates generally have a high need for affiliation.

Achievement Motive: The Need to Achieve

Those who are affected by the achievement motive are somewhat independent, do not depend on others, and find personal satisfaction in performing a task.

Status Motive: The Need to Possess or Acquire Position in a Group

Formal status symbols include titles and privileges; informal status symbols include dress and performed functions. Status and its companion symbols are extremely important to most employees and deserve appropriate recognition.

Security Motive: The Need for Certainty and Protection

The rapid change in today's work environment creates a serious threat for some employees. Communication, understanding, and empathy from the supervisor can be most helpful in easing employee fears in this area.

AGE FACTORS IN MOTIVATION

As we age, our needs change, and so does our perspective. We have different responsibilities, different sets of standards, and a new role in society. The supervisor who understands an individual's needs is closer to discovering what motivates that individual.

Young Workers

Young workers look for praise and recognition

As people embark on their chosen careers, it is likely they want to prove to others and to themselves that they can be successful. It is natural to pull away from parental control and be independent. An early marriage, a new car, a new apartment—all reflect a need to satisfy one's self-esteem drive. A person works hard to develop a self-image consistent with his or her new status. For high school as well as college graduates, this is the period of low income and little responsibility. As a result of experimentation, job changes can be frequent. The young worker is looking for recognition, status, and praise, and often feels his or her idealism is unappreciated. Maslow's self-esteem need is important during this period.

People in their twenties are concerned with personal identity and have the ability to develop intimacy. During this period they reach toward others but they may avoid emotional extremes and rarely bother to analyze commitments. It is also the time when a person is likely to acquire a mentor—a patron and supporter some eight to fifteen years older. The patron can offer advice, give general support, and at the same time satisfy his or her own midlife need to help someone else.

TEST YOURSELF

CAN YOU RECOGNIZE THE NEED?

Each of the following work situations stresses the denial of one of four basic needs: (1) security, (2) social, (3) self-esteem, and (4) self-actualization. After each situation write the number of the need being denied. Refer to the text if necessary. (Answers are given at the end of the chapter.)

1. A rumor of imminent layoffs was being circulated in the company, and the employees were upset. _____
2. A new employee felt left out when she was not asked to join her fellow workers for coffee. _____
3. A machine operator developed a way to cut production time. Her supervisor adopted the plan for operators on similar machines without giving her credit. The woman was resentful. _____
4. A man who had worked hard on behalf of the union wished to be elected shop steward. At the last election, he was not nominated, and he felt let down by his friends. _____
5. A worker received $15 extra in his weekly pay check. He felt ashamed that he did not report the mistake. _____
6. A group of employees liked to go for coffee together. The boss divided them into two groups and made them go at different times. The employees were unhappy about the ruling. _____
7. An employee who felt he could not work smoothly with others wanted to take a human relations course. The course required him to leave work 15 minutes early once a week, and he offered to make up the loss by coming in 15 minutes early on those days. The supervisor denied his request, thereby causing the employee a setback in his plans. _____
8. A store manager set a goal of a 15 percent sales increase in the next six months. She failed to attain her goal, but she did increase sales by 5 percent. She was keenly disappointed. _____
9. A salesperson was worried because he had a substantial drop in sales for no apparent reason. _____
10. A manager resented having to cancel elaborate plans for a camping trip with her family at the last minute because of work commitments. _____

Crisis at 30

Three leading life cycle scholars, UCLA psychiatrist Roger Gould, Yale psychologist Daniel Levinson, and Harvard psychiatrist George Vaillant, agree that a crisis generally develops around the age of 30. Assurance wavers, and life begins to look more difficult and painful. Self-reflection churns up new questions: What is life all about? Why can't I be accepted for what I am, not what others expect of me? An active social life tends to decline during this period.

Marriage becomes particularly vulnerable to infidelity and divorce. The spouse may be viewed as an obstacle instead of an asset. Some behaviorists see crassness, callowness, and materialism at this stage. A struggle can be detected among incompatible drives: one for order and stability, one for freedom from restraints, and one for upward mobility at work.

Midway at 35

Somewhere during this period an emotional awareness develops that death is approaching, and time is running out. Researchers see this stage as an unstable, explosive time resembling a second adolescence. All values are open to question, and the midlifer wonders: Is there time to change? The mentor acquired in the midtwenties is cast aside, and the emphasis is on what some call becoming "one's own person." There is "one last chance to make it big" in one's career. Does all this add up to disaster? Not necessarily; the way out of this turbulent stage often heralds a new stage. Researcher Erik Erikson calls it "generativity": the nurturing, teaching, and serving of others. Successful midlifers can emerge ready to become mentors themselves. During this stage a person may welcome the challenge of being a supervisor.

Settling Down at 45

Belonging need becomes important

As a person passes the midpoint in life or possibly in a career, the need for self-esteem may be tempered by the reality of marriage and children. A need for belonging may now become stronger than a self-esteem need. Some satisfaction for this need may be found through community action groups or perhaps recreational groups such as bowling leagues and softball teams.

The die is cast, decisions must be lived with, and life tends to settle down during the forties. There is increasing attention to a few old values and a few friends. Money is often less important.

Married people tend to turn to their spouses for sympathy as they once did to their parents.

The employer who hires workers past 45 years of age can expect these qualities:

1. Stability that comes with maturity
2. A serious attitude toward the job
3. More reliability, less absenteeism, and steady work habits
4. A sense of responsibility and loyalty
5. Less tendency to be distracted by outside interests or influences

Noting these advantages, many employers include older workers in every working unit. They find that mature employees have a stabilizing influence on the group. Studies have reported a positive correlation between age and general attitude or job satisfaction. As workers grow older, they tend to become more satisfied with their jobs, regardless of the income.

Mellow Fifties

The fifties are marked by a softening of feelings and relationships, a tendency to avoid emotion-laden issues, and a preoccupation with everyday joys, triumphs, and irritations. There is more concern for security, stability, and keeping the "work ship on an even keel."

Need for security dominates the preretirement age

As one approaches the senior citizen years, security becomes a frequent concern. Future plans are connected with pensions, retirement homes, and endowment checks, and the accumulation of savings becomes very important. The security need is a strong and necessary drive for the preretirement person of 55 years or older.

THE WORLD OF WORK

Today's growing pressures to economize put additional stress on labor problems. Absenteeism, turnover, idleness, and featherbedding, along with product defects and errors, are seen first as cost factors and second as the result of a lack of motivation. When motivation is failing, management may consider one of the following "carrot-and-stick" theories:

1. Work is inherently irksome, and thus more interesting carrots are required.
2. Workers are a shiftless and lazy lot, and thus stronger sticks are required.

Positive motivators are often tried during economically good times, when enticing carrots are dangled in front of the employees to encourage them to perform. But during a period of recession, it is more common to motivate negatively. During the recessions of the early seventies and early eighties, for example, the fear of losing one's job was the incentive for many to work harder.

As technological changes continue to characterize American industry, the supervisor's challenge becomes even more complex. Many jobs are becoming obsolete with the increased use of robots, microcomputers, and word processors. Many workers face career changes. Such uncertainty makes workers at all levels in the organization feel uneasy. Motivating workers in such a quickly changing environment is a real challenge for today's supervisor.

Intrinsic and Extrinsic Motivators

During the past 40 years, the growth of fringe benefits has become a sizable part of the payroll. Companies provide sick leave, paid vacations, medical and dental plans, and free legal aid, all in the hopes that employees will show more loyalty and more motivation. Ironically, in most cases an employee can enjoy the fringe benefits only when away from the job. These are called *extrinsic motivators.*

Extrinsic motivators are enjoyed off the job

Intrinsic motivators benefit employees on the job. Logically, people work harder when they are provided with comforts and when work is enjoyable. Coffee breaks, cafeterias, clean restrooms, and safe equipment are classic intrinsic motivators, giving employees the feeling that management cares (see Figure 5–4).

People can indeed be induced to work because they enjoy the environment and the work itself, and educators have long recognized the value of these intrinsic motivators. Often extrinsic motivators are needed to prod people into doing new or more difficult jobs or into acquiring rudimentary skills. In fact, there is a danger that extrinsic rewards may undermine a person's intrinsic interest in an activity by inducing him or her to engage in it only as a means to some extrinsic goal. The joy of performing a task for itself may disappear when it is done simply for the reward offered by the supervisor.

Extrinsic motivators may undermine intrinsic motivators

Interesting work may be the top attraction

In a University of Michigan study 1,533 workers were asked to rate the importance of various aspects of work, and intrinsic motivators led the list. Of the five top-ranked features, as listed below, only the fifth dealt with tangible economic benefits:

1. Interesting work
2. Enough help and equipment to do the job
3. Sufficient information to do the job
4. Enough authority to do the job
5. Good pay

Supervisors' and Subordinates' Views of Motivation

People today are motivated primarily by their self-images. Opportunities for advancement, greater responsibility, promotion, growth, achievement, and interesting work are consistently identified as factors that make the work situation enjoyable. These factors, being primarily associated with higher-order needs, are not easily measured or handled in supervisory strategy.

All too often managers think they know what the employees want, but employees claim otherwise. In one survey, supervisors were asked to rank ten job factors in the order they felt their workers would rank them, and the workers were asked to rank the same factors. When the answers were compared, it was obvious that the supervisors' perception of important job conditions was considerably different from that of their employees.

Supervisors thought pay was most important, whereas workers wanted to be appreciated

The most interesting finding of the survey is that supervisors rated wages as the most important factor, while the employees rated appreciation of work done as the most important. It could be

FIGURE 5–4 Logically people work harder when the job is more enjoyable. Attractive surroundings, pleasant music, coffee breaks, clean restrooms, and safe equipment are all effective intrinsic motivators. (Photo: Courtesy of Steelcase, Grand Rapids, Michigan)

that today most employees take high wages and excellent benefit plans for granted. We know that most collective bargaining sessions do not start from the question of whether there will be a raise in pay; the issue is simply the size of increase. Thus the key to long-term employee motivation is found in the higher-level needs. Only when they are satisfied can a sound, stable working environment be developed.

The Frustration of Motivation

The concept of motivation can be very complicated. If the bridge that serves to narrow the gap between needs, motives, drives, and goals were shorter, then the difficulties of motivation would be far less complicated. Unfortunately, many obstacles in life and on the job prevent motivated drives from reaching goal achievement. When drives are blocked, frustration results (see Figure 5–5). Employees have many reactions to frustration that make the supervisor's job more difficult. Specific approaches to motivation must be developed to prevent frustration and effectively motivate employees.

SUPERVISORY APPROACHES TO MOTIVATION

Delegation

One way to satisfy employees' need for achievement, recognition, and responsibility is to give them a task and the authority to carry it out. Authority is one of the most important positive motivators delegated to employees by supervisors. If workers are allowed to have it, they may be willing to take on new challenges.

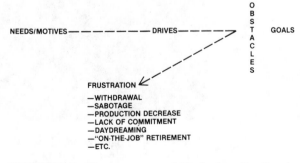

FIGURE 5–5 Consequences of blocked motivational drives

Some leaders, however, are afraid to grant such authority, because an employee may make a poor decision that would embarrass the supervisor.

You should be looking for new ways to expand rather than limit your subordinates' scope of activities. Many supervisors do not use their time wisely because they are not delegating enough duties to their employees.

One company that does try new methods of motivation is Polaroid. It allows its scientists to pursue their own projects and order their own materials without checking with a supervisor. Film-assembly workers are allowed to run their machines at their own pace. At another company, secretaries are allowed to send letters under their own signatures, rather than those of their executives.

Secretaries sign their own letters

Work Involvement

Another motivational tool used widely today is the employee-participation program. Pride and company teamwork are enhanced through the use of employee advice and suggestions. Experiments in group decision making indicate that the guidelines developed from such an approach are more realistic and more tolerable to the employees. Decisions made by employee-oriented committees are more strictly followed and last longer than those dictated by supervisors alone. This does not mean that all decisions should be made by employees, nor that employees should merely be led to believe that they are participating in decisions. Supervisors must actively seek their employees' opinions and be willing to be influenced by their suggestions and criticisms. This may be a difficult task for supervisors who feel insecure, but once a program has been established and accepted by all, it may become a better method of seeking solutions to future problems.

Group decisions can be more tolerable

Participative management may also change manufacturing techniques. Employee involvement can combat boredom by keeping the workers informed and actually participating in decision making. Saab-Scania is one company that has taken a big step in ending dehumanization and dull jobs on the assembly line. Their traditional assembly line has been partly replaced by Swedish-made industrial robots, which will take over many monotonous jobs, allowing teams of four workers to assemble an entire engine alone. A member of the team might choose either to work individually on the assembly line or to work with a partner. Instead of merely operating the electric screwdriver, the worker has learned the entire final stage of engine assembly—adding the carburetor, water pump, spark plugs, flywheel, and other parts to the block.

Teammates decide how to divide their combined 30-minute operation. The engines do not arrive inexorably; the team calls for them. If they quickly assemble three engines in 80 minutes instead of 90 minutes, they may take a supplementary coffee break at the picnic table in their alcove. "There is a greater feeling of relaxation, not so much stress," says one employee. "We help each other out, you know, when somebody has a problem or gets behind."

A similar experiment is being conducted in one Volvo plant, although the number of workers involved is small and the program is closely controlled. If the new assembly technique is successful from the workers' point of view, the union will press for the assembly team concept in other plants.

Chrysler has also shown interest in employee involvement by asking its various plants to consult with workers and come up with individual improvements, keeping in mind such principles as:

1. Fixing the responsibility as far down the organizational structure as possible
2. Giving workers enough authority to go with their responsibility
3. Letting workers know the concrete results of their suggestions and improvements
4. Creating a climate that encourages change

Flexibility

Such giants as General Foods and Motorola banished time clocks years ago. Instead they have five shifts starting every fifteen minutes. The shifts begin at 8:00, 8:15, 8:30, 8:45, and 9:00 A.M., and end at 4:00, 4:15, 4:30; 4:45, and 5:00 P.M. Each group puts in an eight-hour day, but the employee selects his or her own schedule.

In West Germany some 3,500 firms have adopted flextime. In one form of the plan, company doors are open from 7:00 A.M. until 7:00 P.M., and the factory and office workers can come in any time they like, provided that they are around for a core time from 10:00 A.M. to 3:00 P.M., and that they put in a 40-hour week. As a result, productivity is up, staff turnover is down, and absenteeism has fallen as much as 20 percent.

Job Rotation and Job Enrichment

Jobs that are altered to be less confining may actually violate certain efficiency principles but may also yield production gains. If variety in job functions offsets monotony, then it works as well as a rest. Job rotation is an excellent means of counteracting the boredom resulting from automation.

A clerk at a bank remembers her first job well: "My job was to pull invoices and checks out of envelopes and stack them into three piles—one under $10, another between $10 and $25, and a third over $25. Then I passed the piles to the next person. After two months of this, I was bored enough to quit within another month." After two more years she was still at the bank, but instead of performing a tiny task in the paper mill, she handled all the processing for 22 corporate accounts. "Handling your own accounts is a lot more interesting, and you feel like you have accomplished something," she said of her new job. Such job enrichment is essentially a restructuring of jobs to give workers variety, interest, challenge, and a sense of accomplishment.

The bank branch mentioned above had a turnover rate of nearly 60 percent a year, almost double the bank's overall rate of 30 percent. But after a job enrichment program was introduced, the rate plummeted to 24 percent.

The job expansion in one clerical operation in a stockbroker's office cut the error rate from 4 to 1 percent, and enabled 17 clerks to do the work that required 25 the year before. Most people are capable of doing far more than their jobs either allow or require, and this vast resource should be tapped. At the same time, having responsibility for a complete unit of work has given the clerks a chance to obtain feedback on their performance, which boosts productivity and cuts the error rate.

Motivation on the Job

Job enrichment must be carefully developed

Developing job enrichment programs is not easy. They must be accepted at the highest level of management and then trickle down to the lowest level. Many may resist the changes that job enrichment brings, because they see it as a threat to established jobs.

Overspecializing leads to boredom

For at least 50 years, industry has attempted to break jobs down into their smallest possible components and to string them out along assembly lines. Managers, assuming that work was inevitably boring, tried to boost morale and productivity by improving benefits and working conditions. We are now finding that the impact of boredom on productivity outweighs the benefits of extreme specialization.

Positive Reinforcement

Employees should receive praise and recognition for improved performance. Although this sounds like an obvious and elementary principle for any well-managed operation, many companies ignore it. We naturally tend to tell employees when they are doing wrong, but how often do we praise them for doing a good job or even an excellent job? Yet the fact is that we can all be motivated by strokes of praise or "warm fuzzies." Kennett Blanchard and Spencer Johnson, in *The One-Minute Manager*, suggest praising a worker who does something right. They suggest that the praise should be brief but specific—and should occur at the time. The one-minute praisings serve as a motivational reinforcement technique. Some supervisors wait until performance evaluation time to praise, thus losing the benefit of the reinforcement. Even worse, if praise is delayed, some supervisors forget the incident.

Listening Supervisors

Studies seem to indicate that employees who have supervisors who listen to them have higher morale than those who do not. To be an effective communicator, the supervisor must know more than the rules for writing memos or making effective speeches; the supervisor must also know how to listen. Listening helps a supervisor develop an insight into the motives and aspirations of their employees in order to interact with them effectively.

Management needs to exchange information with employees

Xerox and the American Management Society have developed and conducted listening clinics. "Remember," one conference leader points out "the higher you get in management, the more dependent you are on the accurate exchange of information." You can improve the exchange of information as well as increase your employees' morale by having a sympathetic ear and cultivating an interest in their real biases, abilities, ambitions, and needs.

One manager said, "I don't understand why the employees don't perform better." Another manager replied, "Perhaps they don't want to be treated better, but want to be used better, and the only way we can find out how to use them better is to listen to them."

SUMMARY

A major responsibility of supervisors is the constant and continuing attempt to motivate the work force. We must accept the facts that each worker is different and hence that individual needs vary. The last few decades have produced workers with changing views on the meaning of work and what they want out of a job.

Motivation is a three-step process: An internal need is expressed in terms of an action, which in turn leads to the achievement of an external goal. Over time, workers should become better at their jobs. If productivity or output begins to drop off, it could suggest a lack of motivation.

Maslow, the noted behavioral scientist, believes that people strive to satisfy higher needs only after lower needs have been fulfilled. The most basic needs are the physical ones, followed by safety needs, social needs, self-esteem needs, and self-actualization needs.

Motivation can also be analyzed from a motive point of view. Some psychologists maintain that learned needs (motives) are more important to the understanding of today's employee than unlearned needs. Learned needs include the power motive, affiliation motive, achievement motive, status motive, and security motive.

Age factors seem to affect our motivational drives. The young worker wishes to satisfy a self-esteem drive, the middle-aged worker is more likely to try to satisfy a belonging need, and the preretirement worker may find security most important.

Extrinsic motivators are enjoyed off the job; vacation, medical plans, holidays, and sick leaves are examples. *Intrinsic motivators* are enjoyed on the job; work itself, clean working conditions, and a sociable work group are examples.

Managers and supervisors are learning that some workers may be motivated through delegation, participation, flextime, and job enrichment. However, being a caring and listening supervisor is one of the easiest and simplest ways to motivate an employee.

CASE STUDY 8

Flextime for Everyone

Your department is investigating the merits of implementing flextime for all employees. The proposal is for everyone to work four ten-hour days.

QUESTIONS

1. What are the merits of flextime from the standpoint of the employees in the department?

2. What are the merits of flextime from a supervisor's viewpoint?

3. What motivational needs can be met by flextime?

4. What are your personal feelings about this proposed work week?

CASE STUDY **9**

The Disappearing Bonus

A Christmas bonus has been given regularly for the past 18 years. Last year, profits were down, yet management still decided to give the bonus because they did not want to break with tradition. This year profits have again slipped, and the subject of a Christmas bonus is at hand. The following dialogue took place at a recent meeting:

FINANCIAL MANAGER: Tradition or no tradition, profits are down, and we would really be stretching our financial resources if we were to give a bonus.

PERSONNEL MANAGER: The Christmas bonus, because of tradition, is expected. We would seriously injure morale by rescinding the bonus program. But in view of our financial condition, perhaps we should offer half of the typical bonus.

FIRST-LINE SUPERVISOR: My hourly workers don't make that much money in the first place. Heck, most of them have spent their bonuses already. If you want morale problems, wait until you see what happens if the bonus program is discontinued.

EMPLOYEE REPRESENTATIVE: It's not our fault that profits are down! We're working harder than ever. I think management should forgo *its* bonus. From the workers' point of view, we don't think of the bonus as a bonus—you *owe* it to us.

QUESTIONS

1. Discuss the merits of each statement in terms of motivation.
2. If it were your decision, what would you do? Why?

Terms and Concepts Supervisors Should Know

Achievement motive; Affiliation; Learning curve; Maslow's hierarchy of needs; Mentor; Motivation; Physical need; Positive reinforcement; Power motive; Security motive; Security need; Self-actualization need; Self-esteem need; Social need; Status motive.

Questions for Discussion

1. What are the greatest barriers to the achievement of your company's goals? Are those barriers caused by you, your employees, or your supervisors? Why do you think such a situation exists? Is there anything you can do about it?
2. What are the greatest barriers to the achievement of your *personal* goals?
3. What is your strongest need: physical, safety, social, self-esteem, or self-actualization? Can this need be satisfied on the job?

4. Which of Maslow's basic needs seems to be most neglected on the job? What could be done about this?

5. What one thing could you do to motivate your employees that you have not done recently or have never done?

6. What intrinsic motivator could be installed in your firm for your employees' benefit?

Answers to "Test Yourself: Can You Recognize the Need?"

1.	(1)	6.	(2)
2.	(2)	7.	(4)
3.	(3)	8.	(4)
4.	(3)	9.	(1)
5.	(3)	10.	(2)

For Further Reading—And More Ideas

Blanchard, Kenneth, "Finding the Comfort Zone (Some Stress Contributes to Peak Performance)," *Business Credit* (November 1988).

Blanchard, Kenneth, and Spenser Johnson, *The One-Minute Manager*, New York: William Morrow, 1981.

Boyd, Bradford B., *Management-Minded Supervision*, 3rd ed., New York: McGraw-Hill, 1984.

Cavanagh, M. E., "In Search of Motivation," *Personnel Journal* (March 1984).

Christenson, Christina, Thomas W. Johnson, and John E. Stinson, *Supervising*, Reading, MA: Addison-Wesley, 1982.

Collins, J. F., "How to Motivate Your Employees," *Nation's Business* (December 1982).

Crowley, G., "How the Mind Was Designed," *Newsweek* (March 13, 1989).

Davidson, R., "Motivating the Underachiever," *Supervisory Management* (January 1983).

"Employee Motivation for Better Performance," *Supervision* (September 1982).

Fisher, K. K., "Managing in the High-Commitment Workplace," *Organizational Dynamics* (Winter 1989).

Franklin, W. H., and S. G. Franklin, "Employee Motivation," *Security Management* (August 1982).

Galosy, J. R., "Teaching Managers to Motivate:

When Theory Isn't Enough," *Training* (November 1983).

Grant, P. C., "Why Employee Motivation Has Declined in America," *Personnel Journal* (December 1982).

Grensing, L., "Motivating Without Money— Easier Than It Seems," *Supervision* (August 1982).

Harrigan, B. L., "Job Frustration," *Working Women* (June 1983).

Herzberg, Frederick, "One More Time: How Do You Motivate Employees?" *Harvard Business Review* (January–February 1968).

Herzberg, Frederick, G. Mauser, and B. Synderman, *The Motivation to Work*, New York: John Wiley & Sons, 1959.

Kovach, K. A., "Tracking Motivation: Survey Helps Gauge Employee Needs," *Management World* (January 1983).

Maslow, A. H., *Motivation and Personality*, New York: Harper and Row, 1954.

McCreight, R. E., "A Five-Role System for Motivating Improved Performance," *Personnel Journal* (January 1983).

Miklas, D. C., "The Best Ways to Motivate," *Supervisory Management* (September 1982).

Mitchell, T. R., "Motivation: New Directions for Theory, Research, and Practice," *Academy of Management Review* (January 1982).

Nakao, Keiko, "Social Class in the Workplace: The United States Versus Japan," *Society* (January–February 1989).

Naylin, R. D., "Fulfilling Employee Needs—The Key to Motivation," *Supervision* (November 1982).

Phillips, J. J., "Rewarding Employees Effectively: Substance and Style," *Supervision* (November 1982).

Raudsepp, E., "Motivating for Super Performance," *Computer Decisions* (September 1982).

Rosse, Joseph G., "Symptoms of Unhappy Employees," *USA Today* (October 1983).

Steers, Richard M., and Lyman W. Porter, *Motivation and Work Behavior*, 2nd ed., New York: McGraw-Hill, 1979.

Szilagyi, Andrew D., Jr., *Management and Performance*, 2nd ed., Greenview, IL: Scott, Foresman, 1984.

Vroom, V. H., *Work and Motivation*, New York: John Wiley & Sons, 1964.

Williams, B., "The Trusting Heart (Modifying Hostile Behavior, Excerpt)," *Psychology Today* (January–February 1989).

The Functions of Supervision

6

"Now we have some direction."

LEARNING OBJECTIVES

When you complete this chapter, you should be able to:
1. Explain the challenge and importance of the supervisory functions.
2. Understand the phases of planning.
3. Describe the components of organizing.
4. Understand the methods used to obtain and retain qualified personnel.
5. Define and explain the function of directing.
6. Explain what must be controlled and how to control it.

"If we don't know what we are trying to achieve, how will we know if we achieved it?"

Here are a number of questions to contemplate while reading this chapter. Some of the answers are covered in the chapter, whereas others involve reflecting on your experiences and opinions.

To be an effective supervisor, is it important to plan?

What are the consequences of a lack of planning?

Which is more important, planning, organizing, staffing, directing, or controlling?

What are the major components of staffing?

What does controlling involve?

THE CHALLENGE OF PLANNING AND CONTROLLING

Planning and controlling are sometimes called "Siamese twins"

Two of the most important functions performed by the supervisor are planning and controlling. Planning suggests anticipated future actions, while controlling deals with checking to see how effectively those actions have been carried out. Planning and controlling are closely related, sometimes being referred to as the "Siamese twins" of the supervisory-management process. In effect, if you do not have a plan, you cannot control! How would you know what to evaluate?

Planning deals with the future, whereas controlling deals with the present. In practice, they enable the supervisor to determine how well the department measures up to expectations, or, in other words, to evaluate the relationship between expectation and reality. In short, if we fail to plan, we do not know what we are trying to accomplish, and we are prone to experience numerous crises. If we fail to control, we do not know what we have accomplished.

PLANNING AND CONTROLLING PROCESS

As shown in Figure 6–1, there are five steps in the planning and controlling process:

1. Determine objectives
2. Establish plans
3. Put plans into action

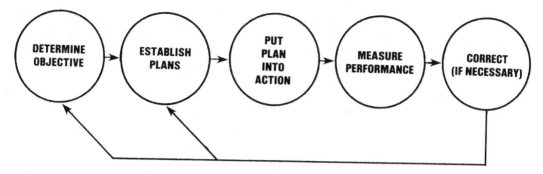

FIGURE 6–1 The planning and controlling process

4. Measure performance
5. Correct (if necessary)

Planning and the need to control set the tone for the functions of supervision. However, to succeed as a supervisor, all five functions must be practiced.

THE PLANNING FUNCTION

Planning is the foundation of the supervisory process

The planning function represents the foundation of the supervisory process. It bridges the gap from where we are to where we wish to go. It is the thinking phase of the process, ensuring that critical activities occur in a timely, deliberate, and systematic fashion that is consistent with predetermined goals.

Guidelines for Planning

Although planning is complex and difficult, the following guidelines can improve planning:

1. *Develop plans that are clear and understandable.* A confusing plan causes waste, and the most effective plan is useless if it is not understandable.
2. *Develop plans with purpose.* The plan must focus on specific goals.
3. *Develop plans that are possible.* The plan must be realistic and practical. If a plan is not possible, it is useless.
4. *Develop plans that are complete.* The plan must be thorough, exact, and detailed.
5. *Develop plans that are flexible.* The plan must be flexible to allow for modifications should circumstances change.

Even if these guidelines are followed, however, there is no guarantee that perfect plans will result. Likewise, good, effective planning will not eliminate all problems, although it can greatly reduce them. But proper planning, even if not perfect, will provide *There is no substitute for* a sense of direction, assist with change, and help coordinate *planning* work. It is a function for which there is no substitute.

The Planning Sequence

The planning function can best be analyzed in sequential phases. When supervisors gain experience in planning sequentially, the process becomes easier and more effective. The planning phases are as follows:

- Phase 1: Select objectives.
- Phase 2: Communicate objectives.
- Phase 3: Review the environment.
- Phase 4: Determine strategies.
- Phase 5: Identify and select an action plan.
- Phase 6: Evaluate the action plan.
- Phase 7: Prepare budgets.
- Phase 8: Determine a timetable.
- Phase 9: Develop standards.
- Phase 10: Involve subordinates.

PHASE 1: SELECT OBJECTIVES

The primary objective of planning in organizations is to establish and accomplish the goals of the enterprise. Supervisors must be cognizant of the organizational objectives, since planning at the department level must be consistent with the overall goals. Orga-*Goals must be clear* nizational goals must be clearly stated and understood so that supervisors can shape departmental objectives according to organizational plan. Department plans are subservient to those of the organization and represent a starting point for the supervisory planning process.

During the first phase, supervisors must never forget that *People do the work* people do the work. Even if objectives are technologically advanced and strategically sound, they will be worthless if the employees are not involved in and committed to the process. Such participation is clearly a vote of confidence for the work force. Objectives developed from this perspective will lead to employee ownership in the objectives and serve as a solid foundation for the remainder of the planning period.

PHASE 2: COMMUNICATE OBJECTIVES

When departmental objectives have been established in concert with organizational objectives, supervisors must communicate those objectives to all departmental members. Frequently, however, this critical step is overlooked. Complete communication of objectives occurs when:

1. All subordinates are aware of the organizational objectives.
2. All subordinates are aware of the departmental objectives.
3. All subordinates are aware of what is expected of them in relation to both the organizational and departmental objectives.

Subordinates must know the objectives

More importantly, subordinates must know about the objectives prior to the implementation of the plan, which offsets the problems that can arise when employees learn about objectives secondhand. Firsthand involvement leads to long-term commitment, loyalty, and ownership.

PHASE 3: REVIEW THE ENVIRONMENT

When the organizational and departmental objectives have been determined, a thorough review of the external and internal environment must occur to evaluate the feasibility of their achievement. For example, if a company decides to mass-produce a product to enhance profitability, the following external and internal variables must be considered:

External Environmental Variables

1. *Interest rates:* Can we afford the cost of automated equipment?
2. *Consumer demand:* Can the demand sustain the objective?
3. *Societal trends:* Is the product a fad or does it fulfill a more stable societal need?
4. *Competition:* Is the competitive environment ripe for the entry of a new product?

Depending on the objective, other external environmental variables may require consideration, including government regulations, community standards, ecology, population trends, legal aspects, and economic climate.

Internal Environmental Variables

1. *Work force:* Are there enough adequately trained workers to achieve the objective?
2. *Budget:* Are sufficient financial resources available?
3. *Capacity:* Are production facilities adequate?
4. *Inventory:* Can appropriate supplies and materials be obtained?

Depending on the objective, other internal environmental variables may require consideration, including unions, storage capacity, and equipment.

STRATEGIC PLANNING IN ACTION

Chrysler Corporation demonstrated excellence in strategic planning when the K car was introduced. From an external environmental standpoint, the car-buying public sought an economic, well-built automobile with room for five adults. Foreign imports threatened Chrysler's continued existence unless it provided such a car.

As Chrysler assessed its internal environment, it determined its strength to be its automation. It saw its weakness as the production of oversized cars of questionable quality.

The K car strategy required both short-term and long-term decisions. On a short-term basis, cost-cutting and human resource strategies were implemented to facilitate the production changeover. Long-term decisions involved retooling, advertising, and production changes aimed at reaching the overall objective.

The economical and quality-oriented aspects of the K car are stressed at all levels of the Chrysler Corporation, and are backed by the policy offer of 7 year/70,000-mile warranty protection plans.

The successful implementation of these strategic decisions enabled Chrysler to engineer one of the most dramatic turnarounds in American business history.

PHASE 4: DETERMINE STRATEGIES

The purpose of a strategy is to carry out the objectives of the enterprise. Organizations use strategy as a comprehensive device to guide the nature and direction of the activities designed to accomplish their goals. G. A. Steiner and J. B. Miner have defined strategic planning as "the process of determining the major objectives of an organization and the policies and strategies that will govern the acquisition, use, and disposition of resources to achieve *Strategies emerge from* those objectives."[1] A strategy results from determining objec-
objectives tives. For example, the K car and the minivan are strategic outcomes of the Chrysler Corporation's objective to provide an economical means of private transportation.

Strategic planning has five distinguishing characteristics:

1. It necessitates an external assessment of opportunities and threats.
2. It necessitates an internal assessment of strengths and weaknesses.
3. It can take both a short-term and long-term perspective.
4. It reflects ideology that is useful at all organizational levels.
5. It requires the development of policy statements.

---

[1] Steiner, G. A. and Miner, J. B. *Management Policy and Strategy* (New York: Macmillan, 1977).

NURTURING CREATIVITY

Review the following statements. Notice how those on the left foster creativity, while those on the right can block creativity.

Paths to Creativity

- Yes, we can.
- You gotta believe.
- We can do it.
- It's worked before.
- We have the ability.
- It's within our grasp.
- It's a goal we can achieve.
- We'll give it our best shot.
- It's worth the effort.
- We can make it work.
- Let's make it happen.
- We've got the spirit.
- It will help the organization.

Roadblocks to Creativity

- It's too costly.
- We don't have the staff.
- It's not logical.
- It's too time-consuming.
- It's not our kind of project.
- It's not realistic.
- It's impractical.
- It's not possible.
- What if we fail?
- It's not worth the effort.
- We don't have the know-how.
- I don't think we can do it.
- It was tried before and didn't work.

PHASE 5: IDENTIFY AND SELECT AN ACTION PLAN

An optimal decision is the goal

The purpose of an action plan is to select the optimal course of action leading to the accomplishment of stated objectives. All possible actions must be identified and analyzed. Alternatives can be best considered when subordinates are included in the process. In turn, supervisors can enhance the generating of alternatives by nurturing subordinate creativity.

Frequently, too many options are identified, thus making their evaluation exceedingly difficult. In-depth analysis should consider such important variables as cash outlay, risk, rate of return, and opportunity cost. Quantitative methods such as operations research and computer techniques can be helpful during this critical phase. Ultimately, the best course of action must be selected for maximum goal accomplishment. The planner must never lose sight of this objective.

The best choice must be selected

PHASE 6: EVALUATE THE ACTION PLAN

At times, the planning process can be so cumbersome that supervisors lose sight of the organizational objectives. In phase 6 planners should step back and evaluate the selected course of action for its ability to achieve the objectives.

Additionally, modifications and improvements can be implemented at this time without causing confusion.

PHASE 7: PREPARE BUDGETS

A budget provides numerical meaning to the plan by establishing monetary limits and expressing its true cost. It also enables the planners to balance spending with the available resources.

PHASE 8: DETERMINE A TIMETABLE

A timetable is closely related to the planning budget. It gauges the degree of accomplishment at various intervals, thus enabling the planners to see if the project is on schedule.

PHASE 9: DEVELOP STANDARDS

Plans should be measurable Whenever possible, a plan should be established in quantitative terms. For example, "to increase market share" and "to decrease cost" are vague objectives. More appropriately expressed plans are "to capture 9 percent of the market" or "to decrease costs by 12 percent." Precise, quantitative standards enable supervisors to measure and monitor the performance of a plan, and to make appropriate corrections if necessary.

PHASE 10: INVOLVE SUBORDINATES

Subordinates should be part of the planning process. From such involvement they are likely to develop the following in regard to the plans:

1. A sense of ownership
2. A sense of loyalty
3. A sense of commitment
4. A desire to achieve
5. An understanding of individual, departmental, and organizational expectations

Subordinate involvement also enables the supervisor to obtain the following:

1. Input from those who will implement the plans
2. Insights that may not have otherwise been considered
3. More accurate plans

Thus both supervisors and subordinates benefit through involvement in the planning.

THE ORGANIZING FUNCTION

Organizing emerges from planning

The organizing function is the second step in the supervisory process. It emerges from planning and centers on the principle that people *can* do the job. Once plans are established, jobs and tasks must be arranged to accomplish goals. The skills and capabilities of people must be accurately assessed, and a flow of work must be established by the supervisor. Plans must be translated into job duties and responsibilities. People will perform the job; therefore principles of human relations must be included in the effective practice of organizing.

Organizing involves four parts:

1. Work tasks and activities broken down into units
2. People who are assigned tasks
3. Coordination of work and people
4. Condition of the environment in which people work

These four components can best be accomplished through six phases:

- Phase 1: Identify all activities necessary to accomplish organizational objectives.
- Phase 2: Divide activities into homogeneous subgroups.
- Phase 3: Assign activities to personnel.
- Phase 4: Express job responsibilities in writing.
- Phase 5: Assign adequate authority.
- Phase 6: Ensure effective coordination of departments and personnel.

Phase 1: Identify All Activities Necessary to Accomplish Organizational Objectives

This step is time-consuming yet vital to the success of the entire process. In an organizational setting, every job is important. *All* people and *all* tasks must be accounted for in the organizing effort; otherwise the plan will fail. Even worse, if a task is overlooked, the person performing it will feel excluded. Ideally, organizations should include rather than exclude people.

Phase 2: Divide Activities into Homogeneous Subgroups

Relationships are formalized through departmentalization

After all activities and personnel duties have been determined, organizations logically group homogeneous activities to create departments. Departmentalization formalizes relationships among the different work units within an organization, which results in the grouping of similar tasks. The major principles according to which departmentalization can occur are:

- Function
- Product
- Geography
- Customer
- Time
- Process
- Task force
- Matrix
- Hybrid-mixed structure

In phase 2 of organizing, departments and work units can accomplish organizational objectives more effectively.

Phase 3: Assign Activities to Personnel

Supervisors must learn to delegate successfully to achieve their objectives. Delegation is the formal assigning of tasks and authority to others. It is a basic tenet of organizing, and frees managers to perform higher-level activities. Additionally, delegation allows managers to develop the skills of departmental personnel.

Tasks are assigned through delegation   Each individual possesses unique talents, skills, knowledge, and other characteristics. Supervisors must ascertain individual strengths and center the organizing function around those abilities. Individuals must be placed in jobs matching their capabilities. Failure to assess talent accurately can lead to improper personnel placement, which causes subordinate frustration.

This consequence must be avoided at all costs. Can you imagine a football coach organizing a passing offense around a quarterback who lacks passing skills? Frustration would be the result. The quarterback loses confidence, the team loses games, and the coach loses a job.

Phase 4: Express Job Responsibilities in Writing

In all cases, job duties must be expressed in the form of a complete and updated written description. Commitment occurs when expectations are clearly defined and fully understood. Job descriptions serve as a contract between the worker and the job. It is difficult to become committed to something that has not been explained and thus is not understood.

Phase 5: Assign Adequate Authority

Authority is the privilege of giving orders

Authority is a major component of organizing. Certain employees, in addition to possessing specific job duties, are cloaked with authority; they have the privilege of giving orders. Supervisors must make sure that authority is granted effectively. If it is assigned in blind fashion, the following are likely to occur:

1. Tasks are not accomplished.
2. Authority is abused.
3. Organizational inefficiency prevails.
4. Objectives are jeopardized.

Authority is a privilege that must be taken seriously. It thus must be assigned and delegated properly.

Phase 6: Ensure Effective Coordination of Departments and Personnel

The function of organizing requires the effective coordination of all parts. When plans are reduced to operational terms, supervisors must envision the tasks to be performed. People and their expected roles are attached to assigned jobs, which, when properly coordinated, work in concert to achieve the harmony required for peak performance.

THE STAFFING FUNCTION

Staffing involves getting and keeping good people

The third step in the supervisory process is staffing. It involves recruiting, selecting, and assigning personnel to the jobs necessary for goal achievement. People *are* the organization; therefore, staffing ultimately determines the quality of the organization. The human contribution should be the nucleus of staffing.

The process of obtaining and retaining qualified personnel involves six phases:

- Phase 1: Identify positions to be filled.
- Phase 2: Initiate a recruiting program.
- Phase 3: Analyze the applicants.
- Phase 4: Develop an effective selection process.
- Phase 5: Implement orientation and training programs.
- Phase 6: Conduct salary surveys.

Phase 1: Identify Positions to Be Filled

A comprehensive analysis of job vacancies must precede the selection of people for those jobs. Job descriptions must be studied to determine:

1. The skills required
2. The experience required
3. The education required

Once assessed, a picture of the ideal candidate begins to form.

Phase 2: Initiate a Recruiting Program

Ideally, an effective recruiting program generates a number of candidates, which greatly increases the chances of an optimal choice. Major recruiting sources include:

1. Advertising (newspapers, trade journals, etc.)
2. Education agencies (colleges, high schools, trade schools, etc.)
3. Employment agencies (state, private, etc.)
4. Internal analysis (applications on file, promotion possibilities, job postings, etc.)
5. Recommendations (from employees and/or community contacts)

Supervisors should work with the human resource department during this phase.

Phase 3: Analyze the Applicants

Skills, experience, and education must be evaluated

Each recruited applicant must be analyzed and compared to the requirements of the job vacancy. Specifically, the person's skills, experience, and education must be evaluated in detail. Additionally, all applicants must be assessed according to individual personality to ensure a match with the organization. Those with a complete composite of skills, experience, education, and personality should be considered further.

Phase 4: Develop an Effective Selection Process

The optimal selection process should include a number of devices to aid in making the appropriate decision. When possible, these selection techniques should include:

1. Reviews of résumés, employment applications, and other credentials
2. Interviews
3. Tests (when applicable)
4. Reference checks
5. Character investigation
6. Education verifications

The use of such techniques is time-consuming and costly. However, if an effective choice is made, it is well worth the time and effort.

Phase 5: Implement Orientation and Training Programs

Orientation programs provide vital information

Research studies indicate employees contribute to the realization of organizational goals when they have a sense of belonging to the organization. The purpose of an orientation program is to foster this feeling by giving new employees the information they need to do the job. The sooner workers are oriented, the sooner they feel committed to the organization. Typical orientation programs include:

1. Introductions of co-workers
2. Explanations of company policies
3. Information on daily worker incidentals (entrances, exits, restrooms, cafeteria, parking lot, etc.)

Training is a never-ending process

After orientation, training and professional development programs must be established. Under most circumstances, new employees require some degree of training to perform the job. After the initial training, the organization and the supervisor must make a long-term commitment to employee training and professional development, which are ongoing, never-ending processes. Such opportunities enhance employees' contributions to the organization. The time and money spent on these programs are worthwhile investments. After all, people are an organization's most valued asset.

Phase 6: Conduct Salary Surveys

Compensation is an important consideration in staffing. Employees seek a fair day's wage for a fair day's work. An equitable pay and benefit system must be established to ensure fairness and consistency. Wage and salary surveys are recommended as a fact-gathering device to guarantee the payment of competitive wages and benefits.

THE DIRECTING FUNCTION

Directing initiates action

Directing is the supervisory function that initiates action. It involves issuing directives, communicating instructions, and guiding and motivating employees. It requires building an effective work team, and motivating each worker to perform at higher levels in a willing and enthusiastic manner.

Directing unites the other supervisory functions

Directing is a part of every supervisor's job, regardless of the number of subordinates. It influences all other functions of the supervisory process. When supervisors direct successfully, plans are accomplished, organizing is achieved, and teamwork occurs. Directing, therefore, unites all other functions. Successful supervisors never cease to direct, teach, motivate, guide, and coach employees to achieve higher levels of performance.

Directing requires the daily understanding and practice of five concepts:

1. Communication
2. Motivation
3. Leadership
4. Teamwork
5. Counseling

Each concept is not explained here since they are discussed in considerable detail in other chapters. A thorough review of these sections is strongly suggested.

THE CONTROLLING FUNCTION

Controlling requires supervisors to determine if objectives are being accomplished by measuring performance against expected standards and taking corrective action if necessary. This function completes the supervisory process.

Controlling is a four-step process

Controlling consists of four phases:

- Phase 1: Determine standards.
- Phase 2: Generate data.
- Phase 3: Compare and evaluate.
- Phase 4: Take corrective action if necessary.

Lost time and money result from a failure to control

Figure 6–2 diagrams the controlling process. As a supervisor, you must control your work situation. Failure to do so results in lost money, lost time, inefficiency, and frustration. Effective controlling, on the other hand, permits the supervisor to make certain that the plan has been properly implemented in an efficient and timely manner.

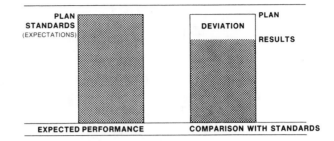

FIGURE 6-2   The controlling process

Controlling Guidelines

For control systems to be effective, the supervisor must put the following guidelines into action. Controls should

1. Be meaningful and have a purpose
2. Be clear and simple
3. Be economical
4. Be action oriented
5. Be timely

What Must Be Controlled and How?

The supervisor must recognize that individual systems of control must be put into effect. Each department is different, so the nature of their tasks may differ. Given the variety of concerns, the supervisor must concentrate on general areas common to all departments and tasks. The application of the following seven critical control measures should provide the supervisor with ample direction:

1. *Quality:* Prepare a record of expected product quality, and evaluate to see if the results are consistent with the record. If not, investigate to determine the cause of the problem, and institute measures that will correct the problem.
2. *Quantity:* Prepare a schedule of expected volume. Analyze the daily results and establish patterns. If variances occur, develop a plan to correct the deviations. This must be done continually.
3. *Cost:* Refer to your department or function budget to determine the operating money that is at your disposal. As money is expended, compare and evaluate the effect of those expenses on your budget. Review all expenses on a daily, weekly, and monthly basis to make sure that spending is in ratio to performance. Evaluate material and equipment costs so that variances can be addressed quickly.
4. *Time:* Deadlines are a fact of life in supervision. Controlling enables

the supervisor to use deadlines beneficially. Needless to say, if the product or service is not completed on time, the organization suffers. Ideally, the deadlines and expected dates of completion should be merged into a schedule that enables the supervisor to identify variances as soon as possible in order to apply corrective measures.

5. *People:* When quantity, quality, or time problems are identified, the problems are frequently traced back to poor employee performance. The supervisor must evaluate the performance of each subordinate on a regular and continuous basis so that appropriate corrections can be made.

6. *Safety:* Supervisors are legally obligated to make sure that employees are provided with safe and healthy working conditions according to the Occupational Safety and Health Act (OSHA). Also, accidents must be kept to an absolute minimum. Control mechanisms for safety must be established, with variances being corrected immediately.

7. *Inventory:* If the complete task is to be done properly, the supervisor must be able to regulate materials, people, and money in a timely manner. If the necessary parts and materials are not available when needed, the job cannot be completed. Excessive inventory, on the other hand, is extremely costly. The supervisor must establish an inventory system that responds to organizational and departmental needs as well as established deadlines.

Resistance to Control Problems

Employees frequently fear control systems, and sometimes resist their application. When this happens, an important function of supervision is neglected, thus creating dangers for the entire organization. Supervisors can ease workers' fear of and resistance to controlling by establishing clear standards of performance. Each employee must know exactly what is expected, so he or she will not be subject to vague and abstract evaluations.

Deadlines, goals, and *quotas* must be communicated to each worker. To surprise a worker with an unexpected expectation is unfair. It is also understandable why an employee would resist and fear control under those circumstances.

Controls should be *rigid* and *tough,* but *fair* and *attainable.* Unrealistic controls will cause the worker to give up; flexible controls may not be taken seriously.

Group and individual meetings should be held to communicate control measures. Question-and-answer sessions should be included so that the supervisor can be sure that all controls are clearly and definitely understood. Any changes that follow should be handled in the same manner. If the employees are totally informed about the control process, fear and resistance can be reduced, and possibly removed.

SUMMARY

Successful supervision requires the effective and systematic application of five functions:

- Planning
- Organizing
- Staffing
- Directing
- Controlling

Planning is setting goals and developing a scheme to accomplish them. Organizing is determining how the work is to be segmented and coordinated. Staffing is selecting, orienting, training, and compensating people consistent with organizational objectives. Directing is leading and motivating people toward successful goal accomplishment. Controlling is measuring performance against standards and taking corrective action as necessary.

These five functions represent a sequential process. While they are distinctly independent, they are also collectively interrelated.

CASE STUDY **10**

Why Aren't We Profitable?

Bill Henry was a very successful insurance salesperson who decided to strike out on his own. After an intensive search for appropriate office space, he decided to locate in the middle of the business district. He felt this location would be best, even though office rent was at a premium in this area. Bill's instinctive reaction was that a key location was central to success, regardless of the cost.

Bill decided to hire two insurance agents. He firmly believed that personalized marketing would result in success, so he sought agents who identified with his approach. Bill was able to hire two exciting and dynamic agents, who were ready to start immediately.

Bill had a general meeting with his agents and told them to do whatever it takes to make the sale. He encouraged them to take potential clients out to dinner, and treat them in a personalized and professional manner. He told them that they had unlimited expense accounts. Bill believed that the long-range profit would greatly offset the expenses needed to obtain the sale in the first place. Bill also reimbursed his agents for gas and mileage. His sales agents accordingly took clients to the finest restaurants in town for lunch and dinner. Their sales results were excellent.

Most of Bill's time was spent paying rent bills, office bills, reimbursing agents for expenses, and establishing effective office *(continued)* procedures. At the end of the first six months of operations, he was extremely pleased with the number of policies sold. As he prepared reports, however, he noticed that despite the sales, his operating losses were extremely high. He asked himself, "How can I be losing money with sales as good as this? I better do something—but what? Heck, I'm not a manager, I am an insurance man. But, I can't afford to lose any more money. If I do, I'll be out of business in no time."

QUESTIONS

1. Where did Bill Henry go wrong?
2. If you were Bill, what would you do now? How would you solve the problem?
3. If you were Bill, what would you have done in the first place to prevent the problem from happening?
4. What if his insurance agents resist his attempts to change? How would you handle this phase?

CASE STUDY 11

Well, It's Budget Time Again!

Harriet Johnson was the office manager at Manis Manufacturing Company. She had two supervisors reporting to her and was very pleased with the way she had delegated the office operation to her supervisors.

About one month ago, Harriet sent a memo to each supervisor reminding them that budget time was rolling around, and that perhaps they should have a preliminary meeting in two weeks. In the interim, Harriet asked the supervisors to prepare information to support their budget needs.

At the meeting, Harriet asked each of them to summarize the progress they had made on their budgets. One of the supervisors, Cathy, indicated she was very pleased with the results of last year. She mentioned the total output was 18 percent above that of the previous year. Delays were down 11 percent, with absenteeism, tardiness, and turnover being less than 2 percent. All things considered, it was an excellent year. In addition to the above achievements, the year ended with expenses being 6 percent under budget. Cathy mentioned that with paper costs going up, she was investigating new vendors and new systems to control costs. "I'll have more on that in a week,"

she said. Cathy then proceeded to hand Harriet a recommended budget for next year, which included deadlines, costs, quotas, and new goals.

The other supervisor, Ann, did not bring details to the meeting. She stated that she was happy with the way her area had performed last year and was very optimistic about next year. There were very few problems—everyone got along very well—and she expected this to continue. Ann mentioned that they were within last year's budget, and that, as a matter of fact, "I think we had a little bit left over. I'll check on that."

QUESTIONS

1. Compare and evaluate the approaches to planning, budgeting, and control used by the two supervisors.
2. Can you recommend ways in which each supervisor can improve?
3. If you were Harriet, what type of information would you request from each supervisor at the next meeting?
4. If you were Cathy and Ann, what type of information would you want to have before the next meeting?

CASE STUDY 12

Obsolete Descriptions

Last week you were promoted to the position of supervisor. As you received the job descriptions for your department, you noticed that they had not been updated for eight years. You find this particularly disturbing because of the massive technological changes that have taken place in your department.

QUESTIONS

1. Consider this dilemma in terms of the staffing function.
2. What other supervisory functions are affected by this problem?

CASE STUDY 13

Conflicting Cues

Recently, you were promoted to the position of assistant supervisor. You have observed the supervisor coming in late and leaving early. Yesterday, one of your employees arrived late for work. You approached the person about the problem, but the employee reminded you that the supervisor was guilty of the same violation. You discussed the matter with your supervisor, who told you, "Do as I say, not as I do."

QUESTIONS

1. Discuss the implications of this problem in terms of directing.
2. What other supervisory functions are affected by this problem?

Terms and Concepts Supervisors Should Know

Controlling; Controlling guidelines; Directing; Guidelines for planning; Organizing; Planning; Planning and control process; Planning sequence; Recruiting; Selection process; Staffing.

Questions for Discussion

1. Why are the functions of supervision sequential? Explain.
2. Explain the relationship between planning and controlling. Can you do one without the other?

3. Do the five supervisory functions apply to all organizations and all supervisors? Why or why not?
4. What is the most difficult aspect of planning? Why?
5. What type of control techniques can you establish for one of your subordinates for the next two weeks?

For Further Reading—And More Ideas

Bass, B. M., and G. V. Barrett, *Man, Work, and Organizations*, Boston: Allyn and Bacon, 1972.

Bennett, C. A., "The Human Factors of Work," *Human Factors* (Winter, 1975).

Drucker, Peter F., *The Practice of Management*, New York: Harper and Row, 1954.

Dubin, R. (Ed.), *Handbook of Work Organization in Society*, Chicago: Rand McNally, 1973.

Dubin, Robert, *Human Relations in Administration*, 4th ed., Englewood Cliffs, NJ: Prentice Hall, 1974.

Dugger, W. M., "Veblen and Kropotkin on Human Evolution," *Economic Issues Journal* (December 1984).

Fayol, Henri, *General Industrial Management*, London: Sir Isaac Pitman and Sons, 1949. Fayol's *General Principles of Management* first appeared in 1916 in an industrial bulletin published in France.

Gellerman, S. W., *Managers and Subordinates*, Hinsdale, IL: Dryden, 1976.

Huneryager, S. G., and I. L. Heckman, Jr., *Human Relations in Management*, 3rd ed., Cincinnati: South-Western, 1972.

Jahoda, M., "A Social-Psychological Approach to the Study of Culture," *Human Relations* (Spring, 1961).

Joseph, B., "How Middle Managers Err as Supervisors," *Supervisory Management* (November 1984).

Locke, Edwin A., "The Ideas of Frederick W. Taylor: An Evaluation," *Academy of Management Review* (January 1982).

Mayo, Elton, *The Human Problems of an Industrial Civilization*, 2nd ed., Boston: Harvard Business School, Division of Research, 1946.

Roethlisberger, Fritz J., and W. J. Dickson, *Management and the Worker*, Cambridge: Harvard University Press, 1939.

Skinner, B. F., *Science and Human Behavior*, New York: The Free Press, 1953.

Taylor, Frederick W., "The Principles of Scientific Management," in H. F. Merril, ed., *Classics in Management*, New York: American Management Associations, 1960.

Taylor, Frederick W., *Scientific Management*, New York: Harper and Row, 1911.

Toffler, A., *Future Shock*, New York: Random House, 1970.

Wren, Daniel A., *The Evolution of Management Thought*, New York: Ronald Press, 1972.

Goal Setting and Management by Objectives

7

"*Now we are mutually committed to our goals!*"

LEARNING OBJECTIVES

When you complete this chapter, you should be able to:
1. Recognize the goal-setting characteristics of self-motivated achievers.
2. Define management by objectives and explain how it can be applied in business.
3. Recognize the advantages of individuals setting their own goals.
4. Determine the advantages of management by objectives.
5. Cite the relationship between motivation and establishing goals.
6. Recognize the need for rewarding yourself for reaching a goal.

"We can accomplish more together than we can individually."

While reading this chapter, keep the following questions in mind:

Which are more important to you: your personal goals or the company's goals? Which are more important to the company?

Do supervisors set higher personal goals than their subordinates do? Why or why not?

What are the essential ideas of management by objectives (MBO)?

How would you establish your MBO approach for the next year? What goals would you set? Would you be content to have your annual review rating based on your goal accomplishments?

Would MBO work in the human resource department as well as in the production department?

THE GOOD SUPERVISOR IS A GOAL SETTER

Studies by psychologist David McClelland have identified three major characteristics of the self-motivated achiever.[1] The achiever tends to follow certain patterns throughout life, beginning at a surprisingly early age.

Good supervisors set own goals

First, achievers like to set their own goals. They are nearly always trying to accomplish *something*. They are seldom content to just drift aimlessly and let life just "happen to them."

Set attainable goals

Second, achievers prefer moderate goals. These goals are not so easy that achieving them provides no satisfaction, nor so difficult that reaching them is more a matter of luck than ability. Achievers gauge what is possible, then select a goal that is a tough but *practical* challenge. This attitude keeps them straining their abilities to realistic limits, but no further. Above all else, achievers want to achieve, so they do not commit themselves to an impossible goal.

Always want feedback

Third, achievers prefer tasks that provide them with immediate feedback—that is, measurement of how well they are progressing toward their goal. They like to know how well they are

---

[1] David C. McClelland, "The Two Faces of Power," *Journal of International Affairs*, 24 (1), 1970, pp. 29–47.

doing at all times. This is one reason why achievers often decide upon a career in sales. The salesperson gets much more rapid feedback about the effectiveness of his or her efforts than do people in most other occupations.

Self-achievers have high price tags

McClelland points out that the monetary incentive affects an achiever in a complex way. Self-achievers usually have a fairly high opinion of their services and prefer to place a high price tag on them. They are unlikely to remain for long in an organization that does not pay them well. On the other hand, it is questionable whether an incentive payment actually increases their output, since they are normally working at peak efficiency anyway.

McClelland's findings can be applied to the supervisory role. Self-achieving supervisors like to set their own goals, which will be realistic and practical. Short-range goals are often more rewarding to them because of the immediate feedback of success or failure. Supervisors who have self-achieving employees should give them room to set their own goals, for greater performance is more likely with such an approach.

WHY MANAGEMENT BY OBJECTIVES?

Supervisors have always been challenged to produce results, and they are judged by the results of subordinates. Today they must produce these results in a time of rapid technical and social change. Both supervisors and the organizations they manage need to anticipate this change and set aggressive, forward-looking goals to make changes occur when and where they want them. They must *use* these changes to gain greater control of their own destinies, or else they will be overwhelmed by them.

The supervisor's most important tool for setting and achieving forward-looking goals is people. To achieve success, supervisors must be able to instill in their workers a sense of vital commitment to organizational goals. They must also coordinate the efforts of their workers toward goal accomplishment, and they must help their subordinates grow in ability so that they can make even greater contributions.

The concept of management by objectives (MBO) was introduced by Peter Drucker in 1954 and has been further developed and advanced by such management theorists as George Odiorne and Douglas McGregor.

MBO is not a recent concept

MBO is a total system of managing

Since the 1950s, the concept of MBO has enjoyed significant popularity with organizations, supervisors, and workers. By definition, *MBO is a total management system in which the superior and subordinates meet to identify and agree on common goals to be performed by the subordinates during a certain period.* At the conclusion of that time, the superior evaluates subordinate success in realizing the goals. MBO requires all employees to set *specific* objectives, and it relies on input from people to provide the organization with vitality, creativity, and commitment. MBO is a formalized management tool with widespread use in all organizations, regardless of type and size. While all organizations can use and benefit from MBO, however, no two organizations apply MBO in the same manner.

THE MBO PROCESS

MBO is a nine-step process. Figure 7–1 illustrates the complete cycle of implementation.

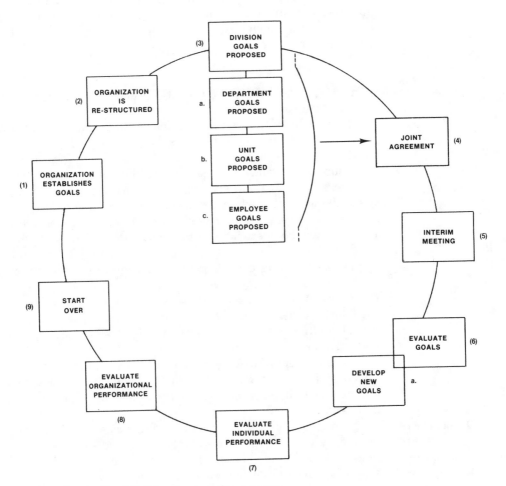

FIGURE 7–1 The MBO implementation process

Step 1: Organization Establishes Goals

The organization's goals may be expressed in terms of profits, sales, market share, or any other viable objective. The board of directors or the chief executive officer typically determines these goals.

Step 2: Organization Is Restructured

Depending upon the goals established in step 1, organizational restructuring may be necessary. If an organization decides to manufacture new products, for example, additional divisions may be needed, thereby changing organizational structure and design. Other goals may not require restructuring.

Step 3: Subunit Goals Proposed

Each division and department within the organization must next determine the degree of performance necessary to achieve the organizational goals. For example, if the organization desires to increase sales by 20 percent, each division and department must set the desired performance for the expected time period. In doing so, they will have defined their "piece of the pie." Superiors then meet with each subordinate to identify individual employee goals. The superior explains organizational and departmental goals to the employees and requests them to propose individual performance goals. This is the core of the MBO process: Individuals have the opportunity to propose their own "piece of the pie." As indicated, managers and supervisors must ensure that individual goals are quantitatively expressed. When the process is implemented properly, individuals have proposed their own performance objectives and understand their role in achieving departmental and organizational goals. Additionally, the superior can objectively measure the performance of each subordinate based on the quantitative goals.

Step 4: Joint Agreement

The superior and the subordinates meet to agree on proposed goals. When joint agreement on specific goals is achieved, linkage occurs between the employees and the organization. The results are expressed in writing and reviewed by both the superior and the subordinates during the evaluation process.

Step 5: Interim Meeting

Periodically, the superior and the subordinates should meet to assess progress. The MBO process does not recommend a specific number of meetings; however, it is inconceivable to evaluate an individual effectively in just one meeting. With monthly meetings, the supervisor can determine a subordinate's degree of success and provide problem-solving advice if needed. If a supervisor waits until the end of the evaluation period, there is no time to make adjustments or offer problem-solving information.

Step 6: Evaluate Goals and Develop New Goals

As a result of interim meetings, goals may require reevaluation. If, for example, unexpected events render initial goals unobtainable, the supervisor and the subordinate need to develop new goals jointly while there is still time.

Step 7: Evaluate Individual Performance

Individual performance is measured and evaluated on its own merit.

Step 8: Evaluate Organizational Performance

Organizational performance is measured and evaluated on its own merit.

Step 9: Start Over

The MBO implementation process begins again, and the same steps are followed.

All organizations exist for a purpose, and to achieve that purpose top management sets goals and objectives for the whole organization. In organizations that do not choose to use MBO, most of the organizational planning, strategy, and goal-setting are directed downward, from one managerial level to another. Subordinates are told what to do and how to do it. They will then be held accountable for those directives.

The MBO process shifts the direction of the communication flow by injecting an element of dialogue in which proposed plans and objectives move upward. Each employee's goals are proposed

Ways to measure for MBO

in relationship to the goals of the organization—and to the unit, department, and division to which the employee belongs. Each subordinate proposes *specific objectives*, which represent what the employee will do in measurable terms. This is sometimes referred to as the "employee's piece of the organizational pie." Together, the superior and subordinates jointly agree on the specific goals in a linking fashion (see Figure 7–2). Together they develop a group of specific *goals, measures of achievement*, and *time frames* for reaching the defined goals and/or improving job performance.

The subordinate is held accountable for the accomplishment of these proposed goals. The supervisor and the subordinate should conduct interim meetings during the process for the purpose of periodic progress review. The added communication and contact at this stage is regarded as a definite benefit. Should less than acceptable progress be identified at this time, reasons for such performance should be identified and discussed. Perhaps it becomes known that the goals and objectives were unrealistic. If this is the case, a new set of realistic goals should be established and agreed upon rather than continuing to strive for unattainable goals.

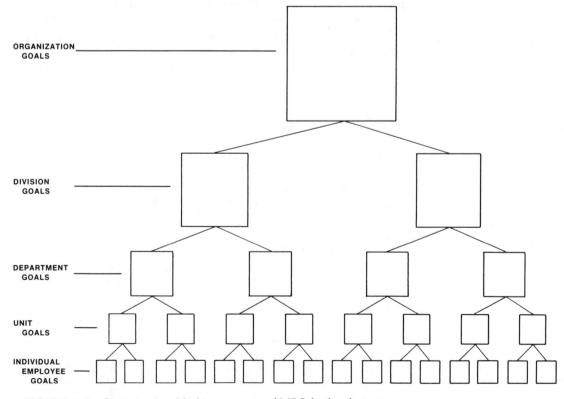

ORGANIZATION GOALS

DIVISION GOALS

DEPARTMENT GOALS

UNIT GOALS

INDIVIDUAL EMPLOYEE GOALS

FIGURE 7–2 Organizational linking aspects of MBO by levels

In the final analysis, the subordinate is judged on the merits of performance. By the same token, the evaluation of the entire organization is done on the same basis.

INDIVIDUALS SET THEIR OWN GOALS

MBO is a management technique that helps supervisors crystallize plans, stay on schedule, initiate ideas, and provide objective evaluation of an employee's performance at the end of the year. The technique of individual goal-setting is based on the belief that employees who help set their own work objectives—and thus have a role in their own destinies—will contribute more to the company.

COMMITMENT

Individual commitment increases through participation

Research indicates that employees are more likely to extend full individual commitment to something if they have had input into its development. A major advantage of the MBO system is that employees propose their goals to the supervisor, in keeping with departmental and organizational goals. As goals are projected, it is recommended that they be expressed in measurable terms, if possible. Dates, percentages, and other similar information should be stated where applicable. Ideally, individuals will not want to let themselves down, and hence they become committed to the objectives.

MODIFICATIONS

Often, an employee will propose plans that are too ambitious. The supervisor and the employee should then discuss the plans and revise them to fit the reality of the situation. It would be very unwise to accept unrealistic goals. The employee will become extremely frustrated once it is discovered that the plans cannot be accomplished, which leads to a lack of commitment to the MBO process. Sometimes the goals appear to be realistic at the time of proposal, yet they turn out to be too ambitious because of other factors. During the interim-meetings phase of the program, such problems should be recognized and modified accordingly.

Variations in Practice

In practice, the MBO approach varies widely, especially in the extent to which it is formalized and structured, and the degree to which subordinates are allowed to set their own goals. In some organizations, MBO is a formal management system with precise review scheduling, set evaluation techniques, and specific formats in which objectives and measures must be presented for review and discussion. In other organizations the system is informal and described simply as "the way we do things when we get together and decide what we've done and what we're going to do." However, in most organizations MBO involves formal objective setting and appraisal meetings held on a regular basis—quarterly, semi-annually, or annually.

The MBO approach is even more varied in the degree to which a subordinate is allowed to set his or her own goals. The kind of work performed by an organization plays a large part here. In some companies an employee is told what to do and is simply asked if he or she will achieve the goal. In other institutions the employee is given great latitude and room for innovation. Contrast, for example, the production company supervisor who informs an employee that he or she must produce 100 diodes a day, to a university president who informs a subordinate of the need to develop more community-oriented programs and asks how he or she thinks this goal can be achieved.

Potential Advantages to the Organization

No matter what form it takes in a given organization, MBO is essentially a process that helps direct attention toward results, emphasizes commitment to specific achievements, and facilitates thinking in terms of the organization's future needs.

By using the MBO approach, supervisors gain three basic advantages:

Greater commitment
1. Supervisors can gain greater commitment from their subordinates by giving them a part in formulating their objectives, a process that also gives the subordinates a sense of where they fit into the organization.

Better control
2. Supervisors can gain better control and coordination of goal achievement by having a clearer picture of who is doing what (or not doing what), and how the parts all fit together.

Development of employee
3. Supervisors can help subordinates develop by being better able to clarify their strengths and weaknesses in terms of future results.

Mutual Benefits to the Supervisor and Employees

The setting of objectives, which is part of the planning of every manager, is partially delegated to employees with the MBO approach. The benefits of mutual agreement of objectives include the following examples.

1. Gives top management increased ability to direct the efforts of the organization
2. Provides employees with a more complete understanding of expected performance
3. Provides assistance for more effective supervision
4. Provides motivation for improved performance
5. Can help supervisors develop
6. Improves communication

Guidelines for Making MBO Work

The following are some principles that have been helpful in making an MBO program effective:

1. Top management should establish overall objectives, which must be discussed with immediate subordinates to assure their understanding and acceptance.
2. Long-range plans should be prepared for each department and division and updated each year.
3. Management at all levels should participate in setting their own objectives.
4. Objectives should be stated in terms of *specific* expectations within a *specific* time frame.
5. Each objective should be stated in *measurable* terms.
6. Goals should be *realistic*. To be most effective, goals should provide for reasonable and outstanding job performance (see Figure 7–3).

Accountability Can Lead to Objectives

Checking the manager's responsibilities against areas of accountability will suggest *key result areas* for which specific objectives may be written. Examples of key result areas to consider are

1. Production (the use of capital, people, machinery, and materials)
2. Personnel development (selection, placement, and training)
3. Innovation (improvement in facilities, service, and methods)
4. Cost effectiveness (control of all expenses)
5. Product development (new and improved products)

Initiating the Program

A total understanding of the philosophy and principles of MBO requires practical experience, which will come only when you have started a program that then becomes well established.

The following points will be helpful in initiating an MBO plan:

MANAGEMENT JOB OBJECTIVES

(Prepared by the) Manager _____   Date _____   Manager's Job Title _____

(Reviewed by his or her) Supervisor _____   Date _____   Supervisor's Job Title _____

Statement of Objective	Priority	Date to Accomplish Objective	Outcome or Results
1. To reduce waste and spoilage to 3% of all raw materials used.	3		
2. To reduce time lost due to accidents to 100 man-hours a year.	5		
3. To reduce operating cost to 10% below budget.	7		
4. To install a quality-control system at a cost of less than $50,000.	2		
5. To improve production schedule and preventive maintenance in order to increase production to 95% of capacity.	6		
6. To complete a 6- to 8-hour training program for every employee.	1		
7. To complete a 2- to 4-week training program for the supervisors.	4		
8. To increase production 3% over this year's production record.	8		

FIGURE 7–3   MBO form for recording goals, priorities, and time frames

1. Start on a limited basis and involve only a small part of the organization. Proceed gradually.
2. Try to involve supervisors who are receptive to an organized approach to their jobs.
3. Use group discussions to get the program under way.
4. Don't require or expect perfection at the start. Experience will show where objectives and measurements may be in error. Adjustments can be made.
5. Hold frequent superior-subordinate discussions to make the program work.
6. Make objectives individualized and accountable.

Potential for Misuse

MBO can easily be misused and often is. What is supposed to be a system that allows for dialogue and growth between the supervisor and the employee often degenerates into a system in which the boss puts constant pressure on the subordinate to produce results. Sometimes even well-intentioned supervisors misuse MBO because they do not have the knowledge of human needs to keep their appraisal sessions from becoming critical, "chewing-out" periods. Finally, many supervisors unrealistically view MBO as a total system that, once installed, can handle all management problems.

An Organizational Goal: To Cut Down on Smoking

Can you command an employee not to smoke?

The following example will describe a positive method for developing a company goal into a commonly held employee goal. A number of company leaders in conference with medical experts have decided to accept some social responsibility and make a moral statement. They have stated that working in a smoke-filled room is undesirable because it is dangerous to everyone's health. This is a moral stand that certainly not everyone will accept. How then can the leaders install a policy that the workers will not openly oppose?

In the past, many companies have instituted incentive programs to encourage workers to stop smoking on the job. More recently, corporate attempts to eliminate smoking entirely are becoming more common. In either example, commitment to an organizational goal becomes the focus. The rationale is that smoking is not only physically unhealthy for the workers but economically unhealthy for the companies.

ESTABLISHING GOALS IS NOT ENOUGH

Discussing the goals and direction of individuals and organizations is not enough. "If we don't know where we want to go, we will make little effort to get there" is a two-pronged statement that implies both a goal and a motivation. Figure 7–4 explains the relationship between goal clarity and goal motivation.

Box A is best

Box A, with high motivation and high goal clarity, presents the optimum situation: "I know where I want to go, and I have the desire to get there." Box B shows high motivation but low goal clarity: "I want to go, but I don't know where." Box C illustrates low motivation but high goal clarity: "I don't want to go where I could or should." Box D diagrams low motivation and low goal clarity: "I don't want to go anywhere."

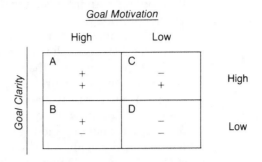

FIGURE 7–4   The relationship between
goal clarity and goal motivation

Escaping from Box D

When employees are laid off, they frequently fall into Box D. They are demotivated, without clear goals, in a "minus-minus" state. However, many who have developed new careers have discovered that setting and pursuing new goals is an exciting, revitalizing process that substitutes adventure for boring routine. A layoff can stimulate employees to widen their choices and multiply

---

HOW DO YOU HANDLE EMPLOYEES IN BOXES C AND D?

As a supervisor you are likely to be rated in Box A. You are highly motivated and have defined goals for your department. Some of your employees may be highly motivated, but unless they took part in developing departmental goals, they may be in Box B.

One of your goals is for the department to develop more teamwork, but suppose one of your employees is a young rugged individualist who prefers to work alone? He or she would clearly fit in Box C. The more you pushed your goal of teamwork, the more he or she would fit in Box C and perhaps even produce less. And there is also the employee in Box D, the near-retirement worker with little reason to generate a teamwork spirit because he or she wants to retire to go fishing. This person doesn't care to produce; retirement is his or her only goal.

1. Should the preretirement employee be told to produce or be released, or should you do nothing and wait for his or her retirement in one year?
2. Should the individualist be allowed to continue working alone, or should he or she be encouraged to leave for the benefit of the department's morale and production?
3. For the benefit of the company, should individual goals ever come before company goals? If so, when?

their options. An interested and considerate supervisor can set this process in motion.

The manager-counselor should point out that the employee who has lost his or her job may be in a position to plan more realistically at this time than at the beginning of his or her career. When the employee first looked for a job, he or she may have accepted what was available and then followed the path of least resistance. But now it's quite possible that his or her experience, broader information, and the opportunity to stand back and decide what he or she really wants to do can steer the person toward more stimulating and satisfying work.

REWARD YOURSELF FOR REACHING A GOAL

A painless way to overcome time-wasting habits is to give your ego the praise and compensation it needs for achieving a goal. We go through life distributing rewards: a morsel to our dog when he performs a trick, a tip to the waitress who serves us promptly, a treat to the child who gets an outstanding report card, a hug for the spouse who gives us a gift. In fact we are generous in rewarding everyone except the one person who is most important to each of us: ourselves.

The concept of rewarding yourself for a desired action may seem contrived, but behavioral scientists tell us it is one of the most effective ways of altering our own behavior. If you would like to change some of your habits (and who wouldn't?), try using some self-bestowed rewards.

Select a habit

The first step in setting up a reward system is to focus on a single habit you want to alter and then decide what specific action constitutes success. For example, do not resolve to reward yourself for being "more prompt" or for "not procrastinating." Desirable as these goals may be, they are not specific enough to serve as re-

Select a specific action

wardable objectives. Instead, select such actions as being at your desk at 8:00 A.M. sharp, starting your day with the most unpleasant task you have to do, or setting up a more efficient system for record keeping. The reward must be tied to a particular action, not to a character trait, even though character is what you hope to influence in the long run.

Select even a trivial reward

Second, recognize that there is usually no relationship between the magnitude of a reward and its effectiveness. Trivial things such as a hot fudge sundae can be more useful than a lobster dinner in providing an incentive for changing habits, because they permit frequent rewards for small successes, which is the key to behavior change.

Of course a major reward such as a trip to Hawaii or a new car can motivate you toward important goals. When your purpose is to change a habit, however, small but frequent rewards are far more effective. The point is to reinforce each small success and thus shape behavior.

Self-rewards can take many forms: a snack, a cup of coffee, a drink of water, a five-minute break, a short walk, a moment to freshen up, reading time, an exercise break, or permission from yourself to purchase a necessity such as a shirt or a luxury such as jewelry. Even a small chore can be a reward if it involves something you would like to finish.

Although tangible rewards are generally the most effective, you can also reward yourself mentally. Give yourself a mental pat on the back for each small accomplishment. Everyone reacts favorably to praise, and your subconscious mind does not care whether that praise comes from you or another person. Be generous in your praise when you've succeeded in achieving even one small step toward your goal.

Another method of mental reinforcement was developed by Joseph R. Cautela, Professor of Psychology at Boston College. Using this method, you imagine yourself performing the action you want to reinforce, and then you imagine yourself getting an appropriate reward. Repeating this process over and over can reinforce your tendency to perform the desired action.

SUMMARY

We have all had the experience of wanting something very badly and working very hard to achieve that goal. People have their own goals on the job as well as off the job, and ideally their individual job goals should coincide with the company goals. One key to matching the goals of the individual with those of the company is to make sure that the company's objectives are clearly explained at the time of hiring.

Goals are clearly spelled out in a process called management by objectives (MBO), which requires all supervisors to state specific objectives to be achieved by some future date, for which the subordinate is then held directly responsible. In many companies the managers and their subordinates work together to develop the specific goals, measures of achievement, and the time frame for accomplishing these goals. Employees are then evaluated on their attainment of goals they helped set and to which they had made a commitment. In some firms individuals set their own goals, which are monitored and modified by their supervisors.

The MBO program has several benefits. it enables top management to better direct the efforts of the company, it provides employees with a more complete understanding of expected performance, and it provides a method of developing managers and improving communication. MBO is misused, however, when management uses it as an excuse to apply constant pressure for results, as a basis for criticizing employees, or as an unrealistic answer to all problems.

"If we don't know where we want to go, we will make little effort to get there" is a two-pronged statement that implies not only a goal but also motivation. Good results depend on both goal clarity and high motivation. The clearer the goal and the stronger the desire, the harder we will work for the objective. As a supervisor you must make sure the department's goals are clear and use many ways to motivate your workers to achieve them.

We are generous in rewarding others for achieving their objectives, but we seldom do the same for ourselves. Self-rewards are a means of self-motivation and can take many forms: a snack, a cup of coffee, a mental pat on the back, or a purchase of some luxury. The next time you achieve a goal, remember to reward yourself as you would others.

CASE STUDY 14

He Established Management by Objectives, but . . .

The consensus of the management team was that productivity in inventory control left much to be desired. During the past several years management had taken various steps to improve the situation. They had changed work standards and had improved the environment with a new acoustic ceiling, new fluorescent lighting, and newly painted walls. However, output remained about the same.

Last month, Jim MacVeer became the new supervisor. He submitted a plan to improve production to his manager, Karen Nau, and asked permission to implement it. The plan is as follows: Each employee, with Jim's approval, will establish his or her own *productivity goal* for the next six months. Jim will meet weekly with each employee, assessing accomplishments and offering suggestions for achieving the mutually set goal. If employees are not reaching their

goals, they will identify hurdles that stand in their way, and Jim will take steps to eliminate some of the hurdles. Employees will receive one honor point a week if they are successful in attaining their goals. Each three honor points accumulated at the end of the six months entitle the employee to either one day off with pay or $25 cash.

Karen Nau was skeptical of the plan, but granted permission because of Jim's enthusiasm and assurance that the employees would cooperate. Jim pointed out that if the plan worked in his department, it might be applied to other departments as well.

Jim explained the program thoroughly and carefully to his employees. They asked to elect a committee of three to help Jim knock down the hurdles that impeded their production, and Jim agreed.

The program got off to a good start. At the
(continued)

end of four months, production showed a 9 percent gain. For some employees the increase ranged from 12 to 14 percent, while for others it was from 4 to 6 percent. Those employees who showed only a 4 percent increase complained that the system wasn't fair. Jim insisted that he was simply applying effective modern supervisory techniques.

QUESTIONS

1. In what types of situation would Jim's plan most likely be successful?
2. What are common sorts of production hurdles?
3. Do you feel Jim's program will have a long life, or will it lose the group's interest and fade away? Why?

CASE STUDY 15

MBO: Shall We—or Shall We Not?

Robert Mullins is the president of Computer and Video House, a chain of 280 company-owned stores located throughout the United States. Each store sells personal computers, computer accessories, video and audio cassettes and accessories, and related equipment.

Mullins attended a workshop/seminar at the local community college that covered the basics of MBO. Mullins became extremely excited about the prospects of implementing the system for Computer and Video House.

In the past five years, Mullins had developed the company's annual sales forecast based on input from the marketing manager, Linda Calhoun. Usually, after a discussion, both agreed that sales would increase by 15 percent per store. Expenses were usually estimated to increase by 3 percent. Neither Mullins nor Calhoun based his or her projections on hard data; they just figured that the forecast would be more effective if it were based on easy-to-understand percentages.

The day after the seminar, Mullins called Calhoun, and they had the following conversation:

MULLINS: I've just returned from an MBO seminar. It sounds exciting and very workable in our operation. Are you familiar with MBO?

CALHOUN: I've heard of it, plus I've read a few articles about it. Some friends of

mine, at other companies, have used it, but I personally have not had any direct experience with MBO.

MULLINS: The system appears easy to use. Since it's time to establish our sales forecast for the next year, I thought we'd give it a try. In the past, you and I established the forecast. Although we've always asked our territory managers and buyers for input, you and I really set the forecast.

CALHOUN: Yes, we simply come up with the same increase in sales and the same increase in expenses every year.

MULLINS: You're right. Perhaps now is the time to change. I'd like to use MBO; I think we can benefit from it. What do you think?

CALHOUN: Can we increase sales and decrease expenses?

MULLINS: We can try! Plus we can get everyone in the organization involved.

CALHOUN: How do you see us implementing MBO?

QUESTIONS

1. Does Computer and Video House sound like a viable company to use MBO?
2. What are the potential benefits to be derived from the system?
3. Specifically, outline a method for implementing MBO at Computer and Video House.

Terms and Concepts Supervisors Should Know

Commitment; Control; Individual goals; Interim meetings; Management by objectives (MBO); Measures of achievement; Modification; Organizational goals; Time frames.

Questions for Discussion

1. Using your own job description and present duties, establish three goals to be accomplished within the next two weeks. In what ways can you measure your accomplishments, particularly if you do not finish the tasks?
2. Make a list of your personal goals, set time frames for achieving them, and establish ways to measure your success in achieving each goal.
3. For which jobs is it difficult to establish MBO goals, and for which positions does it seem easy?
4. What are some of the advantages and disadvantages of employees setting their own goals?
5. What kind of goals and measures of achievement can you establish for one of your subordinates for the next two weeks?

For Further Reading—And More Ideas

Babcock, R., and M. A. Qureshi, "Program for Integrating Budgeting and MBO," *Managerial Planning* (June 1981).

Beuhlmann, D. M., and R. F. Ortman, "'Management by Objectives: Some Evidence on Measuring Objectives," *Management Planning* (July–August 1982).

Carroll, Stephen J., Jr., and Henry L. Tosi, Jr., *Management by Objectives: Applications and Research*, New York: Macmillan, 1973.

David, F. R., "How Companies Define Their Mission," *Long-Range Planning* (February 1989).

Deegan, A. X., and T. R. O'Donovan, "Budgeting and Management by Objectives," *Health Care Management Review* (Winter 1984).

Doran, G. T. "There's a Smart Way to Write Management Goals and Objectives," *Management Review* (November 1981).

Duffy, M. F., "ZZB, MBO, PPB and Their Effectiveness Within the Planning/Marketing Process," *Strategic Management Journal* (March–April 1989).

Fannin, W. R., "Making MBO Work: Matching Management Style to MBO Program," *Supervisory Management* (September 1981).

Ford, R. C., "Ten Questions About MBO," *California Management Review* (Winter 1980).

Granger, C. H., "HBR Retrospect: Excerpts from *The Hierarchy of Objectives*," *Harvard Business Review* (March–April 1989).

Greenwood, R. G., "Management by Objectives: As Developed by Peter Drucker," *Academy of Management Review* (April 1981).

Halatin, T. J., "Targeting Your Audience for Strategic Supervision," *Supervisory Management* (April 1989).

Heshizer, B., "An MBO Approach to Discipline," *Supervisory Management* (March 1984).

Horan, N. J., "Will Your MBO Program Fly or Fizzle?" *Supervisory Management* (December 1981).

"How the Best Get That Way (Codes of Conduct and Mission Statements)," *Training and Development Journal* (March 1989).

Jackson, J. H., "Using Management by Objectives: Case Studies of Four Attempts," *Personnel Administrator* (February 1981).

Kelly, C. M., "Remedial MBO," *Business Horizons* (September–October 1983).

Kondrasuk, J. N., "Studies in MBO Effectiveness," *Academy of Management Review* (July 1981).

Latham, G. P., and E. A. Locke, "Goal Setting: A Motivational Technique That Works," *Organizational Dynamics* (Autumn 1979).

McConkey, Dale D., *How to Manage by Results*, 3rd ed., New York: Amacom, 1980.

McConkey, Dale D., "Twenty Ways to Kill Management by Objectives," *Management Review* (October 1972).

McGliore, R. H., "'MBO Redefined," *Management World* (November 1982).

McGregor, Douglas, *The Human Side of Enterprise*, New York: McGraw-Hill, 1960.

Odiorne, George S., *Management by Objectives*, New York: Pitman, 1965.

Pringle, C. D., and J. G. Longenecker, "Ethics of MBO," *Academy of Management Review* (April 1982).

Raia, Anthony P., *Managing by Objectives*, Glenview IL: Scott, Foresman, 1974.

Ruth, S. R., and W. W. Brooks, "Who's Using MBO in Management," *Journal of Systems Management* (February 1982).

Schaeffer, D., "MBO Pitfalls," *Supervision* (August 1983).

Schaffer, R. H., "Built-in Barriers to High Performance (Excerpts from *The Break-Through Strategy*)," *Management Solutions* (November 1988).

Treece, M. A., "Supervision by Objectives—A Workable Approach," *Supervision* (August 1982).

Weimer, G. A., "MBO Is Tailor Made for Managing in Recession," *Iron Age* (July 21, 1980).

Wilkinson, R., "How to Avoid Getting Lost in the Crowd," *Supervision* (February 1989).

Wright, P. C., "'Management by Objectives—One More Time," *Supervision* (January 1984).

Organizational Structure

"Now to whom do I report—Boss?"

LEARNING OBJECTIVES

When you complete this chapter, you should be able to:
1. Explain the need for an organizational structure.
2. List the advantages and disadvantages for each of the three types of organization: line, line and staff, and matrix.
3. Discuss management hierarchy and its relationship to the organizational chart.
4. Link the organizational chart to the various types of communications.
5. Compare and contrast the general staff and the specialized staff.
6. Compare and contrast tall and flat organizational structures.
7. Summarize the basic points of the span-of-control concept.
8. Know the difference between the styles of centralization and decentralization.
9. Describe the basic elements of the matrix style of organization.
10. In your own words, discuss the advantages of a company policy and an employee's handbook.

"Businesses fail because of people who believe they can rest on past laurels."

Here are a few questions to stimulate your thoughts. The answers to some may be in the text; for others you may need to call on your experiences and personal opinions.

As a company expands, does it become more complex?

Who has more employees to supervise personally: the company president or the line supervisor?

Which is the most complicated organizational system: the line, the line and staff, or the matrix structure?

Who is more motivated to communicate with employees: the line supervisor or the staff personnel? Why?

Would you rather work for a tall or a flat organization? Why?

How many people do you supervise? Does this number seem consistent with your position, duties, situation, and employees? Why or why not?

Are businesses tending to become more centralized or decentralized?

THE NEED FOR ORGANIZATIONAL STRUCTURE

How a supervisor carries out his or her job is defined by the organizational structure and by the structure of the supervisor's particular department. This limitation makes the job difficult, because it does not allow for human variability. If structure limits flexibility, why then does it surface in every organization? Is there an advantage to a structured situation over an unstructured one?

Organization must be built around the firm's long-range goal

An organization's structure limits the freedom of individuals in order to achieve a long-range goal. That goal may be questionable or may conflict with other, larger goals. Workers who object to the organization's purposes will not accept the structure of the organization, because they do not accept the objectives.

Furthermore, a company may become bureaucratic; its structure may become unwieldy and so complicated that it actually obstructs its original purposes. Most people have had unpleasant experiences, at best humorous and at worst tragic, with bureaucratic organizations.

It is important for you, as a supervisor, to understand something about the structure of the organization in which you function. Your understanding will make your working relationships more productive.

THE MANAGEMENT HIERARCHY

Every company ostensibly has a formal hierarchy related to authority and responsibility. Let us examine how managers make up a team within this formal hierarchy.

Management's hierarchy has four levels

A pyramid, our symbol for management's hierarchy, is shown in Figure 8–1. It is divided into four levels: top management, middle management, operating management, and the first-line employees. This pyramid is typical of any business.

In terms of organization, employees today have a tremendous advantage, for they can combine their individual talents to benefit the group, thereby finishing the job more quickly and usually better. Today's businesses may have too many committees that argue over the delegation of responsibilities. However, they do build houses, manufacture cars, perform specialized surgery, and accomplish innumerable other feats that would not have been possible for a lone worker in the Middle Ages.

Structure

Every organization must establish an effective structure to coordinate its human and physical resources. The effectiveness of that structure directly influences the accomplishment of organizational objectives.

Just as fingerprints differ from person to person, so do structures vary from organization to organization. Although every organization requires a structure, no two formal organizational structures are exactly alike. Yet each must be built upon basic principles of organizational theory. As a supervisor you must understand and adapt to this structure as part of your job.

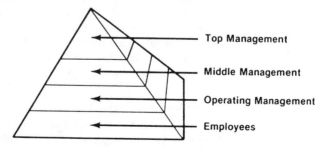

FIGURE 8–1 Management's hierarchical pyramid

Organizational Charts

A chart showing an organization's structure is a kind of an-atomical drawing indicating the formal, *official* channels by which messages must travel. An example is given in Figure 8–2. Flowing around the formal structure are complicated, ever-changing net-works of informal, *unofficial* channels. They are not shown on the chart, because informal channels are basically unstable.

Organizational charts show the formal channel of communication

An organizational chart can indicate only the major formal channels. A chart that showed all formal paths that messages could travel would look more like a maze or puzzle. For example, the positions of secretaries and receptionists are seldom shown on charts, even though in large organizations most messages are routed through these individuals.

In practice, adherence to a chain of command can never be complete. The various levels of management cannot be rigidly com-partmentalized; a president, for example, deals directly with the vice-presidents but also communicates with their subordinates. These contacts involve not only casual personal conversations but also serious business discussions. Associations of this type are not confined to joint conferences of several layers of management; they include the "leapfrogging" or by-passing that runs counter to the chain-of-command concept. The main force contributing to this flexibility is the need for speed, since communications move rather slowly through formal channels. There is a danger, however, in excessive leapfrogging. No supervisor likes to be ignored. Your boss needs to be informed of your actions.

An effective chart illustrates four major aspects of an organi-zation's structure:

1. *The division of work:* Each box indicates an individual or department responsible for a section of the workload.
2. *Managers and subordinates:* The solid lines indicate the chain of com-mand (who reports to whom).
3. *The grouping of work segments:* The entire chart indicates the basis upon which the organization's activities have been divided—on a functional or geographic basis, for example.
4. *The levels of management:* A chart indicates not only individual man-agers and subordinates, but also the entire management pyramid. All persons who report to the same individual are represented on the same management level.

Formal channels provide orderly, predictable routes so that the necessary information quickly reaches the right people, who then make decisions and take action. For example, sales orders sent to factories by traveling salespeople must be processed in the

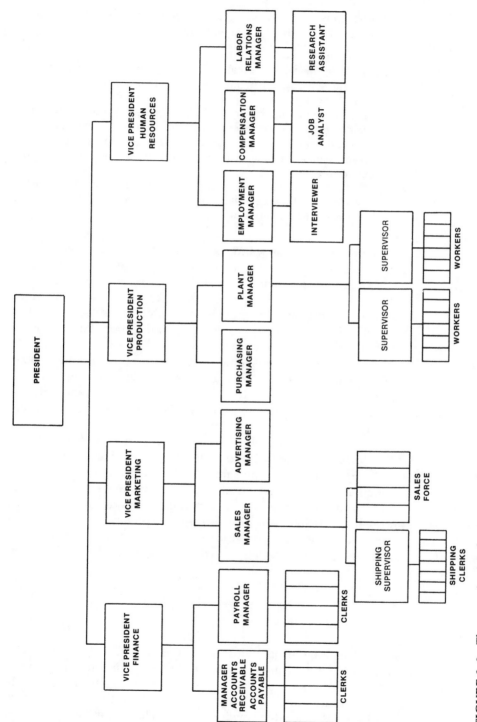

FIGURE 8-2 The organizational structure of an industrial plant

sequence in which they were placed . Figure 8–2 illustrates some of the routes that such processing would travel:

1. The sales manager is notified of the order by the salesperson.
2. The sales manager then informs the shipping supervisor to pack and ship the goods.
3. The shipping supervisor sends the necessary information to the credit and billing manager so that the customer can be billed.
4. Either the sales manager or the shipping supervisor might notify the plant manager in the production department to replace the sold merchandise.
5. If sales are very good, some shipping or stockroom clerks may work overtime, and the payroll manager must be notified to adjust their paychecks for the extra hours.

In complex organizations, the flow of formal communications never stops. Remarkably, a variety of messages travels from department to department, and many of these are far more complex than those involved in the processing of sales orders described above. Communications moving *between* divisions are called *horizontal*, because the messages flow in that direction. Look at Figure 8–2, and this will become clearer.

All organizations should have a current, accurate organizational chart. As duties, roles, and responsibilities change, it is extremely important to update the chart continuously and critically so that it is an accurate reflection of the organization. Depending on the size of the organization, some charts can be cumbersome and complex. Nevertheless, workers must know and understand their place in the organization. Organizational charts can never be 100 percent accurate, since political and social systems cannot be described or illustrated. For this reason, few organizations actually operate the way the organizational chart indicates. Despite this drawback, a chart still provides a basic framework for intended operations. Ideally, supervisors should use it as a blueprint to dictate operational expectations, while recognizing the hidden political and social relationships.

Line Structure

The supervisor, whose job requires him or her to exercise authority, should understand the source of this authority. He or she, regardless of the structure in the total organization, usually functions according to a *line structure* of authority. In other words, authority is delegated downward, in a clearly defined line, from the individual who is the supreme authority, to a subordinate, to a

TALL AND FLAT ORGANIZATIONAL STRUCTURES

In complex organizations, there are usually several levels of management but only one or two levels of workers. Supervisors interact with the employees daily and manage their work closely.

Fewer controls are found in flat structures

A flat or short organizational structure, with widely distributed authority and fewer strict controls, is a good environment for people who like to work independently. A successful flat organization depends primarily on alert supervisors who make good decisions and take responsibility. Poor supervision in a flat organization can quickly lead to management problems because of fewer divisions of labor.

Problems develop faster in a flat structure

Flat structure allows for a wider span of control

Entrusting each supervisor with a greater number of subordinates reduces the number of supervisors needed and thus reduces supervisory salaries, which may constitute a large part of the firm's operating costs. If efficiency can be maintained, then the organization will benefit financially through the use of this broader span of control.

The more management levels that exist, or the taller the structure, the longer it takes for a message to reach the proper level for action, and the possibilities for communication breakdown thus become more numerous. Some companies, as a result, have been trying to reduce the number of their immediate management levels without overloading the managers.

The taller the structure, the poorer the communications

Given an equal number of persons in each organization, an axiom concerning the tall and flat organizational structures is evident: the taller the structure, or the more numerous the levels of management, the poorer the communication; whereas the flatter the structure, or the fewer the levels of management, the better are the chances that accurate information is being transmitted (see Figure 8–4).

In the taller structure, where each manager supervises fewer employees, ideally he or she will pay closer attention to the job, but the extent of this effect is difficult to determine. In a tall organization with many levels of authority, a supervisor can become more "boss oriented."

Span of Control

Studies on organization structure date back to Biblical times when an overseer was made responsible for so many laborers. The number of persons who can be controlled or supervised effectively by a single individual has been discussed through the years. Classical theorists place limits on the number because every supervisor has a limited amount of energy, knowledge, time, and experience.

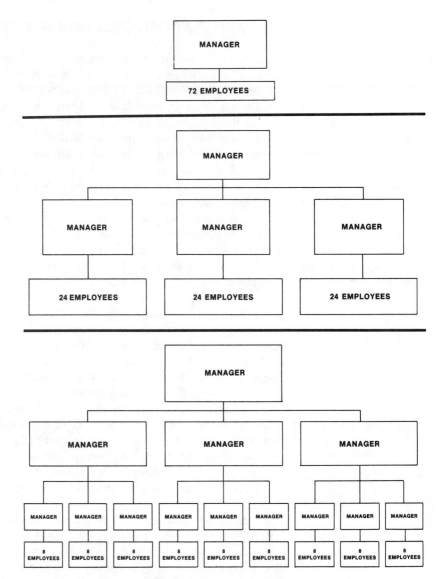

FIGURE 8–4 Organizational differences caused by different spans of management for the same number of employees (72)

Span of control is the number of subordinates a supervisor directly oversees. Face-to-face contact and communication are vital aspects of the span of control. Increased production and improved morale are typical outcomes when the span of control has been correctly determined.

Many theorists have incorrectly described span of control as a fixed number, usually between four and eight persons, but such a rigid view is unrealistic because the capabilities of supervisors and of employees are limited, and because the amounts of training, intelligence, and other factors present on the job vary. Where subordinates are capable, independent, and open to communication, a large span of control is possible. Where the supervisors and employees have less training and intelligence, and a difficult communication process exists, a smaller span of control is likely.

Sears is a company with a large span of control at the top; as many as 40 executives may report to the president. Smaller spans of control exist at lower levels of Sears. The federal government is a classic example of the use of smaller spans of control throughout the organization.

LIMITING THE SPAN OF CONTROL

When a supervisor has extensive responsibilities, the workers may feel that no personal attention is being given to their work and their problems. The supervisor may also have difficulty in training, communicating with, and controlling the workers if the span is too wide. To remedy the situation, a supervisor can break up the span either by delegating some authority to informal team leaders or by asking experienced people to serve as trainers. It is important to organize the work so that there is more time for the human relations aspect that is so vital to any company.

STRETCHING THE SPAN OF CONTROL

Enlarging the span and producing a flatter organization facilitates communications. Bottlenecks caused by too many levels can then be eliminated.

Broadening the span of control lessens the red tape

The advantage of broadening the supervisory span is less red tape. Because the structure is compacted, operations require a shorter chain of command. A broader span also encourages more extensive delegation and more general rather than close supervision. All these factors can raise employee morale.

DIVISION OF WORK

According to some theories of organization, there are advantages to specialization, chiefly in manufacturing. Dividing workers into specialty groups increases production for a number of reasons. First, workers' skills increase when they concentrate on a particular task. Second, little time is lost in shifting from one job to another. Finally, a division of labor encourages the use of specialized machines capable of increased production.

Division of labor leads to specialization

Behavioral scientists, on the other hand, cite the disadvan-

Too much specialization leads to monotony tages of too much specialization. They argue that employees suffer from boredom and dissatisfaction when the job is overspecialized. When labor is divided greatly, people are treated more like machines. Individuals repeating the same operation with monotonous regularity lose interest in their work and cannot relate it to the final product. Creative flair, which could improve production, thus has no opportunity to develop. An area between the two extremes could best satisfy the necessary goals of production and good human relations.

Departmentalization

A major component of any organizational structure is departmentalization. Basically, it means the division of areas of responsibility. In modern business there are four main ways to *Departmentalize by function, geography, product, or customer* departmentalize employees: by function, geography, products, or type of customer. Companies may find it necessary to use a combination of these methods in creating divisions (see Figures 8–5 to 8–8).

Vice-presidents are often chosen by their functional specialization, such as sales, marketing, finance, production, or research and development. Grouping employees by geographic areas is another common method, particularly when better service or coverage is desired. The "Northwest sales district," for example, combines both the functional and geographic methods.

An organizational method used recently by many companies is that of product or product lines. Hormel Meat Packing Company developed the product Dial Soap. Certainly the company staff could not market meat and soap with the same sales staff or the same advertising campaign.

The different types of customers may lead a company to develop separate departments, such as those in cosmetics companies, that sell some items to wholesale companies, others to large retail

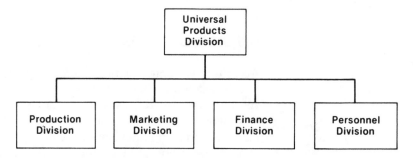

FIGURE 8–5 Functional organizational chart

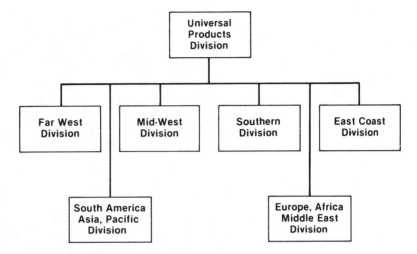

FIGURE 8–6 Geographic organizational chart

outlets, and still others to small mail-order firms. Departments may also be established according to the process or type of equipment used. This is particularly true for manufacturing firms.

Recently, three major factors have caused firms to reexamine and reevaluate existing organizational structures:

- Costs
- Technology
- Changing market conditions

COSTS

When costs increase, firms may respond by consolidating departments, to reduce expenses. Levels of management can be eliminated to trim excess overhead. The Dana Corporation, a major auto parts manufacturer, decreased its levels of management from 11 to 5, thus saving millions of dollars in salaries.

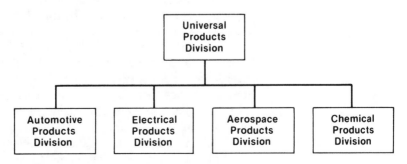

FIGURE 8–7 Product organizational chart

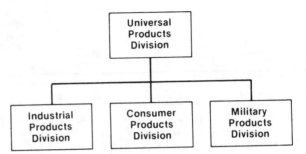

FIGURE 8–8   Type-of-customer organizational chart

TECHNOLOGY

Organizations must be structured to accommodate the daily advances made in new product development and production systems. The twentieth century has been characterized by dynamic technological change, a trend that will continue to influence society. It is imperative for organizations, management, and workers to be aware of this phenomenon to remain competitive.

CHANGING MARKET CONDITIONS

Geographic shifts and other market changes force organizations to alter their structure to meet consumer demand. Production facilities, warehouses, and distribution and service centers must be strategically located to capitalize on customer needs. Successful organizations must be responsive to these and other marketing factors.

As organizations continue to grow in size, consumer needs will become even more complex. They will do more than dictate structural change: they will *mandate* it.

Centralization Versus Decentralization

The concept of centralization refers to the extent to which authority has been retained at the top of the organization, whereas decentralization refers to the extent to which authority has been passed down to lower levels. The greater the delegation of authority, the more decentralized the organization. For example, when lower-level supervisors can expend large sums for supplies, equipment, and wage increases, that company is decentralized.

Centralization can be cost effective

Centralization tends to concentrate control closer to the top of the organizational pyramid. A variety of functions may be centralized, such as engineering, labor negotiations, computer operations, or purchasing. There seems to be a cost effectiveness to centralization.

A decentralized operation has the opposite characteristics. It gives greater independence to departments and managers, thereby lending itself more to those in marketing or sales. It may work well when there are many geographical sales offices. However, when efficiency or profits start to fall, a firm will frequently take steps to establish a more centralized operation.

Delegation

No matter how centralized or decentralized the organization is, delegation must take place, because the supervisor cannot do everything. The nature of delegation suggests that when the supervisor assigns a job or duty to someone, two things have occurred:

- The supervisor has given that person *authority* to get the job done.
- The supervisor has created *responsibility* in the person to whom the task has been delegated.

Delegation involves both authority and responsibility

Delegation involves both authority and responsibility. The amount of authority delegated must agree with the formula: AUTHORITY = RESPONSIBILITY. In effect, if the supervisor makes an employee responsible for completing a job, then the employee must have the authority necessary to complete the job.

Too little authority results in lack of control

Too little authority results in excessive checking with the supervisor; too little authority results in lack of control. To ensure effective task completion, proper delegation of authority must take place within the parameters of organizational practices.

Unity of Command

A sign of a well-structured organization is the presence of clear authority lines from top to bottom. In most organizations, the ultimate scope of authority rests at the top. Through effective delegation, authority is passed down the organization from superior to subordinate. The amount of authority present at each level must agree with the formula in terms of responsibility. It is also important, as a part of organizing, to make sure that a worker does not report to more than one immediate superior. This concept is called *unity of command*. It is impossible to be loyal to more than one boss. To avoid possible conflict, unity of command is a good practice to follow.

FROM LINE TO STAFF TO MATRIX STYLE

The typical corporation is a fairly rigid pyramidal structure, having a commander in chief, subordinates with line responsibility, and a staff that provides the services. Once an organization grows to a certain size, the functional pyramid may develop problems: people have difficulty communicating beyond a fairly small circle, the vastness of the structure obscures the capabilities of its employees, talents are hard to assess, and the people at the top are unaware of the state of affairs within their empire.

A matrix form of organization, on the other hand, can operate effectively with a sizable group of employees. Approximately 250 is considered the threshold number for this form of organization; if there are fewer, you simply will not have the personnel to perform the necessary functions. If the number is greater, the matrix structure can function equally well.

Matrix is a team of workers from different departments

The matrix organization is a team composed of employees from different departments who are working on a common project. The project manager may have no permanent authority in the organizational structure, but he or she is an expert for the specific project and, as such, coordinates, directs, and controls the members of the team. In effect, a matrix organization is a second form of organization overlaid on the chain of command (Figure 8–9). As short-term programs are established, special groups are created to handle them.

Experts work together on a single project for a limited time

The chairperson of a matrix project may find that he or she is supervising employees who are above, below, or at the same hierarchical level. For some hours a day or for months at a time, a worker may find that there is a superior from another department

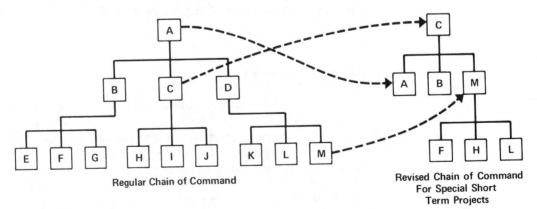

Regular Chain of Command

Revised Chain of Command
For Special Short
Term Projects

Line Organization

Matrix Style

FIGURE 8–9 Matrix style organization can exist within a line organization (*Source:* Adapted from Jack Halloran, *Applied Human Relations* (Englewood Cliffs, NJ: Prentice Hall, 1978), p. 72).

working under his or her direction. This can put a strain on the relationship, or it can break down the rigid barriers of formal communications.

A story is told of a professional service company that underwent a change from a line and staff organization to a matrix organization with little line authority. When this company switched to the market-oriented, matrix-style structure, the total employee profile underwent some subtle, but fundamental modifications.

Rigid people are unhappy in a matrix

People who had come to the company from rigidly structured organizations were unhappy, for they felt insecure. When they reorganized around markets demanding certain skills, some managers, whose technical expertise had diminished and whose primary talent was "pure" administration, were no longer happy. Since the layers of the matrix organization are shallower than those of the line organization, middle-level supervisory personnel were no longer required, and they left the firm.

Matrix needs fewer middle-level supervisors

Matrix employees need flexibility

The new employees entering, although not necessarily younger, had a more flexible orientation; they could adapt to being moved from project to project or city to city. At one time, not more than 30 percent of the professional employees in this firm were willing to travel regularly; now more than 80 percent are willing to share their skills elsewhere for days or weeks at a time.

Matrix structure is more mobile and satisfying for some

Probably the most positive gain for the new employee was the avoidance of the boredom and stagnation that often comes from performing the same function, at the same desk, with the same people, for an indefinite period. Formerly, it was fairly typical to change occupations perhaps three times during a person's working life, but this lack of mobility may not be the best way toward a satisfying, fulfilling career. The matrix organization requires many personal transitions, which keep employees actively involved in their specialties and away from a purely administrative supervisory rut.

Furthermore, the matrix organization allows a dissatisfied employee to change jobs with less upheaval than in a line organization. Without forcing an issue with the boss, an employee can explore other job areas. There is no need to request a formal transfer or make a long-range commitment. One need not change companies in order to change activities.

Self-confidence and flexibility are most important in matrix

If you have never worked under this type of format, you should now see the difference between the matrix and the normal range of experiences you have had under the line or line and staff organizations. Attitudes of confidence and flexibility are the cornerstones to a successful matrix organization. If you decide to work in a company with such a design, first assess your personality to determine if you could be happy there as an employee and a supervisor. One must also be aware that a matrix structure can produce anxiety in employees because of conflicts of authority and some lack in continuity. It is for these reasons that matrix is not common in industrial companies, government, and nonprofit organizations.

ORGANIZATIONAL POSITIONS AND RISK FACTORS

An interesting combination of planning and organizational structure can be related to the amount of risk taken by a supervisor. One's organizational position influences the type of planning and risks involved. Top management must make forecasts for the next five years. These decisions are based on future sales estimates, the availability of semifinished goods, transportation, and the labor supply. Given such indicators, top management may decide to open a new plant in Atlanta, Georgia. A great amount of money will be expended before the plant turns out its first product. The risk is high! The president's position and even the company's existence may be in jeopardy.

By contrast, the operative manager is responsible for short-range goals. His or her responsibility may be to set the wholesale and retail sales figures for a product by next week, to finish the plant payroll by Friday, or to take inventory of several sections in a department store. These duties are important, but the goals are short-range and less risky than those of top management. The relationship among supervision, risk, and planning goals can be seen in Figure 8–10.

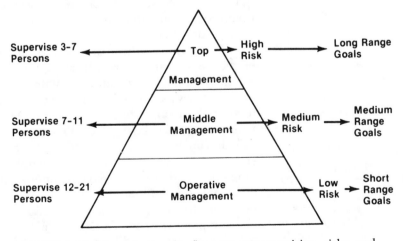

FIGURE 8–10   Organizational influences on supervision, risks, and goals

FROM ORGANIZATIONAL STYLE TO COMPANY POLICY

As an organization grows, certain philosophical ideas are usually developed. Either centralization or decentralization is a management style that begins sprouting in the first year of operation; by the third to the fifth year, one or the other has taken root. The ideas and values of the company leaders will, over time, create impressions and become organizational policies, whether written or implied. For example, an organization that has a policy of promotion from within may have a more competitive climate than one that fills top positions from the outside.

Management's ideas usually are translated into company policies and the employee's handbook.

Company Policies

Company policies are statements of the company's goals and basic principles for operating, and are intended as a job guide for supervisors and employees alike. Some policies, like the following excerpt, are written in general terms to allow the supervisor to use his or her best judgment in their application: "We believe in giving the people closest to the problem the responsibility for solving those problems and expect the supervisor to engage in a solution that is in the best interests of both the company and the employee." Others may be clear-cut rules to be carried out without question. Most are printed in a positive, encouraging manner and do not have a list of dos and don'ts.

In-house procedures are often recorded so that each employee can follow the common and acceptable way of handling routine matters such as the requisition of supplies, preparation of work records, disposition of classified materials, implementation of cost-control measures, establishment of quality control, requests for maintenance and repair, and the acquisition of new equipment.

Certainly every situation cannot be handled by this guideline, and many policies remain implied rather than expressed. The more complex a company becomes, however, the more the policy booklet will tend to become detailed and complex. More rules and policies often lead to a more rigid structure with less freedom for the supervisor.

You, as a supervisor, do set policy at the shop level. You are required to interpret policy at your level as it applies to your employees. The broader the policy, the more discretion you have. Some supervisors do not want to have too much latitude in making decisions, but as you climb the corporate ladder, you will have more and more freedom in solving problems and setting policy.

Employee's Handbook

The most common items covered in an *employee's handbook* are wages, holidays, vacations, absence, termination, safety rules and reports, medical and health insurance, service awards, retirement, and pensions. These points are discussed during a new employee's orientation and are provided in written form for later reference.

THE MATURATION OF AN ORGANIZATION

As a company grows and matures, it may pass through many phases. Certain dimensions that affect its organization are the number of employees, the growth of its parent industry, and its age.

A growth in the number of employees in an organization may force management to approach problems in different ways. As difficulties in coordination and communication increase, new levels of management are likely to emerge, and tasks become more interrelated.

The growth of the industry within which the company is operating will also call for changes within the firm. Rapidly expanding markets, for instance, accelerate certain needs; new employees have to be hired, and plant facilities have to be expanded.

As it matures, a company can undergo various stages and accept various challenges. Growth in a young company occurs as a result of creativity, and the crises are more often in terms of leadership. As the company develops, growth is nurtured through proper delegation of authority, and the crises more often result from improper control. Still later, as the company matures, growth depends more on effective coordination, and the crises result from attempts at cutting the red tape that has developed. At this point, management attitudes and employee behavior have become more predictable and harder to change.

Whether the company is young or old, certain healthy and unhealthy traits can be detected. Review your company's characteristics in relation to the lists in Table 8–1.

THEORY Z ORGANIZATION

William Ouchi of UCLA has proposed a unique organization format called *Theory Z*.[1] In researching why Japanese organizations are so successful, he noted that American and Japanese organi-

---

[1]William Ouchi, *Theory Z: How American Business Can Meet the Japanese Challenge* (Reading, MA: Addison-Wesley, 1981).

TABLE 8–1   Personality traits of organizations

Unhealthy Traits	Healthy Traits
1. Managers feel alone in trying to get things done. Only sometimes are orders carried out as intended.	1. There is a noticeable sense of teamwork in planning, performance, and sharing responsibility.
2. The judgment of lower-level employees is not respected outside the narrow limits of their jobs.	2. The judgment of people on lower levels of the organization is respected.
3. Personal needs and feelings come second to all other problems.	3. Problems tackled include personal as well as organizational ones.
4. When there is a crisis, employees blame one another.	4. When there is a crisis, the employees quickly band together until it is overcome.
5. Conflict is mostly covert, and managed by office politics and other games.	5. Conflicts are considered important to decision making and personal growth. They are dealt with openly.
6. Learning is difficult. People do not willingly learn from their peers; they reject others' experience.	6. There is a great deal of on-the-job learning based on a willingness to give and seek feedback and advice.
7. Feedback is avoided.	7. Comments from others are encouraged.
8. The manager is the parent figure in the organization.	8. Leadership is flexible, shifting to fit the situation.
9. Taking minimum risks has a very high value.	9. Risk is accepted as a condition of growth and change.
10. Tradition!	10. There is a sense of order and yet a high rate of innovation. The organization itself adapts *swiftly* to any opportunities or changes in its marketplace.

zations differ according to seven characteristics (see Table 8–2). Ouchi reported that a few especially successful American organizations, such as Eastman Kodak, IBM, Procter and Gamble, and Hewlett-Packard, did not follow the typical format of American organizations but rather established a middle-of-the-road course that offered long-term employment, collective decision making, individual responsibility, and moderately specialized career paths; he identified this organizational approach as Theory Z. His

TABLE 8–2   Ouchi's comparison of Japanese versus American organizations

Japanese Organizations	American Organizations
Lifetime employment	Short-term employment
Slow evaluation and promotion	Rapid evaluation and promotion
Nonspecialized career paths	Specialized career paths
Implicit control measures	Explicit control measures
Collective decision making	Individual decision making
Collective responsibility	Individual responsibility
Wholistic concern	Segmented concern

ideas have been well received, with many organizations attempting to put his thoughts into action.

SUMMARY

The structure of an organization develops from a set of long-range company goals and short-term personal objectives. Structure limits the freedom of the individual in order to achieve the larger company goal. The management hierarchy is composed of top management, middle management, operative management, and the first-line employee. Each level has its particular role and duties to perform.

An organizational chart is a kind of anatomical drawing indicating the company's formal, official channels. It must be current and accurate, reflecting organizational changes. The rigid chain of command works well in concept, but an informal leapfrogging of information is used to save time.

The military is a prime example of the tightly structured line organization, and such a line of command is easy to understand. The second type of structure is the line and staff form. There are two separate types of staff: general staff assist division managers in a variety of ways, and specialized staff contribute specific skills in a narrow area of expertise. Staff persons are more motivated to communicate to all organizational levels than are the line personnel, because the staff must sell ideas, not give commands.

Tall organizations have more levels of management than flat organizations. The tall organizations supervise fewer people in a span of control than the flat structures. Problems develop more quickly in a flat structure, but morale is often higher. The tall structure with more levels of management has a greater chance of communications breakdowns.

As a person moves up the hierarchy, the number of persons he or she can supervise, or the span of control, quickly diminishes because of the more varied nature of employees' tasks. On the lowest level of supervision, one person may be able to manage as many as 12 to 21 people. A person in middle management can effectively supervise about 7 to 9, while a company president can supervise only about 5.

The matrix style is the newest and most complex organizational structure. It is a team composed of employees from different departments who work on a common project. The project manager may not have permanent authority in the organizational structure but is an expert for this specific assignment. As short-term programs are established, special groups are created to handle them.

CASE STUDY 16

The Organization Versus the Manager's Needs

Some years ago, C. Northcote Parkinson wrote satirically in *Parkinson's Law* that "work expands so as to fill the time available for its completion." He suggested that organizations do not grow merely to keep up with increased workloads. No conclusion about the amount of work performed can be drawn on the basis of an organization's size. "The rise in the total of those employed," he said, "is governed by Parkinson's Law and would be much the same whether the volume of the work were to increase, diminish or even disappear."

There is some truth in this observation, because personal considerations do influence the corporate structure. Those in positions of influence may act on the basis of what is best for them personally rather than what is best for the company. Empire builders often believe their personal power to be derived from the number of people they supervise, and they are more interested in the employees' aggregate numbers than in their output.

QUESTIONS

1. Do you think there is any present validity in Parkinson's law?
2. How can organizations overcome the rise in employment, regardless of work load or profit, as a company ages?
3. In what type of industry is this theory most likely to be applicable: consumer products, manufacturing, the military, civil service, small business, or service industries? Why?

CASE STUDY 17

The Family Business

For the last five years you have worked for a small, family-owned business. During that time the business has been very profitable, and has grown and expanded. The president of the business approaches you and states: "Because of recent sales increases and expansion, we have decided to form a corporation. Since you have been taking business classes at the local college, I'd like you to help us establish an effective structure and an organizational chart. Since you're not a family member, you'd probably be more honest and objective."

QUESTIONS

1. What type of data would you need to design an effective organizational chart?
2. Do you see any problems with the president's request?
3. How should the basis of departmentalization be determined?

Terms and Concepts Supervisors Should Know

Authority formula; Centralization, Decentralization; Delegation; Departmentalization; Flat organizational structure; General staff; Line structure; Management hierarchy; Matrix structure; Organizational chart; Span of control; Specialized staff; Tall organizational structure; Theory Z; Unit of command.

Questions for Discussion

1. What is the most common organizational structure of businesses in your community: the line, line and staff, or matrix? Does there seem to be any trend toward a change from one style to another? If so, why do you think it is happening?
2. Is your position at the line or staff level? What are the advantages and the disadvantages of your position as contrasted to the other type?
3. Does your company have a visible organizational chart? Does it tend to show a tall or flat structure?
4. How many persons are in your span of control? Would you change this span if you could? If so, in what way?
5. Could you work effectively in a matrix-style company? Why or why not?
6. Does your firm have a company policy manual or an employee's handbook? How effective is it for the company and the employees?

For Further Reading—And More Ideas

Barks, J. V., "Flat Is Where It's At (Trend Away from Hierarchical Management)," *Distribution* (November 1988).

Berger, P., "Commonsense Centralization (Combines Centralized Management Control of Business Functions with Decentralized Decision Making)," *Computer Decisions* (January 1989).

Blackburn, R. S., "Dimensions of Structure: A Review and Reappraisal," *Academy of Management Review* (January 1982).

Boudette, N. E., "Networks to Dismantle Old Structures," *Industry Week* (January 16, 1989).

Byrne, J. A., "Is Your Company Too Big?" *Business Week* (March 27, 1989).

Carzo, Rocco, Jr., and John N. Yanouzas, "Effects of Flat and Tall Organization Structures," *Administrative Science Quarterly* (June 1969).

"Decentralization in Management Theory," *Forbes* (August 15, 1983).

"Decentralization—The Reins Are Getting Tighter," *Chemical Week* (May 19, 1982).

"Firms Plan to Decentralize," *Engineering News Record* (March 29, 1984).

Katz, J. H., "The Fact and Causes of Variation in Structural Development Processes," *Journal of Management Studies* (March 1989).

Land, P. A., "Decentralized—Elixir for the Eighties," *Bureaucrat* (Winter 1982–83).

Mathews, G. H., "Run Your Business or Build an Organization," *Harvard Business Review* (March–April 1984).

Ouchi, William, *Theory Z*, Reading, MA: Addison-Wesley, 1981.

Peters, Thomas J., and Robert H. Waterman, Jr., *In Search of Excellence*, New York: Harper and Row, 1982.

"Principles of Modern Management," *Esquire* (December 1983).

Sprague, J. L., "Restructuring and Corporate Renewal: A Manager's Guide," *Management Review* (March 1989).

Stupack, R. J., "Back to the Future: Organizational Effectiveness," *Bureaucrat* (Summer 1988).

Treese, M. A., "Know Your Organization," *Supervisory Management* (November 1982).

Umstot, Denis D., *Understanding Organizational Behavior*, St. Paul, MN: West, 1984.

Vajta, P. G., "When It Comes to Organization, Think Simple (Marketing Departments)," *Business Month* (May 1989).

Vanfleet, David D., and Arthur G. Bedeian, "A History of the Span of Management," *Academy of Management Review* (July 1977).

"Well-Run Companies," *U.S. News & World Report* (October 10, 1983).

Delegation, Responsibility, and Authority

9

"I know you can do the job!"

LEARNING OBJECTIVES

When you complete this chapter, you should be able to:
1. Explain how delegation can reduce cost.
2. Know when you need to delegate.
3. Recognize why supervisors do not delegate and why subordinates are reluctant to accept authority.
4. Describe the attitude of a supervisor who is willing to delegate.
5. Identify some of the guidelines for granting authority and delegating responsibility.
6. Define some delegating techniques.

"The art of delegating is letting the other person have your way."

Before you begin this chapter, answer the following questions:

Should presidents delegate more of their work than first-line supervisors?

Do fast-growing companies tend to delegate more to lower-level personnel than stable companies?

Do older supervisors tend to delegate less than younger supervisors?

Do those who delegate more duties have more problems with discipline?

Does pride and lack of confidence in personnel prevent supervisors from giving more responsibility to subordinates?

If you answered *yes* to every statement, you agree with most of the myths and truths about delegation. Reading this chapter and participating in group discussions should reveal the differences.

DELEGATION AND AUTHORITY

Charles Wilson, the former president of General Motors Corporation, often used colorful expressions to make his points. When he was secretary of defense he was asked whether he gave detailed instructions to any of his key subordinates. Wilson replied: "You never give orders to such a degree; that isn't the way it's done. I mean, it's like telling an artist how to draw. You give him the job and let him draw his own way."

Of course, Wilson was delegating work to trained subordinates, each an expert in his or her field. His job was not exactly the same as that of a supervisor giving an assignment to a new employee, but the basic principle is the same. The main purpose of supervisors is to get results from their people, and this means *An effective delegator is* supervisors must know how to delegate. The ability to delegate *not overworked* separates the effective supervisor from the overworked, complaining boss.

"Go West, young man!" was Horace Greeley's advice for success over a century ago. Today the common advice in management circles is: "Delegate. Decentralize." Experience has shown that subordinates have a remarkable capacity to shoulder responsibility and get results, and that many employees desire responsibility. We also know that wise delegation helps build morale and is an important training device. Yet supervisors frankly admit that they do not delegate as much as they should. In large and small companies we continually hear the comments: "The boss is overworked," or "There's a good person who needs to be given a chance." If we could overcome the obstacles to delegation in cases like these, we would gain resilience and flexibility that add strength to a company. Why, then, is the nature of delegation so difficult?

Delegation allows for flexibility

To clarify the problem, let us set aside the cases where the boss at any level—president, superintendent, or first-line supervisor—does not want to delegate. Some bosses are "little Napoleons," who can satisfy their egos only by making all decisions themselves. In other cases, a supervisor's boss may hold such a tight rein that the supervisor hates to delegate any further. And some bosses haven't given enough thought to management to recognize the advantages of sharing responsibilities. For reasons such as these, a lack of desire to delegate is a problem in itself.

Delegation

Assignment and acceptance make a contract

Delegation is the assignment of a task to another person and that person's acceptance of the task. Like a contract, there must be an offer and an acceptance according to the terms of an agreement. The employee who accepts a job also accepts the responsibility for completing it. The acceptance of an assignment is thus two-sided, carrying both the responsibility and the authority to do the job, although the two sides are not always equal in weight. For example, a subordinate may not have the authority to order the parts or employ the number of people necessary to complete a job he or she has agreed to do.

To have the responsibility but not the authority to complete a task is an aggravating and depressing experience. It is like trying to shear a sheep, but needing permission to use the clippers every time you take a clip of the wool. Employees will eventually resent and resist supervisors who withhold authority when they delegate responsibility. No one wants to do a job unless he or she has some authority to carry it out. Remember, if you do not delegate the authority along with the responsibility, employees will do the job their way, not yours.

Authority and Power

Power and authority are key factors in a supervisor's job. While many consider the terms to be interchangeable, in practice they are quite different. Supervisors must understand this difference and be aware of the effective role each plays in the achievement of job objectives.

Authority is the right or privilege to direct workers to perform job actions. It derives from the organization and is given to a job title or position. In effect, an organization must provide a job function with authority equal to its responsibility. Authority includes the right to take disciplinary action if a subordinate refuses to do as he or she is told.

The source of a supervisor's authority can be considered from two points of view. From one viewpoint, it is the formal structure of an organization that gives authority to the first-line supervisor. From the other viewpoint, authority is conferred by the subordinates when they accept a supervisor's authority. Some humanists say that authority is given from above and that leadership is granted from below. New supervisors should remember both viewpoints, since both have validity in the actual practice of supervision. As shown in Figure 9–1, the amount and scope of authority vary according to the level within the organization. Smaller

Authority is given from above; leadership is granted from below

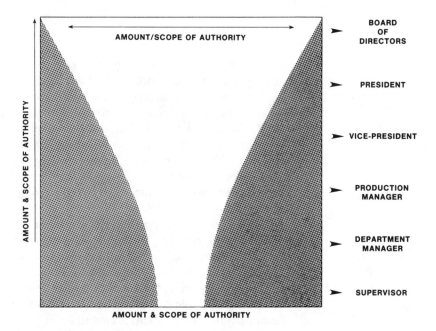

FIGURE 9–1   Amount and scope of authority according to level within the organization

---

POWER BASES

When a supervisor asks you to work overtime:

1. If you comply because supervisors have the traditional right to make such requests, *legitimate power* is the basis of influence.
2. If you comply because you are seeking a promotion, *reward power* is the basis of influence.
3. If you comply because of the fear of being fired, *coercive power* is the basis of influence.
4. If you comply because your superior is competent, *expert power* is the basis of influence.
5. If you comply because you respect your superior, *referent power* is the basis of influence.

---

amounts exist at the bottom. The amount and scope increase as one progresses to the top.

Power is the ability to achieve expected outcomes from supervisory directives. Power is personal and cannot be delegated. In effect, authority is the right to tell a subordinate what to do; power is the ability to get the subordinate to do it.

The organization provides the supervisor with the right to give an order. But why are some orders followed, while others are rejected? The answer rests with power. One popular way to understand power is to review the following types of power that a supervisor may possess proposed by the noted theorists R. French, Jr., and B. Raven:

1. *Legitimate power:* An employee does what is asked because of the supervisor's position within the organization.
2. *Reward power:* An employee does what is asked because of possible rewards (money, praise, promotion) that may result from following the order.
3. *Coercive power:* An employee does what is asked out of fear (demotion, termination) of the results of not following the supervisor's request.
4. *Expert power:* An employee does what is asked because of the special skill, ability, or knowledge of the supervisor.
5. *Referent power.* An employee does what is asked because of admiration for the supervisor.[1]

---

[1] R. French, Jr., and B. Raven, "The Bases of Social Power," in Dorwin Cartwright and Alvin Zandler (eds.), *Group Dynamics*, 2nd ed. (Evanston, IL: Row, Peterson, 1960).

Delegating authority means granting the power subordinates need to accomplish a defined task. In the delegation process, the manager still retains his or her overall authority and can, if need be, revoke all or part of the authority granted to a subordinate.

CRITERIA FOR DELEGATION

Before you delegate tasks, it is wise to determine whether such tasks should be delegated. The four questions below will help you make this decision:

1. *How would you assess the ability of your staff?* If your staff has not had the training needed to handle a job, authority should not be delegated. However, portions of a job may be delegated with minimum instructions. If these parts are done successfully, larger portions of the job can be delegated the next time.
2. *How quickly is the completed task needed?* If a job needs to be done immediately, there is less likelihood it can be delegated. With proper planning, you and your superior can develop more lead time for tasks that must be done. The more time you have, the greater your opportunity to delegate.
3. *How good is your firm's communication system?* The smooth operations of some companies make delegation easy, because the subordinates and the supervisors are able to converse openly and readily. The more clearly a job assignment is outlined, the easier it is for employees to understand—and for you to delegate.
4. *How complex is your firm?* The larger the company, the more complex its structure will be, and the more people will be involved in projects. The more people with whom you must coordinate a project, the more difficult it may be to delegate the tasks. If a company is geographically decentralized, it may require many jobs to be delegated. The complexity of a firm sometimes determines whether a task can be delegated.

WHEN DO YOU NEED TO DELEGATE?

A study of your delegation methods will help you learn whether you delegate too much or too little, and whether you overload a few key employees whom you can trust, while giving only routine assignments to others.

WHY SUPERVISORS ARE RELUCTANT TO DELEGATE

Supervisors resist delegating for many reasons. One common cause of their reluctance is fear: fear of subordinates making costly mistakes, fear of losing control of the activity, or fear of losing prestige or status. Some of the other reasons behind a supervisor's failure to delegate are discussed below.

TEST YOURSELF

ARE YOU A SUCCESSFUL DELEGATOR?

1. Are you willing to fall behind in your work so that you can give every task the personal attention it needs?
2. Do you invest a generous amount of your time straightening out problems that subordinates are not quite able to handle alone?
3. Do your employees frequently come back to you for further instruction, advice, or a decision before they complete a task?
4. Are you a stickler for details when a subordinate hasn't done a job the best way?
5. Do you find you have oversensitive subordinates who make mistakes when you watch them?
6. Do you spend so much of your time getting the details done right that you're not able to plan your work as you would like?

(Answers to these questions are given at the end of the chapter.)

The Expert

You can do it better, but less will be done

Some managers become trapped in the "I-can-do-it-better-myself" fallacy. Supervisors who are conscientious and have high standards usually *can* perform most activities better than their subordinates. But even when they can do better, supervisors must nevertheless reconcile themselves to turning the job over to someone who will perform the task well enough. Supervisors must focus not on the difference in the *quality* of work they and their subordinates could do on a specific task, but on *how much more can be done* when they delegate and devote their attention to more important tasks such as planning and supervising.

Supervisors who believe that no one can do the job as well as they can do not delegate effectively. They keep the important tasks for themselves and give routine and unimportant work to subordinates. The employees know they are at a dead end, as far as doing anything useful is concerned. Since truly capable people will not remain in assignments when they have no chance to develop skills or acquire the experience needed to advance, "expert" supervisors end up with the kind of subordinates they prefer: those who will "fetch and carry" and who feel no responsibility for results.

The Poor Planner

Plan the work, develop the method, and tell the workers

Supervisors must be able to tell subordinates what is to be done, often far in advance. They must visualize and plan the work situation, develop objectives or goals, and then communicate these plans and goals to subordinates. After two people have worked together for a period of time, this process may be informal, but it is still important that these three key elements be present.

Supervisors who don't know what they want employees to do are costing the company money. At the beginning of a work day, employees are apt to waste valuable time waiting around until the supervisor decides what is to be done and who will do it. The only kind of job the poor planner can delegate with confidence is a routine, repetitive one.

Many supervisors stay after work to plan the assignments for the next day. The next morning they are prepared and confident as they assign tasks to people as they come in to work.

The Doubter

The doubter is the manager who hesitates to turn things over to subordinates because: "He'll take care of the details all right, but miss the main point. . . . I'm not sure of her judgment in a pinch. . . . She has ideas, but doesn't follow through. . . . He's too young to command the respect of others."

Supervisors who lack confidence in the ability of their employees to do the work properly may have a good reason; for example, perhaps the workers are not properly trained. But their criticism is really directed at themselves, for the supervisor is responsible for training. When a supervisor doesn't have confidence in his or her people, it shows in his or her actions and methods. He or she is nervous, requires constant progress reports, and even when a problem is trivial, may move in and make decisions.

Delegate, train, or get a new employee

When this kind of situation is open and recognized, the remedy is clear. Training should be started immediately or new subordinates should be found—or the supervisor should start trusting his or her employees. However, the situation is rarely so clear-cut; the supervisor's lack of confidence may be subjective and almost unconscious. When this is the case, the doubter gives lip service to delegation but will not let go in actual working relationships.

The Boomerang Peter Principle Effect

Lawrence Peter developed the theory that people are promoted to their level of inefficiency. For example, the teacher who works hard is rewarded by being made a principal. Although the person was a good teacher, he or she may not be effective as a principal. This theory can be extended to show a "boomerang ef-

One can only do the old job well, so one continues doing it

fect." Employees who are promoted to but ineffective in a supervisory position will revert to performing many of their previous tasks. They cannot delegate their old jobs because those tasks are the only areas where they find winning results.

Boomerang supervisors are people who have been promoted, but who really enjoy the work of their former job and are reluctant to give it up to someone else. Employees who are promoted should be made to realize that they must leave their former job behind them, and they should be sold on the joys of their new job.

WHY SUBORDINATES ARE RELUCTANT TO ACCEPT NEW ASSIGNMENTS

Delegation is a two-sided relationship. Even when the boss is ready and able to turn over responsibility and authority, there may be a reason why the subordinate shrinks from accepting it. Something within the subordinate or in the relationship with the boss may block acceptance. Let us look at some difficulties subordinates have in accepting new assignments.

Too Much Work

"I already do enough"

An initial obstacle to accepting responsibility might simply be that subordinates already have more work than they can do. It may be that they are not using their time properly, but if they already feel overburdened, they will probably shy away from new assignments that call for creative thinking.

Lack of Information and Resources

"That person never tells me what the boss wants"

Most people hesitate to accept responsibility when they believe they lack the necessary information and resources to do a good job. For example, the enthusiasm of a newly appointed training director was dampened when she found she had little equipment and poor secretarial help. Then, when top management officials were not only too busy to see her but also failed to advise her of company planning changes that affected training needs, she lost most of her initiative.

A great deal depends upon the employee's attitudes and expectations. It is unlikely that a person who is given limited funds and personnel will accept responsibility, for he or she knows there will be a battle for each step. Even if the person accepts it, the frustrations that accompany such an assignment will probably discourage him or her from accepting further assignments. Such a barrier makes effective delegation difficult indeed.

Fear of Criticism

Another factor that keeps a person from embracing greater responsibility is the fear of criticism. A great deal depends on the nature of the criticism the person thinks he or she may receive, and that expectation is based on past experience with his or her supervisor.

"I never receive an 'okay' comment"

Negative criticism is more feared than constructive review, and "unreasonable" criticism is likely to evoke an even sharper reaction. Unreasonableness, in this situation, must be defined in terms of the subordinate's feelings. If he or she feels that unfavorable results were beyond control, that duties and authority were not clear, or that there was not an opportunity to explain his or her side of the story, the criticism will have a towering effect and discourage him or her from accepting further responsibility.

Let the Boss Decide

"I can't guess what he wants, so I'll ask"

The subordinate often finds it easier to ask the boss than decide for himself or herself how to deal with a problem. Making a wise decision is usually hard work, and people are perpetually seeking formulas or shortcuts to avoid this labor. If a person finds that he or she can take a half-baked idea or problem to the boss and get an answer, he or she will do it.

In addition, making one's own decision carries with it the responsibility for the outcome. Asking the boss is a way of sharing this burden. Over time, asking the boss becomes a habit, and the subordinates become dependent on their boss rather than on themselves.

A habit of taking tough decisions to the boss can best be broken by an agreement between the two people to change their ways. But if the practice is longstanding, the supervisor may have to resort to a stubborn refusal to give advice. Usually a period of "throwing the person in the water and letting him or her swim" is a healthy way to break the bad habit.

Lack of Self-Confidence

"I'm afraid I can't do it"

A lack of self-confidence sometimes prevents a subordinate from accepting responsibility. When an employee who is capable and willing to do the job is unsure of his or her ability, all the encouragement from the boss will have little effect. In many cases, however, supervisors can build an employee's self-confidence by carefully assigning him or her problems that are increasingly difficult. This does not work for everyone, and you should remember some people may not have the psychological make-up to carry heavy responsibilities.

Lack of Incentives or Rewards

Finally, subordinates may decline assignments because positive incentives or rewards may be inadequate. As noted, accepting additional responsibility usually involves more mental work and greater emotional pressure from the higher risk of failure. For these reasons there should be positive inducements for accepting delegated responsibility. The inducement may be a pay increase, a higher title (status), more pleasant working conditions, and other rewards both tangible and intangible.

THE GENTLE ART OF DELEGATION

The subject of delegation is mentioned in most management manuals and inspirational talks. Executives and supervisors are supposed to be able to delegate wisely, and a high value is placed on this ability. Observation and experience show, however, that the ability to delegate is neither an inborn trait nor an easy skill to acquire.

Job Enrichment

One frequently hears the complaint that the boss has assigned the responsibility for some piece of work but has not delegated the authority to carry it out. Many people will be willing to accept additional duties and new challenges if the supervisor is willing to

Expanding the job is job enrichment

give them the necessary authority. Keeping this in mind, you might look for new ways to expand, rather than limit, the scope of your subordinates' activities. Many supervisors feel they need more time, and the reason may be that they are not using opportunities to spread their duties to their employees.

AT&T's "work-itself" program enriches jobs

American Telephone and Telegraph's "work-itself" program demonstrates the concept of job enrichment. Before the work-itself program was introduced in one keypunching department, for example, each of the operators punched about one-fourteenth of the day's work load. The operators did not identify with the work, and turnover rates were high. The job was redesigned so that the employees had more meaningful responsibility for their work, as follows:

1. Each employee was made responsible for a specific customer or department. For example, one operator would keypunch cards for traffic, another for marketing.
2. Each operator set his or her own verification rates.
3. Operators were allowed to communicate directly with their accounts, instead of going through a supervisor.
4. Operators were given increasing opportunities to schedule their own work.

As a result of these changes, turnover and absenteeism dropped, and production increased so that only ten employees were needed to handle the same amount of work.

Ambivalence Toward Authority

Fromm suggests we want freedom and security

The manager's job is always complicated by the fact that people feel ambivalent toward authority. According to Eric Fromm, most of us have complicated, mixed feelings toward independence and dependence. We value freedom, but sometimes feel lost and anchorless when we have too much. We like protection, but we don't like interference. People are generally willing to tolerate uncertainty and even anxiety in a few areas of their life that are unpredictable and exciting, but they insist that most events occur as expected.

PRINCIPLES OF DELEGATION

Define the Job

Have the job spelled out

Every employee to whom authority is given deserves a statement of the responsibilities that are attached to the position. Then the employee can be held accountable for those duties.

Grant Authority to Complete the Task

If the supervisor can empathize and see the situation through the eyes of a subordinate, he or she will quickly see the need for granting authority needed to complete a task. When a supervisor can't do the job without the authority, he or she shouldn't expect a subordinate to do without it.

Granting authority means that a supervisor confers upon a subordinate the right to make his or her own decisions within predetermined limits. A supervisor should be specific in telling employees what authority they have and what can be done with it. It is a most uncomfortable position for employees to have to guess how far their authority extends, or to test its limits by trial and error. Perhaps you have found yourself in a position where your own boss was not explicit as to how much authority you really had. You then know the frustration and shouldn't let it arise in neophytes.

Be explicit on the amount of authority

Obtain Acceptance of the Responsibility

When you delegate authority to a subordinate, he or she must agree to accept responsibility for performing a given task. Without the subordinate's acceptance, delegation is not complete. The employee agrees to perform his or her duties in return for rewards, such as status or a paycheck. The important point is that the responsibility is something the worker agrees to accept, not something that is imposed by the supervisor.

Set the Goals

Everyone likes to know how he or she is doing. This basic human need can be satisfied when authority is delegated and when the employees know they have accomplished the basic task. This means that they know what the task is in terms of specific goals.

The sales quota illustrates the value of setting goals. Salespeople have been delegated authority to sell in a territory, and no one can tell them how they should see each customer. The sales quota provides them not only with a goal but also with a constant reminder of how well they are doing.

Communicate Ideas

You should convey your plan for delegation as clearly as possible, and remember to allow for feedback. A good way to test your subordinates' grasp of a plan is to ask them to explain it to you. Some people may feel you are quizzing their ability to listen, which perhaps you are. However, it is better to be sure the idea is transmitted clearly at the onset of the project.

Another point to remember is that each of us retains ideas

Show some, tell some,
show and tell others

and facts differently. Some people are audio learners, and others are visual learners. Some learn best by hearing the ideas, while some retain best by reading the concepts. It is wise to understand your people and decide which communication method works best with each person. Of course, some people do best when you show *and* tell. The more channels you use to communicate your ideas, the more effectively you convey the message.

Few of us are content to be at the mercy of forces we do not understand. We all tend to feel insecure in poorly defined situations. Research indicates that high-production supervisors tend to give their subordinates as much information as possible about what is expected on the job and about what is likely to happen to them in the future. This information helps subordinates to do better work by enabling them to make wiser decisions.

It is also important that supervisors let others know that a task has been delegated. To give a fair chance for a subordinate's success, you should let everyone concerned know you have authorized someone else to act for you.

Expect Some Mistakes and Remain Calm

Limit criticism; encourage
other attempts

Delegation becomes a challenge rather than a threat to a subordinate when mistakes are looked upon as an opportunity for further training. You must be sufficiently placid to see others make mistakes and to consider the cost a worthwhile investment in the development of your most important resource: people. To delegate authority you must remain calm and limit your criticism of the individual who tries but fails, for to criticize too heavily is to discourage the person's willingness to try again.

Use Broad Control in Supervision

When you delegate authority, you must be able to exercise a great deal of self-restraint. You must be content with exercising broad controls over results and refrain from telling salespersons how to sell, or accountants how to handle accounts—no matter how expert you have been in either field.

Chairman William Stanfill of Fox Movie Studios stated:

"I believe in delegating authority. In this business you have to give a competent executive the authority to make a quick decision. I have not, as they say, gone Hollywood." Under Stanfill and Alan Ladd, formerly chief movie executive, Fox produced such profitable hits as *Star Wars, Julia,* and *The Turning Point.* Mr. Ladd also believes in delegation—allowing his producers to produce and his directors to direct. Mel Brooks found Fox willing to underwrite his *Young Frankenstein* for $3 million, but it returned $45 million in film rentals. Mel Brooks did it again with a $4 million investment from Fox for a return of $45 million for *Silent Movie*. Gene Wilder, comic actor turned filmmaker, said he likes working at Fox because "they allow me to conceive my own ideas and carry them out without interference."[2]

Establish Controls and Follow-up Procedures

Use follow-up

The fine line between too much supervision and not enough control is hard to establish. When you first delegate a job, frequent checking is often necessary to encourage the employee. The more jobs an employee accomplishes, the less often you need to check on progress.

A supervisor shouldn't delegate a job and then forget it. Mistakes can be minimized by inviting frequent progress reports until both the supervisor and the worker have confidence in the progress being made. The progress and review discussions are also an opportunity for the supervisor to coach a subordinate and to give guidance.

Many supervisors do not delegate because they really do not know how to control the activities of others through an efficient follow-up procedure. Delegation rarely comes easy, and its companion function, follow-up, is also difficult to do without practice. If you are to delegate satisfactorily, you must have a system of follow-up. This requires you to be a well-organized person, one who knows how long to wait before follow-up, how long difficult tasks take, and how to return work that is not of the quality desired.

ADVANTAGES OF DELEGATING

Delegating provides for individual and company growth

The principal advantage of delegating is that it gives an individual the opportunity to grow and advance in a company, and thus gives the company the opportunity to grow. Regardless of the supervisor's effectiveness, he or she can only accomplish so much in a day. When supervisors delegate many of their tasks, they have more time for planning and executing more challenging work. It follows that their subordinates also have even greater opportunities to expand their horizons.

---

[2]"The Big Picture: Fox Film Star Rises with Success of 'Star Wars,' " *Wall Street Journal*, January 1978, pp. 7, 21.

Delegation can improve decisions and cut costs

Delegation often results in having better decisions made more expeditiously by the person who has the facts. It eliminates the need for review after review, cuts paperwork, and saves time in getting things done. It is wasteful for supervisors to clutter their desks and their minds with matters that could be handled by others.

Subordinates can often make better decisions

Many good opportunities are lost for lack of proper delegation, as in the following example. The executive committee of an oil company in New York reserved the right to approve each capital expenditure of $2,000 or more. This meant it voted on the opening of every proposed service station in Central and South America. When the company's country manager located and wanted to buy good corners in San Juan, Bogotà, and Rio, he was in competition with other oil companies. A fast decision was needed, and he was ready to make one; he had the facts on the prospective businesses, the investments needed, and the prospects of a profitable payoff. However, the manager could not act; he could only fill out the forms and send along his recommendations to the paper mill in New York. The executive committee finally made its decision, but it was too late—the stations were sold.

SUMMARY

Delegation is difficult but extremely important for a supervisor. All supervisors have an obligation to delegate, and they must also see that those under them delegate work properly.

Proper delegation is not the answer to all managerial ills, but everyone should take some time, now and then, to sit back and think through the process of delegation. And don't be afraid to delegate the interesting assignment, for that will allow you to take on more assignments, many of which will be even more interesting.

The principle advantage of delegation is that it gives both an individual and a company an opportunity to grow. Regardless of a supervisor's effectiveness, he or she can accomplish only so much in a day. If supervisors delegate many of their tasks, they will have more time for planning and for doing work that is more challenging. It follows that their subordinates will then have even greater opportunities to expand their horizons.

Remember that the subordinate's decision becomes his or her supervisor's decision. If the subordinate makes mistakes, they are the supervisor's mistakes; if the subordinate does well, that success reflects well on the supervisor.

CASE STUDY 18

Work Delegation and Dual Command

Frank Colella works in an aircraft plant as a dispatcher in production control. According to his immediate supervisor, Frank's duty is to determine the priority of shop orders for completion in each department. On this particular Saturday, Frank was assigned to the turret lathe department, where only a few people were working. During this overtime day the supervisor for the department was Martha.

Frank had been told by his supervisor to process the orders needed to facilitate production. However, since her department was behind in production, Martha told Frank to make an inventory of all orders in the shop, and not just those that could be completed quickly to reduce the backlog. Frank told Martha he could not follow the order, since his immediate supervisor had given him specific instructions. Martha replied, "This is my department, I should know what is best; I am the supervisor, and I run the department." Frank again refused, and Martha called his general supervisor, who told Frank the matter would be referred to the superintendent on Monday, and that Frank would be fired.

QUESTIONS

1. Who is right in this situation, Martha or Frank?
2. How would you resolve the problem of dual authority?
3. What action would you take if you were the superintendent, and why?
   a. Fire Frank.
   b. Reprimand him.
   c. Do nothing.
   d. Commend him for following the orders of his immediate supervisor.

CASE STUDY 19

Power Sources

Explain how each of French and Raven's sources of power can be used in the following situations:

1. A teacher wants the class to do a homework assignment.
2. A doctor wants a patient to have an operation.
3. A supervisor wants a worker to work overtime.

Terms and Concepts Supervisors Should Know

Authority; Bases of power; Decentralization; Delegation of authority; Delegation of responsibility; Fear of accepting new assignments; Fear of delegating; Goal; Job enrichment; Peter principle boomerang effect; Power.

Questions for Discussion

1. How would you approach a subordinate whom you feel does not delegate enough of his or her duties?
2. How would you help a person who failed to delegate because he or she was an "expert," a poor planner, or a doubter? Who would benefit most from a training session? Who would benefit most from supervisor-peer conferences?
3. Describe your own observations of the boomerang effect when someone has been promoted to his or her level of inefficiency. Is this very common?
4. Are supervisors more reluctant to delegate, or are subordinates more reluctant to accept the responsibility?

Answers to "Test Yourself: Are You a Successful Delegator?

A *yes* answer to any of the questions is a signal that your skill in delegating could be improved.

For Further Reading—And More Ideas

Arnott N., "When in Doubt, Delegate!" *Executive Female* (November–December 1988).

Blaun, R., "Plugging into the Power Source (How to Gain Power at Work)," *Executive Female* (November–December 1988).

"Decentralized—The Reins Are Getting Tighter," *Chemical Week* (May 19, 1983).

Fast, J., *Body Politics: How to Get Power with Class*, Norwalk, CT: Tower Books, 1980.

Feretic, Eileen, "Power," *Today's Office* (October 1983).

"Firms Plan to Decentralize," *Engineering News Record* (March 29, 1984).

Hersh, Seymour M., "The Price of Power," *The Atlantic* (December 1982).

Hollingsworth, A. T., and A. R. Al-Jafary,

"Why Supervisors Don't Delegate and Employees Won't Accept Responsibility," *Supervisory Management* (April 1983).

Humphreys, L. W., and N. J. Humphreys, "Applying the Management Process to Your Work Day," *Supervisory Management* (March 1983).

Korda, M., *Power! How to Get It, How to Use It*, New York: Ballantine, 1975.

Kozoll, E. C. "Delegations, Instruction, and First-Line Understanding," *Supervision* (October 1983).

Land, P. A., "Decentralized—Elixir for the Eighties," *Bureaucrat* (Winter 1982–83).

Lippert, F. G., "Responsibilities of a Supervisor," *Supervision* (March 1983).

Macleon, J. S., "Some Thoughts on Power,

Powerlessness and Productivity," *Employment Relations Today* (Winter 1983–84).

Mathews, G. H., "Run Your Business or Build an Organization," *Harvard Business Review* (March–April 1984).

McGregor, Douglas, *Human Side of Enterprise,* New York: McGraw-Hill, 1960.

Pascarella, P., et al., "The Power of Being Responsible," *Industry Week* (December 5, 1988).

Polczynski, J. J., "Building a Foundation of Power," *Supervisory Management* (October 1982).

Ragins, B. R., "Power and Gender Congruency Effects in Evaluations of Male and Female Managers," *Journal of Management Studies* (March 1989).

Schilit, W. K., and E. A. Locke, "A Study of Upward Influence in Organizations," *Administrative Science Quarterly* (June 1982).

Sheppard, I. T., "The Art of Delegating," *Management World* (March 1984).

Simon, Herbert A., *Administrative Behavior,* New York: Macmillan, 1961.

Tjosvold, D., "Interdependence and Power Between Managers and Employees: A Study of the Leader Relationship," *Journal of Management Studies* (March 1983).

Weiss, W. H., "Supervise the Job—Don't Do It," *Supervision* (July 1982).

Organizational
Development

10

"Can we make things better?"

LEARNING OBJECTIVES

When you complete this chapter, you should be able to:
1. Define organizational development.
2. Identify each element of the improvement star.
3. Understand the basic concepts of organizational development.
4. Indicate the symptoms of unhealthy organizations.
5. Identify the steps in organizational development.
6. Explain the supervisor's role in organizational development.

"Don't be a victim of organized confusion."

This chapter will help you develop questions for class discussion as you formulate an understanding of organizational development. Some answers to the questions below may be found in the chapter, whereas others may require personal reflection.

Why is organizational development a continual process?

Is it better to react to change or to anticipate change?

Why is trust essential for building good relationships?

Is conflict an unhealthy or healthy organizational characteristic?

What is the relationship between organizational development and supervision?

ORGANIZATIONAL DEVELOPMENT: A DEFINITION

The process of organizational development can be defined as *a planned approach designed to improve the operation of the organization by increasing organizational performance and improving the quality of work life.* For an organizational improvement plan to be effective, it must be carefully developed. It cannot be haphazard, and it must receive the complete support of top management.

An organizational improvement plan must be carefully developed

When the concept of the organization is considered, it must be analyzed in parts. The parts are related internally and externally, and influence each other continually. Interactions occur every minute of every day. It is imperative for the supervisor to understand all of the parts and the dynamic, interrelated quality of their exchange—as well as the consequences.

Complete organizational effectiveness depends on the control and development of each interrelated part. Improving the entire organization can begin by improving any part, but the most effective results occur when all parts are considered simultaneously as integral segments of the organizational structure.

THE ORGANIZATIONAL IMPROVEMENT STAR

The improvement star (Figure 10–1) depicts the five clear-cut organizational points at which improvement may begin:

1. The individual
2. The work group
3. The task

FIGURE 10–1 The improvement star

4. The technology
5. The structure

Successful organizations implement long-range, ongoing improvement plans for each point. All five parts must be continually evaluated, analyzed, and improved for organizational goals to be accomplished.

The Individual

The individual is the most valued asset in any organization. Improvement is not possible unless an organization makes a firm and positive commitment to individuals. If they fail to grow, the organization won't keep pace with its competition and will run the risk of failure.

Supervisors must be committed to individual improvement

An integral part of each supervisor's plan must be a commitment to individual improvement. An analysis of the work force may point to the obsolescence of managerial or technical skills. An example of an organizational improvement plan aimed at solving the problem of managerial skill obsolescence is a supervisory training program. First-line supervisors and others in managerial positions may have received promotions because they were the best workers. However, there is a vast difference between supervising a task and doing it. It is an organization's responsibility to provide new, existing, and potential supervisors with the training necessary to achieve supervisory effectiveness. Such programs help new supervisors cope more effectively with the myriad of people problems that exist in today's organizations. They also provide current supervisors with reinforcement as well as knowledge of new and even better supervisory practices. Finally, potential supervisors can also benefit from such programs.

Technical skill is essential   Technical skill obsolescence can be addressed by providing key production workers with both internal and external training and development opportunities. Formal workshops and seminars can be offered at the work place by contracting the services of training consultants, who will develop a program tailored to specific needs. Another option is to send employees to schools or training facilities. Both are appropriate methods for skill training, and a cost analysis of the alternatives will determine the one with the maximum results. Technical skills in such fields as electronics, engineering, and computers require constant updating to remain current and avoid obsolescence.

The Work Group

The team approach is important   Organizational improvement may begin with the work group. Current supervisory theory stresses the need for a team approach to problem solving and decision making within the organization. Work group improvement may take one of two forms: intergroup or intragroup.

Intergroup improvement is designed to enhance relations between members of different work groups. It occurs when department supervisors are assigned to a task team, which enables them to solve a specific problem and gain an appreciation of the strengths, expertise, and concerns of other departments' members. When future problems occur, members of the organization will share information and ideas more freely as a result of their positive experience on the task team. Intergroup improvement is critical to achieving organizational efficiency.

Intragroup improvement enriches relations among members of the same work group. Many organizations have used regularly scheduled quality circles to achieve this critical objective. Participating employees work together to solve problems that directly affect their jobs. When used properly, quality circles create a spirit of teamwork among their members. Additionally, as individual contributions are recognized, employees gain a greater sense of self-respect and individual worth. Their value to the work group and the organization increases as their greater commitment to the goals of the enterprise develop. A snowballing effect *will* result,

Quality circles create a spirit of teamwork

enabling the group to handle future problems more effectively because of the mutual respect and positive climate gained in the quality circle experience. Such conditions in turn encourage continual networking. While cooperation among *intergroup* members is critical, cooperation among *intragroup* members is essential.

The Task

Jobs and tasks must be constantly updated

Since individuals are constantly changing, so are the jobs they perform. Jobs as well as job descriptions thus need constant updating.

Task improvement may result in the addition or subtraction of responsibilities or the increasing of authority in specific areas. The complexity of some jobs may require the deletion of minor responsibilities, allowing the worker to complete major objectives. Over time, some workers may have become bogged down with trivial matters, preventing them from fulfilling their job responsibilities. This problem may result from underdelegation.

Workers like to be challenged

The increased education of today's work force is one factor that has increased the need for task improvement. Opportunities for using worker skills, abilities, and learning must not be missed! Today workers demand to be challenged. Task improvement may take the form of job enlargement, job rotation, or participative opportunities. To achieve optimum task improvement, the following criteria should be considered:

1. When possible, a task should be "wholistic." A worker will feel more enriched when the individual experiences larger segments of the total job. For example, a greater sense of personal achievement results when a worker makes the whole product instead of a segment.
2. When possible, a worker should be able to dictate the flow and pace of the job, within the parameters of the organization's objectives.
3. When possible, jobs should be challenging, and workers should be encouraged to be creative.

The Technology

Technology plays a vital role in the economic success of every organization. It is an ever-changing applied science present in every functional area. Frequently, technology may cause organizational change, which may result in the restructuring of job roles and job responsibilities. Innovations in technology and production methods require supervisors and organizations to adapt in order to maintain their

1. Competitive advantage
2. Superior job design
3. Maximum product quality
4. Optimal organizational performance

If an organization incorporates adaptive measures in its daily operations, it can maintain a position of industrial leadership. The Japanese have successfully used such adaptations to achieve world-wide success. In terms of technological improvement, an organization may select from four technological strategies:

1. *Leader:* The organization commits resources (time, money, or people) to the development and implementation of new technologies to establish technological superiority in the field.
2. *Enthusiastic follower:* The organization resigns itself to quickly adapting to technological advances designed by others. Such a strategy, although less costly, can be risky, for valuable time is lost while the competitor reaps immediate benefits. Copyrights and patents may create further costly delays.
3. *Reluctant follower:* The organization employs technological changes only when necessary. This strategy is based on the idea that some technological processes are fads, subject to still further change. The reluctant follower opts to wait until technological stability occurs. Then, and only then, will it gear up for the change.
4. *Avoider:* The organization decides that its current system will be injured by change and thus fears change of any type. It is committed to the continuation of current methods and technologies and consequently risks failure by virtue of missing major opportunities.

The Structure

Organizations must strive to improve

Organizations must constantly strive to improve their structure, which is visually depicted in an organizational chart. With time an organizational chart, which illustrates functions, positions, roles, relationships, units, the chain of command, and formal lines of authority, may become obsolete due to environmental, technological and operational considerations. Organizations must constantly monitor their day-to-day operations to ensure that their charts accurately reflect the intended structural operation. When an organization becomes obsolete, structural changes must be employed and the organizational chart adapted to avoid role confusion and authority problems. Organization members should follow the

Members must follow the chain of command

formal chain of command as depicted in the chart. If it is outdated, the organization will fail to perform according to intended expectations.

The organizational chart and structure should be analyzed according to three characteristics:

1. Task
2. Philosophy
3. Product

TASK

Over time, tasks change as a result of technology, worker skill, or competitive demand. It is imperative that job descriptions and organizational charts be updated to reflect changes that may have occurred.

PHILOSOPHY

Frequently, organizations decide to change or modify their management style and philosophy. Some organizations operate on an authoritative basis and decide to change to a participative or democratic philosophy. A structural shift of this nature requires a change in attitudes as well as operation. For a smooth transition, a new philosophy should be introduced through planned orientation meetings. Additionally, job descriptions and the organizational chart must be modified to reflect the intended changes.

PRODUCT

The company's final output affects organizational structure in three ways:

1. The item produced
2. The means of production
3. The intended consumer

The Item Produced   The Coca-Cola Company made a major structural change in terms of what it produced when it began to market New Coke as well as Classic Coke. This change prompted massive structural modifications of job descriptions and organizational charts.

The Means of Production   The Chrysler Corporation made a major structural change in terms of how its products are produced when it decided to use 700 robots to manufacture automobiles.

The Intended Consumer   Coors Brewing Company changed the geographical nature of its operation when it decided to market its

THE IMPROVEMENT STAR CHECKLIST

Is your organization designed for improvement? Your improvement star can shine if you use the following checklist as an appraisal to assist you in moving toward perfection.

DOES YOUR ORGANIZATION HAVE . . .

	Yes	No
1. frequent internal training and development?	_____	_____
2. tuition reimbursement?	_____	_____
3. a full-time personnel and training specialist?	_____	_____
4. a consultant who offers personnel and training programs?	_____	_____
5. a library of curent trade journals and periodicals?	_____	_____
6. a library of current training films?	_____	_____
7. a suitable budget for training?	_____	_____
8. a formal system of recognition for those who complete seminars, workshops, training sessions, certificates, and degrees?	_____	_____
9. an attitude that encourages self-improvement?	_____	_____
10. a system that evaluates and determines training needs?	_____	_____

beer on the East Coast. This shift has far-reaching structural ramifications.

Conclusion

Organizational improvement must be continual

Organizational improvement must be a continual process. Successful companies cannot rest on their laurels; they must strategically strive for perfection. As each point of the improvement star is addressed, organizational relationships can improve. When a work group, via quality circles, stresses the need to alter the task or the technology, such changes have a great impact on individuals, groups, and jobs. The implications are limitless, as are the opportunities for organizational improvement.

ORGANIZATIONAL DEVELOPMENT

Organizational development is complex

Organizational development is a complex process. Attempts to improve individual contributions are influenced by the style of management, the structure of the organization, the nature of the task, and the quality of relationships within the organization. Environmental factors further complicate the issue. Additionally, the work group influences the individual, who is exposed to group values and beliefs that can create conflict and confusion. Individual beliefs and group norms can be further shaped by organizational goals and objectives. In summary, people, groups, and organizations are three important influences on organizational development. As Figure 10–2 shows, organizational development success is a continuum of certain beliefs about people, groups, and organizations.

Belief 1: Employee Performance Is Critically Influenced by the Method of Supervision

Style of supervision will influence performance

Successful companies, like the Disney Corporation, Hewlett-Packard, and IBM, take a positive approach to the supervision of human resources. Ineffective human relations practices negatively affect employee performance, resulting in work stoppages, slowdowns, high turnover, and possible attempts for unionization. By contrast, successful supervisory practices lead to such favorable outcomes as worker commitment, loyalty, positive attitude, and increased productivity.

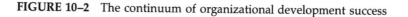

Employee performance is critically influenced by the method of supervision.

Individuals will tend to support what they help to create.

Commitment to organizational goals requires more than just agreement — it requires belief.

Congruency between individual goals and organizational goals should exist.

Change and conflict are positive and inevitable.

Teamwork is essential for organizational success.

People make the difference.

Success

FIGURE 10–2   The continuum of organizational development success

Belief 2: Individuals Will Tend to Support What They Help to Create

People will support what they help to create

Do renters behave differently than owners? If your signature is required on a document, will you read it thoroughly? Owner-ship creates commitment. A supervisor can generate commitment by the effective utilization of participative management. When in-dividuals can become a part of the decision-making process, they tend to take their role seriously.

Belief 3: Commitment to Organizational Goals Requires More Than Just Agreement: It Requires Belief

Organizational goals must be supported

Ideally, individuals must believe in the purpose and objec-tives of the organization. Can a football team tolerate a member who does not believe in winning? Agreement is simply the out-come of negotiation, whereas belief is an extension of devotion. Supervisors need workers who are devoted to the organization's goals.

Belief 4: Individual Goals and Organizational Goals Should Be Congruent

Personal goals and organizational goals should agree

An organization must seek workers who possess a philoso-phy similar to that of the group. A hospital specializing in excellent patient care should not seek a physician individually dedicated to finding the cure for cancer. By the same token, individuals must seek organizations and situations whose goals are compatible with theirs.

Belief 5: Change and Conflict Are Positive and Inevitable

People do not always resist change

The popular belief that people resist change is not true. Ac-tually, people resist *not* being a part of the change. Organizations and individuals must view change as necessary, because it pre-vents stagnation. An organization must always strive for improve-ment. As change is implemented, conflict frequently will occur, and a supervisor must learn to deal with it constructively. It must be treated as a positive and inevitable element of reality.

Early management theorists regarded conflict as a symptom of poor management that should be suppressed, ignored, or re-moved. Current management thinking, however, suggests that conflict is an opportunity to uncover differences of opinion, discuss them, and effectively arrive at the best solution.

Belief 6: Teamwork Is Essential for Organizational Success

Teamwork is essential   No one person is capable of single-handedly achieving the goals of an organization. Organizations succeed as a result of co-operative endeavors. Who won the last Super Bowl? It wasn't the quarterback but rather the entire team.

Belief 7: People Make the Difference

People are the heart of the organization   The technology and structure of an organization are mean-ingless unless people are prepared to make things happen. People are the heart of organizational development and are the invaluable resource making the difference between success and failure.

Conclusion

Organizational development success is based on a continuum of seven beliefs. No organization ever permanently achieves all seven beliefs. However, organizations that search for excellence are perpetually guided by these beliefs.

Results

When organizational development is practiced effectively, both self-improvement and organizational improvement can re-sult. Successful implementation will make the jobs of the execu-tive, middle manager, supervisor, and worker more challenging and rewarding. When the entire organizational development pro-cess is implemented successfully, the organization can expect

1. Informed and involved employees at all levels
2. A clear understanding of organizational goals
3. A better fit between people and work
4. A continuous upward and downward flow of communication
5. Increased teamwork
6. A climate in which problems and differences can be openly dis-cussed and resolved
7. Management by goals instead of by controls
8. Decisions that are better and more widely accepted
9. An organization that acts rather than reacts to change and conflict
10. A built-in mechanism for continual self-examination

SYMPTOMS AND CURES

Change for the sake of change is not the answer

When should organizations use organizational development to bring about change? This is a delicate question that demands thoughtful and considerable analysis. To change just for the sake of changing is not the answer. Consider the following situation:

> A scouting report of your next football opponent reveals a weak defense against the run. During the actual game, you run the ball seven times and score seven touchdowns. Would you change your strategy? Of course not. Change should only be employed for the sake of improvement.

Given the complexity of today's organizations, it is difficult to determine when to change. The list of symptoms (and their cures) in Table 10–1 is designed to help make such determinations. In effect, they indicate unhealthy organizations.

Symptom 1: Restricted Flow of Information

Healthy organizations communicate freely and openly

Healthy organizations communicate in a free and open manner. Unrestricted communication keeps employees at all levels informed and enhances each employee's feeling of worth, resulting in increased worker involvement, commitment, and loyalty. An

TABLE 10–1   Symptoms and cures for organizational development

Symptom	Cure
1. Restricted flow of information	Promote a steady flow of shared information
2. Conflict avoidance	View conflict as an input to be managed through in-depth discussion
3. Lack of recognition and rewards	Continually provide realistic recognition and rewards
4. Unilateral problem solving	Practice multilateral problem solving
5. The concept of individualism	Stress the team concept
6. Inflexible behavior	Perpetuate flexible behavior
7. Lack of trust	Create bonds of trust
8. Reaction management	Institute action management
9. Organizational imbalance	Maintain organizational equilibrium
10. Employee stagnation	Establish policies and procedures for growth and advancement

organization is not healthy if the flow of information is restricted. Supervisors must establish communication as a major priority.

THE CURE

Promote a steady flow of shared information.

Symptom 2: Conflict Avoidance

Conflict is inevitable. It is unrealistic to expect total agreement at all times. When differences of opinion occur, healthy organizations use the varying positions to help determine the best solution.

Conflict should not be avoided

An unhealthy organization regards conflict as a dangerous element to be avoided. When conflict is suppressed, however, the resulting frustration and anxiety endanger the healthy existence of the organization. Effective supervisors do not suppress conflict; they learn to manage it.

THE CURE

View conflict as an input to be managed through in-depth discussion.

Symptom 3: Lack of Recognition and Rewards

Employees like recognition

Lack of recognition is a common complaint of many employees. In some cases, negative reinforcement is the only type of recognition they receive from their supervisors. This is an unhealthy circumstance for both the employees and the organization.

Research suggests that employees respond productively to positive reinforcement. Instead of magnifying their mistakes, why not try "to catch your employees doing something right."[1] When you do, give them a pat on the back or another form of positive reinforcement. This practice can lead to a healthy employee who is willing to contribute to a healthy organization.

THE CURE

Provide realistic recognition and rewards on a continuing basis.

---

[1] Kennett Blanchard and Spencer Johnson, *The One-Minute Manager* (New York: William Morrow, 1981), p. 63.

Symptom 4: Unilateral Problem Solving

Employee input improves decision making

Supervisors do not know all the answers, nor are they expected to. But making a decision with limited worker input is not an effective supervisory practice. A prescription for this problem is regular doses of employee input. When provided with additional information, the supervisor is in a better position to make the quality decisions that are required to maintain the good health of an organization.

THE CURE

Practice multilateral problem solving.

Symptom 5: The Concept of Individualism

Supervisors must convert "me" to "we"

Some workers, especially those who are ego oriented, have a tendency to develop an "I" attitude. Engaging in constant "me deep" conversation can be detrimental to the individual, the department, and the organization. Effective supervisors must learn the transition technique of converting "me" to "we."

THE CURE

Stress the team concept.

Symptom 6: Inflexible Behavior

Think of the number of times you have heard someone say, "That's the way we've always done things around here." Such inflexible thinking and behavior inhibits creativity and innovation. Resisting new ideas puts you on the road to failure. Creativity and innovation are the means of cutting through obsolescence to provide the competitive edge.

THE CURE

Perpetuate flexible behavior.

Symptom 7: Lack of Trust

Trust is a key element

For on-the-job relationships to be effective, "trust is a must." A lack of trust leads to suspicion, which is not conducive to productive group behavior. Action-oriented supervisors must set the pace by displaying trust as an integral part of their day-to-day activities. As employees follow the lead of the supervisor, suspicion dissolves and trust is fostered. Trust is necessary for all cooperative endeavors.

THE CURE

Create bonds of trust.

Symptom 8: Reaction Management

Supervisors must learn to act rather than react

Unhealthy organizations and ineffective supervisors constantly find themselves reacting to events. They move from crisis to crisis, ineffectively trying to put out the fire. This can only lead to dismal results. Effective supervisors have learned to act rather than react. They anticipate problems and develop solutions in advance.

THE CURE

Initiate action management.

Symptom 9: Organizational Imbalance

All departments must be treated equally

Unhealthy organizations are frequently peopled with empire builders who fail to view their departments within their proper perspective. Such supervisors demand a disproportionate amount of resources, money, machines, and personnel to create their artificial importance and a false sense of security. Empire-building practices are detrimental to organizational unity. All departments and units must be viewed as equal, or organizational imbalance will result.

Healthy organizations take a balanced approach and subsequently view each part as an integral piece of the organizational puzzle.

THE CURE

Maintain organizational equilibrium.

Symptom 10: Employee Stagnation

Limited opportunities for growth and advancement result in employee stagnation in the short run and in organizational death in the long run. Restricted training and educational opportunities are major contributors to this serious problem. Every supervisor

Individual growth must be emphasized

must thus place a premium on individual growth and advancement. Healthy organizations work to avoid the short-term and long-term consequences of employee stagnation.

THE CURE

Establish policies and procedures for growth and advancement.

GUIDELINES FOR ACTION

Supervisors are the key to effective organizational development. The following action guidelines are provided to ensure that supervisory impact is positive and in agreement with organizational development principles:

1. Try new approaches.
2. Be an effective communicator.
3. Control your behavior.
4. Distinguish between feelings and facts.
5. Learn to listen.
6. Understand what motivates individuals and groups.
7. Know how things get done as well as what gets done.

Guideline 1: Try New Approaches

Supervisors must not be afraid to try new approaches. As technological and human relations advancements occur, the supervisor must be confident that effective implementation is not only possible but probable. To find new and better ways is not a challenge; it is a requirement.

Guideline 2: Be an Effective Communicator

The supervisor is the vital link in the organizational communication process, serving as a bridge between top management and the work force. In this unique capacity, the supervisor must go beyond the who, what, where, and when of communication and become effective at *how* to communicate. Therefore, the many obstacles to effective communication must be removed. Today's information age can create communication overload, which demands that supervisors review, receive, send, and share relevant information in a timely and accurate manner.

Guideline 3: Control Your Behavior

Every time there is an action, there is an equal and opposite reaction. This principle of physics can be applied to supervisory situations. It is important to realize that your actions affect others. Be sensitive to this phenomenon and take the lead. Set the pace, and provide an example to those who follow.

Guideline 4: Distinguish Between Feelings and Facts

Too many supervisors make decisions based solely on emotion. They fail to separate their feelings from the facts, and subsequently make irrational decisions.

Effective supervisors step back from the emotion of the situation and systematically gather the relevant facts. Once the data are obtained and effectively analyzed, the supervisor can make a rational decision and at the same time anticipate the behavioral consequences of the proposed action. While intuition is to be valued, don't be afraid to confront the facts.

Guideline 5: Learn to Listen

Effective listening is an art that must be practiced and fine-tuned on a regular basis. It is a component of effective supervision for which there is no substitute, for how can you respond to employee ideas and suggestions if you fail to listen when they are introduced? Effective listening is a feedback mechanism that enables the supervisor to gauge and monitor the actions of the individual and the organization.

Guideline 6: Understand What Motivates Individuals and Groups

Periodically, supervisors should review basic human relations concepts. All supervisors should have a basic human relations handbook as part of their self-help library. Basic motivational and leadership principles should be reviewed regularly to improve supervisory action and organizational efficiency.

Guideline 7: Know How Things Get Done As Well As What Gets Done

Many supervisors make the common mistake of placing too much emphasis on results while losing sight of how those results are achieved. While results are a primary responsibility of management, methodology cannot be dismissed. Supervisors must make sure that employees are learning and doing their jobs properly. There is always room for improvement.

THE STEPS OF ORGANIZATIONAL DEVELOPMENT

Improvement requires the following of six steps

Creating improvement through the process of organizational development can best be accomplished by following six separate yet interrelated steps:

1. Foster total organizational commitment.
2. Compile research and diagnoses.
3. Prepare an action plan.
4. Implement the action plan.
5. Receive feedback.
6. Recycle.

Needless to say, no improvement can take place unless the entire organization is committed to the change. The commitment must start at the top.

An action plan will lead to success

Haphazard changes are not the answer. Data must be collected systematically, and an action plan must be followed. Ideally, the action plan should be developed by as many employees as possible. When it is implemented, supervisors must be alert to feedback, which will help them determine whether the process has been successful. Finally, successful plans of action should be recycled to other segments of the organization that can also benefit from the process.

SUMMARY

Organizational development is a strategy to improve the operation of the organization by increasing performance and improving the quality of work life. Complete organizational effectiveness depends on the control and development of each interrelated point on the improvement star: the individual, the work group, the task, the technology, and the structure. It is advisable to use the improvement star checklist as an appraisal instrument.

Organizational development beliefs are best viewed as a continuum, since the ultimate achievement of all the beliefs is elusive.

When the process is implemented successfully, the organization can expect worker involvement, a continuous flow of communication, increased teamwork, a desirable climate, and effective management.

Perhaps the best way to determine the need for change is to analyze an organization in terms of unhealthy symptoms and healthy cures. To ensure that the supervisor's actions are positive and in agreement with organizational development principles, it is best to follow the guidelines for action, which include trying new approaches, controlling your behavior, and learning to listen. Improvement can best be accomplished by following the six steps that lead to the systematic implementation of organizational development concepts. Ideally, successful organizational development principles can be recycled for use in other segments of the organization. In short, organizational development is a dynamic and continuous process that results in both individual and organizational excellence.

CASE STUDY **20**

Organizational Development Questions

At the weekly administrative meeting, it is decided that a training and development program should be implemented for organizational development purposes. The following questions emerged from the meeting.

QUESTIONS

1. How should the company determine which major areas of training should be considered?
2. What steps should be followed in implementing the program?
3. Who should implement the program?
4. How can the company determine the success of the program?

CASE STUDY 21

Try It Out

You have been employed by an accounting firm for the past eight years. After receiving several promotions, you are now a manager of a major department. On your own, you have been taking classes at the local college and are nearing completion of your degree. In a recent supervision course, you were required to do a research paper in which you apply a course topic to your job. You selected the concept of organizational development. Your instructor, after reading the report, suggested that the concepts actually be applied to your department, but you indicated that your organization is conservative and would not approve of organizational development as a mechanism for change.

QUESTIONS

1. Which organizational development principles can be practiced on a departmental level?
2. Which organizational development principles cannot be practiced on a departmental level?

CASE STUDY 22

The Improvement Star

Top management at an assembly plant has indicated a desire to implement organizational development concepts to improve the overall effectiveness of the organization. The improvement star was used as the criteria for an internal audit. Knowing that changes are costly, time-consuming, and difficult, you have been asked to analyze each element of the improvement star and answer the following questions.

QUESTIONS

1. Which element is the most costly to change?
2. Which element is the least costly to change?
3. Which element is the most difficult to change?
4. Which element is the easiest to change?
5. Which element can be changed most quickly?
6. Which element would take the longest to change?

Terms and Concepts Supervisors Should Know

Guidelines for action; Improvement star; Organizational development; Organizational development beliefs; Organizational development cures; Organizational development results; Organizational development steps; Organizational development symptoms.

Questions for Discussion

1. What is the most important element of the improvement star?
2. Does organizational development require workers to be made to fit the job? Discuss.
3. Do people resist change? Discuss.
4. Which symptoms of unhealthy organizations do you feel is most critical?
5. When should plans of action be recycled?

For Further Reading–And More Ideas

"Alignment (Leadership, Employees, and Organizational Goals)," *Training* (December 1988).

Argyris, C., *Integrating the Individual and the Organization*, New York: Wiley, 1964.

Bonsignore, F. N., "Creating and Changing a Firm's Culture (CPA Firms)," *The CPA Journal* (January 1989).

Cunningham, R., "Confront and Engage for Organizational Development," *Training and Development Journal* (February 1989).

Deal, T. E., and A. A. Kennedy, *Corporate Cultures*, Reading, MA: Addison-Wesley, 1982.

Hackman, J. R., and G. R. Oldham, *Work Redesign*, Reading, MA: Addison-Wesley, 1980.

Hampton, David R., Charles E. Summer, and Ross A. Webber, *Organizational Behavior and the Practice of Management*, Glenview, IL: Scott, Foresman, 1987.

Hampton, R., *Behavioral Concepts in Management*, 3rd ed., Belmont, CA: Wadsworth, 1978.

Hampton, R., *Management*, 3rd ed., New York: McGraw-Hill, 1968.

Handy, Charles, "The Changing Shape of Work," *Organizational Dynamics* (Autumn 1980).

Harris, P. R., and D. Harris, "Decision Making for a New Work Culture," *Management Decisions* (August 1988).

Herzberg, F., *The Managerial Choice: To Be Efficient and to Be Human*, Homewood, IL: Irwin, 1976.

Katz, J. H., "The Fact and Causes of Variation in Structural Development Processes," *Journal of Management Studies* (March 1989).

Kimberly, John R., "Initiation, Innovation, and Institutionalization in the Creation Process," in *The Organizational Life Cycle*, J. R. and R. H. Miles, eds., San Francisco: Jossey-Bass, 1980.

Lawrence, P. R., and J. W. Lorsch, *Developing Organizations: Diagnosis and Action*, Reading, MA: Addison-Wesley, 1969.

Likert, Rensis, *New Patterns of Management*, New York: McGraw-Hill, 1961.

Lundberg, C., "Corporate Culture," *Human Resource Management* (Spring 1985).

Luthans, F., and R. Kreitner, *Organizational Behavior Modification and Beyond*, Glenview, IL: Scott, Foresman, 1985.

McGregor, Douglas, *The Human Side of Enterprise*, New York: McGraw-Hill, 1960.

O'Hara, K., C. M. Johnson, and T. A. Beehr, "Organizational Behavior Management in the Private Sector: A Review of Empirical Research and Recommendations for Further Investigations," *Academy of Management Review* (October 1985).

Ouchi, William, *Theory Z: How American Business Can Meet the Japanese Challenge*, Reading, MA: Addison-Wesley, 1981.

Pascale, R. T., "The Paradox of Corporate Culture," *California Management Review* (Winter 1985).

Peters, T. J., and N. Austin, *A Passion for Excellence*, New York: Random House, 1985.

Peters, T. J., and R. H. Waterman, *In Search of Excellence*, New York: Harper & Row, 1982.

Quinn, James B., *Strategic Change*, Homewood, IL: Dow-Jones Irwin, 1980.

Saffold, G. S., "Culture Traits, Strength, and Organizational Performance: Moving Beyond Strong Culture," *The Academy of Management Review* (October 1988).

Sathe, V., "How to Decipher and Change Organizational Culture," *Managing Corporate Cultures*, San Francisco: Jossey-Bass, 1984.

Shanks, D. C., "The Role of Leadership in Strat-

egy Development," *Journal of Business Strategy* (January–February 1989).

Waterman, R. H., T. J. Peters, and J. Phillips, "Structure Is Not Organization," *Business Horizons* (June 1980).

Weick, Karl E., *The Social Psychology of Organizing*, Reading, MA: Addison-Wesley, 1979.

Weinstein, N., "Getting off on the Right Foot (Organizational Development Training Specialists)," *Training and Development Journal* (March 1989).

"What Corporate Culture Is and How Shared Values Contribute to the Success or Failure of Strategy," *Business Week* (October 27, 1980).

Wiener, Y., "Forms of Value Systems: A Focus on Organizational Effectiveness and Cultural Change and Maintenance," *Academy of Management Review* (October 1988).

Wrapp, H. E., "Good Managers Don't Make Policy Decisions," *Harvard Business Review* (July–August 1984).

Recruiting, Selecting, and Training Employees

11

"How to pick and keep a winner!"

LEARNING OBJECTIVES

When you complete this chapter, you should be able to:
1. Identify the components of a good job description and be able to write one for your position.
2. Identify the components of a good job opening and be able to write one for your position.
3. Recall the six steps in selecting a new employee.
4. Compare a job description with a candidate's qualifications.
5. Identify the various ways of recruiting.
6. Understand the value of training programs.
7. Appreciate the need for establishing training goals before the methods of training are established.
8. Define how an on-the-job training (OJT) program might work in your company.

"A company is known by the people it employs."

Below are some questions to stimulate your thoughts before reading the chapter. You may know the answers to some, and you will find others as you read.

Have you seen a written job description for your position? Could you write one right now?

What are the six steps in selection?

When should you test an applicant?

During the interview, who should do more talking: the applicant or the interviewers? Why?

Is there an advantage to a training program, even when the cost seems high?

What would be the best way to train employees in your department? In other areas in your company?

Can you think of areas where training could have saved your company money?

What would you include in the orientation training program in your company?

STAFFING

An important area of supervision is staffing, which includes recruiting, hiring, appraising, orienting, training, promoting, and compensating employees. Staffing directly affects all subordinates, and the supervisor is in complete charge of this function until the firm grows and portions of it can be absorbed by staff personnel.

The human resource department is involved in staffing

As each staffing task becomes more sophisticated, effective coordination is necessary between the supervisor and the human resource department. The latter, using job descriptions or personnel requests provided by the supervisor, may recruit applicants through newspaper or magazine ads. The supervisor may select the final applicant after an initial screening by a selection committee. The company training program may be organized by the human resource division with certain phases handled by an individual supervisor. A promotion is possible after interviews, reviews of the personnel file records, and conferences with several peers. The total compensation package and the wage and fringe benefit system may be established and implemented by the salary and negotiation staff in the human resource division with little or no input from the supervisor.

If you are a supervisor or expect to be one, it is wise to understand the entire staffing system and the various ways of recruiting, interviewing, and selecting employees.

Job Description

The job description lists all duties

A systematic selection starts with a good job description. Human resource directors are often asked to find "a good person" without the faintest indication of what that means. Specifying the job content before the opening is advertised is most important. The supervisor and the person holding a position similar to the one being filled are the best persons to determine the job description. The list of requirements and duties should include the experience, skills, and education needed, as well as the supervisor for the job. A job description for a manufacturing supervisor is shown in Figure 11–1.

Job Opening

Job openings list duties, salary, work conditions, and application deadline

Requirements from the job description are listed in an official job opening. Besides the items listed above, the announcement should specify the final date for submitting applications, salary range, physical requirements, the working conditions, and the occupational characteristics. A sample job announcement is shown in Figure 11–2.

A position description is designed to help the supervisor determine minimum qualifications for the position and ways of assessing an applicant. This method can help the firm select the most qualified candidate.

Recruiting

Recruiting means finding job applicants

The more applicants a supervisor has for a specific job, the better chance he or she has of selecting the most qualified person. Many avenues for recruitment exist. Figure 11–3 lists some ways to begin a search for employees.

Ads can be open or blind

An ad can be *open*, giving the name, address, and perhaps the telephone number of the employer, or it can be *blind*, using only a box number. The open ad usually yields more applicants and also gives exposure to the company name. On the other hand, the blind ad allows the company to recruit confidentially, without informing present employees. It also eliminates the necessity of responding to all applicants and avoids a deluge of telephone calls or personal applications.

POSITION DESCRIPTION

Title: Tool Room Supervisor

Dept./Division: Moving Arm

Objective: To be in charge of the tool room for Manufacturing, Q.C., Q.A., and Engineering. To constantly maintain high-quality tooling. Interface with Engineering and other departments. Recommended Requirements: five years in general tooling of high precision. Experience on lathes, mills and grinders. Able to supervise experienced toolmakers and machinists. Minimum Requirements: three years as toolmaker-machinist, experience on machines; two years in design and drafting.

Reports to: Manufacturing Engineering Manager

Job responsibilities:

1. Be in charge of tool crib and all materials therein (value approx. $50,000). Keep a running inventory of steels, aluminums, taps, drills, reamers, and other materials needed for general tooling.
2. Hire and terminate employees.
3. Evaluate employees; write and give reviews and pay raises.
4. Teach the tool trade and proper machine handling to apprentices and inexperienced machinists.
5. Plan to make delivery on time after receiving tooling requirements. Assign work to employees to high-tolerance tooling.
6. Run machines and build tooling parts when needed.
7. Interface with Engineering on tool design and redesign.
8. Be responsible for tooling being built for inhouse use and outside customers.
9. Take responsibility for shipping anodized and plated parts, and for all outside services for shop.

FIGURE 11–1   The job description lists requirements and responsibilities

PLEASE CIRCULATE AND POST

July 28, 19XX

CLASSIFIED OPEN AND PROMOTIONAL OPPORTUNITY

POSITION

ACCOUNT CLERK, SENIOR (Continuing Education)
SALARY: $892 - $1085/Month (+2½% Swing Shift)

Five-step salary range, initial placement customarily at
first step; advanced placement according to District policy;
full-time, 8 hours/day, 12 months/year; plus fringe benefits;
12 month probation period.
Working Hours: 1:00-10:00 P.M. - Mon-Thurs; 8:00-5:00 P.M. Fri.

JOB SUMMARY

Under general supervision, to perform accounting clerical work
of above average difficulty involved in the maintenance of the
District's financial and statistical records; and to do related
work as required.

EXAMPLES OF DUTIES

Performs financial record keeping operations related to one of
the moderately complex elements of the District's accounting
activities; arranges, posts, and balances financial data;
establishes and maintains subsidiary ledgers; makes routine
verifications in accordance with established procedures;
maintains control accounts; balances accounts and takes trial
balances; checks, assembles, and prepares payroll and accounts
payable data for issuance of warrants; posts and maintains
supportive payroll records involving changes, new employment,
terminations, leaves of absence, time cards, and W-2 and W-4
forms; receives and accounts for cash; prepares daily bank
deposits for various accounts; operates a posting machine in
posting receipts and expenditures to various accounts; prepares financial and statistical reports and statements; interprets and applies appropriate rules and regulations; answers
questions regarding financial and accounting procedures,
account balances, and related matter; may approve checks;
operate typewriter and accounting, adding, calculating and
other office machines.

QUALIFICATIONS

Education and Experience: Any combination equivalent to
graduation from high school, including or supplemented by
courses in bookkeeping, and two years experience in financial
record keeping work.

Knowledges and Abilities: Knowledge of the methods, practices
and terminology used in bookkeeping and financial record keeping; ability to post data and make arithmetic calculations
rapidly and accurately; ability to operate calculating and
adding machines; ability to type at 40 words per minute;
ability to work cooperatively with others.

General Requirements: Good health and physical condition,
including evidence of freedom from active tuberculosis and
satisfactory results from prescribed physical examinations;
from disabling defects that would prevent satisfactory
job requirements; satisfactory fingerprinting

EMPLOYMENT BENEFITS

District paid Medical, Life and Income Protection Insurance;
Dental Insurance available. 12 paid vacation days, 12 paid
sick days, and 15 holidays per year. Shared retirement and
Social Security costs. Tax shelters and credit union available. Many other benefits available for classified employees.

APPLY

Classified Personnel Dept.

Applications must be
received by: August 9, 19XX
(Interview by Invitation Only)

AN AFFIRMATIVE ACTION - TITLE IX EMPLOYER

FIGURE 11–2   A sample job announcement for a community college

1. Advertise in newspapers and trade publications.
2. Let your employees know about the job vacancies. They may be able to find applicants through word of mouth.
3. Use placement services of trade, industrial, and professional associations.
4. Use placement services of colleges, trade schools, and business schools.
5. Ask your friends, customers, suppliers.
6. Use state and commercial employment agencies.
7. Labor unions sometimes have the responsibility of supplying job applicants.
8. Review past applications received.

FIGURE 11–3   Means of recruiting employees

Another type of blind ad gives only the telephone number. Applicants are screened when they call, and appointments are set up for personal interviews only with those who are qualified. This method saves time.

Public employment agencies can screen your applicants

In some sectors of the United States, the public employment service is a good source for recruitment. The service recruits applicants, screens them according to specifications, and sends those qualified to the prospective employer. To save time and still attract more applicants, a retailer can run his or her own ad and let the service do the screening. Applicants report to the service agency, and only the best four or five are interviewed personally by the employer.

Employees usually pay agency fees

Private employment agencies provide another route. Employees usually pay the agency to find the job, but in some instances employers will pay the fee. Charges range from 10 to 50 percent of the first month's or first year's salary.

Contacting associates for help sometimes yields good results, but it can also cause problems. If a person who is recommended by an associate is not satisfactory and must be released, the person who recommended the employee may be unhappy or angry about the outcome.

A competitor can sometimes be a source

Sometimes a friendly competitor or colleague can supply applicants. It may be that he or she has had to lay off a good worker, owing to a slump in business. One dealer spreads the word about an opening by informing suppliers, and they in turn often find applicants.

When recruiting prospective employees, management must keep Equal Employment Opportunity regulations in mind. These require all employers to expand their pool of employment applications so that no one is excluded because of past or present discriminatory practices in regard to race, nationality, sex, or age.

Employers who engage an otherwise well-balanced work force often neglect older people, who in many cases are more experienced and more reliable than younger workers. Nor should handicapped people be overlooked, as they frequently make excellent workers, and customers can appreciate the management's sense of social concern. State employment agencies can supply complete information regarding state and federal vocational rehabilitation programs for the handicapped.

Older people and the handicapped may be ideal candidates

Screening Application Forms

It helps to have an application form ready to be completed by a prospect before an interview. The form offers a good starting point and provides a written record of facts about the applicant's education, work experience, references, and where he or she can be reached.

Contacting Applicants

After reviewing all the applications, you can contact the best prospects by telephone. A few pertinent questions will help you decide whether you wish to pursue this applicant's possibilities by setting up an interview.

Review Testing

In some firms the next step may be testing qualified applicants. Such companies give tests either before or after the initial interview. These devices can screen for personality, aptitude, achievement, and performance; thus they are helpful in ranking candidates and predicting their subsequent success. After these tests are validated, the interviewer knows a considerable amount about the applicant, which saves time in questioning. Aptitude tests are commonly used to measure such abilities as mental and verbal skills, and if given before the interview, to eliminate applicants who do not meet the minimum requirements.

Brief tests of general ability may be used

You may want to give applicants a general ability test. Local colleges and universities can provide excellent referral services to maximize legally appropriate testing procedures.

Employ Reference Checks

An important step in hiring is to check employees' personal and business references. This can shed light on the honesty and personality traits of the applicant. Reference checks can be done before or after the interview, either by telephone or by mail. Gen-

COMPARISONS OF JOB DESCRIPTION WITH APPLICANT'S QUALIFICATIONS

JOB DESCRIPTION	APPLICANT'S QUALIFICATIONS

1. *Physical*
   a. Is appearance important to the job?

   b. Is the ability to converse with employees, customers, and supervisors needed?

   c. Is there a physical strain involved, such as long hours, travel, or hard physical labor?

2. *Education and Experience*
   Does the job call for a specific amount or type of education or experience, or can there be a combination of these? Can two or three years of experience equal one year of college?

3. *General Intelligence and Special Aptitudes*
   a. When there is a large number of candidates for a position, there may be a need for tests of intelligence and performance.

   b. Special aptitude tests for mathematics, writing, and mechanical ability can be used.

4. *Personality and Interests*
   a. What type of role should the applicant be able to fill: a leader, a subleader, or "just one of the group?"

   b. How well will the person fit into the organization? What does the company expect of its employees in the following areas?
      (1) Physical

      (2) Intellectual

      (3) Social

a. INTERVIEW: Note dress and physical appearance.
b. Does the person speak well, and does appearance inspire confidence?

c. RÉSUMÉ: Is there a physical liability that may limit performance?

RÉSUMÉ: Check high school, technical training, college, and prior experience. Contact previous supervisors and personal references.

a. Results of performance tests and a general battery of intelligence tests, usually short form (half-hour).

b. RÉSUMÉ OR WRITTEN/PERFORMANCE TESTS: Give written tests for some skills and performance tests for others, such as shorthand, cooking, custodial, maintenance, and auto mechanics.

a. INTERVIEW OR PERSONALITY TESTS: Does the candidate exhibit evidence of leadership ability? Does the person seek to influence groups? Can the person sustain a leadership role? Does the résumé exhibit such traits? Has the person held an office before in a voluntary organization?
b. RÉSUMÉ AND INTERVIEW:

(1) Does the candidate take part in any organized sport?
(2) Does the candidate read or go to cultural events?
(3) Does the candidate show an interest in people, clubs, and professional associations?

JOB DESCRIPTION	APPLICANT'S QUALIFICATIONS

5. *Circumstances and Contingencies*
  a. Is there a strain in the job that may relate to the person's domestic life? Will he or she have to travel? Will he or she have to entertain out-of-town guests?
  b. How well can the applicant handle unexpected contingencies? How well can he or she work under stress?
	a. INTERVIEW AND RÉSUMÉ: What are the candidate's family's circumstances and upbringing? Does the job correspond to his or her expectations?
	
	b. INTERVIEW: Presented with real or hypothetical problems, how well does the applicant analyze the problem, see possible alternatives, and select the best solutions?

SIX STEPS IN SELECTION

REMEMBER TO S C R E E N APPLICANTS

S   SCREEN the application form.
     Passes if the applicant has the essential qualifications.

C   CONTACT the applicant and set up initial interview.
     Passes if everything on the surface seems satisfactory.

R   REVIEW testing.[1]
     Passes if the test scores are adequate.

E   EMPLOY reference checks.
     Passes if there is evidence of good job performance and an ability to get along with others.

E   ENTER into a comprehensive interview.
     Passes if the applicant seems to have ability, interest, and good work habits, as well as a satisfactory personality.

N   NECESSARY medical check.
     Passes if the applicant is in good physical condition

HIRED

---

[1] The Civil Rights Act of 1964 and its accompanying interpretation by the federal courts have resulted in a reduction in the use of tests for selection. In *Griggs et al.* v. *Duke Power Company,* the U.S. Supreme Court ruled that preemployment tests must show a relationship to job performance, or, in other words, they must possess validity. It is therefore suggested that tests be used only after validation.

Checking references by phone is preferable

erally a telephone call is preferred, as job requirements can then be discussed in some detail. A good question to ask is whether the former employer would consider rehiring the candidate.

After enough candidates have been recruited, the screening and interviewing are done either by the supervisor or by a selection or interviewing team. The team is often composed of subordinates, peers, and supervisors. The number of candidates has usually been pared down to 3 to 12 for comprehensive interviews. The selection may be carried out by the team or by the supervisor. The latter should have a great deal of influence on the selection, because he or she will be most responsible for the employee's actions and duties.

Enter Into a Comprehensive Interview

Interviewing is the most important step

The crucial step in selecting an employee is the interview. Many techniques, strategies, and skills must be used to ensure that the right person is hired.

Employment interviewing is the open exchange between persons of unequal status for a mutually agreed-upon position. Good interviewing depends upon your skills in helping the applicant talk spontaneously, in using the correct questioning techniques, in interpreting the answers appropriately, and in knowing the various interviewing styles.

"CHARLIE, YOU'VE BEEN TRADED TO
PITTSBURGH METAL MANUFACTURING
FOR THREE SALES MANAGERS AND AN
ACCOUNTANT TO BE NAMED LATER."

Review the résumé and application first

Review the candidate's résumé and application *before* the interview. Look for unexplained gaps in time sequences and accomplishments, and try to read between the lines to locate strengths and attributes that should be explored. Then formulate specific questions to ask during the interview.

Develop a Plan for the Interview

Write out questions in advance

Remember that a plan should be established *prior* to the interview. After a thorough review of all data at your disposal, you should consider the questions you will ask. It is recommended that you write out the questions in advance so you will know not only which questions but also the order in which they should be asked. If the same questions are asked of all candidates, a fair and consistent basis for comparison will result. This will add to the efficiency and fairness of your decision. Where possible, ask open-ended questions. Simple answers of *yes* and *no* provide limited information upon which to make a decision. Needless to say, illegal questions must not be asked.

All interviewers have biases and must attempt to suspend them

Know your own biases, and try to set them aside. Almost everyone has biases of some kind. Successful interviewing does not mean that you must overcome your biases immediately, but that you should be conscious of them and attempt to *suspend* them while interviewing.

The interview tests the relevance of the experience and training claimed by the applicant. You, as the interviewer, should try to appraise the candidate's personality, motivation, and character, keeping in mind that his or her answers are screened. They reveal only those facts and attitudes calculated to make a good impression. Because you want to penetrate this screen, it is very important that there be no interruptions or phone calls during the interview so that you can give the applicant your undivided attention.

Rapport can be established by mutually interesting small talk

Establish rapport with the applicant right away by talking *briefly* about a subject of mutual interest. This initial small talk is the key to getting early, spontaneous answers. You should attempt to make the prospective employee as comfortable as possible. The interviewer's use of facial expressions also is very important. Two expressions generally used are the raising of the eyebrows and smiling. When the applicant has revealed impressive achievements, raise the eyebrows in approval to help him or her talk with ease. Smiling frequently during the interview makes delicate questions less obtrusive and gives one the appearance of being receptive.

Let the applicant do 75 percent of the talking

Let the applicant do most of the talking. A good rule of thumb is to let the applicant talk 75 percent of the time, use 15 percent of the time for your questions and comments, and allow 10 percent for describing the position offered and giving details about your company. Your surroundings should be as professional as possible, with a minimum amount of clutter or distraction.

Interviews should move smoothly and in sequence

A well-organized interview is conducted with a sequence in mind. The essential points of *work experience, education,* and *skills* must be covered for an effective evaluation of the applicant. The sequence below is a suggested plan for an in-depth interview including these essential points. Information supplied on the application or résumé will guide you in exploring the candidate's background.

EDUCATION AND TRAINING

Applicant's school record reflects attitudes, hard work, and intelligence

Education is an important factor in hiring employees. An applicant's course of study, his or her likes and dislikes, and participation in extracurricular activities all are informative. The level of intelligence, quality of work, amount of tardiness, and absenteeism are points to consider in school and employment records.

WORK HISTORY

Begin with the first job. Discover whether it was full- or part-time, volunteer or paid, and progress step by step through the applicant's work history. The number of jobs the applicant has had reflects upon his or her stability, satisfaction, and emotional maturity.

OUTSIDE ACTIVITIES

A great deal can be learned about motivation and imagination by discussing how the applicant spends his or her spare time. Extracurricular activities show how involved, active, and interested the applicant can be.

PRESENTATION

Make a specific presentation of the position, salary, and benefits of your organization. Describe as fully as possible the next step in the hiring process. Will there be another interview? Are you interested in the candidate? Do you plan to make an offer? Communicate as much as you can.

Present the job and organization in an accurate, positive way. The interview is really a two-way negotiation between the supervisor and the candidate. Think in advance about some of the aspects of your organization that might be most interesting to an

Assess your company honestly

applicant. Do not glorify your company. If there are problems in your firm, mention them and show how you are coping with them. Encourage the applicant to ask questions and answer them directly.

EXPLORATORY QUESTIONS

Open-ended questions allow the person to expand on ideas and feelings

When you want the applicant to reveal his or her feelings and ideas to the fullest extent, use exploratory or open-ended questions. Ask questions that must be answered with explanations: What do you enjoy most about work? What would you change about your last job if you could change anything? What did you mean when you said that your production record was higher than average?

"Job hoppers" change jobs frequently

People who change jobs frequently are called *job hoppers* and *may* be considered a bad risk. Job hopping can indicate immaturity, signs of which may appear during the interview. Evidence sometimes is found in childish emotional statements, such as: "No one really cared what I did; I was never encouraged or told things were going right, so I figured if they didn't care, I didn't care either." A mature person has the ability to rise above matters such as these, and to handle responsibilities despite personal conflicts or stress.

Why did you leave your last job?

An interviewer must ask personal questions, such as why the applicant wants the job you have to offer, and why the person left the last job. Responses should be evaluated as the discussion proceeds. You should determine if the applicant seems to be knowledgeable, if he or she tends to be evasive, and if there are discrepancies in any statements.

Interpreting the applicant's answers, attitudes, and reactions is very important. You must look for clues to *personality, motivation, work history,* and *personal successes and failures.* One way of going about this is to have the candidate compare his or her previous jobs to the job to be filled. Important factors to compare would be income needs, company policies, and degree of supervision.

CLOSING THE INTERVIEW

Close the interview on a positive note

End the interview on a clear, positive note. One of the biggest complaints from applicants is that they often walk out of interviews without knowing where they stand or what the next step will be. By now, you should have an overall view of the prospective employee's qualifications. Try to clarify your feelings about the applicant, and tell him or her whether you are seriously interested. Communicate clearly as much information as you can.

UNACCEPTABLE PREEMPLOYMENT INQUIRIES

Some of the following facts need not be revealed before hiring, but many may be asked for after hiring if the information is necessary for fringe-benefit programs.

SUBJECT	DO NOT ASK
Age	Questions that allude to age
Religion	"Do you attend religious services or belong to a house of worship?"
	Applicant may not be told, "This is a Catholic/Protestant/Jewish/atheist organization."
Photograph	For a photograph before hiring
Citizenship	Whether applicant's parents and/or spouse are citizens of the United States
Experience	Type of military discharge
National origin or ancestry	Language commonly used by applicant: "What is your native tongue?"
Character	"Have you ever been arrested or had your wages garnished?"
Relatives	Marital status or number of dependents "Who will care for the children while you are working?" "With whom do you reside?" "Do you live with your parents?"
Physical or financial condition	"Do you have any physical disabilities?" "Do you own or rent?"
Maiden name	The maiden name of a female applicant

MEDICAL CHECK

Medical exams protect against future medical claims

Some companies require medical checks at different points along the selection process; however, because of the high cost of medical examinations, many companies use them as the last screening device before hiring. Since many companies provide medical coverage, a medical exam is necessary to protect the firm against compensation claims for injuries or diseases incurred before hiring.

ACCEPTABLE PREEMPLOYMENT INQUIRIES

Subject	Do Ask
Name	"Have you worked for this company under a different name?" "Have you ever been convicted of a crime?"
Birthplace	"Can you, after employment, submit a birth certificate or other proof of U.S. citizenship or age?"
Age	"Can you, after employment, submit a work permit if under 18?" "Are you over 18?"
Citizenship	"If you are not a U.S. citizen, have you the legal right to remain permanently in the U.S.?" "Do you intend to remain permanently in the U.S.?" "Can you, after employment, submit proof of citizenship?"
Education	Academic, vocational, or professional education.
Experience	Work experience
Physical condition	"Do you have any physical condition that may limit your ability to perform the job?"

TRAINING

Once the hiring decision has been made, the supervisor must employ effective training techniques to prepare the employee for work. More and more companies are allocating increased resources for training. They realize that the skill and knowledge necessary to perform today's jobs are rapidly changing. It is generally recognized that this trend will continue.

We must train for the future, not the past

As supervisors, we must meet the challenge of preparing our workers for the future, not the past. As changing work methods and improved technology reduce the segment of our population required to produce the goods and services needed by society, our primary role focuses on teaching and training for today, while keeping a sharp eye on tomorrow.

Since the supervisor accomplishes goals through people, it is obvious that the people must be prepared and equipped to accomplish those goals. For this reason alone, effective training makes good sense.

The faster that workers are trained to reach acceptable levels of performance, the faster that waste is reduced, safety is enhanced, and quality is improved. When workers become secure with the present, they will be more adaptable to the future. As high-tech developments go beyond our wildest expectations, we must keep pace. Learning is a continuous process. As supervisors, we must invest *now* if we expect to receive a payoff. For our own good, we must continue to invest. We owe it to our workers.

Learning is a continuous process

Advantages to Training

The following are five good reasons for initiating a training program:

1. *You get to know your subordinates.* You become familiar with the needs, wants, and potentials of new employees, and you can update your knowledge of present subordinates. This makes for easier personnel decisions concerning promotions, raises, and transfers.
2. *Training promotes good human relations.* Through their training, your employees will gain self-confidence and security, which in turn promote cooperation and respect for you. Many will see you as the impetus behind their improvement and will rely on you more for advice in the future.

Training others can advance your own career

3. *You may further your own career.* As your people expand their abilities, yours also will grow. As individuals increase their efficiency, your group benefits. Your reputation is a product of these positive training effects.
4. *Time can be used more advantageously.* As your subordinates' performances improve, you have more time for the essentials, such as planning, organizing, and controlling. You will also spend less time on corrections.
5. *Training promotes health and safety.* By emphasizing health and safety rules, you will be reducing the likelihood of violations and accidents.

How to Rationalize a Training Program

The most difficult aspect of a training program is to recognize the need for one and to convince management that time and money should be spent for it. You must remember that there is no guarantee that it will be successful and will help production or profits. It is difficult to measure the effectiveness of training programs, but the cost is small when compared to the cost of mistakes that can be made by untrained employees. Another benefit is that companies

Effective training is hard to measure

can test and evaluate personnel after a training program, and the results can help management decide on transfers and promotions.

School Versus Company Training Programs

Some of the courses offered by colleges, adult education schools, trade schools, and technical colleges are very applicable to the job situation; remedial, general education, and certain technical courses are ideal for company employees. They are usually widespread in availability and are offered at a lower fee than what the company would spend to provide its own programs.

Company programs, on the other hand, are usually designed to meet special needs. Short-term programs can be planned and scheduled to best meet the needs of the company and the employees. They are frequently taught on the company grounds during or after work. Because smaller companies in particular often have difficulty finding qualified trainers, these programs usually cost more than those provided by outside schools.

The choice between courses in local schools and a company training program should depend entirely upon the company's goal. If the goal is to develop highly skilled medical laboratory technicians, for example, it may be achievable only through a company training program.

The Expense of Training

The result of money spent on production is visible. The result of money spent on research is uncertain, but the expenditure has a definite practicality. Training, however, is often considered a luxury item, to be indulged in only when profits are high or the expenses are being used as a tax deduction. In some organizations, however, training is considered to be a normal, productive expenditure, and such organizations are among the most successful.

Truly wasteful expenditures occur when people are promoted and then never trained in their new duties. We can then see the Peter Principle being fulfilled within an organization, not because of the inability of the promoted person, but rather because of the lack of training.[2]

Promotion requires
additional training   An organization must commit appropriate training resources to individuals who are promoted. Such practices will reduce the

---

[2] The Peter Principle states that employees are raised (promoted) to their highest levels of incompetence. See Laurence Peter and Raymond Hull, *The Peter Principle* (New York: William Morrow, 1969).

possibility of employee anxiety and frustration frequently associated with increased responsibilities. Failure to adhere to this principle could result in employee failure, demotion, and turnover—
costly characteristics that must be avoided.

Goals and Methods

Whether an employee comes to a job with experience or is
trained by the company after being hired, job training of some
kind, formal or informal, must take place for three reasons: (1) so
that people will be more productive on their present jobs and be
ready for advancement; (2) because the success of the enterprise
requires that everyone perform at an optimum level; and (3) because all "good" personnel, regardless of organizational level, can
do a good job, want to do a good job, and will do a good job, if they
are given a chance.

Supervisors can discover through many sources areas in
which employees need additional training. An annual appraisal of
Ways to find areas where performance helps the supervisor find an employee's weaknesses
employees need more and determine an effective training program for that person. Other
training methods of determining training needs to meet company standards are

1. Brainstorming
2. Committee meetings
3. Conferences
4. Consultants
5. Interviews
6. Observations
7. Surveys
8. Questionnaires

The training director or a training committee may select areas
of need and prepare a priority list such as the following:

Areas Needing Training

1. New employee orientation
2. Stockroom
3. Reservation desk
4. Program evaluation

Once you have established needs, appropriate training programs must be discovered elsewhere or organized by the company. Ways of implementing training programs without upsetting
work schedules have to be investigated.

First select goals, then A distinction must be made between training goals and the
methods methods by which the goals are achieved. Training methods are
effective only when applied to appropriate training goals. For in-

Some learning requires doing

stance, role playing does not help employees learn more about running a drill, although it may help them learn how to become better managers. And one cannot adequately learn human relations skills except by practicing them. Instead of a lecture, some training method involving human interaction must be employed.

Training goals, then, must be clearly defined before a specific program is undertaken. Once the goals are well formed, the methods will fall into place. The following list will help you to see that different methods are better at achieving different goals:

Areas of Training	*Method of Training*
1. New employee orientation	1. Classroom technique, daily from 8 to 10 A.M. or 1 to 2 P.M.
2. Stockroom	2. Closed-circuit TV
3. Reservation desk	3. Programmed manuals
4. Program evaluation	4. Survey of participants and management

The employees must be convinced that these learning experiences can be exciting and stimulating, and are directly related to their growth as both employees and human beings. Negative feelings of tedium resulting from early educational experiences in a regimented classroom should not be associated with this type of learning process. Employers should attempt to encourage participation in educational programs rather than demand attendance.

Education should be conducted during working hours

Learning is a valid part of any job. It is not solely the employee's responsibility to invest time in education. Employee education should preferably be conducted during the working hours on company premises. This gives the employee the much-needed incentive that the company has a vested interest in his or her future.

Managers often have manual skills but no supervisory skills

All too often competent technical people are promoted and expected to function without training in supervision and management. They are expected to become leaders overnight without guidance or education. This is a serious misuse of valuable employees who could perform an outstanding job if guided.

TRAINING NEW EMPLOYEES

General Orientation

When people decide to work for a company, they have already formed some impressions. The job interview will have given them a sense of the company's atmosphere. They may have heard reports from friends about what it is like to work there, and they may have received ideas about the company's policies through newspaper and magazine stories.

The first few days
influence attitudes

Impressions formed during the first few working days greatly influence and solidify employee attitudes toward their jobs and their companies. Orientation is the formal means by which employees learn about their new employer. New employees have a trial period, but the company is on trial for new employees as well. Orientation can have a powerful effect on employees' attitudes and morale.

Orientation is learning
about the company

Induction is learning
about duties

Orientation introduces employees to general company matters. It is concerned with accomplishing two major tasks: (1) to inform employees about company policies and benefits, and (2) to make employees aware of important locations and procedures. Formally, the first point is called *orientation* and the second *induction*. Loosely, however, both tasks fall under the general concept of orientation: acquainting new employees with their job environment, co-workers, and company policies and procedures.

New employees must learn an amazing amount of detail in a short time. Supervisors should be careful not to overwhelm them. However, new workers do need certain basic information that someone should be responsible for providing. Without this general orientation, new employees can easily feel lost or alienated.

After you warmly greet your new employee, explain just where he or she fits into the entire company's operations. Starting with the organizational chart, you can move from the new employee's position in your department up the chain of command to the chief executive. Give the newcomer a good idea as to how his or her job and the department relate to the ultimate success of the company. What are the position's limits? What are the possibilities for advancement?

Discipline starts with the induction and orientation of each new employee. Give the dos and don'ts that you intend to enforce, and explain the penalties attached to each. Present the employee with copies of the company regulations and department rules.

Policy Orientation

New employees must become acquainted with department and company policies and practices, which usually include sick leave, vacations, holidays, disciplinary procedures, and company forms. Employees will need to study the possibilities of medical and other fringe benefits, including the credit union, stock purchase plans, employee purchases and discounts, and retirement and insurance plans. Some companies withhold the detailed infor-

Company orientation
covers many topics

HOW TO GET THE EMPLOYEE STARTED RIGHT

R   RIGHT preparation
       Get the employee's background information.
       Plan the job information for the employee.

I   IMPRESS the need for safety.
       Explain safety rules.
       Stress accident prevention.
       Pinpoint employee responsibilities.

G   GENERATE confidence.
       Explain the employee's role
       Give the employee a tour of the plant.
       Make the necessary introductions.

H   HAVE interest in the employee.
       Put the employee at ease.
       Talk to the employee about his or her interests.

T   TRAIN with a follow-up plan.

---

mation for about a week, or until after new employees have time to feel comfortable with the more immediate concerns of job, co-workers, and the work environment.

Very large companies sometimes carry out the orientation in two phases. The first, or concentrated, phase takes place on the first day of employment. However, if fewer than ten employees are starting on that day, the concentrated orientation may be held a few days later, when a larger group can be gathered. It is usually held in a conference room and consists of a lecture on overall company policies, procedures, fringe benefits, union membership, and other matters common to the corporation, its subsidiaries, and its divisions. Often a film showing company products, work areas, outlying divisions, and other items is of general interest to new employees. Such films are designed to develop a sense of pride and loyalty on the part of the new employees.

Induction Programs

Introduction to the physical plant is important

New employees must also be oriented to the areas of the physical plant pertinent to their jobs: parking spaces, employee entrance and exit, time clock, locker, bathrooms, bulletin boards, cafeteria, coffee and smoking areas, and work-related departments. It is a sad comment on a company's orientation program to encounter a new employee wandering the halls in search of the bathroom or the cafeteria. Further induction should include company procedures on uniforms, safety equipment, rest breaks, and salary and wages.

When you show the cafeteria to an employee, treat him or her to coffee. Some companies pick up the tab for the first day's snacks and lunch. If your firm does not, why not provide the treat yourself? It is a good way to say, "Welcome." Having a relaxed lunch with an employee is a personal way to assess the impact of the morning's events and to provide a chance to clear up any questions.

A checklist such as the following can be very helpful in ensuring a successful orientation.

Checklist for the Orientation of New Employees

1. *Work station:* Introduce the employee to his or her place of work and to as many fellow workers as possible.
2. *Working hours:* Explain starting and quitting time, lunch hour, rest periods, time signals, and the number of hours normally worked each week. Show the employee the time clock and how to punch in and out, or the method of recording time if there are no time clocks.
3. *Restrooms, lockers, and supply cabinets:* Show the new employee where these are located, and issue a key or keys if necessary.
4. *Transportation:* Explain bus schedules, parking lot rules, and share-a-ride possibilities.
5. *Pay status:* Explain hourly rate, weekly rate, and overtime policy. Also explain holiday pay policy. Discuss when the employee can expect the first paycheck.
6. *Safety rules:* Explain any necessary safety equipment to be worn. Explain the wearing of sandals, high heels, and the like that might cause accidents. Note where smoking is permitted.
7. *Grievances:* Explain the procedure for employee complaints and the rights accorded a worker who does not receive satisfaction at the supervisory level.
8. *Absenteeism:* Alert the employee to call in as soon as possible if he or she is unable to report for work. Explain how the company handles unexcused absences and an employee's need for time off.
9. *Quality:* Tell the new employee that quality is as important as quantity. Explain the function of the quality control department (if one exists).
10. *Safety:* Reemphasize safety rules and regulations. Check to see if the employee is wearing safety equipment.
11. *Plant tour:* This tour should occur early in one's employment.

Some managers consider it good practice for an established, responsible co-worker to sponsor a new employee, at least during the first few days. In this way, the newcomer can establish immediate rapport with a person in the same department. The co-worker is available to answer questions and to introduce the new employee to others, thereby helping the newcomer overcome feelings of shyness and strangeness. The use of this procedure does not mean that managers and supervisors should not show concern for the new employee; they can sporadically drop by the work station or have occasional follow-up interviews.

Putting the new man or woman to work and introducing him or her to fellow employees is only a small part of the orientation process. Orientation can continue for the next four to five weeks, even though the formal procedure may be finished within the first week. If a formal appraisal program exists in your company, there is opportunity for follow-up at that time.

Proper orientation by the supervisor can help give a new worker a proper start, aid in reducing turnover, and improve productivity and group morale.

On-the-Job Training

OJT is most effective when supervised

No matter what training is necessary in procuring a job, some on-the-job training is helpful later. Without it, new employees learn only through trial and error. On-the-job training, or OJT, can include informal comments and suggestions from others, but it is most effective when supervised. The apprentice who watched the master work and learned the master's trade was a forerunner of today's on-the-job trainee. Because of the diversity of job tasks and employee turnover, OJT is often neglected. It shouldn't be.

In OJT, the burden is on the trainer: It is generally assumed that when a worker does not learn the job thoroughly, the teacher has not taught properly. For an instructor to present material consistently, OJT should be preplanned. Information should be presented in manageable sections and in a logical sequence. To facilitate this, the trainer should break down *on paper* the job to be learned. All the steps do not have to be covered in the written outline, but the principal ones must be emphasized.

A person new to a job is nervous and has difficulty concentrating. Thus it is especially important that the trainer be at ease and not feel rushed. For training to be most effective, a rapport must be established between trainer and trainee (see Figure 11–4). The trainee should be receptive to the trainer's teaching, and feel that the trainer is sincere in his or her desire to help. Impatience, irritation, or criticism almost completely stops learning, but praise for the learner's accomplishments and efforts helps build self-confidence. A trainer should not interrupt when a trainee is performing correctly, because it will break the concentration.

FIGURE 11–4 Training on technical equipment should be limited to small groups. The use of simulators, flow charts, and other visual aids is helpful. In small groups it is most important that members feel free to ask questions. (Photo courtesy of Litton Industries, Inc.)

However, when a trainer sees that an error is about to be made, he or she should attempt to prevent it. To correct an error, the trainer has to return to the immediately preceding step.

The trainer should observe the employee frequently

When the employee is sufficiently trained to do the job alone, the trainer should be available to answer questions and should continue to observe the employee frequently, but without being overbearing.

SKILLS

Many jobs require the mastery of certain motor skills. The best method of teaching a skill is immediately to involve the learner in performing it. Constant practice is the key to the acquisition of motor skills. In moving from an in-depth understanding of the tools to an actual working knowledge of the trade, the new employee can experience a controlled exposure to both the technical and manipulative sides of the job.

Close supervision helps develop good working habits

Close supervision is essential in preventing poor working habits. Often the trainee must unlearn certain procedures acquired through earlier experiences before he or she can substitute the new methods. This is a time-consuming task that requires a great deal of patience from the supervisor and employee.

ATTITUDES

A trainer's attitude is all-important

As you train, attempt to instill positive attitudes. Attitudes are taught primarily by your example and secondarily by your words. If you talk safety but act in an unsafe manner or treat the issue lightly during the training period, your worker will adopt the same casual attitude.

THE SUPERVISOR AS A TRAINER

Starting with the first day on the job, the employee must learn proper work habits. The supervisor can start this process and establish good rapport with the employee by setting the proper example during the training program.

We must remember that the job is a totally new experience for the employee, and we thus should avoid intimidation at all costs. In general, supervisors are not obligated to do the training themselves. It is important to choose a trainer who is qualified and knows how to teach. If another employee possesses these qualities, then he or she may be chosen to do the training. If the supervisor is the most qualified, then the supervisor should do the training. Regardless of who does the actual training, it is the supervisor's responsibility to make sure that proper training is given. This responsibility cannot be delegated.

A Supervisor's Checklist for Good Instruction

1. *Find out what the employee already knows.* A good instructor does not make assumptions regarding the extent of an employee's job knowledge, but rather checks to verify such information. Work that is easy for you may be hard for an employee, and an employee's prior experience in similar jobs does not automatically translate into familiarity with the new one. If you learn exactly what the employee knows before you begin to explain the work, you will make the learning process easier and head off misunderstandings.

Demonstrate often

2. *Illustrate or demonstrate as much as possible.* Explanations, no matter how accurate, always become clearer if they are accompanied by illustrations or demonstrations. If, after demonstrating the task, you still have doubts about the employee's understanding, ask him or her to perform the task alone.

Encourage questions

3. *Encourage questions.* Establish a pleasant relationship, and make certain the employee understands that you can be interrupted whenever he or she needs clarification.

4. *Explain the purpose of the job.* An employee learns faster when he or she knows the reason for the work. Explanations take time and effort, but an employee who knows why the work is important and how his or her job ties in with company goals can understand the

need for cooperation with other employees. Morale is higher as a result, and more interest is taken in the quality of output.
5. *Follow up carefully.* When you have completed instructions and the employee is working on his or her own, check frequently on progress. In the beginning the worker may need advice and help, and your availability is reassuring. As the assignment is mastered, you can relax your supervision and reduce the extent of follow-up.
6. *Recognize accomplishments.* Recognition builds confidence. Acknowledge the employee's good work, and if criticism is needed, do not be harsh with it. The trick is to build assurance. Start with simple jobs and, when they are finished successfully, assign more difficult ones.

A Checklist to Avoid Training Pitfalls

1. *Attempting to teach too quickly:* This results in frustration. It is not wise to push employees beyond their learning limits.
2. *Trying to teach too much:* There are limits to the amount that one can learn. Teach segments of the job sequentially to develop a greater appreciation and understanding of the whole job.
3. *Viewing all trainees as the same:* All employees are different. Since some workers learn faster or slower than others, these differences must be accounted for in the training program.
4. *Not providing time to practice:* Practice makes perfect. There are no natural-born skilled workers. Adequate practice time must be provided for employees to develop their skills.
5. *Not providing a pat on the back:* It is always a good idea to reinforce employees during the learning process. Encouragement, praise, and reward are highly recommended.

SIX STEPS FOR TRAINING EVALUATION

REMEMBER TO R E V I E W THE PROGRAM

R   REVIEW the training method.
Is it geared to your objectives?

E   EVALUATE worker performance.
Is it what you expected?

V   VISUALIZE changes for improvement.
How can I improve the training?

I   IMPLEMENT new ideas, do not be afraid to experiment.

E   EXAMINE the results.
Is this better?

W   WEIGH the overall results continuously.
On-going improvement is the
overall objective.

6. *Frightening the employee:* As a supervisor, it is possible to know the job for which the employee is training so thoroughly that the new employee may feel inadequate or intimidated.

METHODS OF TRAINING

The type of training to be used is determined by the manpower to be developed, available physical facilities, allocated funds, available instructional personnel, and the urgency of the situation. No single type of presentation is the most effective for all situations.

Many methods exist for developing human resources. Some represent broad approaches to meeting developmental needs, others are narrower and have been designed to meet a special training need or to improve upon present methods, and still others are distinguished by the amount of instruction received on and off the job.

Programmed Instruction

PI is self-teaching

Programmed instruction (PI), also called programmed learning, is a self-teaching method particularly useful for transmitting information or skills that need to be learned and placed in logical order. The "instructor" is either an instruction booklet or a teaching machine, or both. It is possible to present PI entirely in written form, although automated machines are sometimes preferred.

PI courses can be developed to suit the particular learning problem, or they can be purchased ready-made. The American Management Association, for example, has developed a series of "shelf" courses called PRIME, or Programmed Instruction of Management Education. PI has provided learning tools for many businesses and industries. Du Pont Corporation has a library of about 50 courses on how to solve problems in their plants. First National City Bank of New York uses PI to train its tellers and clerks.

The success of programmed instruction, like that of other training programs, is not always easy to determine. National Cash Register Company, however, has reported that its class in computer techniques now takes one week to complete instead of the previous two week program with an instructor.

Simple steps called frames are presented

Immediate feedback is provided

Programmed instruction presents the material to be learned in brief, logical sequence, one step at a time, through either machines or booklets. The technique is to present a small amount of information, called a frame, and to follow with a simple question requiring an answer. The answer may be written or said silently, but in either case there is immediate feedback for each response.

Since the process is designed to have a low error rate, the student is motivated to continue.

PI's biggest advantage is that it is self-pacing

The biggest advantage to such an individualized program is that it is self-pacing. But since it is strictly individualized, motivation can drop quickly. A long program that is the equivalent of an 18-week college course may not be very effective, but for remedial instruction, enrichment material, or short segments, this method works well. Programmed booklets have been developed for reading new instrument dials in cockpits, for doing business mathematics, and for playing bridge.

Advantages and Disadvantages

Programmed instruction has the following *advantages:*

- Employees can proceed at their own paces, without being held back by slower co-workers or being pushed ahead by faster ones.
- Employees are given constant feedback, so that they know what they have accomplished and what is needed to progress further.
- Employees are constantly rewarded for picking correct responses, which encourages them to learn even more.
- Employees can become actively involved with the material, rather than passively reading or listening.

Programmed instruction has the following *disadvantages:*

- It can be costly and time-consuming to prepare.
- The learner may become bored if the program is not well written or if it is too simple.
- It is possible that the programmed instruction will contain erroneous information or end up as a series of unrelated sentences with blanks to be filled.

Videotape

Videotape works well for assembly lines

Showing videotapes on closed-circuit television can be an excellent method for instructing new employees, especially those on assembly lines. An assembly line can be filmed from several positions, and the finished cassette can be installed in a television monitor or screen above the work station. A well-timed video describing a multistep job can supply more understanding than supervised on-the-job training. The new employee can watch the process on the screen several times before he or she tries the project. He or she can learn at his or her own rate by starting or stopping the film at any point. The watchful eyes of the impatient supervisor are not there to cause employee anxiety. Likewise, the supervisor can use this valuable time for other duties, with only reassuring spot checks on the recruit.

Videotape has special advantages over motion pictures in that there is no need for film processing; the tape can be used immediately after recording the training sequence. Also, it can be made in-house, with a limited staff.

Such audiovisual aids are effective teaching devices because they are repetitive. They can be watched or heard many times by the same or other individuals. They also assure that the proper material is presented and usually require less personalized teaching time.

Correspondence Courses and Outside Reading

When carefully selected and controlled, correspondence courses and outside reading can produce positive training results. This is not the most popular training method, however, since employees must be ambitious and willing to work on their own. It essentially means having to learn the hard way. Many experts suggest coupling this method with other approaches to obtain more effective results.

Apprentice Training

Apprenticeship programs have long been a staple of training in the trades and crafts. Their origins can be traced back through many centuries of success. They are expensive and time-consuming, however, and as a result fewer and fewer employees are being trained via apprenticeships. Federal jurisdiction usually determines the length of such programs.

SIMULATION METHODS

The major goal of simulation techniques is to solve problems, particularly those in management. Real work situations are duplicated and studied in order to be dealt with properly. The simulation process can involve written materials, individual study, group discussion, and dramatization. Simulation tries to build problem-solving skills in anticipation of actual work situations.

Case Study

Case studies are written problems that are presented to a group for discussion. They are intended to simulate real work situations and therefore include descriptions of the organizational structure and the personalities involved. Group members study the problem and then offer their solutions. Group participation is effective here because members obtain immediate reactions to their ideas and have a chance to react to the ideas of others. Groups are usually led by a teacher or trainer to ensure that the discussion remains relevant.

Case study offers many solutions

Rather than finding the best solution, which is the basis of the problem-solving method, the case method attempts to use facts to present a logical, convincing position. This approach is based on the assumption that in business there is no one right way to act. It acknowledges that the solutions determined to be the "best" often rely on personal preferences.

The case method usually deals with problems that affect individuals in organizations. It involves the ability to justify management decisions, and to give priorities to problems that are important to the company and its employees. An example would be a case study involving an employee whose supervisor fired him or her for using a company car for personal reasons. The employee has appealed to the grievance committee. Each member of the committee receives the pertinent information needed to decide whether to (1) sustain the firing; (2) suspend the employee without pay; or (3) reinstate the employee with full rights.

Behavior Modeling Training

BMT involves seeing a model perform and then imitating the performance

Industrial psychologists are turning to role playing and videotapes in improving their supervisor's skills. Those with good supervisory skills use a role-playing situation to show how to handle subordinates. Over 300 companies are using this approach, which is called behavior modeling training, or BMT.

BMT proposes that interpersonal skills can be taught to supervisors as easily as reading or typing. Dr. Bernard Rosenbaum, president of New York's Personnel Science Center, is the creator of a specially tailored BMT program used by many retail stores. He believes that people's reaction to the training and development they receive actually determines their productivity.

Courses are conducted over a 12-week period. Participants view videotapes in which people handle situations that arise in the daily running of the business. Participants are then given an opportunity to role play, taking the part of either the supervisor or the subordinate.

You adopt the skill illustrated

This practice of employing the skills that are illustrated is especially important to the success of BMT. The leader acts as a coach, giving the participating supervisors the opportunity to learn and employ the necessary skills in an interplay between supervi-

Positive reinforcement is important

sors and subordinates. Positive reinforcement is offered at the same session in what trainers call "constructive feedback and praise where applicable."

Persuading the trainees to actually use the skills illustrated is the most difficult part of supervisory development programs. At Bloomingdale's department store, the leader and each participant form a contract in which the supervisor agrees to practice the skills on a particular boss or subordinate in an actual situation. At the session, he or she can practice ways of handling the situation; on returning the next week, the person reports on how effectively he or she transferred theory into practice. The system seems to work.

The goal: to become unconsciously competent

BMT trainers feel that people are subconsciously incompetent. The goal is to make them unconsciously competent. Behavior modeling means seeing the ideal way to handle a situation. A videotape can then be made during the role-playing session. Afterward, the trainer and group members can discuss the process and begin to change each trainee's attitudes and behavior. Listening to or watching the tapes made during the session can help the trainees become more aware of their actions. Research has found that role playing for job interviews on videotape is a most successful way to provide helpful insights into interviewing techniques.

WAS THE TRAINING EFFECTIVE?

Regardless of which training method is used, it is extremely important to evaluate the results. A supervisor should not want to have training simply to have training. The goal of training is to prepare workers to do the job properly. At the completion of training, the supervisor must establish a formal evaluation program to make sure that the objective was met.

SUMMARY

The process of recruiting and selecting employees is complex in larger companies, where the chore is shared between the human resource department and the supervisor.

A well-written job description is the basis for writing a job opening. The job description summarizes in general terms what the job entails. It should list the minimum experience, education, knowledge, skill, and physical dexterity required. The job opening should include these items along with the final application date, the salary range, working conditions, occupational characteristics, and information about the company. Recruiting can be done through blind or open ads in newspapers, through various placement agencies, and through friends, customers, suppliers, and labor unions.

There are six steps in the selection process: (1) screen the application forms; (2) contact the applicant and perhaps give an initial interview; (3) require testing—written, oral, or by demonstrating; (4) check references; (5) hold a comprehensive interview; and (6) give any necessary physical exam. These procedures will assist you in finding the best employee in the most logical manner.

The step most vital in selecting an employee is the interview, the open exchange between persons of unequal status for a mutually agreed-upon position. Establish rapport initially by talking briefly about a subject of mutual interest. Let the applicant do most of the talking. A good rule of thumb is to let the applicant talk 75 percent of the time, use 15 percent of the time for your questions and comments, and use 10 percent to describe the position and the company itself.

After selection, the employee must be prepared to work. Training is the practical side of education because it transmits information to improve problem-solving abilities. Effective training depends partly on the attitudes of the employees, instructors, and companies involved. For training to be successful, companies must be clear about their training goals and then use the training methods most applicable to those goals. There is no reliable way to test for training effectiveness, since results often are intangible and can develop over a long period. On the other hand, the lack of training can be costly in terms of both time and money.

Job orientation is a form of training that can greatly affect new employees' attitudes. Orientation familiarizes them with all company matters except those that pertain to actual job performance. Induction is an introduction to the procedures and practical features of the job environment. New employees must also receive some on-the-job training, regardless of their previous job experience. The success of OJT depends on the trainers, who should have a clear idea of training procedures. Instructional training methods include programmed instruction, videotapes, and many kinds of visual aids. These are considered the traditional ways to teach skills.

Well-known simulation techniques are the case study method and behavior modeling training. They offer opportunity to solve problems that are as close as possible to real-life problems. Simulation methods take many different styles, and they are always at least one step removed from reality.

CASE STUDY **23**

Would You Hire an Ex-Con?

The Johnson Packing Company, employing 150 persons, recently underwent a change in ownership and management. At that time the company's operations were expanded, necessitating additional employees.

Helen Luher, in charge of the personnel section, assumed the responsibility of screening the many applicants who applied for the new positions. Each applicant who passed the initial interview would be sent to Paul Kemper, one of the new owners, for the final decision.

One of Helen's first applicants turned out to be a man recently released from a state prison. James Winthrop had been convicted of two counts of robbery and had a prior history of petty thefts. Although Helen did not wish to hire him, he did qualify for a position as a merchandise packer or loader, so Helen sent him to see Paul as instructed. Soon after the interview ended, Helen was called in for a discussion.

"What do you think about hiring an ex-convict?" asked Paul. "Do you think it is a good idea?"

"Well, to be honest with you, Paul, I don't think so. All the employees are a little on edge with the new people coming to work here. And I don't think they'll go for having an ex-con in their midst, especially when we have no adequate facilities to safeguard valuables. We won't be able to keep quiet the fact that he's an ex-convict. You know how word can get around in a small town like this."

"I see your point, Helen, but I think we should hire him anyway. The man's given his word that he won't steal anything. I think we should do our share in getting him back on his feet. Besides, it may even be good for our public relations."

"What happens when something turns up missing out there? There is always something being lost. Last week it was a lunch that fell behind some crates, and Joe raved all day that someone swiped his lunch. Regardless of the circumstances, this new man will be blamed."

QUESTIONS

1. With whom do you agree: Paul or Helen?

2. Give specific reasons for hiring or not hiring James Winthrop.

3. This can work well as a role playing situation. Divide the class into several small groups either for or against hiring the ex-convict. After discussing the reasons for each group's position, have the groups select two people to represent Paul and Helen. The two should carry on a conversation for ten minutes on the pros and cons of hiring the ex-convict.

CASE STUDY 24

How to Select a New Employee

Owen Clement is in charge of a bindery in Santa Paula, California, which employs 15 people, 5 of whom work in the factory. Three of these employees run machines, one supervises, and the fifth moves the blank paper and finished print by handcar. This fifth position, which requires no skill other than driving a handcar, needs to be filled, and 3 applicants have responded.

The first is Mike Lacey, who is 35, unmarried, and a Navy veteran. Mike has a poor work record. During his five years in California, he has worked only seasonal labor and "occasional odd jobs." He drove a forklift in the Navy. He has a strong build, which could help, although the work at the bindery is generally light.

Frank Manea, age 19, recently came to America from Italy. He has done farm labor for many years and assembly line work for one year. His command of English is poor. He resides with his mother and seems certain to remain in the area for some time. After having run farm equipment, he should have no trouble steering a handcar.

Andy Stoneham is a local boy who finished high school six months ago. His work experience is limited to his current job as a service station attendant. His character references are excellent. Andy is small, but he seems quick and was a track star in high school.

QUESTIONS

1. How much consideration should be given to Mike's poor work record? Should Owen verify Mike's work record?
2. How important is the command of English to the job? How quickly could Frank assimilate enough English to be effective?
3. Should Frank be passed over because of his status as a recent immigrant? The other applicants are American citizens.
4. Should Andy get the job? How heavily should his references be weighed against his inexperience?
5. Who should be hired? Why?

CASE STUDY 25

Eager Mike McHugh

One Monday morning Mike McHugh, a recent college graduate, walked into the sales office as a new sales trainee for a business machines company. Liz Noel, the zone sales manager, was there to greet him. Liz's area covered three counties, and ten sales representatives reported to her. The large volume of sales in her area was attributed to recent population growth; industries were finding this area very attractive.

Liz had collected several sales reports, catalogues, and pamphlets detailing the types of office equipment sold by the company. After a pleasant chat about their backgrounds, Liz gave Mike the collected material and showed him to his assigned desk. Soon afterward, the sales manager excused herself and did not return. Mike spent the day reading over the material, and at 5:00 he picked up his things and went home.

QUESTIONS

1. What can you say about Liz's training program?

2. What type of sales training program would you suggest?

3. What method of training would have been best under the circumstances? Would you consider OJT, simulation, or other methods?

CASE STUDY **26**

Just Another Job Transfer

When Luthans Computer Systems moved one of their divisions to Texas, the president decided to transfer those employees who did not wish to go to Texas to other local divisions. Twelve of the 25 chose to stay and be transferred to another division. Maria Buettgenback was one of those. She was assigned to the computer assembly division.

When Maria reported to the new job, Norman Nelson, her new supervisor, told her he did not know whether he would have a permanent spot for her. For three days Maria sat and watched the other employees do their work. On Friday Norman announced that their division had received another big contract, and he would brief Maria on her new assignment on Monday.

Maria arrived at 8:30 Monday morning and waited anxiously to learn her new job. Norman did not arrive until 10:30. He was being briefed on the new contract, he said, and would not have time to tell Maria about her assignment until after lunch. At 1:30 Norman returned to show Maria the operation. "We are reworking model 10-F, and it only requires changing two spot welds. With this jig, you can turn one out in about three to five minutes," Norm said offhandedly. "Oh, by the way, you will be the quality control person on this job. Just double check these six spots on the blueprint." He did not write on the blueprints or mark the areas in any way. Maria was given no idea how important the checks might be.

"Here—watch me," said Norm to Maria, taking up the welding torch. "Any moron can do it." He repeated the operation five or six times. Maria tried it and had no difficulty. Neither of them checked their reworked pieces with the blueprint to see if they would pass the quality control check, and as a result, Maria never checked any pieces after that demonstration. Norman did not see Maria again until Friday.

Between Monday and Friday several things happened. More than half the motors did not work correctly by the time they reached the final assembly. It could not be determined whether the faulty motors were the result of Maria's work or the result of a lack of quality checks. A box of 20 parts had been approved by Maria since her initials were on the inspection card, but she had not made the necessary alterations. That was when Norman found time to talk to Maria again.

QUESTIONS

1. What incidents showed that Norman was not performing well as a trainer?

2. How do you think Maria feels about Norman and her new job?

3. If you were Norman, what would you have done to improve Maria's performance?

4. Would a mentor or a buddy system have helped the situation? How? Why?

CASE STUDY **27**

Does Richard Renteria Need Training?

Richard Renteria has been employed for six months in the accounts receivable department of a large aircraft manufacturing firm. You have been his supervisor for the past three months, and you have conducted a random sampling of the quantity and quality of all employee output. With the exception of Richard, all seem to be producing at or close to the standards set earlier in the year. Along with numerous errors, Richard's work is characterized by low performance; often he does 20 percent less than the other clerks in the department.

As you examine Richard's work, you begin to think about some sort of remedial training for people like him.

QUESTIONS

1. As Richard's supervisor, can you determine if his poor performance is due to poor training or to some other cause?

2. If you find Richard has been inadequately trained, how do you go about introducing a remedial training program?

3. If he has been with the company six months, what kind of remedial program would be best?

4. Should you supervise him more closely? Can you do this without making it obvious to him and his co-workers?

5. Should you discuss the situation with Richard?

Terms and Concepts Supervisors Should Know

Applicant's qualifications; Apprenticeship programs; Assessment; Behavior modeling training (BMT); Case study; Comprehensive interviews; Correspondence courses; Induction; Job description; Job hoppers; Job opening; Medical checks; On-the-job training (OJT); Open and blind ads; Orientation; Private employment agencies; Programmed instruction (PI); Recruiting; Reference checks; Screening; Simulation methods; Staffing; Videotapes.

Questions for Discussion

1. How does your company recruit applicants? Are these the best ways for recruiting the most qualified applicants?

2. Does your company have job descriptions for every position?

3. What are the advantages of job descriptions when you are recruiting, selecting, and interviewing applicants?

4. How do you put applicants at ease during the interview? Is it important to put them at ease? Why?

5. What are the essential points to be covered in a comprehensive job interview?

6. Describe job situations you have encountered in which there was a lack of adequate training. What type of training could have remedied each situation?
7. Have you acted as a trainer? What were some of your experiences, both good and bad? How could they have been different?

For Further Reading—And More Ideas

Anderson, N., and V. Shackleton, "The Chosen Few (Systems of Recruitment and Selection: Britain)," *Management Today* (November 1988).

Anderson, R. H., and K. J. Snyder, "Team Training," *Training and Development Journal* (February 1989).

"The Arduous Process of Filling a Position," *Journal of Accountancy* (March 1989).

Baker, G., "A Checklist for Training Programs," *Training and Development Journal* (February 1989).

Bargerstock, A. S., "Recruitment Options That Work," *Personnel Administrator* (March 1989).

Burns, T. J., "Tests to Target Dependability," *Nation's Business* (March 1989).

Case, R., "Interview Techniques for Hiring the Right Graduates," *Journal of Accountancy* (November 1988).

Cellich, C., "Six Key Checks for Designing Training Programs," *International Trade Forum* (January–March 1989).

Courtis, J., "Watching Out for Bias in Interviews," *Personnel Management* (November 1988).

Cowan, R. A., "Losing New Hires," *Supervisory Management* (March 1989).

Cox, J. A., et al., "A Look Behind Corporate Doors: Examining the Interview Process from the Organization's Point of View," *Personnel Administrator* (March 1989).

Elliot, B., "Psychology and the Selection Process," *Accountancy* (March 1989).

"Employee Testing Services (Directory)," *Personnel* (January 1989).

Fleishman, E. A., "Some New Frontiers in Personnel Selection Research," *Personnel Psychology* (Winter 1988).

Forbes, P. M., "Guidelines for Checking References," *National Petroleum News* (December 1988).

Fritz, N. R., "Honest Answers—Postpolygraph," *Personnel* (April 1989).

Gordon, J., "Where's the Line Between Training and Intrusion?" *Training* (March 1989).

Gorman, B., "Becoming a Better Interviewer," *Journal of Property Management* (January–February 1989).

Hallett, J. J., "Hiring Job Spirit: How Do We Recruit Energy, Enthusiasm, Inventiveness, and Desire?" *Personnel Administrator* (February 1989).

Harrison, R., "Making the Case for Training," *Personnel Management* (February 1989).

Hawk, K., "When Training Doesn't Work," *United States Banker* (March 1989).

Lansing, R. L., "Training New Employees," *Supervisory Management* (January 1989).

Lee, C., "Testing Makes a Comeback," *Training* (December 1988).

Markowich, M. M., "Every Manager a Trainer," *Supervision* (April 1989).

Melnick, J., "Resilience Training: Reaping Success from Failure," *Personnel* (March 1989).

Miklas, D. C., "High-Performance HRD Staffing," *Training and Development Journal* (January 1989).

"Paper-and-Pencil Honesty Tests Fill the Polygraph Gap," *Savings Institutions* (February 1989).

Posner, B. G., "Hiring the Best," *Inc.* (April 1989).

Preer, R. M., Jr., "The Impact of Drug Testing," *Labor Law Journal* (January 1989).

Russell, M. L., "Toward Ethical Training," *Training* (November 1988).

Sherer, R. D., "Hiring for Profit," *Security Management* (January 1989).

Sinai, L., "Employers Use a Variety of Tests (Honesty Testing)," *Business Insurance* (September 19, 1988).

Sloman, M., "On-the-Job Training—A Costly Poor Relation," *Personnel Management* (February 1989).

Zetlin, M., "How to Hire Retirees," *Management Review* (January 1989).

Appraisals, Promotions, Discipline, Demotions, and Dismissals

12

"Do I keep, promote, or fire the employee?"

LEARNING OBJECTIVES

When you complete this chapter, you should be able to:
1. Understand why appraisals are necessary.
2. Appreciate the value of performance evaluations.
3. Identify the various types of appraisal methods.
4. Recall the pitfalls of evaluation in order to avoid them.
5. Understand the basics of conducting a good appraisal interview.
6. Understand the meaning of positive discipline.
7. Define where, when, and how to discipline an employee.
8. Identify the various stages of discipline and the order in which they should be used.
9. Recall how best to handle warnings on dismissals and demotions.

"The goal of evaluating is to leave the person with the feeling that he or she has been helped."

Few duties are more disagreeable to supervisors than the employee evaluation, which requires that they put on paper their feelings and opinions about employees. Perhaps you have asked yourself the questions listed below. Hopefully you will find the answers in the text and in class discussion.

Why should supervisors evaluate personnel?

How are evaluations valuable to the supervisor and the employee?

How can supervisors overcome their fear of making appraisals?

How do supervisors tell employees they are not doing very well?

What are some good techniques to use in the evaluation interview?

Can supervisors really measure an employee's performance?

APPRAISALS

Appraising subordinates is a significant part of the supervisor's duties. The supervisor must decide whether the employee is worthy of continued employment, and if so, whether he or she should receive a bonus, a pay raise, or even a promotion. Appraisals are important, and the manner in which they are performed is vital to both the supervisor and the employee.

Why Evaluate Personnel?

There are five basic reasons why supervisors should periodically evaluate their personnel:

1. To determine whether their subordinates are doing their jobs
2. To measure each employee's performance and to reward those who are doing well
3. To establish corrective action plans for those employees whose performance falls short of expectations
4. To measure an employee's potential for a possible promotion
5. To assess an employee's attitudes and to deepen their own understanding of their subordinates

In addition to meeting these objectives, the evaluation process also fortifies the supervisor-subordinate relationships.

When Must We Evaluate?

Evaluate probationary employees more often

As a general rule, supervisors should evaluate permanent employees at least once a year. However, it is a better and more reliable practice to evaluate formally at least twice a year and informally on a continuous basis. Employees who have probationary status should be evaluated more often. It is customary for many companies and civil service organizations to evaluate probationary employees at least once and preferably twice before they are given permanent status. Ideally, during a six-month probation period, an employee should be evaluated after the first, third, and fifth month of service. After three evaluations it is usually clear to both the supervisor and the employee whether permanent status will be attained at six months.

Use evaluation reminders

Companies use different methods to alert the supervisor that it is time for evaluations. In some companies the personnel department sends reminders to the supervisors, using bright yellow forms for probationary employees. In another company, where the supervisor keeps the payroll records, the review dates for a probationary employee's performance are circled in red.

Who Should Make the Evaluation?

Evaluations must be in writing

Each supervisor under whom the employee has directly served for at least 60 working days during any rating period should contribute a performance evaluation, even though the employee may no longer be under that supervisor's direction. Performance evaluation reports should be made in writing and should be prepared by the employee's immediate supervisor, if possible. Evaluation reports should then be reviewed by the next supervisory level.

How Is Performance Evaluation Valuable to the Supervisor?

Time to praise

An evaluation gives the supervisor a chance to thank and praise employees for their efforts. Too frequently, we forget to tell people they have done a fine job. Employees value praise in frequent doses, and not just during evaluation time. How you praise your employees is important to their egos and future performance.

When you compliment employees, you might remember the words of Bishop Fulton Sheen: "Baloney is the unvarnished lie laid on so thick you hate it. Blarney is flattery laid on so thin you love it."

Time to clarify your expectations

An evaluation is also an opportunity for you to list and clarify your expectations for the employee's job performance. All employees want to know what is expected of them, so you should not limit the evaluation conference to only what has been done in the past. Discuss your expectations for the future as well.

Evaluations are also valuable because they force you to recognize employees' faults early enough to help them try to correct them. Employees' weaknesses, and ways to change them, can then be discussed in a rational rather than an emotional time and setting. For this reason, the communication is more likely to be positive.

Focus on why

Performance evaluation also forces you to give specific reasons why a person has or has not done well. In making evaluations, the supervisor must look at the process and not at the end product. A supervisor for a school cafeteria, for example, may remark that a lunch was poor (the end product), but he or she should know *why* it was poor (the process) before firing the cook. Perhaps directions were not followed or there were fewer people working on the floor, or any number of other mitigating circumstances. Thus the supervisor should focus on the process—the reason why a performance is good or bad—rather than just on the performance itself.

How is Performance Evaluation Valuable to the Employee?

A performance evaluation tells the employee where he or she stands. This is important to an individual's security and ego. Employees want to know how they measure up to the supervisor's standards, not just to their own. Establishing a common standard of expectations between the supervisor and the employees reduces the employees' fears and lets them know the limits of their responsibilities.

Reduces fears and uncertainties

An evaluation is also a time for giving an employee a pat on the back. In addition to regular evaluations, special, unscheduled reports can be used to commend outstanding performance. Written commendations are a valuable asset to a deserving employee's candidacy for promotion.

How to Overcome the Fear of Evaluating

Few employees realize that supervisors actually dread evaluating them. For this reason, evaluations are often not performed at all, even when company policy "requires" that they be done every six months or every year.

Evaluation requires a supervisor to say how he or she feels about an employee and how well he or she believes that person is performing tasks. There is a risk involved in giving an evaluation, but it is a responsibility the supervisor must accept.

Accept the risk and responsibility

Some supervisors fear that a poor evaluation reflects on them rather than on the employee. It is important to shed this psychological burden. When employees accept a job, they also accept the responsibility of performing the tasks listed in their job description. As a supervisor, it is your job to determine how well the employee has performed the tasks, and you must have faith in your ability to do this. If you were not able to evaluate an employee, your superior wouldn't have promoted you to the position.

Have faith in your ability to evaluate

As a supervisor, you must also accept the fact that an employee will judge your evaluation. You may feel, "Oh, if I give Heather a bad rating, she will think less of me." In the long run, however, an employee will think more of you because you gave an honest, straightforward appraisal.

If you want to change your fear of evaluating into your success as a supervisor, you must be willing to hear any reaction to your evaluation. Some employees will complain bitterly with the hope that you will give in and raise the rating. However, the employee will respect you less if you give in to his or her plea.

Be prepared to hear complaints

Supervisors use all kinds of excuses to avoid evaluating subordinates. They say that it takes too much time, harms working relationships, really doesn't do any good, or creates employee resentment. However, *top supervisors do evaluate* their employees, and they do it frequently, thereby weeding out incompetent workers and appraising the better ones. They also use appraisals to make corrections in production, coordination, and morale. These are the supervisors who receive promotions!

Does Evaluation Relate to Money?

Performance evaluation should be thought of in terms of a report card. It provides a graded assessment of one's performance and represents a progress report with respect to all aspects of the job. Whether a raise results from the evaluation is strictly a question of company policy. In some companies, only those employees with above average or superior performance advance to maximum pay for the job.

APPRAISAL METHODS

Narrative Method

Write an essay, giving concrete examples

The most flexible but most difficult way to appraise workers is the essay or narrative method, which requires the supervisor to refer to specific situations that illustrate a worker's abilities or performance. When you use this approach, you use your personal observations to dramatize a particular point. For example, you may write, "Connie has demonstrated her initiative on numerous occasions by requesting additional work and by lending a hand to others."

The narrative method offers the maximum degree of expression for a precise evaluation. However, this is difficult to do because it demands an in-depth knowledge of the employee, which can be acquired only from regular and frequent observation of your subordinates. Close observation is highly desirable but not always possible, since some employees are separated by great distances from supervision (for example, salespeople may be geographically separated from the sales manager).

Field Review

Several people evaluate

Field review is an evaluation of an employee by a group of people rather than by a single person. The group may consist of fellow employees, several supervisors, or a combination of both. This method is sometimes used when there is reason to suspect a supervisor is biased or when an employee wishes to appeal an appraisal.

The judgment of a group is fairer

The judgment of the group will usually be fairer and more valid than that of an individual. For this reason, some companies use the field method for all middle-management personnel. However, a field review is time-consuming, and it is not always easy to find more than one supervisor who has a firsthand knowledge of the employee.

Graphic Rating Scale

A scale is simply a checklist

Used by most supervisors, the graphic rating scale is simply a list of factors to be considered and of terms to be used in the evaluation. Figures 12–1 and 12–2 show on example of a rating scale.

This method has advantages and disadvantages. Since the supervisor makes only checks on the form, it is easy to prepare.

When all supervisors use the same form and all employees are judged in the same terms, comparisons are easy to make but not necessarily fair, because the appraiser's opinions and prejudices can still influence the rating. However, this is not necessarily a drawback, for the only way to remove the element of subjectivity from an appraisal method is to eliminate the appraiser.

Used with the narrative
method

There are some clear disadvantages of the rating scale method. Categories and factors listed on the form often overlap, which makes it difficult for the conscientious supervisor to use. Also, the graphic method is fairly rigid, and it does not give a complete picture of the individual. For these reasons the method is often used in conjunction with the narrative appraisal. The combined graphic rating scale and narrative evaluation is probably the most frequently used because it is thought to combine the best characteristics of both methods.

TECHNIQUES OF EVALUATING

Understand the Duties

When you evaluate employees, you should thoroughly understand the duties and requirements of their particular positions. It will be helpful to review the job descriptions on file in the human resource department.

Consider Each Category Separately

Halo error

The phenomenon of assuming that an employee who is above average in one area is above average in all areas is known as the constant error, or halo error. This is an evaluating pitfall you should avoid.

Quantity is not quality

Do not assume that an employee's excellence in one area implies excellence in all areas. Objectively observe and analyze the employee's performance in terms of *each* factor listed on the evaluation form. Remember to consider each trait and each analysis statement listed beneath the trait separately. For example, an employee's output may be large by your standards and when compared to the output of other employees, but the quality of work may be relatively poor. Thus the employee's high rating on "quantity of work" should not influence his or her rating on "quality of work," which should be low.

NONEXEMPT
HOURLY REVIEW FORM

Employee _____ Job Assignment _____

Supervisor _____ Dept. _____

Date Hired _____ Prior Appraisal Date _____

AREAS OF PERFORMANCE	Outstanding 9–10	Above Average 6–8	Average 3–5	Below Average 1–2	Unsatisfactory 0	N/A
JOB KNOWLEDGE: Comment:						
QUALITY OF WORK: Ability to meet standards.						
QUALITY OF WORK: Ability to effectively use time and materials.						
SAFETY: Result of work under safe/unsafe practices.						
ATTENDANCE: Indicate hours off the job since the date of last appraisal due to: Personal _____ Illness _____ Punctuality (tardiness) _____ Comment:						

PERSONAL FACTORS	5	4	2–3	1	0	N/A
INITIATIVE: How person handles new skills or improvements. Comment:						
ADAPTABILITY TO CHANGE: Ability to adjust to new situations. Comment:						
COOPERATION: Ability to get along with employees and supervisor. Comment:						
DEPENDABILITY: Ability to complete the job. Comment:						

FIGURE 12–1   A sample appraisal form for an hourly employee (page 1)

EMPLOYEE'S PRESENT JOB DUTIES: _____

_____

COUNSELING SUMMARY

EMPLOYEE'S STRENGTHS	SUGGESTED IMPROVEMENTS
1. _____	1. _____
2. _____	2. _____
3. _____	3. _____

Improvement Activity

Consider how this employee has reacted to the counseling and suggestions that were prompted by the last formal appraisal. What has been accomplished toward the goals and objectives established in the previous interview? If the person has failed to follow through, indicate why.

Comment: _____

_____

_____

_____

_____

OVERALL RATING:

_____ Results achieved far exceed the requirements of the job in all areas.

_____ Results achieved are above average.

_____ Consistently performed the job to the requirements of the position.

_____ Results did not always meet the requirements of the position.

_____ Results frequently did not meet the requirements of the position.

OVERALL RATING Comment:

_____

_____

_____

Company-related activities (Safety Committee, Christmas party, picnic, etc.): _____

EMPLOYEE'S COMMENT:

_____

_____

| Employee's Signature | Date | Supervisor's Signature |

Comments by next level of supervision: _____

_____

Manager's Signature

FIGURE 12–2   A sample appraisal form for an hourly employee (page 2)

Evaluate on Entire Rating Period

It is best not to focus on single accomplishments or failures, or on the most recent performance of an employee. Single instances of faulty or brilliant performance should not be ignored, but they should be considered in the context of the total performance for the evaluation period. The employee must not be penalized unfairly and disproportionately for isolated errors in judgment, honest mistakes, or misinterpretations of responsibility.

Avoid rating on recent behavior

It is easy to fall into the syndrome of rating employees on their most recent behavior. Favorable and unfavorable appraisal must be kept in true proportion to time. Do not allow unusual incidents to color your evaluation. An employee who slips once near the end of the rating period may still deserve a high rating on the trait in question.

Consider Longevity Apart from Performance

An employee with a short service record may not necessarily be less effective than one with a longer one. Longevity does not guarantee excellence.

Consider the Requirements of the Position

A junior clerk may be meeting the requirements of his or her position more effectively than does his or her immediate supervisor.

Be Fair to the Company

You must be fair to your employees, but you must also remember your obligation to get the best possible return for your company's payroll dollars. Do not overlook poor performance in the hope that it will improve by itself; wishful thinking cannot be counted on to meet your expectations.

Critical Incident Technique

One of the best techniques for evaluating an employee's performance and focusing on the important aspects of behavior is the *critical incident technique* (CIT). A critical incident is an employee behavior that significantly assists or prevents the accomplishment

Reports significant employee action

of the duties of the position. As the term implies, CITs are simply written reports of an employee's actions that were especially effective or ineffective in accomplishing his or her job. Such incidents are actually behavioral accounts recorded as anecdotes and put in the employee's personal file.

Dennis, a new deep-sea diver, was talking to a hard-hat worker on the oil platforms in the North Sea. "You know, Joe, I don't understand how little notes about my actions have popped up in my personnel folder back in Aberdeen, Scotland. Why, that's more than five hundred miles away!" This true story is an example of how even phone calls put the CIT to work in the evaluation of employees, even when they are 500 miles away and out at sea.

Using the CIT, you can accumulate records of actual behavior for each person you supervise. When you write your monthly, quarterly, or yearly evaluations, you will have in your files the dates and incidents that support the general comments in your evaluation. Another advantage of the CIT is that after reading all of your notes about an individual's behavior, you are not likely to make sweeping generalizations in the evaluation. Both the em-

CIT adds meaningful detail

ployee and upper management appreciate reading about actual incidents that show areas where the employee needs to improve and where he or she is strongest. A general comment that an employee is doing "a great job" it not as meaningful as "Pete, your quick thinking in moving the paper goods from the receiving dock during the rainy period probably saved our company several hundreds of dollars."

Discuss the Good Points as Well as the Bad

Employees should be advised of their strong points as well as their weak ones. They should be commended for past improvement in addition to being told where they could still improve. A fundamental objective of the evaluation discussion is to maintain employees' self-respect and increase their pride in their work.

Talk about the employee's strengths first, covering each point in some detail. Remember that your aim is to encourage or sustain high-quality performance, not to scold the employee. After building upon the employee's strengths, do not fail to discuss his or her weaknesses and how to improve them. Introduce your suggestions for a specific improvement if the worker has not already volunteered good ideas of his or her own.

The "positive sandwich" is bad news between two slices of good feelings

When you have bad news to tell the employee, you should use the "positive sandwich" technique. Start with a "slice of bread" spread generously with good news and supportive information. Then express the bad news quickly and simply as a "slice of thin ham," and follow this with another "slice of bread" bearing explanations and assurances. For example, if a subordinate's request for a new assignment has been turned down, he or she should be told why. However, it is wise to buffer the denial by detailing the subordinate's assets. Then he or she can be informed of the bad news, followed by your supportive attitude. If a more experienced person was selected, for example, you can discuss the subordinate's future potential, should the employee acquire more experience.

Whether the message is written or oral, you must prevent disappointing news from turning your subordinate against you. Your opening sentences should strengthen whatever good feeling exists. When you assert the bad news at the beginning, you place too much emphasis on it, and you jeopardize existing good will. When you come to the bad news, however, you should be explicit and not leave the employee guessing about what you really meant. Equally vital is the latter half of the "positive sandwich," for a positive closing can tip the scales toward the retention of the employee's good will, as is shown in the following letter:

Example of a "positive sandwich"

> We are glad you applied for the position, Ken, because that shows you have ambition and fortitude. You have been an enthusiastic employee, always on time, and willing to work hard. However, I feel you need more experience in company operations, particularly in your present position. We have selected someone with more experience, but this does not mean we cannot consider you for other positions in the future. I want you to know we consider you a valuable employee and a real member of the team.

It should be pointed out that this information should be conveyed to the employee as soon as the decision was made; it should not be delayed to the time of the appraisal two days later.

Management by Objectives

MBO is a contract for future performance

Management by objectives (MBO) is a management technique that has been used for many years for evaluating employees (see Chapter 7). Rather than focusing only on past performance, with MBO the supervisor and the subordinate plan the worker's future objectives. Together they develop a group of specific goals, measures of achievement, and the time frames in which the objectives will be accomplished. The employee's next appraisal is then based on how well he or she has met these expectations.

Objectives must be measurable and set in a time frame

The MBO approach to analyzing the effectiveness and performance of employees can be understood by both the employee and the supervisor, because they developed the objectives together. In addition to forming a common ground, the job objectives should fulfill the following requirements:

1. They should be compatible with the overall company plans.
2. They should represent sufficient challenge to the employee.
3. They should be attainable through the employee's own efforts.
4. They should be realistic and achievable before the next appraisal.
5. They should be clearly defined and measurable, so that achievement can be determined. An unmeasurable phrase such as "develop better human relations among the staff" is not an adequate objective. However, goals such as "to increase production by 3 percent, decrease customer complaints by 5 percent, decrease employee turnover, and reduce staff conflicts to one a month" are all measurable and clearly defined.

Too often evaluations are based on vague abstractions of past performance. By contrast, MBO sets standards for the future. The employees know they will be rated by such standards.

Which Appraisal System Is Best?

All appraisal systems have good and bad points

No one appraisal system is best for all circumstances. Each of those discussed possesses both good and bad points. The supervisor should not select just one method and automatically eliminate the others. Ideally, the unique aspects of all systems should be evaluated, and one that will produce the best results should be selected.

Do Employees Fear Evaluation?

Employees like to know where they stand

By and large, employees like to know where they stand. It is important for workers to possess a clear understanding of their performances and how well they measured up to job expectations. Evaluations also provide an opportunity for them to ask questions and resolve any misunderstandings that might exist.

Appraisals should not be subjective

Many supervisors are afraid that employees will react negatively to criticism. This fear can be removed if the appraisal is based on facts instead of subjective opinions.

APPRAISAL PITFALLS

If a supervisor is not careful, several common pitfalls may occur during the appraisal process. Unfortunately, falling prey to one or more of these dangers can result in faulty appraisal. The following pitfalls should be avoided at all costs:

Halo Effect

Supervisors must guard against the development of the halo effect, in which one dominant trait about a person influences the overall appraisal. It is possible, for example, that the supervisor overlooks specific areas of performance because an employee always arrives early for work and stays late.

Everybody's Satisfactory

Supervisors should not yield to the temptation to classify everyone as satisfactory in order to avoid having to justify high or low ratings. This deprives excellent performers of appropriate recognition and poor performers of an honest assessment. The supervisor must use facts and integrity as the bases for appraisal.

Bias and Prejudice

Such factors as race, religion, accent, gender, or nationality have no place in the appraisal process. The employee's performance must be compared to job standards, not personal aspects with discriminatory overtones.

People Comparisons

No two people are the same. It would be a gross mistake to compare one worker to another. Job standards must be used for evaluation.

Time Problems

Appraisal requires more than just a few minutes of the supervisor's time and should not be put off until the last minute. Since so much depends on formal appraisal, it is important that supervisors give it the valuable time deserved.

CONDUCTING THE APPRAISAL INTERVIEW

Avoid Interruptions

When you conduct an appraisal interview, you should complete your review in one sitting, if at all possible. The evaluation forms are designed to guide you through a continuous process of evaluation and recommendation. Plenty of time should be allowed (half an hour at an absolute minimum), and both you and the employee should be free from interruptions, undue strain, or pressure.

Choose the Right Time and Place

You should conduct the interview on company time and in private. It is important to pick the right day, time, and place for the appraisal. Don't conduct the interview too soon after a disciplinary action or reprimand. Pick a time when you are in a good mood and when you have reason to believe the employee feels the same.

Put the Employee at Ease

Some people suggest that you begin the interview with remarks about the employee's hobbies or interests, or with commendations for good work. What is crucial, however, is that the employee sees the value of the interview, and is prepared to participate actively. As soon as the employee starts to think and talk for himself or herself, he or she will probably forget to be self-conscious.

You should first create the impression that *you* have time for the interview and that you consider it highly important. Next, help the employee feel that the interview is a constructive, cooperative one by placing primary emphasis on his or her development and growth. Avoid any implication that the meeting was arranged to warn or reprimand the employee (unless it was in fact especially arranged for that purpose). If this is the employee's first evaluation interview, you should anticipate curiosity, tension, or anxiety, and be prepared to minimize these feelings.

Be Prepared

A supervisor should be thoroughly prepared for an interview. You should know why you have certain notations on the evaluation form and be prepared to explain them. You should have reviewed the employee's duties and be ready to discuss any aspect of his or her job.

Know your objectives Determine what you want to accomplish in the interview and plan your discussion thoroughly. Your main objectives should be an improvement in the employee's performance and willingness to work. If these are already superior, the objective shifts to one of commendation and maintenance of excellence.

Organize a simple, straightforward plan of presentation that suits the individual employee and the circumstances. Be convinced of the value of the interview, and make your conviction clear to the employee. It is almost impossible to sell anything on which you have not sold yourself.

Use the Appraisal Form as a Guide

You should have the performance appraisal form in front of you during the interview, and you may want to glance at it from time to time to make sure that you are covering all the items. However, avoid reading from the form, for this may make the employee feel that he or she is on trial and that you are a judge handing down a sentence. Your purpose is to counsel, not to judge. Restate the items on the form into your own words. Try to keep the interview friendly, natural, and informal.

Purpose is to counsel, not to judge

Discuss Facts

The discussion should be based on observed instances of job behavior and actual performance, not on the worker's personal characteristics. Employees will be more likely to recognize the validity of criticism made on the basis of facts than to accept vague remarks about their '"potentiality," "cooperation," or "attitude."

Consult documentary evidence when it is available. Almost every job requires some concrete evidence of performance from which quantity and quality can be assayed, whether it be a report, a progress statement, or actual production. Also useful for the formal documentation of appraisals are attendance and punctuality records that supplement those required for payroll purposes, and notations of when employees have been praised or reprimanded during the evaluation period.

Some supervisors keep a critical incident file that documents reasons for the praise or reprimand of each employee. This file contains quick notes about how "Mary saved the day by discovering a serious mathematical error," or how "Peter came in over 30 minutes late three times last month." These notes help keep your evaluation in balance and may help you avoid the recent-behavior syndrome.

Keep the evaluation balanced

Encourage Reaction

Encourage the employee to express his or her reaction to your comments. As you cover each main point, invite the employee to give you his or her point of view. Some supervisors find it useful to ask the employees for their opinions first. Avoid saying, "Do

"How do you feel about it?" you agree?" It is better to ask "How do you feel about that?" Should you decide to revise any of the statements you had made on the form, do so in the employee's presence. This is one purpose for the interview.

It is often a good idea to let the employee offer some plan for improvement, rather than just giving your ideas. Being human, employees will be more likely to carry out their own ideas. This is also a way of helping them maintain their self-respect.

Close the Interview Effectively

After all the points have been discussed, summarize an employee's strong points and weak ones. This will enable the employee to carry away in one-two-three order the main points that the supervisor and the employee have agreed should be improved.

You should close the interview when the following requirements have been met:

1. You have made clear whatever points you intend to cover.
2. The employee has had a chance to review his or her problems, and release any emotional tensions that may exist.
3. Plans of action have been cooperatively developed.
4. You and the employee are at a natural stopping point.

After covering all the items on the form and working out a plan for improvement with the employee, make sure the employee sees a copy of the appraisal form. Always reassure the employee of your interests in his or her progress, and indicate a willingness to take up the discussion again at any time.

PROMOTIONS

Tradition, laws, collective bargaining agreements, and the availability of qualified candidates within a company influence whether a position becomes open to the general public or is filled by an in-house promotion. First-level management positions are usually filled by in-house promotions, which are often determined by the immediate supervisor. For middle-management positions, competition is usually also opened to people outside the organization.

It is common practice for companies to check first for internal talent before searching elsewhere. Frequently, employees will be given expanded duties as an opportunity to prove their potential promotional merit.

How to Nurture Management Potential

A person will learn how to manage from a good supervisor. At first he or she should just observe how the supervisor gets things done. Later he or she should actually work with the supervisor and be given the basic responsibility for one or two projects.

Provide learning opportunity

A company can help a person learn whether he or she likes to supervise the work of others. In one engineering company, for example, the president usually places the supervisor-trainee in charge of junior engineers, since this presents less of a strain than if he or she were supervising more highly skilled people. As he or she masters the initial responsibilities, the supervisory load is slightly increased, although he or she still continues to function primarily as an engineer.

A supervisor is often called a multiplier: The supervisor multiplies the efforts of others by providing the facilities and environment that help other people increase their direct contributions.

Promotion requires a transition

A supervisory position requires a person who is willing to accept the challenge and do the proper planning to make the transition from employee to manager. Engineering firms, for example, have discovered that some engineers have difficulty in making the transition from the role of engineer to that of a supervisor or manager. The following six-step program that has been developed to help newly appointed engineer-managers might help you prepare your subordinate for a promotion:

1. Define exactly what will be required of the potential manager and explain the key measures of performance that will be used to evaluate his or her work.
2. As a form of training, assign increased managerial responsibilities.
3. Help the employee design the organizational structure to carry out these responsibilities.
4. Help the employee define the goals for the component he or she will be managing.
5. Help the employee break the departmental goals into subgoals for each person on the staff.
6. Help the person measure his or her performance against goals.

What Promotion Means

To many people, job improvement or promotion means regular wage increases, more security, and perhaps an easier job. However, this is not always true. An easier job is not possible in some industries because of the fast-paced demand for new technology, and increased security is never guaranteed. As for wage increases, some people turn down promotions because the increase in pay does not seem to equal the increased responsibilities.

Merit and Ability

Merit is based on performance

If promotion is to be an incentive for an employee, the best-performing employee should be advanced. However, differences in employee merit may not be readily measurable, so that when you make a promotion based on merit, the person who was not promoted may feel that favoritism was involved. Another difficulty with merit promotions is that it is hard to evaluate many on-the-job performances, such as that of the salesperson trying to sell a product that is in short supply.

Ability is based on potential

In awarding promotions, there is also the question of ability; the potential to perform well in advanced jobs. Susan may be doing a good or even great job in her present position, but on the surface she does not show the potential for additional responsibility. Charlie, however, is doing only adequate work, but he has poor supervision and his job is unchallenging in nature. A promotion to a more difficult assignment may cause him to blossom.

Seniority

The number of years an employee has been on the job is an easy criterion for judging whether he or she should be promoted. Promotion by seniority helps to overcome the favoritism and discrimination that lead to low morale and production.

Seniority overcomes favoritism, but may lead to mediocrity

Unions have generally been advocates of seniority, because it gives everyone an equal chance, whether he or she deserves it. In some cases, managers may reserve the right to make the final decision regardless of seniority. While seniority may be the criterion for consideration, ability should be the major determinant.

The Employee Who Doesn't Want to Be Promoted

Our culture encourages promotion

In our culture a person who doesn't want a promotion is considered to be either weird or lazy. People who really do not want to be promoted may come to feel that a failure to show interest in advancement is a black mark against their record. Thus some individuals accept a promotion when they are not suited for it, thereby putting the Peter Principle into practice. Unfortunately, it is at a high cost to themselves and to the organization. For these

Promotion doesn't satisfy everyone

reasons, a clear recognition of each employee's psychological need is valuable both to the person and to the company.

Compensation

Hourly wages or monthly salaries are usually established by the company or by the unions and company representatives. However, many items of compensation fall within the realm of the supervisor, for example, assigning overtime, scheduling vacations, setting work hours, and making more flexible schedules. "Comp time" (excused time from scheduled work for personal business that is made up during the employee's free time) is usually given at the supervisor's discretion, as are many other fringe benefits.

In awarding compensation benefits, the supervisor should remember to be fair and consistent, and to treat all employees equally within the company's policy. The wise supervisor will take advantage of all the company aids in the area of compensation. The more clearly defined the pay schedule and fringe benefits are in an employee's handbook, the easier it is for the boss to solve the emotional problems related to money.

POSITIVE DISCIPLINE

Meaning of Discipline

The words *discipline* and *disciple* share the same root, which means *to teach* or *to mold.* True discipline should teach a correct action, yet many supervisors think of discipline merely as punishing or reprimanding a person for a mistake. Certainly the element of teaching has been forgotten.

Disciplining employees is much like the problem faced in our prisons. The most progressive penal institutions try to be corrective, and the inmates who pass out of their gates are at least somewhat prepared to become useful members of our society. Unfortunately, most of our penal institutions only punish their inmates. When they are released, these inmates have a revengeful attitude and want to "get even" with society.

We often find the same attitude in business. When the wrong type of disciplinary measures are used, the worker feels he or she has been treated unfairly and develops a resentful attitude toward the supervisor. Although he or she risks repeated discipline, he or she may try to repeat the same "crime," only this time the employee will try to be more secretive so he or she will not get caught.

This revengeful attitude can become part of the employee's personality.

Effective discipline is not just a reprimand or the inflicting of penalties. True discipline involves an entire program that teaches or guides the employee to become a loyal, devoted, responsible person. When you discipline an employee, remember the constructive rather than the destructive elements of this part of your job. Both you and the employee being disciplined should profit from the experience.

Discipline should be constructive, not destructive

Supervisor's Role

Probably no supervisor relishes the idea of having to discipline, but it is an unavoidable part of a supervisory job at any level. Your job may run along smoothly, with all your employees performing their tasks well and sticking to their work assignments. Then something goes wrong; someone is responsible for an accident, or is careless with his or her work. Then you know that you must take some form of disciplinary action.

Practicing sound human relations and demonstrating leadership ability should minimize your need to be punitive. If your subordinates respect you and like their jobs, you have the best insurance available to head off problems. Workers who know that you are interested in their welfare are not bent on disruption and will not let you down intentionally.

The great majority of employees accept rules and directions as a condition of employment, and would not knowingly break a rule. These same people, however, will observe how you conduct yourself with those few who do get out of line. Everyone is concerned with getting fair treatment. It hurts morale for employees either to see someone get away with violating rules or to witness unduly harsh disciplinary action. As a supervisor you should ask yourself whether your disciplinary methods contribute to or threaten good departmental control.

Violations of rules hurt morale

Where to Discipline

In general, reprimands should be made in private, away from the listening ears of other employees. The cardinal rule is to *discipline in private and praise in public.* Each employee has a reputation to uphold both with you and with peers. An employee's pride and self-esteem need your protection. Most people fear public embarrassment more than discipline itself.

There are exceptions to the rule, however, when you must

Discipline in private, praise in public

reprimand in public, as, for example, when an immediate correction is necessary to protect the workers or when company property may be ruined. When it is necessary to correct the employee right on the spot, it is best to soften the reprimand as much as possible. The important point is to stop the employee from continuing the harmful action.

A public reprimand is usually considered unwise for reasons that go beyond consideration of the employee's feelings. The recalcitrant employee may retaliate in some fashion, by arguing and humiliating you or by adopting an obstinate attitude. If the employee doesn't express his or her feelings at the time, he or she may express them later in stronger language.

Why Discipline?

Like surgery, reprimands sometimes are necessary

A reprimand is like a surgical operation: There are times when it must be performed. Many times a suggestion, some additional instructions, or a casual remark may correct a situation or an employee's attitude. A mistake can even be overlooked at times. But when the infraction is serious or when a bad habit has become chronic, then discipline is necessary.

Discipline for chronic problems and insubordination

Discipline is required when the employee loses his or her temper or shows signs of insubordination. It is often necessary for habitual problems such as chronic absenteeism or tardiness, violations of safety regulations, or poor workmanship.

When to Discipline

Discipline soon after the infraction

Discipline should be administered as soon as possible after the infraction has taken place or has been noticed, and after the supervisor has obtained all the facts related to the incident. If discipline is not prompt, the employee may experience unnecessary anxiety.

How to Discipline

In giving a reprimand, you must recognize that each case is different and that each employee must be handled differently. The better you know your employees and how each one reacts, the better you can handle personal infractions. With some employees, supervisors must be firm or even hard-boiled, for it is the only type of discipline they will understand.

Here are a few ideas you might try when you are required to impose disciplinary action:

Try to discipline
informally

1. The interview should be as informal as possible, to put both you and the employee at ease and to enable you to discuss the matter calmly. This does not mean you should not be firm or treat the problem seriously.
2. You should first ask the employee to tell his or her side of the story. Ask questions to get further details, but try not to interrupt too often until the employee has finished.
3. Listen with an open mind, with as few preconceptions as possible. It is easy to prejudge the worker without hearing his or her case.
4. After you evaluate all sides of the case, give a constructive reprimand. Don't overlecture. Make your reprimand fair and clear, so that the employee knows what will happen and what he or she must do in the future.

Keep emotions under
control

5. Try to keep your emotions under control, and do not argue. You may win an argument but lose the productivity of a valuable, loyal employee.
6. Be sure to inform the employee and, if applicable, the union of your decision. You don't need permission from the union or your steward to discipline, but it is wise to let them know your decision. Don't ask the steward for advice. If the union is dissatisfied with your decision, it will file a grievance.
7. Remember that you are not the final voice in matters of discipline. Your company and the unions will have provisions for the review of your decision, since matters of discipline are too important to entrust to any one person.

GUIDELINES FOR HANDLING DISCIPLINE

Give Credit to Employees

Most supervisors will admit that they criticize more often than they give credit. Some supervisors say it is their job to criticize and correct. But giving credit is just as important, particularly since sound discipline depends on gaining the respect of the employees. As Mark Twain once said, "When a man has credit due him, now is the time to give it to him, for he cannot read his tombstone when he's dead."

Try to be alert to the opportunities for giving credit to your employees, as, for example, when a worker shows initiative, sets a good example for other employees, performs better than was expected, shows evidence of good planning, extends help to fellow workers, or keeps his or her temper under stress. When these and other opportunities present themselves, why not give proper credit to the deserving person?

Be Firm but Fair

Being firm does not mean getting tough or throwing your weight around. Being firm but fair includes explaining why an employee's behavior is unacceptable, how it violates the rules of good conduct, and why the rules exist.

A fair reprimand requires the supervisor to tell the employee what behavior *is* acceptable. Even in the extreme situation of discharge, there is little justification for humiliating an employee. A highly respected personnel director maintains that the real test in discharging an employee is to do it in such a way that he or she says, "Thank you."

Enforce Rules Consistently

Rules are made to be followed by everyone in the department. It's extremely difficult for an employee to understand on-again, off-again enforcement. The supervisor's position in enforcing rules becomes untenable if the violator can respond, "Yeah, but you didn't say anything when Joe did the same thing last week." Reprimands may not be necessary with every violation, but it is important that you remember that consistency prevents minor infractions from becoming a serious problem, as in the office situation described below:

> Shirley, a supervisor, noticed that Bill was making a personal telephone call, but said nothing. The next day the same thing happened, and Shirley felt a little annoyed. When Bill made a personal call for the third day in a row, Shirley was determined to lower the boom the next time it happened. Sure enough, Bill made another phone call, and the fireworks started to fly.
>
> Bill was shocked to find himself the victim of the boss's anger. He thought to himself, "I've been doing it right along, so why should she made such a fuss about it now?" Bill assumed that Shirley was upset about something else and was taking her anger out on him. So Bill said he would try not to make so many personal calls on company time. Shirley was somewhat ashamed for losing her temper, so when Bill was chatting to a friend on the phone the next day, she overlooked the violation. The pattern was repeated, and the following week another stormy session took place.

Rules can be stated simply and as frequently as necessary. Establishing good work habits is as important with employees as it is with children. It is surprising how many supervisors who are successful in instilling good habits in their children forget that the same principle applies to training employees.

Make the Disciplinary Action Fit the "Crime"

When disciplinary action is taken, it soon becomes common knowledge in the department. It is thus important that the action you choose fits the offense. Most plants have certain rules that, if violated, mean automatic discharge. Examples are theft of company property, gross insubordination, fighting, sabotage, intoxication on the job, and smoking in hazardous areas. Although discharge is authorized on the first offense, a supervisor should carefully weigh all the circumstances surrounding the incident before taking such drastic action.

Determining the appropriateness of disciplinary action involves serious consideration of the following factors:

1. The circumstances surrounding the violation
2. The seriousness of the offense
3. The record and intent of the offender
4. Disciplinary action taken in similar situations

Do Not Act When You Are Angry

How many times have you wished you could replay scenes when you made comments in anger? Our emotions influence our observations and our judgment. Poor decisions made in anger force us to back down and apologize for our lack of self-control.

When you are angry, you should wait before you make any decision. It often helps to move away from the environment to regain your composure. Tell the employee to report to you in your office in 10 to 15 minutes, as this will give you both time to recapture your reason.

Follow Up after the Reprimand

If the disciplinary action was necessary because of poor quality work, it is easy to check to see whether the employee's work has improved. If an employee was disciplined because he or she did not comply with a regulation, you must observe the employee's actions for a while to see that the discipline was successful.

STAGES OF DISCIPLINARY ACTION

Most labor contracts outline the steps to be taken in applying disciplinary action. Even in the nonunion organization, company manuals usually describe disciplinary procedures to be used. These steps are designed to ensure fair treatment and to protect employees from impulsive, harsh punishment. In industry as in society, the rights of the individual must be protected.

First Offense: Oral Warning

For the first offense, it is presumed that the employee did not understand why he or she erred, and so the standard of conduct is explained. It is made clear that such misconduct will not be condoned and that further violations will require stronger action. Many companies recommend that a written record of the warning be made. The critical incident technique is a valuable tool for supervisors to use after the first oral warning.

Second Offense: Written Warning

For the second offense, the employee is informed in writing that his or her misconduct is in violation of company standards and that the next infraction will result in the loss of pay or work. All concerned parties are informed of the action taken. A copy of the warning is placed in the employee's personnel file. Others are given to the supervisor's boss and, if a union exists, to the steward.

Copy of warning goes to the human resource department

Third Offense: Disciplinary Layoff

For the third offense, the employee is suspended from the job without pay for a period that is consistent with the seriousness of the offense. The employee is told that another violation will call for discharge.

Fourth Offense: Discharge

After the third offense, it is presumed that the employee has been given every opportunity to conform. For a fourth offense, then, termination is considered to be in the best interests of both the company and the employee. Some infractions are so serious that discharge is permitted with the first violation. In other cases the seriousness of the offense might dictate a shortcutting of these steps.

Cases where employees have been discharged without warnings are few and far between. Employees must be given an opportunity in which to improve, and specific reasons for discharge must be documented. Thus in a case where an employee was dismissed because her continued employment "was not conducive to harmonious staff relations," it was ruled that she should have been given more time for reflection and that the charges should have been more specific. In another case, described below, a court ruled that an employee had been fired in an unfair manner and demanded reinstatement. Do you agree with the court's decision?

> Mrs. O'Brien had merchandise in her purse. Even though she had purchased the merchandise, she had not handled the goods through staff purchase forms. The court found that the written rules she had been given were general, that individual warnings are required, and that there had been inconsistent enforcement of the rules for all the employees. This was Mrs. O'Brien's first offense, and she had received no warning before she was fired.

In determining the action to be taken after an infraction, many supervisors have been guided by the following questions:

1. What is the past record of the employee?
2. Has the employee had a reasonable chance to improve?
3. When was the employee given a fair warning of the seriousness of the misconduct?
4. What actions have been taken in similar cases?
5. What effects will this action have on the rest of the department?
6. Should I consult anyone else before taking action?

It is a good idea to discuss contemplated disciplinary action with your manager, or with members of the personnel or labor relations department. These are the people who have to support your actions. A person who is not emotionally involved and whose judgment you respect can help you establish a better perspective for your decision.

PUNITIVE VERSUS NONPUNITIVE DISCIPLINE

Punishment

Supervisors, especially those new at the job, are apt to equate being lenient with being liked. They sometimes feel that if they "look the other way," or give a lesser penalty for an infraction, the employees will like them more. Nothing could be further from the truth. In reality, a supervisor's leniency will bring more trouble. For example, if you say nothing when Lance arrives late, he is encouraged to do it again, as are others who know of the event.

If you say nothing, infractions will continue

It is always easier to begin with a firm approach and with an emphasis on the letter of the law. As you gain self-confidence and knowledge of your duties, you can shift your emphasis to the spirit of the law and temper your judgments within the framework of the company policies.

Nonpunitive Discipline

One approach to disciplinary action is positive discipline, or discipline without punishment, an idea originally developed by John Huberman, a Canadian psychologist. Punitive and positive disciplines differ in both attitude and procedure.

Suspended employee is paid for the time off!

A few companies are so concerned with teaching their supervisors the importance of a positive discipline concept that they continue to pay employees who are laid off for disciplinary reasons. These companies maintain that the purpose of the suspension is to give employees time to think over the consequences of their behavior, and to decide whether they want to be a part of the team and abide by the rules. Loss of pay is punishment, and the companies contend that time to think without loss of pay is more constructive.

Does positive discipline sound expensive? The companies do not think so. Under the old program, a grievance was filed every time an employee was sent home without pay. Under the new program, grievances seldom follow suspensions because there is no punishment involved. The expense of grievance meetings was much greater than the cost of paying an employee for time off to think about his future with the company.

This positive discipline approach is being applied successfully in plants around the country. During the first year it was used in one plant, the number of employees fired dropped from 58 to 19 and has remained low. Similar results occurred in other plants. Some managers balked at the idea of paying for a day off, but they soon found the company loses more when a worker suspended without pay returns feeling angry, disruptive, and hostile.

A surprising side effect of this approach is that suspension days off with pay have been fewer than expected, seldom more than three to five days a year. The companies report that workers appreciate being treated like adults, who are reasoned with rather than threatened. Thus matters seldom reach the suspension stage. Companies have also found that since supervisors aren't required to be punitive or threatening, they tend to confront and resolve a problem earlier, rather than simply hoping it will go away.

When the purpose of discipline is to teach and to mold, the employee will see that it is for his or her welfare as well as the company's. Positive discipline shows employees that obeying company rules and safety regulations benefits them as well as the company.

DEMOTIONS AND DISMISSALS

Warnings

Employees should be given written warnings of their potential demotion or dismissal. In many cases involving unsatisfactory performance, particularly for permanent employees, warnings *in addition* to the scheduled evaluation reports should be given before action is taken.

In most cases, permanent employees may not be dismissed for reasons of unsatisfactory performance unless there is specific documented evidence. Performance evaluation reports—scheduled and unscheduled—provide a written record of specified deficiencies. *Employee deficiencies affecting job performance that are not recorded on performance evaluation reports cannot properly be used as a basis for dismissal.*

Must provide written warnings for a dismissal

How to Handle a Demotion

A demotion is required when an employee does not have the ability to perform specific tasks or when economic conditions within the company dictate staff changes. In the former case, an employee is usually aware that he or she is not performing to your expectations. There is no need to be abusive about the poor performance, especially if you have encouraged him or her to perform better and provided written warnings of a possible demotion. Your best approach is to be *firm*.

Be firm, be honest

Be honest and straightforward about his or her performance. Make clear statements about the poor performance, using actual incidents. If you are not clear, the employee may feel the demotion is your fault and attribute the demotion to personality problems between the two of you. Remember, it is the performance that is unacceptable, not the employee. An assignment that is less taxing physically or emotionally, or that requires less current technology may be the answer. Remember, a demotion is not a firing.

The "positive sandwich" technique is ideal in a demotion situation, as in this example:

The "positive sandwich" technique in practice

Charlie, you have been with us about six months now. You have been able to adapt to the company and the employees seem to like you. You have a sincere desire to put out an honest day's work. That I like, Charlie! However, I wouldn't be fair if I told you that your performance has been up to par. We can't have so many mathematical errors in your docking and loading reports. As you have discovered, it has a domino effect all the way up to the accounting department. Now, we don't want to let you go because we feel you have potential, but not in your present position. I was thinking, Charlie, perhaps things would work out better for both you and the firm if we moved you to another position. Here is a description of the job I had in mind. I feel it is the type of job that is more suited to your nature and ability. Unfortunately, the pay is a little less, but if you can do the job well you can be making as much in three months as you are now. They have a good crew over there, and you would still be reporting to me. I want you to know I have confidence in you, Charlie.

This approach leaves Charlie some self-respect and also gives him the alternative of either accepting the demotion or leaving the firm. Using this technique, you seem to put the employee in charge of his destiny, although you as the supervisor have decided that Charlie is no longer going to continue in the present position.

How Do You Fire an Employee?

Place yourself in a typical supervisory situation. When you realistically analyze your department and plan for its future goals, you come to the conclusion that loyal people in your department are shouldering the responsibility for one person who is not producing. You can see that it is unfair for others to continually support the burden of the freeloader. In time, both morale and production will be lower if the problem continues. The solution to your problem is to "unhire" an employee.

Don't fail yourself and the company

If you are like most supervisors, firing an employee is a painful experience that makes you feel you have failed the employee in some way. However, if you don't fire the worker, you are failing yourself, the department, and the company.

Before you reach the decision to terminate a person's employment, ask yourself some questions:

1. Did you give ample warning? You are not being fair with the individual unless in performance reviews you have given him or her constructive criticism on how to improve his or her work or mend his or her ways. If the person fails to improve, then you have an honest basis for sterner measures.
2. Do you have a qualified replacement ready to step into the vacancy? You must be certain that the change will bring about a significant improvement. As least the *potential* for improvement must exist.
3. Ask yourself whether the *primary* responsibility for failure was the employee's—or yours. Did you pick the right person for the job? Did the person receive the necessary training and supervision? Perhaps all the person needs is a new manager, not a new employer.

When you have decided to fire an employee, here are some points to keep in mind:

1. Do not say to the employee, "You're not happy here." The employee may respond, "But I *am* happy." Against this response you have no defense.
2. If the employee denies that he or she is having problems, support and agree with him. You can afford to be charitable since you have made up your mind. If you wish, let him or her think that it is all your fault.
3. Conclude with the offer to write a letter of reference or to help the employee find another job. Both of you should be aware that your company is not his or her last salvation, and that he or she may do better under a different manager in another company or in another line of work.

Being fired can be a creative experience for an employee, although it is initially painful. Remember that it is a terrible burden for an employee to know that he or she is not doing well. Also remember that it is important to let an employee go in a way that gives him or her a platform for self-esteem. You are not judging an employee's capability when you fire him or her. You are simply saying this job and the employee do not seem to match. There may be other areas where he or she can perform more effectively and be happier. Thus, on the positive side, you may help an employee to recognize the opportunities involved in being fired and open new avenues to be explored.

SUMMARY

Appraisals are a significant part of the supervisor's duties, for the supervisor must decide whether the employee is worthy of continued employment, a raise, or even a promotion. Most importantly, a performance evaluation tells the employee where he or she stands. Employees want to know how they measure up to the supervisor's standards. An evaluation is also a way of giving someone a pat on the back.

The narrative method of appraising involves writing your feelings about a person on paper. It is precise but requires a great deal of time. The field review is an evaluation done by a group of people rather than an individual. The graphic rating form is simply a checklist of various performance standards. It is perhaps the most popular type of appraisal and is often used with the narrative method.

One good way to gather information for an evaluation is through the critical incident technique. This method uses written reports of especially effective or ineffective employee actions that were noted when the behaviors occurred. Management by objectives is a technique used to help develop a foundation for future appraisals. The important key in making appraisals is to counsel, not to judge.

Tradition, laws, and the availability of in-house candidates influence whether a position is opened to the general public or is filled internally. Supervisors soon learn, however, that not all employees want to be promoted. Some promotions are based on merit and ability, while others are based on seniority.

Discipline means *to mold* or *to teach*. Most employees can accept and profit from constructive discipline. The key is *how* you discipline—the method you use. As a supervisor you should ask yourself whether your disciplinary methods contribute to or threaten good departmental control.

The cardinal rule is to discipline in private and praise in public. Make the disciplinary interview as informal as possible, and allow the employee to tell his or her side of the story. After you have obtained all the facts, your reprimand should be fair and expressed in a calm manner. Try not to argue with the employee.

Other guidelines for handling discipline problems are to enforce rules consistently, make the discipline fit the transgression, never act in anger, and follow up after the reprimand.

The four stages of disciplinary action are the oral warning, the written warning, a disciplinary layoff, and finally discharge. Hopefully you will seldom have to resort to such actions.

Written warnings of substandard performance should be given before you recommend a demotion or a dismissal. Before firing an employee you must think of the employee, the department, the company, and your role as a supervisor. If you do not release an incompetent worker, you are failing yourself, the department, and the company. The best way to release an employee is to say that the job and his or her abilities do not seem to match. On the positive side, you may help an employee to recognize that the firing may open new avenues to explore.

CASE STUDY 28

Self-Appraisal

Joan Mills is a very eager supervisor. She is vitally interested in improving herself so that she can continue to grow and someday hold a top job in the company. She feels that self-assessment is helpful in her effort to achieve her goals. In her reading, Joan found a self-rating form. Each month she rates herself and gives serious thought to improving her supervisory methods.

QUESTIONS

1. Do you feel that self-rating is desirable? Why or why not?
2. Evaluate the self-rating chart that Joan uses.
3. What questions would you add to or subtract from the form?

SELF-RATING CHART

Supervisory Activities and Results	Rating			
	Excellent	Good	Fair	Poor
1. Does each employee know precisely what is expected in terms of the quantity and quality of work?				
2. Do I involve my employees in matters that affect them?				
3. Do I delegate responsibility, encourage employees to ask questions, and attend training courses?				
4. Do I try to become better acquainted with my employees, and to learn more about their duties, goals, and problems?				
5. What have I done lately to become more tolerant and more interested in my employee's welfare?				
6. What new ideas have I developed to improve my present situation?				
7. Am I keeping up-to-date on developments that may affect my job as a supervisor?				
8. Do I give adequate attention to the work environment, and strive to improve both the mental and physical conditions?				

CASE STUDY 29

Promotion Based upon Supervisory Characteristics

You are asked by your superior to recommend someone in your department to supervise the staff of ten salespersons. You think of three people in the department and consider their backgrounds. Which person would you chose? What characteristics (either demonstrated or inferred) will help you make the choice?

1. John McVean has been a sales representative for five years, and shows initiative and drive. He is friendly, loves to tell stories, and is basically easy to understand. He has exceeded his sales quota for the last four years. His major disadvantage is his overaggressive nature. Fellow salespeople have recently complained about his aggressive or rude manner in front of customers, and customers have complained about John's inability to deliver what he promises.

2. Kathy Crevier, a sales representative for three years, is very personable, is outgoing, and tends to be the life of the party when she is in a group. However, when discussing business with you, she tends to become quiet and reserved. Her contribution to the discussion is often limited, and you wonder if you are doing something wrong. Kathy's sales record is outstanding, and her peers believe she is a valuable member of the crew.

3. Bob Kayne, a sales rep, has been with the company for seven years. The last six years have been outstanding sales years. Bob, in contrast to John and Kathy, is a steady, quiet producer. He is a "team man" in his conversations with you, and he feels uncomfortable when the discussion turns to him as an individual.

QUESTIONS

1. How do you feel the new supervisor should relate to the employees?

2. Is it important for a first-line supervisor to have technical competence?

3. Does the fact that a first-line supervisor has initiative and drive have any effect on subordinates?

4. Is emotional stability important for a supervisor? Why?

Terms and Concepts Supervisors Should Know

Appraisal pitfalls; Bias and prejudice; Compensation; Critical incident technique; Demotion; Discharge; Disciplinary layoff; Discipline; Field review; Graphic rating sheet; Halo effect; Job performance; Longevity versus performance; Management by objectives; Narrative appraisal; Nonpunitive discipline; Oral review; People comparison; "Positive sandwich"; Promotion; Punitive discipline; Quantity versus quality; Rating period; Recent-behavior syndrome; Time problems; Written warning.

Questions for Discussion

1. What are the advantages and disadvantages of placing time limits on appraisal interviews?
2. What appears to be more important in your company in regard to appraisals: longevity or performance? Should that attitude be changed? Is it in your power to change it?
3. Do you use the critical incident technique or management by objectives? Is either of these being used anywhere in your company?
4. Discuss a negative situation that may emerge in the work place and develop your response into a "positive sandwich." Then have two people role play the situation.
5. Discuss how demotion or dismissal practices vary among companies in your area. How many warnings, written and oral, must be given before a person can be released?
6. Have members of the class bring in copies of their company's appraisal forms so that the class can observe and discuss the differences.
7. Discuss how you would handle a situation in which an employee was rated below average but strongly claimed to be above average. Have two members of the class role play the situation, and observe the assertiveness or aggressiveness of each person.
8. How many oral warnings should you give an employee for being ten minutes late before you submit a written warning?
9. Rank the seriousness of the following discipline problems, with the most serious as number one: being a half-hour late three times in one week; having an unopened bottle of Scotch in the lunch pail; reporting to work hungover; stealing office supplies worth $20; swearing at the supervisor; threatening one of the employees with bodily harm; making sexual advances to an employee.
10. List the type of disciplinary actions appropriate for each of the problems in the question above. Would any merit an immediate discharge?
11. Every time you discipline an employee, your supervisor reverses your decision. How would you handle this problem?

For Further Reading—And More Ideas

Aikin, O., "Problems over Disciplinary Procedure," *Personnel Management* (March 1989).

Alexander, J. O., "Toward Real Performance: The Circuit-Breaker Technique," *Supervisory Management* (April 1989).

"Appraisals Surveyed," *Personnel Administrator* (June 1983).

Brumback, G. B., "Some Ideas, Issues, and Predictions About Performance Management," *Public Personnel Management* (Winter 1988).

Bunning, R. L., "Rewarding a Job Well Done," *Personnel Administrator* (January 1989).

Clarke, J. R., "The Salvation Manager: Rescuing Poor-Performing Employees," *Management World* (January–February 1989).

"Evaluating Results: Ideal vs. Real," *Training* (April 1984).

Fedor, D. B., and M. R. Buckley, "Issues Surrounding the Need for More Frequent Monitoring of Individual Performance in Organizations (Frequent Organizational Resource Monitoring Systems)," *Public Personnel Management* (Winter 1988).

Fowler, A., "New Directions in Performance Pay," *Personnel Management* (November 1988).

Gabis, G. T., and K. Mitchell, "The Impact of Merit Raise Scores on Employee Attitudes: The Matthew Effect of Performance Appraisal," *Public Personnel Management* (Winter 1988).

Goddard, R. W., "Is Your Appraisal System Headed for Court?" *Personnel Journal* (January 1989).

Greene, R., "Fear of Firing," *Forbes* (April 25, 1983).

Harper, S. C., "A Development Approach to Performance Appraisal," *Business Horizons* (September–October 1983).

Harris, C., "A Comparison of Employee Attitudes Toward Two Performance Appraisal Systems (Trait-Rating Scale and Performance Standards Systems)," *Public Personnel Management* (Winter 1988).

Herman, S. M., "Ready, Aim, Fire (Handling Poor Performers)," *Training and Development Journal* (March 1989).

Herring, K., "Coaches for the Bottom Line (to Motivate and Encourage Employees to Perform Better)," *Personnel Administrator* (January 1989).

Heshizer, B., "An MBO Approach to Discipline," *Supervisory Management* (March 1984).

Horton, T. R., "Accurate Self-Appraisal—A Key to Success," *Security Management* (March 1984).

Jacobs, D., "Exploring Causes of Problem Performance," *Management Solutions* (December 1988).

Kipnis, D., and S. M. Schmidt, "Upward-Influence Styles: Relationship with Performance Evaluations, Salary, and Stress," *Administrative Science Quarterly* (December 1988).

Krantz, S., "Five Steps to Making Performance Appraisal Writing Easier," *Supervisory Management* (December 1983).

Laumeyer, J., and T. Beebe, "Employees and Their Appraisal (Minnesota Department of Transportation Survey)," *Personnel Administrator* (December 1988).

Laurie, J. W., "Your Performance: Appraise It Yourself!" *Personnel* (January 1989).

Laurie, J. W., "Steps Toward an Objective Appraisal," *Supervisory Management* (May 1989).

Lissy, W. E., "Necessity of Documentation to Support Discipline," *Supervision* (January 1989).

Mumford, J., and T. Buley, "Rewarding Behavioral Skills as Part of Performance (Birmingham Midshires Building Society)," *Personnel Management* (December 1988).

Premeaux, S. R., et al., "The Need for Discipline," *Supervisory Management* (March 1989).

Romanoff, K. E., "The Ten Commandments of Performance Management," *Personnel* (January 1989).

True, L. P., "A Practitioner's View of Performance Appraisal," *Bureaucrat* (Winter 1988–89).

Welty, G., "The Power of Positive Discipline," *Railway Age* (April 1989).

Counseling

13

"It is better to give than to receive."

LEARNING OBJECTIVES

When you complete this chapter, you should be able to:
1. Understand the value and purpose of counseling.
2. Appreciate the role of the supervisor in the counseling process.
3. Compare and contrast the types of counseling techniques.
4. Understand and explain the core dimensions of counseling.

"The best way to forget your own problems is to help someone else solve his or hers."

This chapter will help you develop questions for class discussion, while also helping you formulate an understanding of counseling. Some answers to the questions below may be found in the chapter, whereas others may require personal reflection:

> Should the supervisor try to solve all employee problems?
> Are counseling and discipline related? If so, in what ways?
> Should all counseling problems be referred to a professional?
> What are the major causes of work-related problems? Discuss and explain.

COUNSELING AND THE SUPERVISOR

Counseling is an integral part of the supervisor's job

Unfortunately, many supervisors do not regard counseling as an integral part of their jobs. They believe that a worker has an obligation to perform job objectives and that personal problems should not interfere with that performance. While there is some logic to this statement, it is impossible for a worker to report to work and leave personal problems at home. Supervisors who place a premium on human relations recognize the complexity of the worker and realize that counseling is vital to effective supervision. A worker's personal problem is likely to affect the person's job performance. Rather than reprimand the employee for poor performance, the supervisor might be wiser to determine the reason for poor performance. If the problem is identified and removed through counseling, the employee is likely to experience the following:

1. Increased respect for the supervisor
2. Positive feelings for the organization
3. Improved productivity and job satisfaction
4. Decreased tension and stress
5. Enhanced self-image
6. Renewed self-confidence

Effective supervisors counsel regularly

Effective supervisors not only recognize the positive outcomes of counseling but also practice it on a continuous basis. Through careful guidance and effective counseling, a subordinate's growth and development can be enhanced. More importantly, a climate of trust and confidence is built, thus providing the foundation for improved future relationships and interactions. Since personal problems are likely to affect employee performance, it is in the best interest of the organization, the supervisor, and the worker to attempt to solve the problem. When this occurs, the employee returns to full effectiveness.

WHAT IS COUNSELING?

Counseling is a process that changes behavior

Counseling is an extremely difficult term to define. Since several counseling approaches and schools of thought exist, general acceptance of one definition is hard to achieve. Counseling may be regarded as an attempt to change behavior or perhaps as an attempt to influence behavior. More specifically, it may be seen as "an effort which maximizes human effectiveness through facilitating human growth and development."[1] Counseling is a process performed by many people. Parents, ministers, psychiatrists, and others frequently engage in counseling. In each case the intention is to assist a troubled individual.

All employees experience problems

By nature, counseling is a professional skill requiring many years of training. Because the average supervisor does not have this background, it is important to develop a workable definition of supervisory counseling. In an organizational setting, counseling is *the process of identifying employee problems with the intention of resolving them.* Inherent in the definition is the fact that all employees will at some time experience some problems that will affect job performance. The role of the supervisor in the counseling process is to help the employee resolve the problem. Once the obstacle is removed, the employee will again be able to perform as expected.

Supervisors frequently encounter co-workers and subordinates who need counseling services. When this occurs, the supervisor has two options:

1. To ignore the problem by assuming that the individual is responsible for solving problems that affect job performance, or
2. To recognize the need for counseling and explore alternatives that best serve the needs of the employee.

SUPERVISORY RESPONSE

Supervisors must be ready and willing to help a troubled employee

When a supervisor identifies an employee experiencing a problem, a personal sense of obligation to help the person should emerge. This can best be accomplished by carefully answering some delicate yet critical questions.

---

[1] Donald H. Blocker, *Developmental Counseling* (New York: The Ronald Press, 1966), p. v.

- Is it a serious problem requiring professional attention?
- Is it a work-related problem that I can solve?
- Is it a temporary problem that requires only monitoring and observation?

Answers will provide the supervisor with a course for action to follow.

Ignoring a Problem

If a supervisor chooses to ignore a problem, the following outcomes are likely:

1. It is doubtful that the problem will just go away.
2. In many cases, the problem will get worse before it gets better.
3. Frequently, the problem becomes compounded, leading to other problems.
4. Other employees become affected by the unresolved problem, especially when it becomes compounded.
5. Individual and departmental productivity will suffer.
6. The organization will not be able to perform to its potential.

Choosing to ignore an employee problem can also result in

1. The subordinate losing confidence in the supervisor
2. The subordinate losing self-confidence and self-respect
3. A poor work climate and atmosphere
4. A diminished flow of communication between the supervisor and the worker

Professional Attention

Supervisors cannot solve every problem

Supervisors cannot be all things to all people. It is unrealistic to believe that a supervisor will be able to solve every employee problem. Additionally, it may actually be very dangerous to try to do so, since some problems require professional attention. The supervisor should not attempt to solve emotional, domestic, or psychological problems, all of which require professional intervention. In such cases, the supervisor should refer the employee to a

1. Professional counselor
2. Psychologist
3. Psychiatrist
4. Member of the clergy
5. Company-sponsored counseling service (if available)

> **FOUR STEPS IN HELPING WORKERS C O P E**
>
> C Continually observe to recognize work-related problems when they occur.
>
> O Objectively determine the source of work-related problems.
>
> P Propose and apply the appropriate counseling technique.
>
> E Evaluate the implemented procedure, seeking feedback and providing follow-up.

Supervisory Attention

The supervisor must be able to solve work-related problems

For work-related problems, however, the most logical person to provide counseling is the supervisor. The depression and frustration that emerge from the failure to meet job expectations can be resolved through the supervisor's technical expertise.

Such counseling can be most effective if a four-step procedure designed to help employees cope with work-related problems is followed.

STEP 1: CONTINUALLY OBSERVE TO RECOGNIZE WORK-RELATED PROBLEMS

Supervisors should always observe worker behavior

The supervisor must observe the daily actions of subordinates to be able to perceive variances in their behavior, which suggest that problems exist. Some common indications of problems include the following:

Employee habits must be understood

Erratic Behavior Change Supervisors should get to know their subordinates, and understand their habits and expected modes of behavior. This knowledge is valuable in identifying sudden changes in behavior, which frequently warn of a problem.

A decline in productivity is a sign of a problem

Decline in Productivity A sustained decline in worker productivity becomes a symptom of problems when it exists for a period of time. Failure to take appropriate action when employee output falls can only lead to more serious trouble. Effective supervisors possess a unique understanding of human relations and know when to intervene.

Increased Absenteeism Perfect work attendance is an unrealistic objective. Sick days, vacation, and personal days are common. Ideally, a supervisor will closely monitor subordinate attendance

Excessive absences require investigation

and investigate excessive absenteeism. Sometimes a quiet investigation can yield the needed information. Effective human relations practitioners learn when to intervene in such situations. Since some employees attempt to avoid job-related problems through absenteeism, prompt and effective supervisory counseling will help to resolve the problems.

Excessive Lateness   Excessive lateness, which is closely related to absenteeism, can be a symptom of more deeply rooted problems. A quiet and gentle investigation may determine the real source of the problem.

An increase in accidents is a symptom of a larger problem

Frequent Accidents   Frequent accidents must also be monitored. Unfortunately, while some accidents will occur, a noticeable increase may suggest a lack of attention to job details caused by the burden of a personal problem. When this condition exists, the supervisor must be prepared to take appropriate action.

Quality Problems   Observed increases in the number of rejects and defects may be further evidence that an employee problem exists. A supervisor cannot allow quality problems to persist. Sometimes, such problems take the form of administrative errors and mistakes. Regardless of the type of quality mishap, prompt and effective action is imperative.

Noticeable Fatigue   Employees who constantly complain about fatigue may be experiencing a physical or personal problem, which employees frequently attempt to camouflage. Visible signs of fatigue may serve as a supervisory cue to investigate the situation quietly to determine if a problem exists.

Employees must concentrate on their jobs

Daydreaming   If an employee's attention appears to be directed to something other than the job task, the person may be preoccupied with a personal problem. A supervisor must be perceptive and able to identify blank stares and other nonverbal cues as indications of a troubled employee.

Sudden Change in Appearance   One of the easiest signs of problems to observe is a sudden change in personal appearance. When a neat and impeccably dressed employee suddenly begins to wear sloppy attire, the supervisor should discreetly investigate the situation.

STEP 2: OBJECTIVELY DETERMINE THE SOURCE OF THE WORK-RELATED PROBLEMS

The sources of work-related problems fall into five categories:

Ineffective Hiring Decisions   An organization must make sure that appropriate employees are hired. Workers must possess the necessary skills, knowledge, training, and experience. If unqualified workers are hired, work-related problems are sure to arise.

Insufficient Orientation   When an employee joins an organization, positive efforts must be taken to promote feelings of belonging. Orientation programs are designed to provide the information required for job success. It is very difficult to assume job responsibilities if you have not been introduced to co-workers or given an explanation of company regulations.

Inadequate Training   In most cases, employees require training. It is unrealistic to think that an organization can survive without a planned and formalized training program. Ineffective or nonexistent training results in employees who are unprepared to perform the job. Organizations must do more than simply develop training programs for new employees, however. They must also make a commitment to provide continuous training to accommodate a constantly changing work environment.

Inconsistent Explanation of Job Expectations   Most employees are willing to perform the job to the best of their abilities. However, problems arise when job expectations have not been properly explained. Supervisors must take time to clarify job objectives and performance standards. Job descriptions must be carefully developed and discussed to avoid discrepancies.

Improper Attitude   On occasion, a supervisor will encounter an employee who has no desire to do the job. Such an attitude usually stems from one or more of the following factors:

1. Poor motivation
2. Dislike of the supervisor
3. Job dissatisfaction
4. Displaced organizational loyalty
5. Obsolete resources, tools, and equipment
6. Insufficient growth and advancement opportunities
7. Inadequate pay and benefits
8. Dislike of co-workers
9. Absence of job challenge

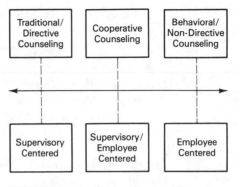

FIGURE 13–1   Counseling continuum

STEP 3: PROPOSE AND APPLY THE APPROPRIATE COUNSELING
TECHNIQUE

When attempting to help an employee with a problem, the supervisor may draw from a unique continuum of counseling methods (see Figure 13–1):

Traditional/Directive Counseling The traditional/directive approach rests on the belief that the supervisor can provide advice that will lead to problem resolution. If the problem is technical and work related, the traditional/directive technique is recommended. If the problem is personal or emotional, the supervisor should refer the employee to a professional counselor.

Behavioral/Nondirective Counseling The behavioral/nondirective approach is based on the assumption that the employee is in the best position to solve the problem. Specifically, the supervisor listens, allowing the employee to express the problem and propose viable solutions. In short, the supervisor serves as a sounding board.

This type of counseling is frequently used by professionally trained counselors. It requires the counselor to refrain from giving advice and offering solutions. Supervisors may apply this technique when an employee is experiencing a work-related problem, but if the problem is personal or emotional, the person should be referred to a professional. If the employee is provided with an open and free environment in which to communicate, viable solutions are likely to result. If an employee is able to solve the problem, this system serves as a confidence builder. To ensure the success of behavioral/nondirective counseling, some guidelines are recommended:

1. Make sure the employee is at ease.
2. Make it understood that all statements will be made in strict privacy and confidence.
3. Eliminate reprimands.
4. Encourage free and open communication.
5. Refrain from interrupting.

BEHAVIORAL/NONDIRECTIVE COUNSELING IN PRACTICE

Recently one of your subordinates has been experiencing some problems producing the end-of-month reports. You regard the subordinate as one of your better employees and want to help. You sense employee frustration and decide to employ behavioral/nondirective counseling techniques to solve the problems. The counseling session dialogue is as follows:

SUPERVISOR: I just thought we'd meet to discuss your upcoming performance evaluation. Are there any issues or areas that you'd like to talk about? How's everything going?

EMPLOYEE: By and large, I think everything is going ok.

SUPERVISOR: Just ok?

EMPLOYEE: Yeah! There are a couple areas that aren't going so smoothly.

SUPERVISOR: Really?

EMPLOYEE: Well, I suppose I could do better with the monthly reports. I just can't seem to get the hang of it.

SUPERVISOR: What do you think is causing the problem?

EMPLOYEE: I have trouble making the calculations. I've never been good with numbers. Plus, it's been years since I had a basic math course.

SUPERVISOR: What do you suggest?

EMPLOYEE: Well, I suppose I could take a refresher course in basic math concepts. Maybe I could purchase a desk calculator.

SUPERVISOR: I'm sure the company's tuition reimbursement program would cover the cost of the math course. How much do you think a calculator will cost?

EMPLOYEE: About $45.

SUPERVISOR: I'm sure that our petty cash budget can afford such a worthwhile investment.

EMPLOYEE: I'll see if I can order the calculator tomorrow. I think it'll help—especially with the math course. I'm sure glad we had this talk.

SUPERVISOR: So am I.

6. Avoid giving advice.
7. Listen attentively.
8. Do not pass judgment.

Cooperative counseling is a middle-of-the-road approach

Cooperative Counseling   The cooperative counseling approach represents a compromise between directive and nondirective techniques. As Keith Davis[2] suggests, the goal is to integrate the advantages of each technique while disregarding their disadvantages. The cooperative technique is neither directive nor nondirective. Instead, the supervisor and employee confer in an attempt to solve the problem. As traditional/directive counseling declines in popularity, the cooperative technique has become a more common alternative. Research further indicates that the behavioral/nondirective method does not enjoy widespread use because today's busy supervisor does not have unlimited amounts of time to devote to employee problems.

Cooperative counseling involves active listening at the onset. However, as the session progresses, the supervisor begins to take a more dominant role in the search for a solution. Whereas the behavioral/nondirective technique requires professional training and experience, the cooperative method allows the supervisor, with minimum training, to establish a proper climate conducive to effective counseling within a realistic amount of time. Additionally, the cooperative method eliminates the autocratic structure of the traditional approach. Figure 13–2 illustrates the three types of counseling, with the circles depicting the advice offered.

STEP 4: EVALUATE THE IMPLEMENTED PROCEDURE, SEEKING FEEDBACK AND PROVIDING FOLLOW-UP

The counseling process does not end when the session is completed. Usually, a good counseling session will yield a suggested course of action. It is not advisable, however, for the supervisor to assume that the employee will always follow this course of action. Thus the supervisor must schedule follow-up meetings to

1. Evaluate the relative effectiveness of the suggestion
2. Determine the degree of progress achieved
3. Recognize accomplishment and provide reinforcement
4. Modify or adjust the course of action, if necessary
5. Schedule additional meetings to reassess the process, provide additional follow-up, and receive additional feedback.

---

[2]Keith Davis, *Human Behavior at Work: Human Relations and Organizational Behavior* (New York: McGraw-Hill, 1972), pp. 431–432.

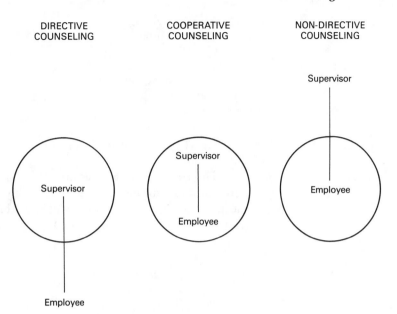

DIRECTIVE COUNSELING

COOPERATIVE COUNSELING

NON-DIRECTIVE COUNSELING

Supervisor

Supervisor

Supervisor

Employee

Employee

Employee

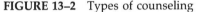

FIGURE 13–2 Types of counseling

FORMAL AND INFORMAL COUNSELING

Counseling can be formal or informal

Counseling can occur on either a formal or informal basis. Formal counseling is a planned process of regularly scheduled meetings for the purpose of bringing about a desired outcome. Informal counseling involves a supervisor's normal, day-to-day contact with subordinates.

The significance of informal counseling cannot be understated. Frequent contact with subordinates allows the supervisor to identify discrepancies in the normal flow of work performance. However, while informal counseling is extremely important, supervisors should not depend totally on such a spontaneous system. Strategies must also be developed for a systematic program of formal counseling.

THE POSITIVE OUTCOMES OF COUNSELING

Both parties may derive many positive outcomes from effective counseling, including

1. Confidence and reassurance
2. Consultation
3. Communication
4. Feelings of relief

5. Employee change
6. Clarity of thought
7. Goal direction
8. Cooperation
9. A sense of accomplishment
10. Improved human relations

Confidence and Reassurance

Counseling can provide confidence and reassurance

The counseling experience often fosters a degree of confidence and reassurance in both the employee and the supervisor. A mutual sense of self-belief develops, enabling both parties to confront future problems in a more aggressive manner.

Consultation

The counseling process provides an employee with information that may be used for personal benefit.

Communication

Open lines of communication are healthy

Counseling facilitates open lines of communication, which contribute to a conducive and healthy work environment. Additionally, it fosters upward communication, providing the supervisor with valuable insights. Effective downward communication is also encouraged, allowing the supervisor to interpret and explain company goals and policies.

Feelings of Relief

Depending on the nature of the problem, through counseling the supervisor and the employee may be able to work out a solution. However, even if they do not resolve the problem, they can experience a sense of relief just by sharing their concern.

Employee Change

Counseling can change employee values

At times, employee values become distorted, and a change is thus necessary. Counseling is designed to bring about such modifications. For example, if an employee is guilty of chronic lateness, the supervisor can use counseling sessions to explain the importance of being on time. In doing so, the employee will recognize the value of promptness and modify habits to comply with company rules.

Clarity of Thought

The burden of a problem may impair the employee's ability to think clearly. By discussing the problem in counseling, however, the employee may obtain a sense of relief. Additionally, anxiety, tension, and frustration are removed, thereby eliminating the mental blockage caused by the problem. This permits clear and logical thinking to take place.

EMPATHY IN ACTION

A company rule clearly states that three days' leave will be granted to an employee who experiences a death in the family. During the end-of-year inventory, one of your employees requests five days off because of a family death.

EMPLOYEE:
I would like to request five days' leave because of a death in the family. Unfortunately, cross-country travel is involved, which explains why I think I'll need the two extra days.

SUPERVISOR: (failing to display empathy):
Five days! Have you lost your mind? I'm in the middle of year-end inventory, and you want to take five days off. How do you expect me to get the inventory done with you gone? I'll only approve the three days leave because you're entitled to it.

SUPERVISOR: (displaying empathy)
I can imagine the sorrow you must be experiencing. Death is a terrible experience and makes things very difficult on the immediate family. Under the circumstances, I can understand why you want five days off. Unfortunately, company policy only allows three days' leave. Therefore that's all I'm able to approve. If you like, I'll submit a request to top management asking for an exception. I doubt it would be approved, but I'd be happy to try. Is there anything else I can do to help?

POSITIVE REGARD IN ACTION

During a busy period, one of your subordinates reports to work one hour late. Upon arrival, you question the employee and ask for an explanation, because it is the third such incident this month.

SUPERVISOR: Can you tell me why you are one hour late? You're holding everybody up.

EMPLOYEE: Actually, I was rushing to get to work a little early so I could get a head start on the job, but went through a stop sign and had an accident. It never fails, whenever I try to do things right, everything goes wrong.

SUPERVISOR: (failing to display positive regard) Why do you think they put stop signs on corners? For decoration? Had you been careful and cautious, it wouldn't have happened.

SUPERVISOR: (displaying positive regard) I hope you're ok! Accidents happen all the time. You should be thankful that you're only one hour late. I'm sure things will be a little inconvenient until you get your car fixed, but that's no big thing. You're a valuable asset to this department, and I don't know what we'd do without you.

Goal Direction

Supervisors are held accountable for achieving a company's goals. When employees experience problems, counseling enables those problems to be identified, minimized, and resolved. In doing so, the employees become more goal directed, and work in concert with departmental objectives and organizational philosophy.

Cooperation

The counseling process activates cooperation by developing the rapport between supervisor and subordinate, which leads to mutual understanding and improved teamwork.

A Sense of Accomplishment

When an employee problem is identified and solved, both the worker and the supervisor experience a tremendous sense of accomplishment. Counseling must be viewed in terms of the positive outcomes. The negative need for counseling can be greatly over-shadowed by the positive results.

Improved Human Relations

Since counseling is a two-way communication process, it offers an opportunity to promote positive human relations. The process is built on honesty and openness, and can enhance the development of healthy future interactions between the superior and the subordinate.

DIMENSIONS OF EFFECTIVE COUNSELING

Supervisors must develop a positive climate

It is important for supervisors to be aware of the basic principles underlying the practice and application of counseling. More importantly, they must appreciate the need to develop a positive climate conducive to counseling.

Robert R. Carkuff and Bernard G. Berenson suggest that there are four basic dimensions of the counseling process.[3]

1. Empathy
2. Positive regard
3. Genuineness
4. Concreteness

Their research reveals that the effectiveness of a counselor is not related to the person's education or theoretical orientation, but rather to his or her ability to create a climate that fosters the core dimensions of the helping relationship.

Empathy

Empathy, which is the ability to understand another person's point of view, positively influences the counseling relationship. When the supervisor displays this dimension, the groundwork for creating an atmosphere of trust and understanding is established. This element is crucial to ongoing, interpersonal relationships.

---

[3] Robert R. Carkuff and Bernard G. Berenson, *Beyond Counseling and Therapy* (New York: Holt, Rinehart, and Winston, 1967).

Positive Regard

Positive regard involves respecting the employee as a human being who has the potential to improve. Frequently, an employee with a problem develops feelings of inferiority. The supervisor must make it clear that everybody experiences problems at one time or another, and that there is no reason for an employee to feel a sense of failure.

Genuineness

Genuineness is the ability to communicate true feelings and reactions. The genuine supervisor does not play a role, but is honest and straightforward.

Concreteness

Concreteness involves being direct, specific, and accurate in communicating a feeling or experience. This dimension ensures that the supervisor and the employee are communicating on the same level and from the same frame of reference. Concreteness eliminates or minimizes misunderstandings between the two parties.

SUMMARY

Counseling is an integral part of a supervisor's job. While it is difficult to define, it is a process that identifies and solves employee problems.

GENUINENESS IN ACTION

Many supervisors tell their subordinates, "If you ever have any problems, remember that my door is always open." Most employees accept this statement as authentic. Thus if an employee comes to the supervisor's office and reveals a problem, it is imperative that the supervisor devote full attention to the employee. If the supervisor continues to fill out a report while the employee is talking, the supervisor displays a nongenuine attitude. The employee may feel unimportant and reluctant to approach the supervisor with future problems.

CONCRETENESS IN ACTION

Many times statements have a double meaning and thus can be misinterpreted. Suppose an employee tells a superior, "I hate my job." A statement of this type may have varied meaning. A supervisor may pursue the comment and discover that the employee is having a personality conflict with a co-worker or does not agree with a company rule. In reality, then, the employee does not dislike the job but rather is having problems with these two relatively minor concerns. As a result of this obtaining information, the supervisor is in a better position to understand and help solve the employee's problem. Had the employee been specific and concrete from the onset, the supervisor could have helped the employee more promptly.

As seen in Figure 13–3, after employee problems are identified, a supervisor must delicately determine an appropriate course of action. A supervisor may choose to monitor and observe, refer for professional attention, or provide supervisory counseling services. Ignoring the problem is never an acceptable alternative.

When supervisory attention is recommended, the supervisor should follow the four-step COPE model. The initial step encourages the supervisor to observe subordinates and watch for cues that indicate work-related problems. The supervisor must then be concerned with locating their source. Three supervisory counseling techniques that may be applied are: (1) the traditional/directive approach, (2) the behavioral/nondirective approach, and (3) the cooperative approach. Feedback and follow-up procedures are a critical part of the counseling process.

While formal counseling is a planned program, informal counseling is a spontaneous, day-to-day practice. The ten positive outcomes of counseling must be recognized. Carkuff and Berenson identified four sequential core dimensions of counseling: (1) empathy, (2) positive regard, (3) genuineness, and (4) concreteness. They define the helping relationship and create a positive work and counseling environment.

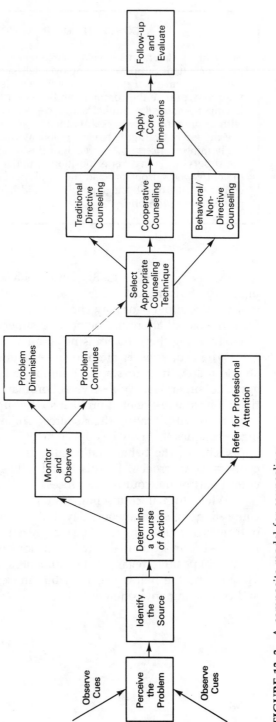

FIGURE 13–3 A composite model for counseling

CASE STUDY 30

What Do I Do Now?

Your superior attends a three-day seminar on supervisory counseling. Since your company has no policy on the supervisor's role in the counseling process, your superior asks you to develop an effective policy and to discuss its strengths and weaknesses.

QUESTION

1. What is your response?

CASE STUDY 31

The Late Employee

One of your employees has missed work five times during the past three weeks. The same employee showed up 30 minutes late today. You request a meeting with the subordinate. At the meeting, you reprimand the employee and indicate that continued absenteeism and lateness will result in dismissal. The employee reveals that the problem is caused by terminal illness in the family.

QUESTIONS

1. Suggest a more appropriate course of supervisory action.
2. How should a supervisor handle the new problem?

CASE STUDY 32

Who Is Right?

Two supervisors recently had the following conversation:

SUPERVISOR A: Since I'm not a college graduate, I don't feel I have a background in counseling. I'm afraid I'd do more harm than good.

SUPERVISOR B: I'm not that comfortable with counseling either, but I do think it's part of my job. The more I do it, the better I become. It's really a case of knowing my own limitations.

SUPERVISOR A: "I don't want my limitations to result in more complicated employee problems. I'd prefer to let the counselors counsel and the supervisors supervise."

QUESTIONS

1. Evaluate the above dialogue.
2. Who is right?

Terms and Concepts Supervisors Should Know

Action plan; Behavioral/nondirective counseling; Concreteness; Cooperative counseling; COPE; Counseling; Counseling cues; Empathy; Formal counseling; Genuineness; Helping relationship; Informal counseling; Positive outcomes of counseling; Positive regard; Professional attention; Sources of work-related problems; Supervisory counseling; Supervisory response; Traditional/directive counseling.

Questions for Discussion

1. Counseling can be expensive and time-consuming. Should companies consider hiring a professional counselor? Why or why not?
2. In terms of counseling, clearly differentiate monitoring and observing from a decision to ignore the problem. Provide examples of each approach.
3. Why is cooperative counseling regarded as a compromise? Explain.
4. Has a supervisor failed when an employee is referred to a professional counselor? Why or why not?
5. Why are the core dimensions of counseling sequential? Explain.

For Further Reading—And More Ideas

Axmith, M., "Coaching and Counseling: A Vital Role for Managers," *Business Quarterly* (October 1982).

"Caution: Drugs at Work (DIW Survey)," *Security Management* (November 1988).

Dryer, R. S., "The Trouble with Mary," *Supervision* (January 1983).

"Employee Assistance Programs (Directory)," *Personnel* (January 1989).

English, C., "Getting Tough on Worker Abuse of Drugs and Alcohol," *U.S. News and World Report* (December 5, 1983).

Greff, J., "When an Employee's Performance Slumps," *Nation's Business* (January 1989).

Hoffer, W., "How to Help a Troubled Employee," *Association Management* (March 1983).

Jaspan, N., "Breaking the Addiction," *Security Management* (April 1988).

Kiechel, W., "Looking Out for the Executive Alcoholic," *Fortune* (January 11, 1982).

McLaughlin, P., "Desktop Drinking," *Canadian Business* (February 1988).

Mann, P., "The Hidden Scourge of Drugs in the Workplace," *Readers Digest* (February 1984).

Marshall, C., "Getting the Drugs Out (Wells Fargo's Employee Assistance Program)," *Business Month* (May 1989).

Morris, S., and N. Charney, "Stop It! Workaholism: Thank God It's Monday," *Psychology Today* (June 1983).

Muczyk, J. P., and B. P. Heshizer, "Mandatory Drug Testing: Managing the Latest Pandora's Box," *Business Horizons* (March–April 1988).

O'Donnell, M., "An Easy Way to Assess Whether Drinking Is a Problem and Some Simple Ways of Coping with It," *International Management* (March 1988).

Quick, R. C., "Employee Assistance Programs: Beating Alcoholism in the Dish Room and the Board Room," *Cornell Hotel Restaurant Administration Quarterly* (February 1989).

Ray, J. S., "Coping with Stress on the Job," *Nation's Business* (February 1984).

Shalowitz, D., "Treating Mental Illness, Drug Abuse Costly," *Business Insurance* (April 25, 1988).

Stein, P. M., and P. S. Gray, "The Drug and Alcohol Body Count," *Across the Board* (May 1988).

Tuthill, M., "Joining the War on Drug Abuse," *Nation's Business* (June 1982).

Watts, P., "Effective Employee Assistance Hinges on Trained Managers," *Management Review* (January 1988).

Weiss, H., "Supervising Employees with Personality Problems," *Supervisory Management* (February 1983).

"Workaholics," *Current Health* (October 1981).

Leadership

14

"Either lead, follow, or get out of the way."

LEARNING OBJECTIVES

When you complete this chapter, you should be able to:
1. Discuss the importance of personality traits in leadership.
2. Explain the relationship between leadership and popularity.
3. Determine which is best to use in a given situation: close supervision or general supervision.
4. Explain the advantages and disadvantages of autocratic, participative, and free-reign leadership styles.
5. Determine whether you are primarily an X-style or a Y-style leader.
6. Understand Fiedler's philosophy of matching the person to the job.

"A leader is more willing to be respected than loved."

Consider the following questions before reading the chapter. Answers to some of them are in the text, whereas others are matters of personal opinion.

Is there an ideal type of leader for all situations?

What type of personality do leaders have?

What kind of leader is needed for a crisis?

Does a leader have to be highly intelligent?

Do all leaders have charisma?

Is the leader the most popular member of a group?

Does the leader reflect the group goals, or does the group impose their goals on the leader?

Which is best for most Americans: close supervision or general supervision?

Under what circumstances should employees be under close supervision?

What is meant by X- and Y-style leadership?

What is the Fiedler contingency model?

In matching one to the other, is it easier to change an organization's or a leader's style?

LEADERSHIP IS SEEN EVERYWHERE

Did you ever think you'd like to coach a football team? It isn't much different from running a business. In fact, according to coach George Allen, it *is* a business. Allen had a magnificent career, with one of the best records in the National Football League: 89 victories, 32 defeats, and 5 ties.

There are differences between football and industry, of course. During a football game there is excitement, shouting, and fast action. Decisions must be made quickly, and communications must be fast. In business and industry the pace rarely is that rapid. Still, a good leader from any walk of life can lead any type of group, because the same fundamental leadership qualities are required.

Research studies in the past 40 years have tested many different concepts of leadership, but they all show that leadership is not nearly as mysterious as is commonly thought. Leadership can be defined as a person's ability to cause others to follow him or her willingly, usually in initiating change. The ability to cause others to

Leadership is the ability to get others to follow

TEST YOURSELF

<small>ARE YOU WILLING TO ACCEPT A LEADERSHIP ROLE?</small>

Here are some questions that may show whether you are willing
to accept a leadership role. (Answers are given at the end of the
chapter.)

1. An employee enters the company dispensary. She tells the
   nurse that she has a severe headache and would like an aspirin. The nurse replies that she is not a doctor and cannot pre-
   scribe medication. The employee replies that she gets these
   headaches all the time and that an aspirin cures them immediately. The nurse should
   _____ a. Give her an aspirin
   _____ b. Call a doctor
   _____ c. Refuse to give the employee an aspirin
2. It is late in the fourth quarter of the football game. The co-
   captains have both been injured and are not on the field. A
   penalty is called against the opposition. The referee walks up
   to the quarterback and says, "Are you the acting captain?" The
   quarterback should
   _____ a. Say he is the acting captain and make the decision on
      the penalty
   _____ b. Call time out and ask his coach if he is the acting
      captain
   _____ c. Say he has not been appointed acting captain
3. A teller is responsible for accepting payments. A customer enters and wants to know her balance. The person who would
   normally get this information is not at work. The teller should
   _____ a. Get the customer's balance
   _____ b. Tell the customer he can't give such information
   _____ c. Refer the customer to his supervisor
4. A supervisor wishes to set objectives for her unit. She knows
   that those objectives should tie into the objectives set by her
   superior. The superior, however, is uninterested in setting objectives and will not do so. Therefore, the supervisor is not
   sure what objectives she should set for her own unit. The supervisor should
   _____ a. Go ahead and set her unit objectives as she sees fit
   _____ b. Abandon her desire to set objectives
   _____ c. Tell her subordinates that the boss considers objec-
      tives to be unimportant

follow to achieve a common goal is one sure indication of leadership.

WHAT IS LEADERSHIP?

According to Daniel Katz and Robert L. Kahn, research centers on three aspects of leadership:

1. As it is related to *position or level in the organization*
2. As it is related to *qualities or traits of a person*
3. As it is related to *categories or types of behavior*[1]

As we analyze the three elements, we must recognize that a supervisor is in a position within the organization at which leadership is expected. The supervisor must cause others to follow so that the job tasks are accomplished. This immediately raises the following questions in the supervisor's mind:

1. How do I get my workers to do the job?
2. Am I a leader?
3. Can I become a leader?
4. Are leaders born or made?
5. Do I possess the traits of a leader?
6. How does a leader behave?

LEADERSHIP TRAITS

For many years social scientists have tried to isolate and analyze the personal characteristics of effective leaders. Most of the research conclusions, however, were found to be unsound because they were based on predetermined leadership models. The resulting lists of "leadership traits" have been helpful only in clarifying what people *think* leaders *should* be. Even with the advanced research methods of today, remarkably few consistent leadership traits have been isolated.

From the many tests given to identify leadership traits, Murray Ross and Charles Hendry designed a personality profile of a leader as summarized below:

Leaders accept responsibility

1. Leaders are self-confident, well integrated, and emotionally stable.
2. Leaders want to take leadership responsibility and are competent in handling new situations.

---

[1] Daniel Katz and Robert L. Kahn, *The Social Psychology of Organization*, 2nd ed. (New York: John Wiley & Sons, 1978).

WHAT ARE THE TWELVE BEST LEADERSHIP TRAITS?

Lists of desirable managerial traits gleaned from many sources seem to include just about every human virtue. A research report asked over 200 personnel managers and executives in a metropolitan gas company to rate 120 adjectives describing the "type of person most likely to succeed as a key leader." From the list below, can you check the 12 traits that the 200 people judged as most descriptive, and the 12 judged as least descriptive? (The answers are listed at the end of the chapter.)

PERSONALITY TRAIT	MOST DESCRIPTIVE OF SUCCESSFUL LEADERS	LEAST DESCRIPTIVE OF SUCCESSFUL LEADERS
Decisive	_____	_____
Amiable	_____	_____
Conforming	_____	_____
Aggressive	_____	_____
Self-starting	_____	_____
Neat	_____	_____
Productive	_____	_____
Reserved	_____	_____
Well informed	_____	_____
Determined	_____	_____
Agreeable	_____	_____
Energetic	_____	_____
Creative	_____	_____
Conservative	_____	_____
Kindly	_____	_____
Intelligent	_____	_____
Cheerful	_____	_____
Responsible	_____	_____
Enterprising	_____	_____
Formal	_____	_____
Clear thinking	_____	_____
Modest	_____	_____
Mannerly	_____	_____
Courteous	_____	_____

Leaders identify with group goals

3. Leaders identify with the goals and values of the groups they lead.
4. Leaders are warm, sensitive, and sympathetic toward other people, and they give practical, helpful suggestions.
5. Leaders are intelligent in relation to the other group members.
6. Leaders can be relied on to perform leadership functions continuously.
7. Leaders in elected or public positions usually possess more enthusiasm and capacity for expression than do other types of leaders.

The profile shows that such traits as height, weight, appearance, self-control, dominance, alertness, cheerfulness, and geniality have little relation to leadership.

Leaders' intelligence usually exceeds the group average

Intelligence requirements for leadership are not absolute but are relative. Leaders usually have a higher intelligence than the average intelligence of the group they lead, whether it is a group of manual laborers or of professional technicians. Intelligence includes native ability and environmental factors such as education and past experience. A leader is able to see relationships between tasks and the personalities of those who must perform them. A leader's perception of others enables him or her to motivate them into action. A leader also tends to have more abstract-reasoning ability than do members of the group.

The leader reflects the group's values

A leader's personality reveals just as much about the group as it does about the leader, because a leader always reflects the group's standards and values. For example, the members of a chamber of commerce might choose to be influenced by the president of a large bank, while the members of a group studying crime in the cities might accept the leadership of a person in the criminal justice profession.

In spite of their role in groups, leaders often are thought of only in terms of their personal abilities. They are admired as extraordinary beings who do not have much in common with nonleaders. However, if you study the personality profile of a leader, you will see that the person's abilities are the same as those of "normal" people. Individuals who become leaders are merely presumed to have developed these abilities to a greater degree.

Charisma

Charisma, a personal magnetic quality that arouses employee loyalty and enthusiasm, can be attributed as much to a situation as to the leader's personal assets. In times of emergency people depend more on chosen leaders than they do in times of stability. During times of great disorganization and when the stakes are high, leaders can gain followers by aggressively manipulating the situation. Emotional dependency on leaders originates in the followers' feelings of inadequacy, their desire to accomplish large goals quickly, and the uncertain and painful pressures of the situation.

Most leadership, however, takes place in a far less emotional atmosphere than charismatic leadership requires. When people are not in a crisis and can act more from reason than emotion, leaders must either follow the will of the group or try to persuade it to change its mind by using reasonable appeals.

Social Popularity

The desire to be well liked may inhibit certain leadership abilities. For example, at a two-week training session at the National Training Laboratory in Bethel, Maine, one observer noticed that the most popular person in a group of 20 did not contribute to formulating group goals: "The individual in question was, in everybody's opinion, a 'nice guy.' He was pleasant to everyone. But he never suggested what the group should do, nor did he give strong support to any position stated by any other member of the group."

The most popular person may contribute little to group goals

Group members concerned primarily with social relations often act as leaders in attempting to keep the group unified. One study reported that the best-liked people rate higher than average in releasing group tension—mainly by smiling and laughing—and in indicating agreement rather than disagreement.

The leadership role involves presenting new ideas and helping to make decisions, and often it requires a leader to take a stand. Part of the risk of leadership is that taking a stand does not always make a person popular with all members of the group. In assuming the leadership role, it is thus more important to be respected than to be well liked.

The group leader is not likely to be the most popular

Robert Bales found that it is difficult for people ranked as leaders in ideas to be also ranked as well liked. In one set of experiments involving a series of group meetings, the leader in ideas had an even chance of being best liked at the first meeting. By the end of the fourth meeting, however, those chances had fallen to about one in ten. Bales found that in most groups the best-liked person is second or third in the hierarchy of group participation.

Leaders Identify with Goals

Group goals create group bonds. The more firmly leaders are identified with those goals, the more likely followers are to identify with the leaders. Additional trust and loyalty result when the leader is at least partially responsible for articulating group goals. Nonleaders may want their leader to take the major responsibility for determining the group goals. However, setting goals is not a requisite for leadership. Some groups have long-established goals and choose a leader whom they feel will help to attain them.

Whether a leader has helped to formulate group goals, he or she must always help the group attain them.

Leaders Make Decisions

When a group cannot easily reach a decision, some leaders simply make the decision, for better or worse, with group compliance. The leader's wishes definitely carry weight in a group's decision-making process, and the degree of influence depends on the distribution of power within the group. Leaders can help clarify possible alternatives of action, and they can prevent a group from stalemating or turning into a debating society.

Leaders clarify possible alternatives

Leaders Resolve Differences

When groups experience internal conflicts, either emotional or intellectual, a leader can often resolve the differences. In this function, the leader does not usually participate directly in the group process, as when group decisions are being made, but tries to stay neutral. The leader listens to all sides of the argument and helps group members arrive at a solution, or ultimately decides the issue alone. A leader is often placed in the arbitrator role to *prevent* serious group splintering. To be effective in this role a leader must be aware of and agree with the group goals, the standards by which the group operates, and the sensitivities of its members. When individual and group goals are in conflict, the leader usually resolves issues in favor of the group goals.

A leader can act as an arbitrator

"AND JUST HOW LONG HAVE YOU BEEN ACCUSED OF BEING A 'TAKE CHARGE' TYPE?"

CLOSE SUPERVISION VERSUS GENERAL SUPERVISION

The amount of direction a supervisor provides may vary. Supervisors are accountable to the company for their subordinates' rate, quantity, and quality of work. The effects of these controllable factors can clearly be measured in cost accounting. If supervisors were working only with machines, they might decide to monitor them continuously. Since they work with people, however, they must understand how their subordinates respond to close supervision.

Workers want enough supervision to know they are doing the job correctly

In most cases, close supervision reduces the effectiveness of the workers. Employees waste time in responding to close supervision, and they feel threatened by a system that seems to evaluate them continuously or unnecessarily. Most workers want enough supervision to be sure that they are doing their work correctly. They may even ask for direction to be sure of performing well enough to keep their jobs or to advance. Systems that allow for workers to check themselves thus help ease the strain of direction and control.

The supervisor must devise systems that fit their employees' supervisory needs, which can vary. For example, studies show that, because of their social conditioning, some women may want more control or direction than do men. Studies also show that cultural differences may affect the amount of control necessary for optimal productivity. American workers appear to want less supervision than do people in foreign lands, a fact that may or may not be correlated with the democratic patterns of American society. It is also interesting that close mangement of the supervisor may result in poor supervision. Like the workers, supervisors may feel that close supervision implies they are incompetent, or they may rely too heavily on their supervisor's direction for what should be done. Upper-level management thus sets the style for the first-line supervisor.

Top management sets the style

The supervisor must also know when direction is *needed*, regardless of whether it is *wanted*. New workers will need closer supervision than experienced workers. Projects that require a very high level of quality, such as missile programs, require a correspondingly complex and tight control system. The same is true for jobs that are planned on a very tight schedule, as in the typing of government proposals. The amount of direction called for in a control system should be adapted, whenever possible, to the conditions of the job. The supervisor should keep in mind that close supervision, while necessary under certain conditions, may be counterproductive in terms of people, time, and money.

Advantages of General Supervision

There are significant advantages to general rather than close supervision. If you direct your subordinates' work in broad, general terms, you will have more time for your other duties. In addition, it is likely that your employees' detailed decisions will be better than yours, since they are usually closest to the problems. General supervision also gives employees a chance to develop their talents; they learn how to make decisions by being placed in a position to make them. Finally, broad supervision motivates employees to take more pride in their work, because it is a result of their own decisions.

POWER RELATIONSHIPS

Leaders obtain authority from groups

People who have authority are not necessarily leaders. All leaders have authority, but not all authoritarians are leaders. Leaders derive their authority *from* the group rather than by imposing it *upon* the group.

The Origin of Leadership Power

It is common practice to grant leadership power to people who already have some authority, but leaders derive power only from group consensus. Leaders do not necessarily have a special, prior status such as position, skill, or education that qualifies them for the leadership role. Leaders gain power within a group gradually, by establishing trust and recognition. Consider, for example, a group that is concerned with obtaining a grant. They discuss ways and means to achieve their goal with a person who is experienced in obtaining grants. One of the group members, who is experienced in this area, keeps coming up with one logical suggestion after another. By accepting the merit of this person's ideas, the group becomes willingly influenced by and thus grants leadership to that person.

Authority is conferred; leadership is earned

The distinguishing difference between a leader and an authority figure is that the group *chooses* the leader. It is well accepted in management thinking today that leadership cannot be conferred but must be earned.

Research and practice have shown that when a supervisor gives up or is not capable of leadership, informal leadership will automatically develop in its place. Groups tend to develop group loyalty and team spirit, which encourages informal leadership roles. However, the goals established by informal leadership are likely to run counter to organizational goals.

Supervisors and Leaders

Supervisors have a legitimate right to act authoritatively because they have an official position that carries specified kinds of authority over others. For example, many supervisors have the authority to hire and fire. Supervisors may abuse their authority by harassing employees and making the work environment miserable. However, such supervisors are not displaying leadership but only their authority. They are misusing the power of their official role, and their coercion is *not* leadership.

Coercion is not leadership

On the other hand, the power of leaders is not necessarily legitimate. Leaders can exercise their power regardless of their formal role within the organization. A revolutionary is an extreme example of a leader who acts with power but without the legitimate right or formal authority to do so.

Power can be illegitimate

The formal authority of supervision and leadership power can occur together, which naturally is the most desirable situation. Supervisors with true leadership qualities have the power to motivate their group to act. For example, supervisors who have a high regard for their employees are often leaders. These supervisors have definite ideas about what they want done, but they make sure to communicate their goals *carefully*. They are usually sure of their decisions but are interested in hearing their subordinates' opinions, especially when deciding the best way to carry out the group's goals. Such supervisors have authority but are able to be leaders as well, because their employees follow the direction they set.

Supervisor-leaders value their employees

Leadership Functions

Groups need leadership to reduce uncertainty and confusion, although very little leadership may be required if a group is functioning smoothly. Since one of the chief functions of leadership is to keep the group focused on its goals, leadership can have an important effect on a group's morale. And when it becomes necessary to stabilize situations, aggressive leadership is required.

Leaders initiate change

Leaders initiate change by making decisions or by encouraging others to make them. A group's trust in its leader is affected by the quality of his or her decisions. Whether the leader's decisions are good or bad, however, the followers must accept them and the process by which they were reached.

LEADERSHIP STYLES

Along with different leadership traits and functions, the *styles* in which leaders perform can also be described. Leadership styles are based on the type of *control* leaders use in a group and their *behavior* toward group members (see Figure 14–1).

Leaders use the style that fits their personality

Social scientists have found that leaders use leadership styles that are consistent with their personalities. However, personalities are complex, and leaders choose many different kinds of behavior to satisfy a wide spectrum of needs and desires. For example, a leader may choose to be authoritarian simply to save time. Thus this style reflects the leader's desire to be efficient, not the need to be autocratic.

Leaders are not "born," but developed

Given the wide variety of personality differences, studying the personal reasoning behind the adoption of particular styles becomes a complex problem. Some researchers decided that it would be more productive to examine the *structure* of the interactions between leaders and their followers. This examination indicates that people are not born leaders but can be trained to develop leadership techniques. Some researchers believe that teaching specific leadership skills and ignoring the significance of personality traits will create mechanical leadership behavior, or a robotlike version of true leadership. Others believe that knowing how to analyze leader-follower interactions helps to dispel some of the mystery associated with leadership. They also believe that learning leadership skills instills confidence and helps people to more readily assume leadership roles.

McGregor's X and Y theory

Douglas McGregor developed what is popularly known as the X and Y theory of leadership.[2] In the sweatshops of the early twentieth century, the leadership style of the supervisors was primarily autocratic, or X, in nature. This style continues today, and it is accompanied by the belief that people work mostly for money and status rewards. In contrast, McGregor believed that leaders can have a genuine concern for both the employee and the accomplishment of the company goals. This participative, or Y, leader believes that many people naturally aspire to independence, responsibility, and self-fulfillment, and that they are capable of correcting their own mistakes. Stated briefly, the X leader is interested in production and the Y leader is interested in employees.

The X leader is interested in production, the Y leader in employees

---

[2]Douglas McGregor, *The Human Side of Enterprise* (New York: McGraw-Hill, 1960).

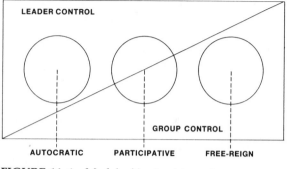

FIGURE 14–1 Model of leadership styles

Autocratic Leaders

Autocratic leaders give orders

Autocratic, or X, leaders leave no doubt about who is in charge. They use the power they have acquired through rank, knowledge, or skills to reward and punish as they see fit. Their ability to command is the major or sole method by which they get things done. This posture does not imply hostility or negativity, but rather sureness of will. Authoritarian leaders give orders and assume that people will respond obediently. Their style can be "soft sell" but is usually "hard sell." In either case, subordinates are permitted little freedom (see Table 14–1).

The autocratic style is efficient. Little time is allowed for other people to influence the decision-making process. This style works particularly well in crises, when decisions must be made quickly and carried through without question. A situation in which an autocratic style *could have been* used but *was not* is seen in the following example:

> Dr. W. is a 62-year-old general practitioner who works one or two days a week in a hospital emergency room. He is not totally familiar with current emergency practices, and he asks opinions of medical personnel who fall under his leadership. For example, he asks X-ray technicians to interpret the X-rays and EKG technicians to interpret EKG charts.
>
> This practice, combined with Dr. W.'s strong aversion to making decisions, is not well suited to an emergency room, as the hospital administrator was well aware:
>
> "It is an uncomforting feeling for the staff, including myself, to have Dr. W. in a leadership position in a true emergency. This may be a setting which, in my opinion, could be fatal for an emergency patient.
>
> "One comforting point is that Dr. W. knows his limitations. This unfortunately means the leadership position is often filled by a nurse or other medical person, and not a doctor."

TABLE 14–1   The relationships between leaders and followers

Description	Leader's Style	Follower's Style
Very autocratic	Boss decides and announces decisions, rules, and orientation.	Can't function well without programs and procedures; needs feedback.
Moderately autocratic	Boss announces decisions but asks for questions; makes exceptions to rules.	Needs solid structure and feedback but can also carry on independently.
Mixed	Boss suggests ideas and consults group; many exceptions to regulations.	Mixture of traits described above and below.
Moderately participative	Group decides on basis of boss's suggestions; rules are few; group proceeds as it sees fit.	Work independently; doesn't need close supervision, just a bit of feedback.
Very democratic	Group is in charge of decisions; boss is coordinator; group makes any rules.	Self-starter; likes to attempt new tasks alone.

Autocratic orders are clear and detailed

Some employees adapt well to an autocratic system, because instructions are clear and often detailed; any ambiguity can be straightened out easily. These employees would feel unfair demands were being made on them if they were given more freedom to make their own decisions. Other employees, however, resent and resist leadership that excludes them from any involvement in decision making.

Since autocratic communication is essentially a one-way process, the lack of feedback can lead to misunderstandings and subsequent errors. It also means that the leader does not always know what subordinates are thinking. Making decisions without first listening to the advice of others can result in poor decisions.

Participative Leaders

Participative, or Y, leaders invite decision sharing. Their style calls for subordinates to exercise high degrees of both responsibility and freedom. They use as little authoritarian control as possible and are concerned with relationships within the group as well as with goal achievement.

There are two types of participative leaders. *Democratic* lead-

Final authority differs in democratic and consultative styles

ers confer final authority on the group; they abide by whatever the group decides, with no exceptions. *Consultative* leaders require a high degree of involvement from employees but make it clear that they alone have the authority to make final decisions.

Participative leaders do not try to disguise their power to make the ultimate decisions, particularly when faced with crises. They do encourage employees to contribute opinions and information, and to participate in the decision-making process as much as possible.

Participative leaders expect constant feedback

Participative leaders request and expect constant feedback to obtain the best available information, ideas, suggestions, talent, and experience. When people participate in making the decisions that affect their lives, they support those decisions more enthusiastically and try harder to make them work. Most people demonstrate high productivity when they are given a fair amount of freedom. They maximize their potential in creative and productive ways, and experience personal satisfaction and accomplishment in their tasks. Further, most people, when given freedom, develop and grow both personally and professionally. Often they will take on more responsibility than is required because of the pleasure they take in their work.

Participative style is time-consuming

Participative leadership can be time-consuming and requires a great deal of energy. Participation sometimes means that little or no planning is done at all, and a situation can thus go out of control. In some circumstances, the participative style can be inefficient. In others, the relaxed atmosphere that accompanies the style may give the appearance of inefficiency, while in fact the work is being accomplished very effectively.

There are certain ambiguities attached to participative leadership. It does not mean that one considers the employee first and the company second. Employee-centered supervisors who get the best results recognize that high production is also one of their responsibilities. Another ambiguity involves the supervisor's responsibility. Participation can be used by supervisors as a guise for shirking their responsibilities and passing the buck to others. Participative leaders must take care that, when they call for it, *real* participation occurs. People resent acts of bad faith. If asked for recommendations, employees do not like to see them ignored or rejected without further discussion.

CHOOSING BETWEEN STYLES X AND Y

In studying the problem of leading employees and maintaining a satisfactory level of production, we come to the issue of deciding which style is better: the autocratic leader who is task oriented or the participative leader who is employee oriented. In actual practice, each leadership role has its place, depending upon the group of followers, the time span of the job, the problem, and the environment (see Table 14–2).

Take the accompanying test, "Your Leadership Attitudes," and see which leadership style is most comfortable for you.

Free-Reign Leaders

Free-reign leaders, also referred to as *laissez-faire* or *group-centered* leaders, are almost completely nondirective. They communicate goals and guidelines, and then allow employees to meet them. They do not give further directions unless specifically requested. One group goal is to involve all nonleaders in participating as equally as possible in a project. Although free-reign leaders have ultimate decision-making authority, they often choose not to use it because the stated group goal is to solve problems together.

This leadership system offers the greatest use of time and resources. The highest possible degree of authority is vested in the group. The theory of participation can extend so far that some groups seem to be leaderless or at least led by the group rather than by an individual. This laissez-faire atmosphere can motivate people to initiate and carry out complex work plans efficiently and responsibly.

Guidelines are established by an effective free-reign leader,

TABLE 14–2   Traits of X and Y leaders

Autocratic Style: X Traits	Participative Style: Y Traits
Task oriented	Employee oriented
Interested in details	Interested in generalizing
Efficiency minded	Morale minded
Knows the product	Knows the people
Interested in promoting him- or herself	Trains his or her replacement
Fast in arriving at decisions	Slow in decisions
Tends to be an extrovert	Tends to be an introvert
Self-appointed or company appointed	Group appointed
Employee knows where he or she stands	Employee is not always sure where he or she stands
Close supervision	General supervision
Task specialist	Maintenance specialist
Paternalistic	Democratic
Calls for time and motion studies	Sensitive to individual's needs

but day-to-day direction is seldom used. Free-reign leadership can be found to some degree with certain professional workers such as engineers, scientists, and teachers; there is a limited amount of supervision of people in these areas. Also, in some research organizations a supervisor may develop a pattern of leadership that to the outsider may appear laissez-faire.

THE VROOM AND YETTON MODEL

Victor Vroom and Philip Yetton have developed a useful decision-making model that can help the supervisor understand the three leadership styles. When supervisors analyze the way decisions are made within their area, they can assess their own leadership style. The model can also help supervisors alter their leadership style. The styles are as follows.

Autocratic

- *Autocratic method I (AI):* The supervisor makes the decision by using whatever information is available at the time.
- *Autocratic method II (AII):* The supervisor obtains necessary information and input from subordinates, and then makes the decision.

Participative (Consulting Methods)

- *Consulting method I (CI):* The supervisor shares the problem with subordinates on an individual basis. After obtaining ideas and suggestions, the supervisor makes the decision.
- *Consulting method II (CII):* The supervisor shares the problem with subordinates collectively (at a group meeting), and then makes the decision.
- *Group method I (GI):* The supervisor serves as a chairperson of a group meeting designed to reach a consensus for action.[3]

Degrees of Leadership

In every organization a different style of leadership will be demonstrated, from the strongly autocratic to the liberal free-reign. In studies done by Tannenbaum, Weschler, and Massarik, leadership styles are viewed on a continuum, as shown in Figure 14–2.[4] The autocratic leader makes and announces the decision. The benevolent autocratic, or X, leader presents the decision (subject to

---

[3] Victor Vroom and Philip Yetton, *Leadership and Decision Making* (Pittsburgh: University of Pittsburgh Press, 1973).

[4] Robert Tannenbaum, Irving Weschler, and Fred Massarik *Leadership and Organization: A Behavioral Science Approach* (New York: McGraw-Hill, 1961), pp. 88–100.

TEST YOURSELF

The following are various kinds of behavior that a supervisor may engage in. Read each item carefully and then put a check on the line that reflects your feelings.

	MAKE A GREAT EFFORT TO DO THIS	TEND TO DO THIS	TEND TO AVOID DOING THIS	MAKE A GREAT EFFORT TO AVOID DOING THIS

If I were the supervisor, I would:

	MAKE A GREAT EFFORT TO DO THIS	TEND TO DO THIS	TEND TO AVOID DOING THIS	MAKE A GREAT EFFORT TO AVOID DOING THIS
1. Closely supervise my subordinates to get better work from them.	_____	_____	_____	_____
2. Set the goals and objectives for my subordinates and sell them on the merits of my plans.	_____	_____	_____	_____
3. Set up controls to assure that my subordinates are getting the job done.	_____	_____	_____	_____
4. Encourage my subordinates to set their own goals and objectives.	_____	_____	_____	_____
5. Make sure that my subordinates' work is planned out for them.	_____	_____	_____	_____
6. Check with my subordinates daily to see if they need any help.	_____	_____	_____	_____
7. Step in as soon as reports indicate that the job is slipping.	_____	_____	_____	_____
8. Push my people to meet schedules if necessary.	_____	_____	_____	_____
9. Have frequent meetings to keep in touch with what is going on.	_____	_____	_____	_____
10. Allow subordinates to make important decisions.	_____	_____	_____	_____

          Theory X   Theory Y

Add up your points for each column. The highest number will indicate where your talents fall on the leadership continuum scale. Are you more of an X leader or a Y leader?

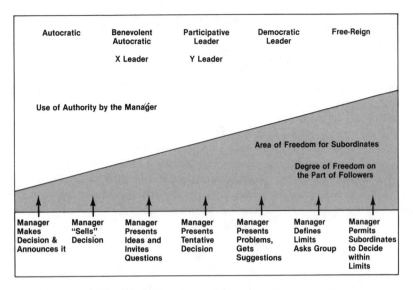

FIGURE 14–2 Degrees of freedom given to employees by the supervisor (*Source:* Reprinted by permission of the *Harvard Business Review.* Exhibit adapted from "How to Choose a Leadership Pattern" by Robert Tannenbaum and Warren H. Schmidt (May–June 1973). Copyright © 1973 by the President and Fellows of Harvard College; all rights reserved.)

changes), seeks ideas, and sells the decision. The participative, or Y, leader or consultative supervisor seeks ideas before making decisions. The democratic leader makes decisions with the group, on a one-person, one-vote basis. The free-reign leader asks the group to decide on its own.

Self-Fulfilling Prophecy

Employees live up to your expectations

The theory of the self-fulfilling prophecy asserts that what you expect of others will determine their performance. If you expect low achievement, your employees will produce little. In some organizational settings people become "X-minded" because they are treated as inferior, lazy, materialistic, dependent, and irresponsible. In other organizational settings employees become "Y-minded" when they are treated as responsible, independent, understanding, goal-achieving, growing, and creative people. Do you feel there is some truth in this theory? Do leaders' actions and attitudes express expectations that are sensed and ultimately fulfilled by their subordinates?

LEADERSHIP EMPHASIS

In addition to their style, leaders can also be characterized according to their concern. While some leaders are concerned with the task, others are concerned with people.

Task-Oriented Leaders

Task-oriented leaders are concerned with results

Task-oriented leaders emphasize the job at hand. Planning, organizing, scheduling, and processing are the blueprint for action. Quality control is a major concern. The focus of task-oriented leaders is measurable results. They consider the task more important than people, with productivity and efficiency to be achieved through better methods and systems. People are viewed as part of this process.

Task-oriented leaders are referred to as "task masters" and are considered to be production oriented. By personality they are not necessarily hard nosed, for being task oriented is an outlook, not always a character type.

Employee-Oriented Leaders

Employee-oriented leaders value people

Employee-oriented leaders are the complete opposite of task-oriented leaders. They view people as the most valuable asset in the organization, and focus on their welfare, morale, and feelings. Employee-oriented leaders convey trust and confidence, and take a team approach to supervising. They view the worker as a person who is capable of development and cultivation.

The University of Michigan Studies

The Institute for Social Research at the University of Michigan, under the direction of Rensis Likert, conducted extensive research on supervisor attitudes and styles.[5] Two types of supervisors were analyzed:

1. Production-centered supervisors who use close supervision, are autocratic, and apply pressure for production
2. Employee-centered supervisors who establish good personal relationships with their subordinates and attempt to motivate them to produce

---

[5] Rensis Likert, *The Human Organization* (New York: McGraw-Hill, 1967).

The study found that the highest-producing supervisors possessed the following characteristics:

1. They supervised but did not do the work.
2. They did *not* practice close supervision.
3. They delegated authority and responsibility.
4. They were employee centered.
5. They maintained group harmony.

Additional research by the University of Michigan divided supervisors into three groups:

1. *Production centered:* These supervisors feel fully responsible for production and believe that subordinates should do only what they are told.
2. *Employee centered:* These supervisors feel that subordinates could assume responsibility after they know what they are expected to accomplish.
3. *Mixed pattern:* These supervisors display both production-centered and employee-centered tendencies.

The findings of this study, which was designed to determine what effect certain supervisory styles had on productivity, were as follows:

1. Highly productive groups usually had an employee-centered supervisor.
2. Groups low in productivity had production-centered supervisors.
3. Even when autocratically controlled groups showed high productivity, the results were only short-term. Such control also produced high turnover and poor morale.
4. Not many supervisors were exclusively production centered or employee centered. Many exhibited mixed styles, which they adapted to the needs of the job and of the people being supervised.

Both task and people need to be considered

The short-term and long-term implications of task-oriented leadership versus employee-oriented leadership are obviously quite different. In reality, there is a need to fuse the two approaches. Leadership does not occur effectively and efficiently in a vacuum. It is difficult to view the task and the people in independent terms. In other words, both have to be involved and considered for high productivity and task accomplishment. Unfortunately, many supervisors tend to stress one at the expense of the other. The effective supervisor, however, achieves a delicate balance between the two areas of leadership emphasis.

Individual Implications

No one style works best in every situation

The effectiveness of the various leadership styles and emphases may vary according to the situation. Even within the same organization, both autocratic and democratic leadership styles as well as task-oriented and employee-oriented leaders can be successful. Supervisors must realize that no one style or emphasis works best in every circumstance.

In situations in which the completion of the job is paramount, an autocratic, task-oriented leader may be the most effective. With such a style, raises, bonuses, and other economic incentives can play a major role in motivating people. Employee performance should be monitored closely, since employees are viewed as instruments to get the job done. The task-oriented leader will probably decide *how* and *when* work is to be accomplished by developing policies, procedures, rules, and regulations that assure standardization. Rigid control systems and productivity quotas may be imposed.

However, in different situations, other styles of leadership may work best. Supervisors concerned with teamwork, employee welfare, and participation will take a more democratic, employee-oriented approach. Such supervisors create a climate of mutual trust and respect, and focus on job satisfaction. Expressions of gratitude and positive reinforcement for good performance are common motivational techniques used by these supervisors. As a result, many employees will respond favorably, share information, and contribute in this open climate for communication.

Selecting a leadership style depends on the situation

The leadership style chosen thus depends on the situation. One approach may prove effective in one setting while ineffective in another. In a war, when the command is given to attack, group discussion is not appropriate. An autocratic, task-oriented leadership style is mandatory. However, in nonemergency situations, group input and discussion can lead to better decisions. Additionally, employee-centered practices under similar circumstances can lead to increased productivity and commitment.

Effective supervisors are able to assess the situation accurately and employ the appropriate style and orientation. At times the supervisor is forced to abandon personal preference in favor of situational demands.

Organizational Implications

A major criticism—and cause of the decline—of many American businesses has been that the chief executive officer, top management, middle management, and supervisors are held accountable for immediate results. Many organizations implement traditional, short-term productivity measurements of a leader's success. A leadership style that increases short-term productivity is therefore likely to be followed. Careful analysis, however, may reveal that such a focus produces some of the following negative employee characteristics:

- Poor morale
- Increased grievances
- Job dissatisfaction
- High absenteeism
- High turnover
- Stagnation
- Stress
- Poor communication

Leaders must take a long-term view

For organizations to measure a leader's effectiveness more accurately, a broader view of productivity must be taken.

As organizations grow, leadership style may change. In family-run businesses, sole proprietorships, and small organizations, one person may be directing all of the activities. This person, whether supervisor or owner, will make most decisions. The company, if financially successful, may grow in size but will be limited to the capabilities of that leader. For maximum growth, top management must delegate responsibility to lower levels. A shift from an autocratic to a democratic style of leadership is essential.

THE CONTINGENCY APPROACH

Since there are significant differences among situations, personalities, individuals, and leadership styles, how does an organization match its needs with the skills and styles of its leaders? Operationally, this can be accomplished in one of three ways:

1. The organization can seek supervisors who believe and practice leadership styles that are congruent with company philosophy.
2. The organization can identify potential supervisors who, through indoctrination and training, can develop leadership styles that are consistent with company philosophy.
3. The organization can seek flexible supervisors who are capable of adapting personal styles of leadership to agree with company philosophy.

The third choice is the contingency approach to leadership. By definition, this style is contingent upon the situation, the task, the employees, and the leader. Leaders who apply the contingency approach are capable of playing various roles and wearing many hats. Leadership style may vary from autocratic to democratic to free reign, depending upon the climate and the situation. The situation is defined by six key environmental factors:

1. *Task characteristics:* Is the work structured or flexible? Is teamwork required? To what degree can workers be challenged? Is the task repetitive?
2. *Technological_classification:* Is the work automated or are craft skills needed? What is the total amount of time spent on the task? How much specialization exists?
3. *Organizational characteristics:* How clear are organizational goals and objectives? Do people interact on a continual basis? What is the size of the organization? What is the structure and philosophy of the organization?
4. *Subordinate characteristics:* How do subordinates react to a particular leadership style? To what degree do they require close supervision? What level of training and education do they possess? How congruent are personal and organizational goals?
5. *Personal characteristics:* How does the leader view people? What style of leadership is preferred? How much power does the leader possess? How is the leader influenced by experience, values, backgrounds, and personality traits?
6. *Existing conditions:* Do seasonal production demands exist? What is the current financial status of the organization? Do emergency circumstances exist? What unusual environmental variables may have current or future impact?

Advocates of the contingency approach believe that leaders must adjust their leadership style and emphasis to the *total* environment. Figure 14–3 illustrates the dynamics of situation leadership.

Fiedler's Contingency Model of Leadership

Fred E. Fiedler[6] is one of the foremost researchers of situational analysis. According to Fiedler, anyone can become a good leader, given the right circumstances. Effective leadership is not the function of any one particular management style, but rather of matching the right style to the right job at the right time (see Figure 14–4). His theory is based on humanistic expediency. As Fiedler points out, "It's far easier to change an organization than it is to change the personality of a leader—especially if, by making this

It is easier to change the company than the leader's personality

---

[6]Fred E. Fiedler, *A Theory of Leadership Effectiveness* (New York: McGraw-Hill, 1967).

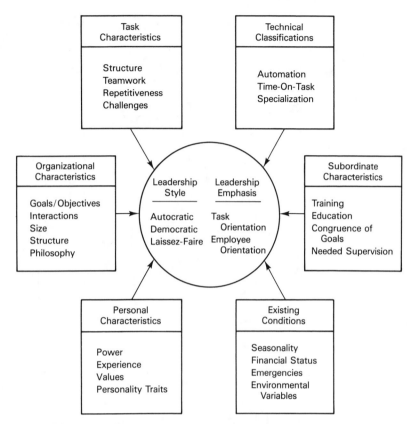

FIGURE 14–3 The dynamics of situational leadership

organizational change, we are able to create a circumstance that will stimulate a person's positive leadership potential."[7]

To use the contingency model we must first identify a leader's style. We must then analyze the job situation, and determine the best possible combination of leader and job for that particular moment.

According to Fiedler, there are two basic leadership styles: relationship motivated and task motivated. The relationship-motivated leader is primarily concerned with relating to people. These leaders are chiefly stimulated by forming and maintaining good work relationships with their subordinates, and in doing this can get jobs done very well—in certain situations.

The relationship-motivated leader is interested in people

In a certain stage of its development a company needs relationship-motivated leadership. When the company is sufficiently established to know its goals and work routines, but is many years away from reaching its final growth, a good, steady

[7] Ibid., p. 146.

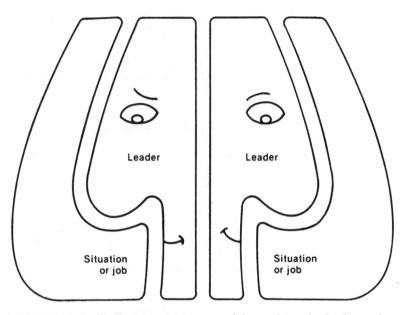

FIGURE 14–4 Fiedler's contingency model: matching the leader to the job

forward drive must be maintained, for the present and the foreseeable future. It thus needs leaders who can find their motivation in people rather than in pursuing high-risk goals or saving an organization on the verge of collapse.

At the other side of the scale are the task-motivated leaders, who could never just "babysit" a company. They need many task challenges to be stimulated. The companies and situations that require task-style leaders involve risk taking and crises, such as a business in the film industry that has daily crises or an organization that requires rapid growth for survival.

We usually think of relationship-motivated leaders as tending toward permissive, nondirective behavior. In the best of circumstances, this is often true. However, when placed in charge of a collapsing organization these leaders may suddenly become aggressive autocrats. They want to do a good job and realize that their group needs a firm direction, but such a task is not easy for them. Because they do not have time to form intimate relationships, their primary motivation has been stymied. And because they have never been particularly interested in the dynamics of uniting a collapsing group, they are not especially effective in performing the task.

The task-motivated leader is more aggressive   Similarly, the aggressive, authoritative behavior of task-motivated leaders can be drastically affected by the job situation. It appears that their behavior is distorted when circumstances stymie their primary motivation, but it is stimulated and enriched when

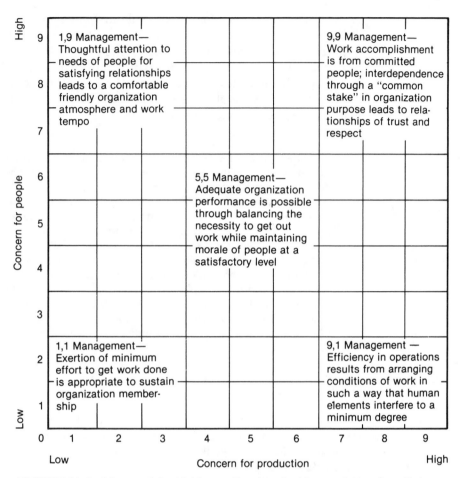

High

9 | 1,9 Management— Thoughtful attention to needs of people for satisfying relationships leads to a comfortable friendly organization atmosphere and work tempo

8

7

Concern for people

6 | 5,5 Management— Adequate organization performance is possible through balancing the necessity to get out work while maintaining morale of people at a satisfactory level

5

4

3

2 | 1,1 Management— Exertion of minimum effort to get work done is appropriate to sustain organization membership

Low 1

0   1   2   3   4   5   6   7   8   9

Low   Concern for production   High

9,9 Management— Work accomplishment is from committed people; interdependence through a "common stake" in organization purpose leads to relationships of trust and respect

9,1 Management — Efficiency in operations results from arranging conditions of work in such a way that human elements interfere to a minimum degree

FIGURE 14–5 Managerial grid (*Source:* Reprinted with permission from Robert R. Blake and Jane S. Mouton, "Managerial Facades," *Advanced Management Journal* (2331 Victory Parkway, Cincinnati, Ohio: Society for Advancement of Management, July 1966), p. 31.)

circumstances call for it. As Fiedler points out, if companies do not want their leaders to engage in destructive leadership behavior, it is far easier to change the job circumstance than it is to change the leaders' motivating styles.

The Managerial Grid

The managerial grid[8] is a tool to help supervisors assess their leadership style (see Figure 14–5). The grid was developed by Rob-

[8] Robert R. Blake and Jane S. Mouton, "Managerial Facades," *Advanced Managerment Journal*, July 1966, p. 31.

ert R. Blake and Jane S. Mouton to point out the two major aspects of the supervisor's job: *concern for people* and *concern for the job.* Typically, these variables are plotted on the chart based on supervisory self-assessment to determine which of the five styles of leadership best characterizes the supervisor. The possible combinations range from a 1,1 style of leadership to the 9,9 style. A brief summary of the five possible styles are as follows:

- *1,1:* Low concern for employees and low concern for production. This style suggests that maximum production is not possible because employees are lazy and indifferent.
- *1,9:* High concern for employees and low concern for production. Here the supervisor works at creating good fellowship and pleasant relationships instead of getting the job done.
- *9,1:* High concern for the job and low concern for the employees. The employees are expected to produce or suffer the consequences. The workers are thought of as machines—work or else!
- *9,9:* High concern for employees and high concern for production. This is the best style. It views the supervisor's job as one that requires a blend of job interests *and* people interests.
- *5,5:* Some concern for employees and some concern for production. This is a middle-of-the-road style. The supervisor does not go all out for either production or the people, but does not ignore either category.

As supervisors, we must always be trying to reach the 9,9 position. As we work at promoting free, open communication and at developing mutually shared goals, we stand a good chance of approaching the 9,9 style.

Identifying the Style

Least-Preferred Co-Worker Test identifies style

Identifying a leader's style can often be difficult. To make the task easier, Fiedler devised a "Least-Preferred Co-Worker Test," in which people are asked to characterize their least-preferred co-worker, past or present. From over 15 years of test data, Fiedler found that relationship-motivated leaders usually describe their least-preferred co-worker as "untrustworthy" or "unreliable personally," whereas task-motivated leaders describe their least-preferred co-worker as "lazy," "unintelligent," or inhibiting the completion of difficult jobs. In this test leaders usually fall somewhere between the two extremes, but the findings do allow us to identify their styles.

Analyzing the Job: Matching the Style

Fiedler analyzed job situations to discover the degree to which they demand a strong work relationship and the completion of difficult jobs. His conclusion is that relationship-motivated leaders do best in situations that are relatively difficult—but not too difficult—to lead, while task-motivated leaders do best in situations that are either very difficult or very easy to lead.

A situation that is relatively difficult to lead is usually one in which there are few major crises but in which primary goals are still far from being achieved. A relationship-motivated leader is obviously perfect for this group. There are no gigantic task challenges, and there is plenty of time to form and maintain the numerous work relationships that challenge this leader.

The contingency model matches the job and the leader

In situations that involve very difficult tasks, the group needs the kind of direction that can come only from a person who is stimulated by crises. The task-motivated leader is a troubleshooter, someone you call in for an emergency. Such troubleshooters also function quite well in easy-task situations, where *speed* becomes important. Task-motivated leaders are challenged to give their people the push they need to continue to do their jobs both quickly and well (see Table 14–3).

Easy-task groups should have a task leader

Job situations do not remain constant, and when they change, their leadership needs change as well. A company group may begin as a very difficult situation to lead, and a task-motivated leader is put in charge. Because the leader is so skilled at giving the kind of direction that is needed, the group quickly becomes organized and becomes only relatively difficult to lead. Ironically, the task-motivated leader has just worked himself out of a job. The situation now requires a relationship-motivated leader. If by improving work relationships this leader turns the group into one that is very easy to lead, the situation again needs a task leader.

Fiedler advises businesses to make frequent evaluations of both jobs and leaders, and to not be afraid to change leadership positions. In business psychology, such manipulation is called *organizational engineering*, which is a method of creating and maintaining effective leadership. The approach is a lot easier than firing

TABLE 14–3 Using Fiedler's contingency model to match the leader to the situation

Situation	Leader Needed
Very difficult to lead	Task-motivated leader
Relatively difficult to lead	Relationship-motivated leader
Very easy to lead	Task-motivated leader

or trying to change supervisors who lose their effectiveness because the leadership needs of their job situation have changed.

Leadership Training

Sensible leadership training should teach people to recognize their style of leadership, the nature of their individual jobs, and the needs of their followers. Promoting and hiring for leadership positions should also be accomplished in the context of good leadership theory. The more aware an individual is of his or her style and its inherent strengths and weaknesses, the less likely he or she is to make supervisory errors. In general, leaders who naturally tend to operate with a broad range of behavior patterns tend to be more successful and more comfortable.

THE QUADIKA OF LEADERSHIP

The group, the environment, and the problem determine the best leadership style

The nature of the group to be led, the job environment and situation, and the goal or possible solution all help determine which leadership style is most effective in a given situation. The leader, the group, and the problem are all dynamic forces, and with each passing day they affect the best possible goal or solution.

Leadership qualities are based on (1) the forces at work within a leader, (2) the forces at work within followers, and (3) the situation within which the leader and followers interact. Consequently the interaction among the leader, the group, and the situation will affect (4) the outcome or solution (see Figure 14–6).

A leader in one situation is not necessarily a leader in all

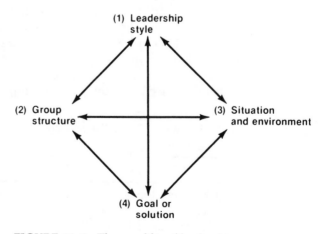

FIGURE 14–6   The quadika of leadership

situations, even when the same group of people is involved. Various situations call for various leadership responses. This doesn't mean the group must change leaders; the same leader can display different personality traits to deal with different problems.

Effective leaders must be able to understand a situation from the points of view of all those involved, including their own. Further, leaders must be aware of their impact on others and the impact of others on them. A low degree of defensiveness makes it possible for a leader to measure many relevant factors that must otherwise be ignored. Leaders must be able to assess all relevant factors in a situation, including their personal needs and anxieties.

Leaders must assess the situation, and their personal needs and anxieties

Effective Leadership

Today, most workers are looking for more than just a paycheck. They want challenging, satisfying work. They seek supportive work relationships and the opportunity to make an effective contribution. As a result, to be successful, leaders must place a premium on worker participation. This is the foundation of positive supervision.

Worker participation leads to positive supervision

Additionally, the two essential components of effective leadership are the ability to understand the situation and to work with human resources on a daily basis. Employees at all levels are the vital asset of an organization that must continually be nurtured and developed. Perhaps the role of the leader was best summarized by Tom Peters,[9] who identified what leadership *is* and *is not* in effective companies:

A Leader Is a . . .	*A Leader Is Not a . . .*
Cheerleader	Cop
Enthusiast	Referee
Nurturer	Devil's advocate
Coach	Naysayer
Facilitator	Pronouncer

In short, the unifying force leading to organizational success is effective leadership.

SUMMARY

Many people admire or fear leadership and do not recognize the leadership potential in themselves. Leaders initiate and facilitate change by interacting with members of groups to make decisions

---

[9]Tom Peters, "A Passion for Excellence," 1985.

about matters having a high-risk or uncertainty factor. Others follow either because they already agree with the changes the leader is initiating or because they want to be changed.

Leadership is not always aggressive or autocratic; often the best test of effective leadership is how smoothly a group functions. Groups *always* have leaders, and new leaders emerge as a group changes. In fact, every situation calls for different leadership responses. Because of the many variables inherent in each situation, there are plenty of opportunities to demonstrate different leadership traits and styles.

Authority that is derived from position, knowledge, or expertise may be very advantageous to leaders, but it is not a measure of leadership skill. Leaders gain their authority over a group by group consensus alone.

Research studies have led to the conclusion that leadership is attributable to only a few personality traits such as self-confidence, responsibility, sensitivity, relative intelligence, reliability, and enthusiasm. These personality traits are not out of the ordinary, but they are more highly developed in leaders. Charisma—that special, magnetic ability to influence that leaders are expected to have—is as much a product of the total emotional climate as it is of the leader, gifted though he or she may be. And being well liked and respected are quite different; being respected is more important to a leader.

The main function of leaders is to help groups achieve their objectives. Leaders initiate changes, help make decisions, and resolve differences. Because of vast and rapid technological and social changes, modern organizations must find new ways for leaders to function more flexibly in organizational structures.

Leaders should choose leadership behavior patterns that are most consistent with their personalities, the function to be performed, and the situation at hand. The most common behavioral types are autocratic, participative, and free-reign leaders. On a continuum scale, they fall somewhere between strict authoritarianism and completely open group participation.

Leadership emphasis can be characterized according to concern. While some leaders are more concerned with the task, others are more concerned with people. The University of Michigan studies analyzed these implications for supervisors and the need to fuse the two approaches.

According to Fiedler, anyone can become a good leader, given the right circumstances. Effective leadership, he argued, is not the function of any one particular management style, but rather of matching the right style to the right job at the right time. It is far easier to change an organization than it is to change the personality of a leader. The task-motivated leader can best handle a situation that is either very difficult or very easy to lead, but a relatively difficult situation is best led by the relationship-motivated leader.

CASE STUDY 33

Who Leads: The Chosen Leader or the Informal Leader?

The Landau Construction Company recently contracted to erect the frames of houses as part of a federal housing project. Loren Franks is the supervisor for the company on this project, and the 12 people working for him were hired from the local union hall. Loren receives bonuses that are based on how rapidly projects are completed. The faster this project is completed, the more money he will get. Because of rain, he is falling a little behind his schedule on this job.

Loren has supervised most of these workers in the past, and on the whole he considers them good, skilled carpenters. One of the men, a young and relatively new carpenter named Brian Baxter, has not worked for Loren before.

Soon after work began on the project, Loren became aware of Brian and his popularity with the other workers. In the beginning, during coffee and lunch breaks, Brian was constantly asking the more experienced workers questions about the carpentry field. Because of his easygoing manner and his desire to learn, Brian soon became popular with all of the workers.

After a few weeks, Loren noticed that Brian began to ask fewer questions about carpentry, and instead began to tell many humorous stories and jokes for the workers' entertainment, which presented no problem in itself. Loren became increasingly aware, however, that the workers were taking longer lunch hours and coffee breaks to lis-

ten to Brian speak. It seemed that he always had a story to finish or one last joke to tell before going back to work.

Loren counseled Brian twice about the problem, but this failed to produce results. During the two counseling conversations Loren got the impression that Brian was enjoying both his popularity and the situation, which worsened. Usually after an extended break, Loren would find many workers grouped around a single operation for which only one worker was needed, such as sweeping shavings. Loren found that the center of the group would invariably be Brian. On these occasions, when Loren was forced to remind the carpenters that their work was not getting done, Brian would always laugh it off and have one last comment to make, which the men would wait to hear.

From all appearances, Brian has assumed informal control of the group. If you were Loren, how would you go about correcting the situation that exists?

QUESTIONS

1. Do you continue to counsel Brian, or do you now go to the workers?
2. If you talk with the other carpenters, what do you say to them?
3. Are there other alternatives?
4. Would you "blacklist" Brian, that is, tell other supervisors not to hire him because he doesn't work hard enough?

CASE STUDY 34

Situational Choices

In each situation described below, decide whether the autocratic, democratic, or free-reign style of management would be appropriate. Be sure to explain your choices.

Situation 1: The production line breaks down and 10 employees are needed to work overtime to repair it.

Situation 2: Your top advertising executive, who is handling the company's largest account, just called in sick. Someone else must be selected to make a major sales presentation.

Situation 3: A decision is needed next month on where to hold the company picnic.

Situation 4: You are the vice-president of a major automotive company. Recently, your top researchers presented you with three style designs. You must decide which one to implement.

CASE STUDY 35

Which Leader Would You Pick?

Laura Lockwood is the president of the Preston Plastics Corporation. The board of directors recently decided that it would be profitable for the corporation to open its own marketing department. Laura has been directed to select a person whom she feels is capable of heading the department and then to put this person in charge of getting the department on its feet. After considering a number of good people, Laura has narrowed the field to two choices: Ted Edmonds and Jessa Hernandez.

Ted Edmonds has a good record with the company. He was hired eight years ago, and through the years has shown drive and initiative in all his endeavors. An aggressive young man, Ted has been nicknamed "Go-getter" in his department. Although at times he seems to be more concerned with ends rather than means, he is very efficient and is considered a good leader by those who work under him. As one worker stated, "Although he can get rough with you at times, you always know where you stand with him, and when you've done a good job,

he lets you know it." Ted is also credited with always accepting full responsibility and with making quick decisions when needed.

Jessa Hernandez has been with the company for 11 years. She is well liked by all in her department, and her work is first rate. In leadership style, Jessa is not as aggressive and quick to act as Ted. Before Jessa makes a decision, she generally consults others whom she feels can contribute further information on a given subject. This often includes those who work under her. Her subordinates consider her a good leader, and state that the atmosphere of participation she has established really encourages their utmost individual output. This can be seen by the production increase that occurred soon after Jessa became the head of her work force.

QUESTION

1. Which person should Laura choose to head the new department?

CASE STUDY **36**

Who Is Promoted?

You overhear two middle-level managers talking about which employee should be promoted to the current supervisory vacancy:

SUPERVISOR A: I think Mike Smith should get the job. After all, he has a college degree in management, and has been eager and enthusiastic since he was hired two months ago. Now that he's familiar with our company, that degree will make him a good manager.

SUPERVISOR B: College degrees mean nothing. It's experience that counts, and you know very well that Mary Stevens is the best candidate. She's been with us for eight years, and knows this company inside and out. It's experience that counts.

QUESTIONS

1. If you were asked your opinion on the two candidates, what would you say?
2. Upon what criteria should leadership positions be filled?

Terms and Concepts Supervisors Should Know

Authority; Autocratic leadership; Charisma; Close supervision; Contingency model of leadership; Democratic leadership; Employee-oriented leaders; Free-reign leadership; General supervision; Leadership; Managerial grid; Participative leadership; Self-fulfilling prophecy; Situational leadership; Task-oriented leaders; Social popularity; University of Michigan studies; Vroom and Yetton model; X-style leadership; Y-style leadership.

Questions for Discussion

1. What style of leadership would be the most effective in your company: X or Y? Why?
2. Is close supervision more often found at the lower, middle, or top level of management? Why? Can you justify your stand?
3. Have you seen Fiedler's contingency model in action? Does his theory help explain some promotions, demotions, transfers, and firings that you have seen in your company?
4. What kind of industries or businesses would ideally operate under:
   a. Autocratic leadership
   b. Participative leadership
   c. Free-reign leadership
5. How does McGregor's X and Y theory of leadership relate to Fiedler's contingency model?

Answers to "Test Yourself: Are You Willing to Accept a Leadership Role?"

If you selected *a* as the best answer to all the questions, you are willing to assume a leadership role, even at the risk of failure and embarrassment.

Answers to "What Are the Twelve Best Leadership Traits?"

The traits most and least descriptive of successful leaders are as follows:

Most Descriptive	Least Descriptive
Decisive	Amiable
Aggressive	Conforming
Self-starting	Neat
Productive	Reserved
Well informed	Agreeable
Determined	Conservative
Energetic	Kindly
Creative	Mannerly
Intelligent	Cheerful
Responsible	Formal
Enterprising	Courteous
Clear thinking	Modest

For Further Reading—And More Ideas

Blake, R. R., and J. S. Mouton, "Management by Grid Principles or Situationalism: Which?" *Group and Organization Studies* (June 1981).

Brache, A., "Seven Prevailing Myths About Leadership," *Training and Development Journal* (June 1983).

Dimma, W. A., "On Leadership." *Business Quarterly* (Winter 1989).

Evans, J., "Will Women Lead?" *Management World* (December 1983).

Fleenor, C. P., "The Changing Profile of Business Leadership," *Business Horizons* (July–August 1983).

Gardner, J. W., "Mastering the Fine Art of Leadership (Excerpt from Leadership Papers by J. W. Gardner)," *Business Month* (May 1989).

Glassman, E., "Creative Problem Solving: Your Role as Leader," *Supervisory Management* (April 1989).

Gluck, F. W., "Vision and Leadership," *Interfaces* (January–February 1984).

Graeff, C. L., "The Situational Leadership Theory: A Critical View," *Academy of Management Review* (August 1983).

Hopkins-Doerr, M., "Getting More out of MBWA (Management by Walking Around)," *Supervisory Management* (February 1989).

Horton, T. R., "Beyond Charisma," *Supervisory Management* (April 1989).

House, R. J., and T. R. Mitchell, "Path-Goal Theory of Leadership," *Journal of Contemporary Business* (Autumn 1981).

"How Women Manage (Interview with F. N. Schwartz)," *Business Monthly* (April 1989).

Johnson, N. P., "Leadership: The Manager's

Principle Role," *Management Planning* (July–August 1983).

Jones, G. R., "Forms of Control and Leader Behavior," *Journal of Management* (Fall–Winter 1983).

"The Keys to Leadership," *Management World* (October 1983).

Lansing, R. L., "Football Coach's Lessons Can Lead Your Team to Victory (University of Notre Dame's Football Coach, L. Holtz)," *Management Review* (April 1989).

Lippitt, G., "Leadership: A Performing Art in a Complex Society," *Training and Development Journal* (March 1983).

Maccoby, M., "A New Model for Leadership (in R & D)," *Research Technology Management* (November–December 1988).

McGrath, G. E., "Leadership Means Planning, Not Discipline," *Safety & Health* (January 1989).

Nelton, S., "Look for Leaders on the Job," *Nation's Business* (October 1988).

Tannenbaum, R., and W. H. Schmidt, "How to Choose a Leadership Pattern," *Harvard Business Review* (March–April 1958).

Watson, C. M., "Leadership, Management, and the Seven Keys," *McKinsey Quarterly* (Autumn 1983).

Zaleznik, A., "Managers and Leaders: Are They Different?" *Harvard Business Review* (May–June 1977).

Communications with Employees

15

"How are you perceived by your subordinates?"

LEARNING OBJECTIVES

When you complete this chapter, you should be able to:
1. Understand why meaning resides within the speaker and the listener rather than in the words themselves.
2. Recognize conversational feedback and why it is beneficial.
3. Determine the four styles of speaking as defined by Carl Jung. Understand why using these styles may help us to communicate effectively.
4. Recognize why listening well may be a better key to success than speaking well.
5. Understand how to provide for individual differences in perception when you communicate.
6. Recognize how upward, downward, horizontal, and diagonal communications differ.
7. Understand the need for an informal grapevine and learn how to end rumors.

"The trouble with people who talk too fast is that they often say something they haven't thought of yet."

Here are a few questions to contemplate as you read this chapter. You can find the answers to some of these questions in your reading; for the answers to others you must look to your own experiences. Share your feelings and ideas about these questions with other students.

Is it easier for you to speak or to listen?

Is one method of communication better than another?

Should you use the grapevine to communicate?

Do employees believe what you tell them?

Are there some things you should not talk about?

How can you be sure that people understand what you mean?

How can you handle rumors?

COMMUNICATION AND THE SUPERVISORY PROCESS

Supervisory success depends upon the effective and efficient practice of at least these five supervisory functions:

1. Planning
2. Organizing
3. Staffing
4. Directing
5. Controlling

Supervisors must communicate plans   The initial function of the supervisory process is to develop an effective plan, which serves as a guideline for achieving organizational objectives. If plans are not properly communicated, the sequence of the supervisory process is seriously jeopardized. Consequently, the supervisor will be unable to organize, staff, direct, and control adequately. More appropriately, when open lines of effective communication exist, the functions are linked in sequence and action. The communication process increases the chances for organizational success by linking the supervisory functions with goal accomplishment (see Figure 15–1).

Studies show that the average supervisor spends about 80 percent of his or her time communicating; of this, 10 percent is spent writing, 15 percent reading, 30 percent speaking, and 45

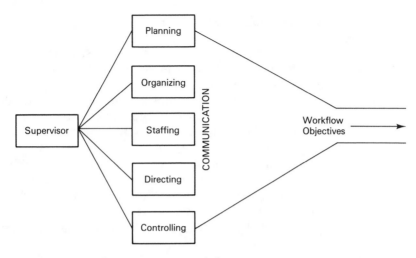

FIGURE 15–1   Communication and the supervisory process

percent listening. A supervisor communicates in words, of course, but also by his or her tone of voice, expression, and mannerisms.

A successful supervisor has to be a good communicator

A study of several plants on the west coast found that the high-producing supervisor was consistently a good communicator. To this we may add that when communications are lacking in an organization, the problem is not a lack of knowledge about good communication but the failure to apply the knowledge that does exist.

"I KNOW THAT YOU BELIEVE YOU UNDERSTAND WHAT YOU THINK I SAID, BUT I AM NOT SURE YOU REALIZE THAT WHAT YOU HEARD IS NOT WHAT I MEANT."

The Meaning of Meaning

Communication is the process of transferring information and understanding *from* one or more people *to* another or others. In simplest form, communication transfers information from one person to another. In more complex kinds of communication, members of a group transfer information to other members. Comprehension of the message is the only test of its success as communication.

How many times have you asked someone, "What do you mean by that?" How many times have you had to answer that question yourself? How do you answer it? Most people confonted with the question assemble their thoughts into new combinations of words and phrases. The meaning doesn't change, but the words do. *Meaning exists within ourselves*, not in the words we use to express that meaning.

Meaning exists within ourselves

The more our messages relate to and overlap the other person's mental and emotional experiences, the more effectively we can communicate. And just as experiences are constantly changing, so are meanings. They are never permanently fixed.

THE COMMUNICATION PROCESS

Consultant John Keltner has estimated that speaking and listening account for 74 percent of the time people spend interacting. Considering this figure, one might think good communication is frequent.

Models

One way to find out what takes place during the communication process is to construct a model of it. Figure 15–2 shows a simple model of an exchange in which a speaker (sender) transmits a message to a listener (receiver), who sends back another message.

This simple model omits so many parts of the communication process that it could be applied just as logically to a temperature control system. Figure 15–3, although still quite simple, shows a more sophisticated model of human communication. This model illustrates the clarity of the transmission as a function of the way in which the listener's attitudes, emotions, role, and nonverbal behavior relate to those of the speaker. Additionally, the listener is shown as responding to the message by means of positive or negative feedback or both.

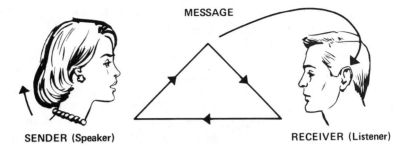

MESSAGE

SENDER (Speaker)   RECEIVER (Listener)

FIGURE 15–2   A simple model of the communication process (*Source:* Jack Halloran, *Applied Human Relations* (Englewood Cliffs, NJ: Prentice Hall, 1978), p. 96.)

Until an idea is communicated, it does not exist. The purpose of communicating is to establish a common understanding between the sender and receiver. Real communication flows freely in both directions. In practice, however, supervisors tend to devote far more attention to *telling, informing,* and *commanding* than they do to *listening, asking,* and *interpreting.* Too often, communication with

Supervisors too often tell, inform, and command

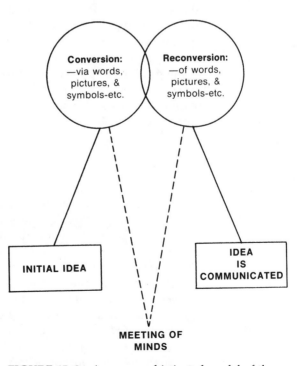

Conversion:
—via words, pictures, & symbols-etc.

Reconversion:
—of words, pictures, & symbols-etc.

INITIAL IDEA

IDEA IS COMMUNICATED

MEETING OF MINDS

FIGURE 15–3   A more sophisticated model of the communication process

management is obscured, because supervisors will not or cannot hear what is being transmitted.

Speaking

Speaking is a form of communication that should be confirmed in writing if the subject is lengthy, complex, or technical. Studies have shown that immediately following a 10-minute lecture, first-year college students retain only 50 percent of the information and forget half of that material in 48 hours.

Matters important to a subordinate are particularly susceptible to misinterpretation and thus should be confirmed in writing. The most common example is the spoken promise of a raise or promotion, which is often misinterpreted after a lapse of time.

About 30 percent of a message is lost or distorted after having passed through two people. If a communication is important, the message should be given directly to those affected.

VOICE TONE

Often the tone of our voice will indicate our emotional state to others even if we are not aware of it. To those who know how to interpret them, voice tones can transmit as much or more emotional information as words. Loudly pitched voices can communicate anger no matter how emotionally neutral the dictionary meanings of the words being shouted. Anger can also be conveyed by very intense whispering. The same emotion can be expressed by different tones of voice, and people differ in their reactions to these tones.

Feedback

Feedback influences and interacts with all other parts of the communication process. In computer technology, the term is used to describe a computer's coded responses to messages. These responses are usually very simple: "correct," "incorrect," and "not enough data" are the most common. In this manner the computer tells the source of the message whether the message has been received accurately. In similar fashion, people tell each other whether their messages are being correctly received.

In its narrow usage, feedback means only those specific responses that correct misunderstandings. The following conversation illustrates the concept of corrective feedback:

SPOUSE: You are not interested in bowling tonight?

SUPERVISOR: No, I'd like to go bowling some other time. I'm worried about the work I need to get done for tomorrow.

SPOUSE: You'd like to go bowling, but you're worried about not being prepared tomorrow, and you'd like to spend tonight getting ready.

SUPERVISOR: Yes, that's what I mean.

SPOUSE: Well, I can understand that you wouldn't enjoy bowling with that on your mind. Maybe we can go another time.

Mirroring

When two or more people are talking, each person's emotions influence the other's, and these in turn affect communication. If we parade our tastes, biases, and prejudices as proof of our moral superiority, such behavior is often interpreted as threatening, and serves to distort understanding and cut off communication. A threatening sender automatically puts the receiver on the defensive. When defenses are raised, arguments or silences follow, and good communication ceases.

If we believe that our messages are being received with warmth, respect, and concern, we tend to become more relaxed and more articulate. If our messages are received with signs of coldness, disrespect, and indifference, we become tense and have difficulty in expressing our thoughts. Face-to-face communicators tend to *mirror* each other's moods.

Some of you may feel that you speak well and that none of the above applies to you. Test yourself. The next time you get into an argument with someone, stop for a minute and try Carl Rogers' famous communication game. The only rule is that each person *Restating one's ideas* can speak only after *restating* to the other's satisfaction the ideas *helps in good* and feelings that person has expressed during the argument. In *communication* other words, you have to present the other person's point of view in terms that will be acceptable to him or her.

Once you can satisfactorily state the other person's point of view, you may find that you have to revise your own responses drastically and that the emotional intensities of the argument will decrease. It takes courage to play this game, because you may be forced to change your mind, which for most of us is a humiliating experience. When you can play this game successfully, you are really communicating. You may not reach an agreement—communication does not always bring agreement—but you are communicating, fully and effectively.

FOUR STYLES OF SPEAKERS

Carl Jung's *Psychological Types* is a landmark text for understanding communication problems. The differences in the four basic types of people described by Jung—thinkers, feelers, intuitors, and sensors—may explain why we have difficulty talking with some people and are immediately able to establish rapport with others. As you read these descriptions, try to identify your basic style of communicating.

Thinkers

Thinkers are organized and have the facts

Thinkers can be rigid

Thinkers like to be organized, be structured, and have all the facts before taking action. They seldom reach hasty conclusions, and once they have made a decision, it is final. Thinkers dress conservatively, have an orderly office, and keep accurate records. They give the company a sense of direction and unity. However, thinkers can get bogged down in details, and at their worst they can be rigid and dogmatic. You might know engineers, data-processing specialists, lawyers, or accountants that fit the description.

Feelers

Feelers are adventuresome and empathetic, and at times impulsive and erratic

Feelers are emotional and adventurous, and they love involvement. To these people, the biggest enemy is boredom; they are always trying something new. Feelers tend to be egotistical, but their style is usually warm, and they have real empathy for their employees. Their choices of styles and colors are reflected in their bright, sunny, and optimistic attitudes. Their decisions are based on feelings, however, which can upset subordinates and superiors alike. Many supervisors think that the feelers can be real nuisances when they are impulsive, erratic, or cavalier.

Intuitors

Intuitors are imaginative but are irritated by those who don't understand their futuristic ideas

Intuitors are imaginative and futuristic, and they enjoy mind-testing games. People of other styles are easily irritated by intuitors, and intuitors are often irritated by others. This is because intuitors are impatient with anyone who fails to see the immediate value of their ideas. The technical details relished by the thinkers would bore the intuitors. Often they are rigid, uncompromising, and impractical. There are few intuitors; you may see them as inventors, scientists, researchers, architects, artists, and planners of one type or another.

Sensors

Sensors are moving and goal oriented

Sensors are easy to spot. This style, more than any other, characterizes about 40 percent of our population. Sensors are spirited, moving, and goal minded. Our heroes with the broadest following have always been the Teddy Roosevelts, Amelia Earharts, and John Waynes—the doers and achievers. Sensors enjoy the thrill of the chase plus a fast payoff. Their remedy for feelings of doubt or anxiety is action. Many supervisors are sensors, and so are many of our best athletes. Vince Lombardi, the great NFL coach, adhered to the belief that "winning isn't everything—it's the only thing."

Sensors can react blindly

Sensors demand total loyalty

Sensors are dynamic, but at their worst they react blindly. "Damn the torpedoes!" they may shout, and then steer straight into a financial blunder. Sensors tend to give and demand total loyalty, and if subordinates fail, sensors blame them for being unaggressive.

By understanding our own communicating style, we will know ourselves better and have a better relationship with others. The clues to people's styles are everywhere. A person's home or office is always a giveaway: thinkers are tidy, with everything in its place; intuitors are unpredictable; feelers fill their surroundings with bright colors and personal mementos; and sensors settle for the basics. Even over the telephone, you can quickly tell whether a person sounds like a warm and friendly feeler, an erratic intuitor, an in-a-hurry sensor, or a cautious thinker.

Once you pinpoint someone's style, you can communicate with that person on his or her own particular "channel," rather than on yours. With a sensor businessperson who wants to know the "bottom line," you might speed up the conversation to hit the high points, using sensor catchwords such as *urgent*, *today*, and *results*. For the logical thinker, slow down your conversation and use words such as *cautious*, *specific*, and *analysis*. The visionary intuitor likes the broad sweep of the horizon and words such as *new*, *creative*, and *sensitive*.

Can an understanding of psychological types help you function as a supervisor? Let us look at an example. A supervisor was trying to convince his manager of the value of a new production concept. Operating like the thinker he was, the supervisor had been piling fact upon fact. For some reason the manager would not give her approval. Frustrated, the supervisor thought, "I'm going to give it one last try. I'll dig up every single fact and figure there

TEST YOURSELF

WHAT'S YOUR STYLE?

For a clue to your own communication style, complete this quiz. For each statement, write the number (4) on the line next to the answer that best describes you, write (3) next to the one that relates often to you, (2) next to the one that relates somewhat to you, and (1) next to the one that is least descriptive of you.

1. I like to think of myself as
   _____ a. A doer.
   _____ b. Sympathetic.
   _____ c. Rational.
   _____ d. Creative.
2. I want my career to be
   _____ a. Results oriented, so that my time and energy will be justified.
   _____ b. Concerned with working with and helping other people.
   _____ c. Oriented toward giving my company a sense of direction and unity.
   _____ d. Designed toward contributing something new.
3. My time is important, so I want to make sure that
   _____ a. Something gets accomplished today.
   _____ b. My employees have a fulfilling experience.
   _____ c. I have a well-developed plan for everyone.
   _____ d. My personality and company goals are being developed.
4. I feel satisfied when I can
   _____ a. Accomplish more than I had planned.
   _____ b. Help a friend.
   _____ c. Logically think a problem through to a proper conclusion.
   _____ d. Develop a new idea.
5. When I am promoted, I think it will be because I
   _____ a. Get things done.
   _____ b. Know how to delegate and empathize.
   _____ c. Keep accurate records and obtain all information before making decisions.
   _____ d. Can develop new ideas to help the company.
6. When asked to make a decision, I am likely to
   _____ a. React immediately.
   _____ b. Give my "gut reaction" or make an intuitive decision.
   _____ c. Ask for plenty of time to develop the correct answer.
   _____ d. Want to make my decision without the advice of others.

Now, find the sum of the numbers on the *a* lines, which refer to the sensor style. Then add the numbers on the *b* lines (feeler), *c* lines (thinker), and *d* lines (intuitor). The highest score indicates your primary communicating style, the second-highest your secondary style, and so on.

is, and bombard her till she crumbles." But then he remembered the matter of psychological types. A few moments' thought suggested that his boss was a person of action—a doer, a sensor. "Why don't I let her take action, then?" the supervisor reflected. He left his facts and figures behind, and returned to his manager's office. "Kathy," he said, "you're in charge here. You're the one who decides what happens next. I can start the new process in two weeks, if you want me to. Just let me know what you decide." The manager asked a few questions, and within five minutes she gave her approval. And she added, with a smile, "I was wondering when you'd get around to letting *me* make up my mind!"

NONVERBAL COMMUNICATION

Nonverbal communication is communication

Nonverbal communication, despite popular belief, is indeed communication. Many individuals think that communication occurs only when a written or verbal expression is conveyed. This is far from the truth, since nonverbal communication frequently carries more importance than verbal messages. For example, facial expressions, body posture, clothing, appearance, body movements, behavior, and physical structure serve as vehicles for sending messages.

Frequently, nonverbal messages contradict verbal messages, thus creating a communication paradox. Supervisors must be cautious in sending and receiving messages to avoid such contradictions. An employee experiences frustration when the message is interpreted in a manner other than that which was intended. This can lead to morale problems and general dissatisfaction. Think of

---

A COMMUNICATION PARADOX

Each day, the maître d' of a famous French restaurant comes to work dressed impeccably: A tuxedo, cuff links, and patent leather shoes are indicative of his first-class appearance. The restaurant's decor is in keeping with the maître d's style of dress. It is highly ornamental, with bronze, silver, and gold furnishings meticulously placed throughout the facility.

Each waiter and waitress is required to wear appropriate attire consistent with the existing environment. At a recent orientation for newly hired waiters and waitresses, the maître d' emphasized the critical need to dress and act properly at all times. He also mentioned the importance of treating customers with the utmost dignity and respect. He ended the orientation by telling the waiters and waitresses, "If you have any problems, please feel free to bring them to my attention. My door is always open; we are very informal around here."

an employee who is given job instructions and carries them out as they are understood, only to discover that something else was expected. The employee runs the risk of reprimand and poor evaluation, even though the intention was to follow the directive with proper attitude and enthusiasm.

Supervisors must be equally adept at interpreting nonverbal feedback, which is an integral part of the communication process. Frequently, peers and subordinates will relay signals of understanding during the transmission phase. At this critical point, supervisors must be able to decipher facial expressions, gestures, and other nonverbal cues given during the message exchange. Expressions relaying confusion, misunderstanding, disillusionment, or frustration cannot be camouflaged. Hence supervisors must train themselves to interpret these valuable signals. Unique awareness of this aspect provides the manager with a dual feedback mechanism to correct the existing communication misunderstanding while preventing subsequent problems.

Supervisors must interpret nonverbal cues

COMMUNICATION OBSTACLES

Unfortunately, communication problems can occur without provocation. The communication system is so dynamic that it is particularly vulnerable to a multitude of problems extremely difficult to prevent. Supervisors must thus constantly work at preventing miscommunication. Success or failure in communication depends on the supervisor's ability to control the major obstacles that can occur at all stages of the communication process. Control may not be gained quickly since it is the culmination of practice, effort, and a desire to communicate accurately and effectively.

Supervisors must work to control communication obstacles

To avoid communication obstacles, it is imperative to become familiar with some of the major barriers:

Value Judgments

Many individuals have a tendency to judge a statement that in fact requires no judgmental action. For example, consider the following dialogue between a supervisor and a worker:

WORKER: I can't wait until tonight. I am picking up my brand-new motorcycle. I've been waiting so long for this day to arrive.

SUPERVISOR: You're getting a motorcycle? Have you lost your mind? What will you do when it rains—get wet? Nobody with any sense would buy a motorcycle.

WORKER: (Says nothing, shrugs shoulders, and slowly walks away in a dejected manner.)

This conversation points to the danger in making an unnecessary value judgment. In this instance, all the supervisor needed to do was acknowledge that the employee had bought a new motorcycle. Instead, the supervisor's comments depressed the employee. Furthermore, the employee reasoned that if a reprimand resulted from such a happy occasion, even worse could be expected for a mistake on the job. The employee therefore decided to avoid future communication with the supervisor.

Language

Supervisors frequently falsely assume that workers will understand what they mean. As a result, they do not choose words with caution and selectivity. Consequently, the result can be confusion and misunderstanding. Consider the following dialogue:

BOSS: I'd like you to come into my office and take a letter.
SECRETARY: All right, I'll take *E*.

Choose your words carefully

This humorous example points out how easily misunderstood language can lead to faulty conclusions. Needless to say, the boss did not want the secretary to pick a letter of the alphabet, but rather intended to dictate a letter of correspondence. Words must be chosen carefully to ensure that proper meaning is conveyed. Consider the consequences when poor wording is selected when issuing a job directive. In addition to the workers becoming frustrated, the organization experiences a negative contribution.

Listening

Listening is an active, not a passive, activity

Many people fail to realize that listening is an active, not a passive, activity. It can be described as a combination of (1) *hearing*—the physical reception of sound; (2) *comprehending*—the interpretation and understanding of the message; and (3) *remembering*—the retention of what has been heard.

How many times have you had a conversation with someone but not heard a word that was said? Have you ever wanted to shake someone and force him or her to pay attention to you while you were speaking? Most people have such experiences from time to time. Listening is a form of *paying attention,* which is an active process involving much more than hearing and seeing. When we pay attention to each other, we are *focusing* our awareness on what is being said to the exclusion of other external and internal stimuli.

Most people are enchanted by the sound of their own voices and would much rather be talking than listening. In fact, some psychological studies have shown that we think favorably of those people who encourage us to talk and who appear to be very interested in what we have to say. The more people agree with what we say, the smarter they seem to us. This facet of human behavior can work to either the advantage or the disadvantage of a salesperson.

The salespeople who listened were the most successful

One sales manager tried to judge the percentage of the sales presentation dialogue that was carried out by his own salespeople and the percentage done by prospective clients, who were generally hospital purchasing agents, heads of housekeeping, and department heads. He found that there was usually an inverse correlation between the amount of talking by his salespeople and the amount of the resulting order. The "high-percentage talkers" tended to be the newer people in the field, while the "low-percentage talkers" were the more experienced and successful ones.

Poor listening skills pose several problems that hinder individual and organizational performance. Listening problems can be grouped into three categories:

1. Divided listening
2. Poor listening
3. Selective listening

DIVIDED LISTENING

Divided listening can lead to only partial understanding

Divided listening occurs when an individual fails to commit undivided attention to the communicator. When a worker enters the boss's office to reveal a personal problem and the boss continues to work on an expense report while the worker is talking, the boss is guilty of divided listening. Because the boss has divided the listening between the worker and the expense report, partial understanding may result. This presents a dual disaster. In addition to the partially understood message, the worker experiences feelings of worthlessness and unimportance, since the manager failed to provide undivided attention. Future communication may be seriously impaired.

POOR LISTENING

Poor listening habits are the result of not realizing the importance of every piece of communication. Like a puzzle, if one piece of communication is missing, the picture is not complete. It is easy to listen only superficially and not seriously consider the implications

Listening is an active process of what the other person is saying. Listening is an active and not a passive process. We have to listen to everything that is being said to get the full picture.

SELECTIVE LISTENING

Selective listening has two variations:

1. Hearing what you want to hear
2. Hearing what you would like to hear

Hearing What You Want to Hear A supervisor informs the work group, "Profits are up, but so are expenses. Raises may be affected." Some employees may interpret the statement to mean that raises will be affected by the higher profits. The phenomenon of selective listening serves to filter out the fact that expenses have also increased, which means that raises may be lower than expected.

Hearing What You Would Like to Hear A worker asks for tomorrow off. The manager responds by saying, "I'll think about it." Because the worker did not receive an outright negative answer, through selective listening the person can believe that the request was granted.

There are no specific rules for effective listening, because what may work well for one person may not work well for another. However, certain general guidelines will help you listen more successfully:

Good Listening Habits

1. *Listen without evaluating.* Avoid passing judgment. A listener who is not critical, evaluative, or moralizing creates an atmosphere of understanding, acceptance, and warmth.
2. *Do not anticipate.* Sometimes we think we know what people are going to say before they say it, and we say it for them. Often we are wrong. Do not anticipate the next moment; stay in the present and listen.
3. *Do not try to retain everything.* Listen for the major points being made. Don't try to memorize details as you listen.
4. *Do not fake attention.* The same time and energy used to fake attention can be better invested in *really* paying attention.
5. *Do not be a "know-it-all."* Often a supervisor assumes an air of superiority, which hampers communication.
6. *Review.* Periodically review what has already been said.

Authority and Status

Some individuals tend to attach an undeserved degree of accuracy to communication emerging from a source of high authority or status. This obstacle can handicap the communication process. Keep in mind that while following directives, policies, procedures, practices, and rules are essential, blind obedience can be detrimental.

Status can hinder upward communication

Communication obstacles can also emerge when lower-level individuals are afraid to communicate with upper levels because of the aura associated with authority and status. Such a circumstance not only serves as a communication obstacle but also hinders the flow of upward communication.

Perceptions

Have you experienced the frustration of learning a new process? Have you told your supervisor, "I don't understand," and had the supervisor proceed to tell you exactly what he or she said, using the same terms, after which you still don't understand? Part of the problem is that we always perceive the situation from our own vantage point. Our perceptions of what we see, hear, read, or feel are based on our own experiences, background, and culture.

Try reading the message in Figure 15–4. Not everyone will be able to read it. For the person who cannot, having it repeated in exactly the same manner will not necessarily increase understanding.

The person who knows how to read the message in Figure 15–4 finds the task to be easy. In the same way, the experienced supervisor may believe that the procedure he or she follows is simple because he or she has been doing it for many years. The jargon used is customary for the people in the field. Psychologically this person is attuned to the problem and has had many experiences related to it. Were he or she to explain the procedure to you, however, you might not have the background or perceptions related to the subject to follow the explanation. The chosen

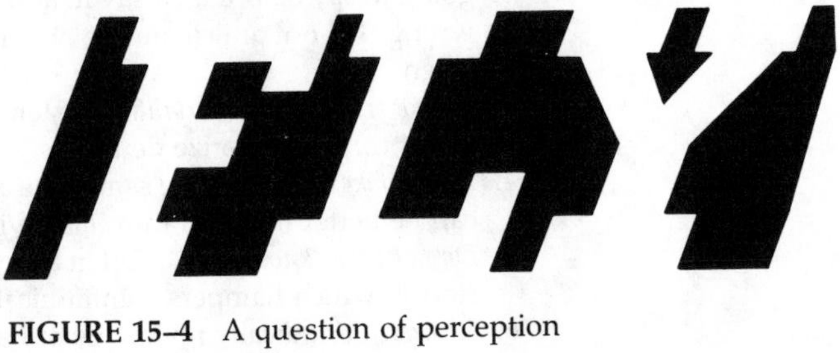

FIGURE 15–4   A question of perception

words might be inappropriate and probably insufficient. Understanding the employee's background, semantics, and perceptions is very important in helping the supervisor find a way to communicate.

Our role and position in the organization greatly influences the way we perceive circumstances on the job. Consider the following example. After 35 years of faithful service, the top sales representative decides to retire. The retirement can be perceived in various ways, depending on the person's status in the organization:

1. *Sales manager:* Views the retirement as the loss of an experienced, dedicated, and effective salesperson.
2. *Human resource manager:* Views the retirement as a problem since a replacement must be found.
3. *Benefits administrator:* Views the retirement as a headache since retirement calculations and loads of paperwork must be processed.
4. *Peer worker 1:* Views the retirement as the loss of a good friend and confidant.
5. *Peer worker 2:* Views the retirement as an opportunity to move up and obtain a better sales territory.
6. *Peer worker 3:* Views the retirement as a cause to celebrate since this worker and the retiree had many disagreements over the years.

Perception, indeed, is an individual phenomenon.

Generalizations

Effective communicators avoid generalizations

To simplify a complex world, individuals tend to categorize, group, or stereotype information into predictable cases or patterns. Such generalizations are often improperly and randomly applied to people, groups, places, and things. Such arbitrary applications can lead to dangerous conclusions. Many people have stereotyped views about ethnic groups, union leaders, politicians, athletes, lawyers, and others. Effective communicators are able to remove such generalizations from their communication patterns, and deal with people and groups on an objective and individual basis.

Defensiveness

Putting someone on the defense or being on the defense is a barrier that can lead to dual distortion. A defensive attitude may cause an individual to be tense and hence unable to express thoughts and ideas properly and fully. It is always advisable to establish a proper climate for communication. Taking a few mo-

---

YOGI BERRA'S BEST "YOGI-ISMS"

1. When he was honored at Yogi Berra Night in St. Louis: "I want to thank all those who made this night necessary."
2. To a young player trying to emulate the batting style of a veteran: "If you can't imitate him, don't copy him."
3. About a popular Minneapolis restaurant: "Nobody goes there anymore, it's too crowded."
4. Talking about a pennant race: "It's not over until it's over."
5. Explaining why left field in Yankee Stadium is difficult to play when shadows fall during day games in October: "It gets late early out there."
6. Explaining declining attendance in Kansas City: "If people don't want to come to the ball park, how are you gonna stop them?"
7. Explaining in 1964 why he expected to be a successful rookie manager with the Yankees despite his lack of managerial experience: "You observe a lot by watching."
8. When asked what he does on the afternoon of a night game: "I usually take a two-hour nap, from one o'clock to four."
9. In an argument with an umpire who ruled that a ball hit a concrete outfield wall and was thus in play, while Berra said that it hit a wooden barricade beyond the wall and was thus a home run: "Anybody who can't tell the difference between a ball hitting wood and a ball hitting concrete must be blind."

Note: Yogi Berra was an all-star catcher for the New York Yankees and former major-league manager. He is reported to have a "unique" way with words.

---

ments to put the person at ease enhances the prospect of effective communication.

COMMUNICATION CHANNELS

All companies have formal communications

Formal communication chains determine the direction and flow of official messages among members of an organization and are an integral part of any company structure. These chains stem from the rules and customs governing the distribution of authority, rank, and type of work within the organization.

The grapevine is an informal channel

Informal communication channels are created by friendships and social associations within the work place. The channel known as the grapevine is perhaps the most important informal channel.

Communication channels have been compared to the nervous systems of organisms, because they perform the same function. Both carry messages, or impulses, from one place to another to keep the organism, or company, informed about any changes in the internal or external environment.

Downward Communications

The most common flow of communication is downward

The most common flow of communication in organizations is downward. It usually starts at or near the top, and disseminates through the levels until it reaches its ultimate destination. This is a powerful flow of information since messages from the top usually carry the weight of authority. The major purpose of downward communication is to inform, assign, describe, and direct the work flow by means of policies, procedures, instructions, and rules. Downward communication also serves to monitor employee performance.

Generally, downward communication tends to be broad and general during its initial stage at the top of the organization. A unique characteristic of downward communication is the detail it picks up as it descends through the levels. For example, suppose top management is dissatisfied with employee attendance. A broad directive is initiated at the top that informs lower levels to control the problem. In turn, each specific manager talks to supervisors, who talk to individual workers about the problem.

Downward communication is the fastest

Downward communication is the fastest form in the vertical chain of communication. It is accepted at face value and is reacted to vigorously.

The importance of downward communication can be appreciated as we look at its types and purposes. In their book, *The Social Psychology of Organization,* noted theorists Daniel Katz and Robert L. Kahn indicate that there are five types of communication from supervisor to employee:

1. Communication about task and job instructions
2. Communication about the rationale and purpose of the job
3. Communication about company procedures and practices
4. Communication about worker performance
5. Communication about company goals and objectives[1]

Although downward communication is essential and works in a somewhat efficient manner, it has some major drawbacks. Directives issued by top management pass down with little direct contact between the top and bottom levels. Thus the lower levels feel isolated and removed from the top echelons, and their feelings of importance are diminished. Also, downward communication from top management runs the risk of misinterpretation since other members of the organization are relied upon to convey the message.

---

[1] Daniel Katz and Robert L. Kahn, *The Social Psychology of Organization* (New York: John Wiley & Sons, 1978).

Another problem in downward communiqués is that supervisors understanding of the problems of their subordinates may not be accurate. Fundamental differences in perception tend to exist at each level in an organization, thereby making communication more difficult.

Supervisors may not know the problems of their employees

Some employees are best informed through written communication, and some are best informed orally. Some must be told repeatedly before the message makes an impression. Tender topics, such as the firing of an employee or the arbitration of conflicts between workers, are best handled in person rather than in writing. When emotions are high or financial stakes are great, face-to-face communications are a must.

Handle emotional problems in person

Some information can only be effectively handled in a downward flow. But organizations cannot exclusively rely on downward communication. They must learn to use it for its maximum potential, while cultivating other directional flows.

Upward Communication

Upward communication occurs when someone in a lower position in the organizational hierarchy passes along information, suggestions, opinions, or grievances to someone higher. Examples of upward communication include

1. Advancing ideas, suggestions, and input
2. Requesting help
3. Expressing feelings, attitudes, and morale
4. Providing feedback

A typist dropping a suggestion in the suggestion box, a supervisor reporting a machinery breakdown to the plant manager, or a copywriter suggesting a sales campaign to the advertising manager are all launching upward communication.

Upward communications are briefer and more guarded

Upward communication occurs less frequently than downward communication. It tends to be briefer and is designed to protect the employee from any possible backlash. Therefore, such communication may lack some facts that are needed to present the superior with the total picture.

Upward communication serves as a reflector to top management by providing it with information pertaining to the workers' attitudes and morale. It also generates ideas, suggestions, and input from lower levels. All levels of management must work diligently to create an atmosphere that permits, fosters, and encourages upward communication.

Unhealthy organizations stifle upward communication. Unless management takes special measures and precautions, upward communication may not exist. If an organization desires to be healthy, it must establish a prescription for upward communication. It must openly seek and actively respond to such communication or it will be terminated. There is no automatic quality to upward communication. This is in direct contradiction to downward communication, since management can inform all employees about a particular matter by issuing a directive. Employees must want to send upward messages, which will only be sent if the climate is conducive to receiving such information. Why should employees talk if top management fails to listen?

Horizontal Communication

Horizontal channels are used when members at the same level of authority communicate with each other. These channels operate both formally and informally, and officially and unofficially. Examples of horizontal communication include

1. Committees and task forces
2. Conferences and departmental meetings
3. Quality circles and other participative management techniques
4. Project groups
5. Inter- and intradepartmental communication
6. Peer communication within the same work group

A sales manager who tells a plant manager to increase production next month because a clever advertising campaign has paid off and sales are pouring in uses formal channels for the message. But the plant manager may have given the idea for the campaign to the sales manager at lunch a few months previously, which is surely an informal situation. Many workers and supervisors use informal horizontal channels often and with great success. They rely on friendships and favors as means of ignoring or expediting requests, evading rules, or changing the work flow. Table 15–1 shows these kinds of communication.

Horizontal communication represents management's plans to secure a lateral flow of communication to promote efficient coordination. For functional units within the organization to achieve their maximum, they must interact with each other. This can only occur if top management establishes conditions fostering horizontal communication. Like upward communication, it will not happen on its own. Management must take the initiative to establish a network for this purpose. For example, the production department, marketing department, and research department all benefit

TABLE 15–1   Examples of communication channels

Downward	Upward	Horizontal
Top management policy	Suggestion programs	Work-flow contacts
Decisions	Grievances	Committees
Orders and directives	Surveys	Quality circles
Instructions	Performance reports	Interoffice memos
Procedures	Self-evaluation	Staff meetings
Strategies	Committees	Wider distribution of written reports
Bulletins	Quality circles	
Performance evaluations	Participative management	
Reprimands	Exit interviews	

from budgeting information provided by the accounting department in a horizontal fashion.

Absence of horizontal communication can result in a multitude of problems, including

1. A lack of cooperation among organizational members and departments
2. An unwillingness to share vital information
3. A tendency to engage in empire building
4. A misunderstanding of departmental roles and purposes
5. A feeling of departmental isolation
6. A likelihood to develop tunnel vision in thought and actions
7. A high probability of not appreciating the work of others
8. A failure to see the total organizational picture

Diagonal Communication

Diagonal communication leads to maximum efficiency

Diagonal communication is a unique directional flow. It purposefully disregards the chain of command to cut through the organizational structure (see Figure 15–5). The purpose of diagonal communication is to provide staff and advisory-type information that will improve the effectiveness and efficiency of the organization. If cultivated properly, this channel of information has no substitute. Although many organizations exist and prosper without it, maximum efficiency can be achieved through the proper use of diagonal communication.

Examples of diagonal communication include

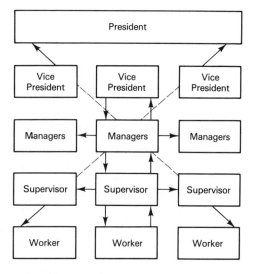

FIGURE 15-5 Organizational communication flow

1. Staff specialists who provide expert opinions and information to other departments
2. Advice that freely flows from one individual or department to another individual or department, regardless of the source or destination

Informal Channels of Communication

Informal communications grow out of the social interactions among people who work together. Informal relationships are complex and change rapidly. A major function of informal channels is to provide communication routes for members of small groups. Every successful business has at least one healthy, if invisible, channel to conduct the messages of its informal organization. This mysterious entity is the *real* organization—the means of coordinating people's energies to solve problems and get things accomplished.

The importance of informal communication is discussed in the best-selling book *In Search of Excellence*. The authors, Thomas Peters and Robert Waterman, report some of the informal communication practices of successful companies:

- *Corning Glass:* This company installed escalators instead of elevators to promote more face-to-face contact.
- *Walt Disney Productions:* Everyone, including the president, wears a name tag that bears only his or her first name.

GO WITH THE FLOW

Profit and loss statements recently compiled by the finance department revealed that the company had exceeded all sales and profit goals for the fiscal year. At the monthly management meeting, the president expressed delight and indicated that all employees should be rewarded for their excellent effort. It was suggested that employees receive an extra paid holiday in addition to a salary bonus.

The president assigned the human resource director the task of determining whether the day should be Christmas Eve or New Year's Eve. The personnel director was asked to determine this information as quickly as possible so that production scheduling could be implemented accordingly.

Shortly after the president left the meeting, the human resource director discussed the matter with department managers and supervisors to determine the most equitable way of allowing the employees to choose the holiday of preference.

The next morning, employees were informed of the salary bonus and asked to vote on which day they wish to be their paid holiday. After the votes were tabulated, the president was informed that workers had selected Christmas Eve as the holiday. The president issued an official memo to that effect.

In the situation described above, indicate examples of

1. Downward communication
2. Upward communication
3. Horizontal communication
4. Diagonal communication

- *Levi Strauss Co.:* This company refers to its open-door policy as "the fifth freedom."
- *IBM:* The open-door policy is a vital part of the company philosophy. The chairman continues to answer all complaints that come to him from any employee.[2]

Occasionally, communication channels may be structured to appear informal when in truth they are not. The so-called informal contacts that supervisors are sometimes *required* to maintain with subordinates are an example. When supervisors are ordered to associate with workers socially, a true informal channel seldom emerges, and communications remain formal and perhaps even stilted. A supervisor's success often depends on the degree to which he or she accepts and uses the existing informal channels.

---

[2] Thomas J. Peters and Robert H. Waterman, Jr., *In Search of Excellence* (New York: Harper and Row, 1982), pp. 319–355.

One company spent much time and money publishing a company newsletter on glossy paper with beautiful photographs. It contained items such as "Mary B. receives a five-year pin" and "Steve H. has a new addition to his family." Yet morale remained poor, so consultants were called in. They found that the employees were not as interested in personal news as they were in company contract prospects and explanations of the profit-sharing plan.

The consultants suggested abandoning the company newsletter and starting a program resembling the "Personnel Council" at Pitney-Bowes. Pitney-Bowes, which boasts very low absenteeism and turnover, has monthly forums, known as Personnel Councils, during which representatives of management and employees sit down to discuss mutual problems and opportunities. The minutes are then posted for all to read. At one meeting employees received answers to questions such as "Can we have more pictures on the cafeteria walls?", "What happens when a promoted employee can't perform his or her new job?", and "Why haven't our insurance claims been settled?"

Studies show that workers receive 60 percent of their technical information from informal sources. The right conditions for informal meetings among people can be created. One way is to remove coffeepots from separate offices and substitute a central coffee area where people from different units can meet informally.

The Grapevine

The grapevine is the unofficial news carrier

The grapevine is a universal method of transmitting messages by unofficial means. Graffiti on ancient Roman walls and modern buildings and messages tapped out by prisoners are examples of a grapevine.

The communication chains formed by friendship cliques or casual associations, which carry daily gossip at work, are frequently used grapevines. In a large and complex organization there can be hundreds of these chains that carry information that is not or cannot be transmitted by formal means. An example is one employee telling another, "I wouldn't ask for that raise today, if I were you. The boss is in a foul mood, and you'd better wait until her mood changes."

Periods of instability or excitement in the organization, layoffs, and rumors of impending automation or electronic data processing all tend to foster an active grapevine. At such times, supervisors should take care to "feed" accurate information to the grapevine. This keeps the rumor level down from the fever pitch that could interfere with morale or production rates.

Rumors

What are rumors? Communications expert Gordon Mc-Closkey defines rumors as "any careless or malicious dissemination of inaccurate facts or impressions which tend to evoke irrational individual or group responses." Gordon Allport and Leo Postman, in their extensive studies, discovered that rumors develop and grow in direct relationship with their importance to people and with the lack of news on the subject from official channels.

Lack of official news causes rumors to grow

What can management do when untrue and malicious reports are circulating? One approach has been to use a rumor control center, which proponents believe can squelch rumors. This concept was used by Serv-Air Aviation Corporation in North Carolina during the 1950s. This company mounted two bulletin boards within an old outhouse: one board was used for rumors and the other for officials' replies. In a two-month period, more than 100 questions were answered. When weeks went by without a posted rumor, the officials staged a mock funeral for the outhouse.

Employees tend to believe the first message they hear. If false rumors run through the grapevine before the company releases an official statement, the employees will tend to believe the rumor regardless of how convincing the official presentation sounds. If the official word reaches them first, employees will tend to ignore rumors. When a supervisor discovers that rumors are beginning to circulate, he or she should make an official announcement immediately.

Stop rumors quickly

Supervisors wishing to stop rumor mongering should concern themselves only with the important ones: those affecting morale and productivity. Immediate face-to-face conversations or group meetings are the best methods for stopping dangerous rumors from spreading.

Upward-moving rumors can provide managers with an understanding of the emotional feelings of the work force. Supervisors who ask questions such as "What does that rumor mean—is someone insecure and afraid of being fired?" or "Is someone really quitting?" are often provided with truthful answers via the grapevine.

Rumors can be projections of fears

Labor relations mediators are always careful to listen to the rumors that union officials and company officials spread about each other. They believe that such rumors are projections of fears and that if they can learn what each side is afraid of, they can better understand the complex issues.

An Effective Supervisor Is a Listening Supervisor

Every supervisor should become a communications expert, one who thinks before he or she speaks or writes, gets plenty of feedback, and is a good listener. Ralph Nichols of Loyola University made a study on effective management. The most common report he received from the thousands of employees who testified that they liked their supervisors ran this way: "I like my boss. He (or she) listens to me. I can talk to him (or her)."

SUMMARY

Communication is the process by which information and understanding are transferred from one person to another. Effective communication enables people to exercise control over their environment. It is an essential tool for the establishment and maintenance of good social and working relationships. If the messages being communicated are not understood, then communication is poor or nonexistent.

The semantic content of a message is always subjective, because meanings reside in people, not in words. A word has meaning only in the significance it has for both the speaker and the listener, and that significance varies greatly from person to person. In good communication you must pay as much attention to the tone of the speaker as to the verbal message itself.

The obstacles to communication must be understood and overcome. Listening is an active, not a passive, activity. To listen effectively, you must pay strict attention.

Understanding the four basic styles of speaking may help you converse more effectively. Some people are *thinkers*, who are well organized and slow in making decisions. Some are *feelers*, who like to be adventurous, and are involved with people and their problems. Such people may be impulsive and cavalier. The *intuitor* is imaginative and creative, but also impatient and uncompromising. The *sensor* is a fast-moving, goal-minded achiever. Sensors demand loyalty and may act blindly. Developing your style of speech to match the styles of others may be a way of establishing that special rapport.

Most downward communication consists of orders and information for subordinates. This type of formal communication gets the quickest results. Upward communication tends to be briefer and is formed to protect the employee. Horizontal communication can be formal or informal, but tends to be more truthful than vertical communications. Diagonal communication cuts through the organizational structure, and provides staff and advisory-type information.

The grapevine is the unofficial carrier of informal communication. Rumors may develop and grow because of the lack of official news. Rumors tend to be malicious and inaccurate, and attempt to evoke individual or group response. Supervisors wishing to stop rumor mongering should try to stop only rumors that are important: those affecting morale and productivity. Conversations and group meetings are the best methods for ending dangerous rumors, and truth is the best weapon against them.

CASE STUDY 37

Talking over Their Heads

Ray Duncan is program director at a summer camp for boys. The camp works in conjunction with juvenile homes in neighboring counties and operates for 10 weeks each summer. Counselors, who work at the camp on a volunteer basis, are concerned citizens from the local area.

Bob Moreau is one of the volunteers. He works in the arts-and-crafts room on a rotating schedule and has been doing so since the camp opened three weeks ago. Unfortunately, though, Bob and the boys are having trouble communicating.

Ray is aware of these difficulties. On several occasions he has overhead the boys' conversations concerning Bob. One comment that he remembers went like this: "He always knows the best way to do something, regardless of what anyone else thinks. He wasn't even listening to my idea. And how about all the jargon he throws at you? Half the guys sit there and act like they understand him. Who are they kidding?"

Ray sat in on one of Bob's sessions and soon realized that there was indeed a problem. Instructing a group on woodcarving techniques, Bob tended to be impatient with questions he felt were not reasonable. In addition, he seemed stern and withdrawn, and his use of vocabulary was sometimes far beyond the boys' understanding. Now Ray could understand some of the hostility the boys felt toward Bob.

Ray naturally feels that he must talk to Bob about this problem, as the purpose of the camp is to provide a pleasant and friendly atmosphere for the boys.

QUESTIONS

1. What is Bob's general problem in communicating with the boys?
2. What steps can he take to improve his method of communicating?
3. How would you approach Bob?
4. Should this problem be discussed personally with Bob, or should it be a general topic during a staff meeting?

CASE STUDY 38

There's a Rumor About My Promotion

Lois Hackaday has worked for the Denver branch of the Tamlon Corporation for three years and is now a junior executive in the Engineering Department. She has just returned from a two-week vacation.

This morning Randy Meyers, a co-worker and good friend, stops Lois on her way into the building. "Congratulations, Lois! From what I hear, apparently you'll be in your own office soon."

"What are you talking about, Randy? I'm not due for a promotion yet."

"I didn't think you were, but the rumor is that Mr. Lundquist is going to promote you."

This information puzzles Lois. She knows there are others in line for promotion before her. But she knows her work is good, and a promotion at this time would be ideal, for she is about to be married. With the promotion she could consider purchasing a new home.

In the hallway Lois passes Mr. Lundquist, who greets her but says nothing about a promotion.

That evening, as Lois prepares to leave work, Mary Stewart, a co-worker in the department, asks, "Is it true that you'll be leaving us soon, Lois? I heard that you were being transferred to the Atlanta branch this summer."

"I haven't been told anything about it. Where did you hear about it?" she asked.

"Oh, I don't know, someone mentioned it last week and said to keep it quiet until you got back. The word is that you'll be promoted and transferred to the Atlanta branch."

"But don't you think someone would have said something to me by now?" inquires Lois.

"It sure seems so," answers Mary. "I suppose it could be another false rumor."

This information has Lois concerned. She'd like a promotion, but the last thing she wants right now is a transfer. If you were Lois, would you:

QUESTIONS

1. Ask Mr. Lundquist directly about the rumor?

2. Ignore the rumor and go ahead with your plans?

3. Try to track down the source of the rumor?

4. Discuss your personal plans with Mr. Lundquist?

5. Try some other ways of checking the validity of the rumor? How would you go about this?

CASE STUDY 39

"Phone-y" Communication

Your company is considering a policy requiring all managers and supervisors to answer their own phones. Arguments that favor the policy suggest it will speed up communication, since most calls are for these people anyway. It was also suggested that the policy will increase efficiency since secretaries will have more time to do other work. Additionally, it will create a feeling of informality.

QUESTIONS

1. What other benefits are associated with the policy?
2. What disadvantages exist?
3. Do you favor this plan? Why or why not?

CASE STUDY 40

One-Way Meetings

You have been a supervisor for four years. Last month you were promoted and transferred to another department. During the past two weeks, you have had two meetings with your workers and you are confused; you did all the talking and they did not get involved. They do not participate in the discussions in the way the workers did in your previous department. You view the meetings as a vehicle for identifying and solving problems while building teamwork. You also anticipate receiving feedback about your ideas. Your subordinates' lack of participation concerns you greatly.

QUESTIONS

1. What are some of the reasons for the above circumstance?
2. What course of action should you employ?
3. Could the problem be your fault? If so, how?

Terms and Concepts Supervisors Should Know

Communication obstacles; Diagonal communication; Feedback; Feelers; Formal communication; Grapevine; Horizontal communication; Intuitors; Lateral communication; Informal communication; Mirroring; Nonverbal communication; Perceptions; Role problems; Rumors; Sensors; Status problems; Thinkers.

Questions for Discussion

1. Find a topic in the news today. Team up with a classmate and discuss your point of view; then have the listener "mirror" those views. The listener must accurately express your own views before discussing his or her own views.
2. Discuss Jung's psychological types of speakers. What kind of speaker are you? What type is your supervisor? Can you better understand your supervisor when you understand his or her style of speaking? Can you—and should you—alter yours to match his or hers? Can you help him or her understand your point of departure?
3. Which is the best way for downward communications to reach your staff: in writing, orally, or through a combination of the two? Why?
4. Which is the best way for you to communicate with your supervisor: orally or in writing? When is the best time to communicate with him or her—in the early morning or late in the afternoon?
5. In your company, who is most likely to spread information through the grapevine? Why? Should you try to stop it? Why?

For Further Reading—And More Ideas

Ahearn, B., "Employee Communications," Personnel (July–August 1982).

Anderson, E. M., "Communication Patterns: A Tool for Memorable Leadership Training," Training (January 1984).

Barry, R. A., "Crisis Communications: What to Do When the Roof Falls in," Business Marketing (March 1984).

Bell, G. R., "Listen and You Shall Hear," Association Management (March 1984).

Budd, J. F., Jr., "Is the Focus of Communication on Target?" Sloan Management Review (Fall 1982).

Byers, J. B., "Five-Step Checklist Helps Communicate Goals," Supervision (June 1982).

D'Aprix, R., "The Oldest and Best Way to Communicate with Employees," Harvard Business Review (September–October 1982).

DiGaetani, J. L., "A Systems Solution to Communication Problems," Business Horizons (September–October 1983).

Dunn, D. H., "How to Grab—and Hold—an Audience," Business Week (April 3, 1989).

Fahs, M. L., "Communication Strategies for Anticipating and Managing Conflict," Personnel Administrator (October 1982).

Fisher, D. W., "A Model for Better Communication," Supervisory Management (June 1982).

Foltz, R. G., "Communication Concerns," Personnel Administrator (September 1982).

Halatin, T., "Upward Communication," Supervisory Management (October 1982).

Harris, R. D., "Communications and the Supervisor," Supervision (October 1982).

Katz, Daniel, and Robert L. Kahn, The Social Psychology of Organization, New York: John Wiley & Sons, 1978.

Kikoski, J. F., and J. A. Litterer, "Effective Communication in Performance Appraisal Interview," Public Personnel Management (Spring 1983).

Kimbell, J. A., Jr., "Some Thoughts on Communications," Journal of Accountancy (March 1984).

Leipzig, J. S., and E. More, "Organizational Communication: A Review and Analysis to Three Current Approaches to the Field," Journal of Business Communication (Fall 1982).

Lipert, F. G., "Communications Up?" Supervision (March 1984).

Lutz, W., "Doublespeak (Political Language)," Public Relations Quarterly (Winter 1988–89).

Lyncott, W. J., "The Upward Communication Barrier," Supervision (December 1983).

McKenzie, C. L., and C. J. Qazi, "Communication Barriers in the Workplace," Business Horizons (March–April 1983).

Peters, Thomas J., and Robert H. Waterman, Jr., In Search of Excellence, New York: Harper and Row, 1982.

Reznik, L. B., "Balancing Your Life (Reducing Stress Through Compromise and Communication: Interview with L. Shapiro and J. Shapiro)," *Business Credit* (November 1988).

Savage, W. G., "Sharpening Your Communication," *Management World* (August 1982).

Smith, R., and R. Ross, "Learing to Be a Great Communicator," *Journal of Property Management* (January–February 1989).

St. John, W. D., "Successful Communications Between Supervisor and Employees," *Personnel Journal* (January 1983).

Thomas, J. G., "Communication: New Thoughts on an Old Subject," *Supervisory Management* (April 1982).

Wackowski, S., "The Trend Toward Language Simplification," *Bank Marketing* (September 1983).

Decision Making and Problem Solving

16

"Where do we go from here?"

LEARNING OBJECTIVES

When you complete this chapter, you should be able to:
1. Explain the different types of decisions.
2. Describe and give examples of the problem-solving aids that a supervisor may use.
3. Describe the differences between humanistic and environmental approaches to decision making.
4. Define and give examples of the fundamental steps in decision making.
5. Discus the various ways in which the following personality traits influence decision making: ability to take risks, attitudes toward success and failure, decisiveness, ability to decide on the basis of experience, willingness to seek advice, and ability to take a break when you are stuck.
6. Discuss the advantages and disadvantages of the two types of centralized decision making: one-person decisions and group decisions.
7. Understand the process and benefits of quality circles.

"Learn to act—not react!"

While reading this chapter, give some consideration to the following questions. Some answers can be drawn from personal experiences, others from the text, and still others from a combination of the two.

Why is management so concerned with decision making?

How can you improve your ability to make decisions?

How can the manager or supervisor make sure that his or her subordinates have practice in making decisions?

Is it ever possible to correct a bad decision? Can you think of any examples?

What might be some early indicators of a bad decision?

Can decision making involve emotions, past experiences, prejudices, and personality traits?

Is problem solving a process concerned with the concrete realities of a specific situation?

WHY DO I HAVE TO MAKE DECISIONS?

Supervisors and managers spend a great deal of time making decisions and solving problems. As a matter of fact, the two roles that best describe a supervisor or a manager are those of decision maker and a problem solver. They represent the major activities for which a supervisor is paid, and in many ways serve to measure the degree of success attained. There is no substitute for good decision making.

All too often the busy, day-to-day hustle of supervisory demands forces hasty decisions. Sometimes these decisions are made with incomplete data. A supervisor must rise above this type of situation and employ systematic approaches to decision making, since good decisions are critical to the success of every organization.

How can we become better decision makers? This chapter offers some guidelines to help us overcome the difficulties in making decisions and solving problems.

Defining a Decision

What is a decision? A decision is a *choice between two or more alternatives.* However, before we can make a choice, we have to know and understand the exact nature of the problem. A supervisor must know exactly what is wrong before attempts can be made to correct the situation. Another common pitfall, once the problem has been identified, is to fail to use the information we do have. For example, consider the truck that was stuck in an underpass. Various onlookers tried to be helpful by suggesting ways to pull the truck out, but all these suggestions involved major changes to the truck or the underpass. Then a little boy suggested letting the air out of the tires!

Sometimes we overlook the obvious

Sometimes we fail to use available information to solve a problem because we start our search by looking at the wrong elements. We must make sure we look in the right direction. Think again about the truck: The onlookers' attention was directed to the top of the truck, since this was where the problem was. However, their thoughts were channeled in the wrong direction.

How can the decision maker be helped to look in the *right* direction? One way is to point out the advantage of trying several approaches. Another way is to view some of the factors that limit our abilities to make good decisions, including

- Our past experiences
- Our roles in the organization
- Our immediate environment

Sometimes the supervisor gets trapped by limitations

At times, these limitations form barriers that prevent us from making the best decision. At other times, we are faced with personal barriers that limit our actions and negatively affect our decision making, such as restrictions on

- Time
- Knowledge
- Intellect
- Authority
- Company resources

Only when you, as a supervisor, escape the limitations and recognize the barriers are you in a position to begin the decision-making process. However, some supervisors fear decisions and try to avoid them. This is one of the most serious problems that jeopardizes the effectiveness of today's organizations.

Decisive or Indecisive

Supervisors need to be decisive. When the time for action arrives, the supervisor must take action. If the supervisor fails to decide, many things can go wrong. The workers may not know

What happens when I don't make a decision?

what to do. A general sense of confusion may exist, and work may not be completed. Also, subordinates lose respect for the indecisive supervisor because they sense that the supervisor does not know what to do. Subordinates are reluctant to follow an indecisive supervisor.

Like any other type of skill, decision-making skills can be learned. With proper instruction, you can learn to be a good and effective decision maker. There is no need to be indecisive. Learn to be decisive, and learn to pass along this skill to subordinates. A supervisor cannot make all the decisions necessary to run the department. It is best to involve the subordinates in the decision-making process. Many times it results in arriving at a better solution.

TYPES OF DECISIONS

To understand the decision-making process, a classification of decisions according to the following systems is helpful:

1. Simple versus complex
2. Short-term versus long-term
3. Individual versus organizational
4. Urgent versus nonurgent
5. Programmed versus nonprogrammed

Simple Versus Complex Decisions

Simple decisions are made quickly

Some decisions can be classified as simple since they require minimal fact gathering and research. Simple decisions are usually made quickly and involve minor problems. A typical example is a decision on whose turn is it to work overtime that is made by rotating the responsibility. Complex decisions, by contrast, require an orderly, systematic, and comprehensive investigation of the facts and related information. Complex decisions are more time-consuming, and have departmental and/or organizational importance. For example, the decision on whether to use overtime to meet upcoming deadlines can only be made after an in depth analysis of the financial, production, and human resource data.

Complex-decisions require time

Short-Term Versus Long-Term Decisions

Short-term decisions are usually measured in terms of time. For example, a supervisor makes a short-term decision when a one-day replacement is hired for a worker who is out sick. A long-term decision is made when a permanent replacement is chosen for a worker who has retired.

Individual Versus Organizational Decisions

Organizational decisions affect the entire organization. A decision to close the plant is organizational, whereas a decision to lay off certain workers is individual.

Urgent Versus Nonurgent Decisions

Some problems have a greater sense of urgency than others. Occasionally, supervisors are afforded the luxury of having weeks, months, or even years to make a decision. On the other hand, some problems crop up suddenly and require an immediate answer. The state police have the luxury of time when determining the type of radar systems used to control traffic. On the other hand, an individual police officer must act with a sense of urgency during a holdup.

Programmed Versus Nonprogrammed Decisions

Programmed decisions are routine and repetitive

Herbert A. Simon,[1] the noted management theorist, categorizes decisions as either programmed or nonprogrammed. A *programmed* decision is routine and repetitive. For example, a bank manager is faced with a number of decisions pertaining to the opening of individual checking accounts. However, procedures can be established that enable the bank manager to delegate the work and be confident it will be handled in a consistent and satisfactory manner.

New decisions are nonprogrammed

A *nonprogrammed* decision is new and novel. No procedures or guidelines exist for handling the situation, since it is not a common, frequent occurrence. The decision-making process requires creativity and good judgment. Chrysler Corporation's introduction of the K-car is an example of a nonprogrammed decision.

DECISION-MAKING CONDITIONS

Decision making would be easy if the outcome were known beforehand. Although this condition exists in a few instances, it is rare. Sometimes a supervisor has no idea of the outcome of a

[1] Herbert A. Simon, *Administrative Behavior: A Study of Decision Making Processes in Administrative Organization*, 2nd ed. (New York: The Free Press, 1957), pp. 97–99.

decision, but most of the time a supervisor will have some idea of the probable result. In practice, decisions are made under three conditions:

1. Uncertainty
2. Risk
3. Certainty

Uncertainty

Under conditions of uncertainty you have no idea of the outcome

When uncertainty exists, the decision maker has absolutely no idea of the outcome before making the decision. For example, suppose an emergency production problem forces the temporary hiring of a worker immediately. Two walk-in candidates indicate their desire to work. The emergency is so critical that an on-the-spot decision must be made, without the luxury of further investigation. At this point the outcome is somewhat uncertain.

Risk

Under risk, you have some idea of the outcome

When a condition of risk exists, the decision maker has some idea of the outcome before making the decision. For example, with sufficient time, the two walk-in candidates can be asked to submit résumés that list their work experience, educational background, and references. By investigating this information, a less uncertain decision can be made. At this point, a decision is made under conditions of risk.

Certainty

Under certainty, you know the outcome

When certainty exists, the decision maker knows the outcome before making the decision. For example, when considering two workers who are currently employed in your department for the production emergency, you have the benefit of firsthand job performance knowledge. Previous evaluations and analyses of their employment records give the decision conditions of certainty.

STEPS OF THE DECISION-MAKING PROCESS

Decision making should follow a prescribed set of steps, as illustrated in Figure 16–1 and described on pages 393–396.

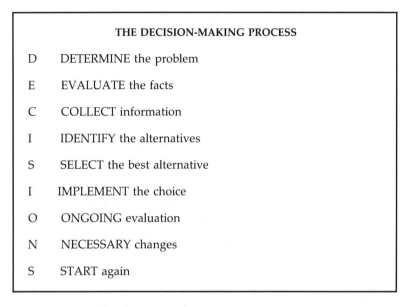

THE DECISION-MAKING PROCESS	
D	DETERMINE the problem
E	EVALUATE the facts
C	COLLECT information
I	IDENTIFY the alternatives
S	SELECT the best alternative
I	IMPLEMENT the choice
O	ONGOING evaluation
N	NECESSARY changes
S	START again

FIGURE 16-1   The decision-making process

Step 1: Determine the Problem

Deal with the problem, not the symptom

The decision maker should ask the question, Why? Frequently, decision makers confuse symptoms with problems. For example, a patient's temperature is a symptom of a problem, not the problem itself. To determine the problem, the physician must identify the reason for the fever. Once the cause is identified, the problem has been determined. In a business setting, a decline in sales is not the problem. The decision maker must approach the situation by asking *why* sales are down. Once that question has been answered, the decision maker has located the problem. In effect, declining sales are but a symptom that provides the decision maker with a clue. Before the decision-making process can continue to a satisfactory conclusion, the decision maker must know the reason for declining sales.

Step 2: Evaluate the Facts

Sometimes, the problem cannot clearly be determined without evaluating the facts. If sales are declining, the decision maker should evaluate the facts at hand. When did the decline begin? Is the decline limited to one product? If so, which one? Perhaps at this point, the decision maker may be able to determine that products A, B, and C have excellent sales figures, while sales of product

D are declining at a rapid rate. Thus in fact, all sales are *not* down. The problem actually focuses on product D.

Step 3: Collect Information

Once the problem has been determined, information must be collected. For example, since sales for product D are declining, answers to the following questions would be helpful:

1. Is product D priced properly?
2. How does product D compete in the marketplace?
3. Are competitor products better? cheaper? more durable?
4. Is the advertising for product D effective?
5. Are all markets for product D being effectively nurtured?
6. Is product D obsolete?
7. Does product D need to be modified?
8. Are other societal factors affecting product D's sales now and in the future?

The collection of this and other pertinent information must occur before possible solutions are identified. Frequently, the first three steps in the decision-making process are approached with haste, which jeopardizes the quality of the eventual decision. These steps should not be taken for granted. Spending time on them increases the chances of arriving at an optimal solution.

Step 4: Identify the Alternatives

Generate as many alternatives as possible

After relevant data have been gathered, the decision maker should generate a full range of alternatives to solve the problem. If problem D is obsolete, some obvious courses of action would be to

1. Discontinue the production and sale of product D.
2. Modify product D.
3. Introduce a new product.

Of course, the more alternatives generated, the greater the likelihood of including the best choice among the possibilities. All alternatives must be considered, and the advantages and disadvantages of each evaluated. Imagination and creativity are needed here to develop as many alternatives as possible. If the decision maker lacks creativity and fails to enter the best choice among the alternatives, an optimal decision cannot be made. Brainstorming and quality circles enhance the selection of alternatives while simultaneously improving the quality of decisions that emerge.

Step 5: Select the Best Alternatives

After intensively reviewing each alternative, the decision maker must select the best. In some cases, it may be a combination of the alternatives. If product D is obsolete, the decision might be to discontinue production and sales while simultaneously introducing a new product that does what product D did—only better.

Step 6: Implement the Choice

Simply making a choice does not complete the decision-making process. Once the best alternative is selected, the decision maker must carefully implement the choice by establishing a plan that considers the following questions:

1. *When* will the decision be implemented?
2. *Who* will be involved?
3. *What* is involved?
4. *What* changes will take place?
5. *How* will they occur?

For example, since product D will be phased out, have the appropriate people been informed? Do they understand their new responsibilities? Have time frames and schedules been established and communicated?

Step 7: Ongoing Evaluation

Ongoing evaluation helps judge the quality of the decision

The consequences and ramifications of a selected course of action cannot all be totally known until the plan is put into action. Once a choice is implemented, the decision maker must continually monitor its outcome. For example, when the replacement for product D is introduced, its acceptance by consumers must be watched closely and accurately. Ongoing evaluation provides the decision maker with information to judge the quality of the decision.

Step 8: Necessary Changes

Effective, ongoing evaluation provides the decision maker with the information needed to fine-tune the decision. For example, perhaps the product replacement is not selling as originally anticipated. Ongoing evaluation may lead the decision maker to identify a breakdown in advertising or distribution. Perhaps it's a pricing problem that can be remedied with slight modification. Or maybe a change in the advertising and promotion strategy is the answer.

Step 9: Start Again

If all necessary changes have been exhausted and the problem remains unsolved, the decision maker may have to start the process again. It may be that the best choice was not selected, that the problem was not accurately defined, or that other changes have occurred in the marketplace since the problem was identified and the course of action selected.

The decision-making process is a continuum

The steps of the decision-making process should be viewed on a continuum that demands constant evaluation (see Figure 16–2). Decisions should not be considered permanent. Societal, market, technological, and human changes impose a temporary quality to every decision.

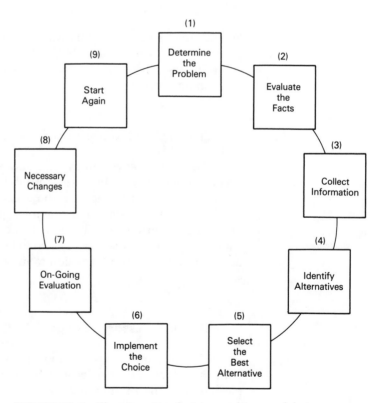

FIGURE 16–2 The nine-step decision-making model

HUMANISTIC VERSUS ENVIRONMENTAL DECISIONS

Some years ago, during a severe electrical shortage in New York City, two methods were used to reduce the heavy use of electricity. One was to put a card stating "Save a Watt" on the wall above the light switch to encourage people to turn off the lights when they were not being used. The second was to take out some of the light bulbs in the corridors. This method assumed that people would not voluntarily turn off the lights, so the environment was changed instead.

Humanistic approach: people make the change

The humanistic approach to making decisions about problems places emphasis on the changes that *people* can make. Environmental decisions affect the environment without any interaction with the people concerned.

It is sometimes difficult to separate decisions that affect people from those that affect the environment. Nevertheless, problems can be approached in terms of either humans or the environment, and both approaches are appropriate, depending on the situation. Frequently one approach follows or is mixed with the other.

Humanistic Decisions

When employees working under similar conditions consistently perform similar tasks differently, it can reasonably be assumed that the environment needs less change than the employees. Training is a common way to change job-related behavior. An inefficient or slow employee may need only a little more education about his or her job or a little more skill development to be able to perform tasks as well as other employees.

Humanists use training programs

Humanists are concerned that people express their points of view before decisions that affect them are made. For instance, if production is low, the employees are given the opportunity to weigh their attitudes and to raise production on their own initiative. As might be expected from its greater emphasis on interpersonal relations, the humanistic approach to decision making focuses on participatory methods.

Environmental Decisions

The solution is in society, not in the person

The environmentalist focuses attention on the external forces that determine a situation. In dealing with employees who perform the same job at different levels of competence, the environmentalist would check to make sure the conditions were appreciably similar. For example, environmental thinking would be responsible for the introduction of safety devices, adequate lighting, and improved methods of maintaining equipment.

Policy is more important than the person

The environmental approach studies decision making from the point of view of long-range goals, with the best interests of the company in mind. Very little emphasis is placed on authority, structure, and evaluation of performance. In other words, policy is more important than employee happiness.

J. Victor Baldridge of Stanford University lists five assumptions that are essential to making decisions from an environmental approach.[2]

Conflict is natural

1. *Conflict is natural.* It is to be expected in any dynamic company. Conflict is not abnormal, nor is it always a result of a breakdown in communication.

A few make the major decisions

2. *An organization is pluralist.* The organization is fragmented into many power blocs. Various groups will attempt to influence plans so that their values will be given primary consideration.

3. *Small groups of political elites make most major decisions.* This does not mean that one elite group governs everything; the responsibility for decisions may be divided, with different groups controlling different decisions.

4. *Bargaining is a major factor.* The formal authority defined by the bureaucratic system is limited by the political pressure and bargaining tactics that groups can exert against authorities. Decisions are not simply bureaucratic orders, but are instead negotiated compromises among competing groups. Officials are not free simply to order decisions but must jockey among interest groups, hoping to build viable compromises among powerful blocs.

Outside groups can influence decisions

5. *External groups can influence decisions.* Outside interest groups have a great deal of influence over an organization, for internal groups do not make policies in a vacuum.

Classes of Decisions

In terms of organizational hierarchy, decisions can originate in three distinct ways:

1. *Decisions that follow executive orders* involve interpreting and carrying out instructions, and can sometimes be delegated further down the hierarchical chain. This can create a chain of nondecisions commonly called "passing the buck."
2. *Cases referred by subordinates* for decisions usually arise from a conflict of orders or of jurisdiction, or from uncertainty of instruction. These decisions usually require judicial decision making.

---

[2] Victor Baldridge, "Organizational Change: The Human Relations Perspective Versus the Political Systems Perspective," *Economic Record,* February 1972 (vol. II.), p. 154.

3. *Other decisions are made on a person's own initiative.* Decisions of this type are the most revealing test of someone's ability to make decisions. A good decision maker knows when to decide and when not to; often *no* decision is the best decision for the moment. The executive who succeeds in business often turns out to be the one who has the knack of saying *no.* The wrong way of saying *no* may leave the no-sayer with a lifelong legacy of ill will, but choosing the right words can save time and heartache. The highest form of the art of saying *no* is convincing the other person that your decision is in his or her best interests.

AIDS FOR DECISION MAKING

Many supervisors use different methods to aid them in making good decisions. There is *no one method* that is best. It is up to each supervisor to study the situation and then determine which method is best for that type of problem.

Mathematical Decision Making

Mathematical decision making helps to analyze

Mathematical decision making is the use of mathematical, statistical, or quantitative methods as an aid in decision making. The methods *do not make the decision;* they are only aids. They allow the decision maker to group numerical data for analysis. The supervisor must make the final decision based on the evaluation of the data. Many popular mathematical decision-making methods exist. Some of the more popular ones include break-even analysis, decision trees, cost-benefit analysis, and operations research.

BREAK-EVEN ANALYSIS

Break-even analysis helps to predict profits

Break-even analysis allows a supervisor to determine the point at which revenue equals cost (see Figure 16–3). Although break-even analysis is done mathematically, it is presented in graph form because it allows management to see more clearly the break-even point and the possible profits and losses that will result in changes in expenses and sales. By using this aid, a supervisor or manager can predict profits and control expenses.

DECISION TREES

Decision trees allow the supervisor to visualize what might happen

Decision trees are graphic illustrations of how different alternatives result in various possibilities. The decision tree helps the supervisor to visualize what could happen, given the choice of several options. For example, suppose that a supervisor is faced

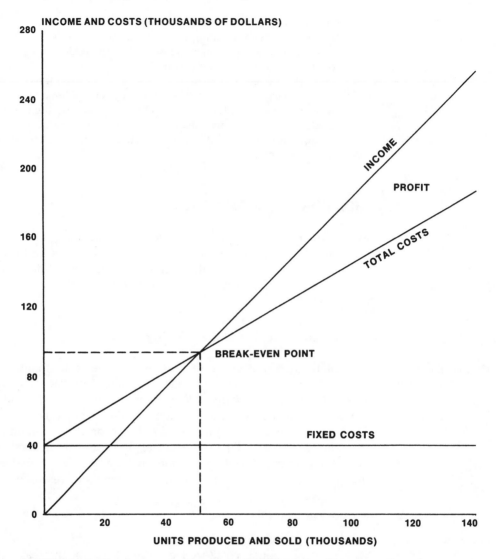

FIGURE 16–3   Break-even chart analysis. This illustrates the preparation of a break-even chart for projected sales of $280,000, fixed costs of $40,000, and variable costs of $1.20 per unit, with a sale price of $2.00 per unit.

with a problem employee who has a habit of being late. The supervisor may consider three ways of handling the problem:

1. One alternative (A1) is to discipline the employee by docking his or her pay.
2. A second alternative (A2) is to encourage the employee to be on time.
3. A third alternative (A3) is to try a combination of both.

DECISION ALTERNATIVES   EMPLOYEE REACTIONS   PROBABLE CHANGE IN BEHAVIOR OF EMPLOYEE

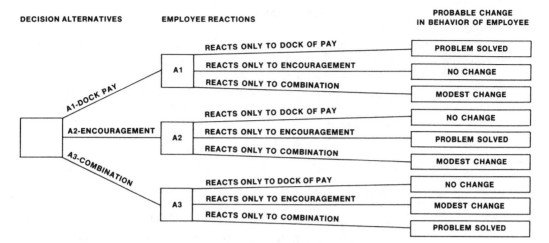

FIGURE 16–4   Decision tree analysis

Figure 16–4 illustrates how these alternatives project on a decision tree by attempting to visualize the probable change in an employee's behavior with each choice.

COST-BENEFIT ANALYSIS

Cost-benefit analysis compares the pluses and minuses

Cost-benefit analysis is a problem-solving aid that allows the supervisor to compare the pluses and minuses of a proposed solution. This technique has become popular in all types of businesses and organizations. For example, suppose a supervisor is considering the purchase of a new piece of equipment for the department. Cost-benefit analysis involves adding all the costs involved in buying the equipment and comparing them with the value of services to be gained by the equipment. It is a method of control that enables the supervisor to balance the costs and the benefits of a proposed alternative.

OPERATIONS RESEARCH

Operations research uses mathematics to explain relationships

Although the name *operations research* is a relatively new one, the methodology used in the technique is not. Operations research draws heavily on mathematics and attempts to explain relationships among the major aspects of the organization. A statistician is usually involved in operations research. A supervisor can use this aid when trying to deal with problems related to the following:

• Inventory
• Equipment replacement
• Production process
• Material ordering

The Final Decision

Although aids are helpful, the supervisor must make the final decision

It should be emphasized that the supervisor must make the final decision. The aids presented are just that—aids! All they can do is place the supervisor in a better position to make the decision. When used effectively and cautiously, they provide real help to the supervisor. But remember, the supervisor must make the decision!

TRAITS THAT INFLUENCE DECISIONS

The decision-making process is either helped or hindered by the basic philosophies and personalities of the decision makers. People react to problems in many different ways; the solutions they choose reflect some of the assumptions they make. Some of the personality traits that are particularly influential in the decision-making process are discussed next.

Taking Risks

Most are averse to 50-50 gambles

There is no such thing as a riskless decision, but the degree of risk can vary. Many decision makers have an aversion to taking risks. When offered a 50-50 chance that a gamble will succeed, most people would choose not to gamble because they do not want to jeopardize the gains they have made.

A graphic way to illustrate the degree of risk would be to offer a group of decision makers a high payoff on an even-chance gamble. A majority would turn down such a proposition, even if the payoff were ten times as high as the sum at risk. If the sum at risk involved all or most of the corporate resources, this attitude would be entirely rational. Mature corporations would not gamble their existence on a 50 percent chance of high returns.

Returns on many small 50-50 gambles can justify the risk

Most business decisions, however, involve only a small fraction of total corporate resources. Taking several 50 percent chances every month to risk a small percent of total resources for a tenfold return would appear to be very good business practice and should pay off handsomely in the long run. However, whether the risk is low or high, decision makers often act as if their fate, or their company's fate, hung in the balance with each decision. Thus many decisions that should be made are often suppressed because of the decision maker's irrational fear of losing everything.

Success and Failure Attitudes

Fear of failure can inhibit bids for great success

Fear of failure can also stalemate the decision-making process. Worrying about the unknown results of a decision can be paralyzing. As long as no decision is made, no judgment can be made as to whether the decision is good or bad; people lose the opportunity to learn either from their failures or from their successes. Only by making decisions can you learn how to make successful ones.

So many things can discourage us that we often find ourselves quoting some of Murphy's laws:

If anything can go wrong . . .

- *Murphy's Law:* If anything can go wrong, it will.
- *Murphy's Second Law:* Nothing is as easy as it looks.
- *Murphy's Third Law:* Everything takes longer than you think.
- *Murphy's Fourth Law:* It always costs more than first estimated.
- *Murphy's Fifth Law:* Blame will never be placed if enough people are involved.[3]

But above all we should remember B. F. Sinner's comment:

A failure is not always a mistake; it may be simply the best one can do in the circumstances. The real mistake is to stop trying.[4]

Experience

Decisions become easier with experience

Knowledge gained from experience is a helpful guide to decision making, and its importance should not be underestimated. On the other hand, it is dangerous merely to follow experience. It is easy for people with many years of experience to fail to listen to innovative ideas from others. Their biases insulate them from trying anything new.

Experience must be put into perspective according to the demands of new situations. Experience is not always useful in evaluating the circumstances of the present and the future. Even when it is helpful, it will seldom apply in a direct way. For experience to be useful, it must be viewed as just one of the many ingredients of the decision-making process.

---

[3] These and other laws attributed to Murphy can be found in Laurence J. Peter, "Murphy's Mystery Solved," *Human Behavior,* June 1978 (vol. II), p. 70.

[4] B. F. Skinner. *Contingencies of Reinforcement* (New York: Appleton-Century-Crofts, 1969), p. 93.

Seeking Advice

It is one thing to be aware that you are the only one who can make a decision, but it is quite another to seek opinions about what action should be taken. Listening with an open mind to what other people have to say increases your potential for making a good decision. You can also use other people as sounding boards for your ideas.

People who make a practice of not consulting others take greater risks in making decisions because they isolate themselves from feedback. Those who go to the other extreme and seek too much advice, too often, can appear to be incapable of making a decision on their own and also can undermine their own confidence in their decision-making ability.

Take a Break When You Are Stuck

The advice given most frequently to problem solvers is to take a break when you are stuck. But does a break really do any good? If you are getting nowhere with a problem, it may be that your plan of attack is inappropriate or that your information cannot be adapted to your plan. If you cannot think of another approach, then you *are* stuck, and this is a good time to take a break. A change of environment may bring a new attitude, and a rest can do wonders for developing a fresh new approach.

WHO MAKES THE DECISIONS?

The relationship between individual decisions and organizational policy is not always simple, for the decisions of top management can meet resistance. A strongly motivated person will form factions and cliques to work for a desired change. Those opposed to that change will also band together. Many people today still think for themselves—even in large corporations; the sabotaging of top management's decisions with lower-level decisions is quite common.

Sabotaging top management

A successful organization is built on setting and meeting realistic goals. Meeting organizational goals requires well-defined administrative relationships, including the assignment of authority and the responsibility for making rational decisions. Even so, the question of who should make the decisions has never been adequately answered. In most businesses, responsibility for decision making is measured by the significance of the decision: how much money and how many people will be affected. Thus decision making follows the organizational hierarchy, with those at the top responsible for the most important decisions.

Major decision making tends to be highly centralized in most large companies, especially when the decisions concern financial, legal, and industrial relations problems. The two main ways in which this centralized control operates are one-person decisions and small-group decisions.

One-Person Decisions

Let the lowest level possible make the decision

Organizations that are controlled by one person are more widespread than most people think. The owner-manager may have difficulty delegating decision-making power to subordinates because of a belief that power and prestige are lost when authority is delegated. Unfortunately, this control method is inefficient. More work can be accomplished and more experience can be gained by the subordinate when decision making is delegated. Many theorists advocate making decisions at the lowest possible level in the organization.

Group Decisions

Major decisions in many organizations are made by a small, elite group consisting of at least three but no more than seven people. In addition to participating in joint decisions, each person usually has an area in which he or she has the final say, such as sales or production. Group control can cause delay and even bring action to a standstill when a deadlock occurs and no one has the final power to decide.

Participative decisions are usually friendly and informal

Decisions made by many people have been called *integrative* or *participative* decisions. These terms are preferable to *democratic decision making* because "democratic" implies an equality that does not exist in this context—certainly not equality in income or status, and usually not in the power to influence major decisions. Participatory action normally takes the form of friendly, informal consultation among top management, and sometimes it includes their subordinates. The real test of participation is the extent to which disagreement is tolerated, especially by those who are superior in rank.

Many firms use consultative decision making to bring those employees with technical background and skill to the conference table. The technical staff is more likely to participate in making decisions when specific skills are involved rather than when long-range planning is required.

Few decisions have total group consensus

Group decision making can be an exceedingly complex affair, but two principles hold true. First, majority decisions usually represent something less than total group commitment. Few groups, other than some religious orders, operate with total group consensus.

The more abstract, the greater the chance for agreement

Second, the more abstract the matter being considered, the greater are the chances of agreement. Put another way, the more concrete the matter, the less the chances are for full agreement. For example, at one company contract negotiations came to a halt over a clause about hiring part-time employees. The term needed definition. One proposed definition was "one who works less than 40 hours a week, on irregular schedules, and is not subject to the benefits of regular employees." Another definition was "anyone who works less than 40 hours a week." The second definition clearly covered many more people than did the first and offered a wider range of interpretation.

The company wanted the broad definition so that it could choose who would be entitled to regular benefits. The union wanted the narrow definition so that it could then claim all employees as dues payers. An agreement was reached only when the definition was restructured more abstractly than either party wanted: "Part-time employees are all those employees who are not regular employees." While this more abstract definition did not solve any concrete problems, it did allow negotiations to continue.

QUALITY CIRCLES

Over the past decade, quality circles have found widespread acceptance in all types of organizations. The concept was conceived in Japan; but many American organizations have benefited greatly from this form of participative decision making. Honeywell and Lockheed were among the first organizations in the United States to implement the quality circle.

Quality circles are a form of participative decision making

By definition, quality circles are *groups of employees who meet voluntarily on a frequent basis to identify, analyze, and solve problems in their area of interest and expertise.* Usually, the objective of a quality circle is to improve quality and productivity.

Under the leadership of Kaoru Ishikawa of Tokyo University, behavioral concepts advanced by Maslow, McGregor, and Herzberg were linked to the quality sciences introduced by Deming and Juran, thereby creating the quality circle concept. In practice, a small work group selects projects and/or problems that

require analysis for improvement. Since the work group is most knowledgeable about the job it performs, its members are in the best position to advance viable suggestions for solutions. By the same token, the work group will be committed to the recommen-
Quality circles have positive outcomes
dations that it advances. Quality circles can be implemented in any and every type of organization. The common outcomes of quality circles are usually cost reductions, quality improvements, and productivity increases. They are most successful when certain criteria are met:

1. Quality circle groups should be small (approximately eight to ten members).
2. Quality circles should be voluntary.
3. Members should come from the same work area.
4. Members should be actively supported by management.
5. Quality circles should have a facilitator to help establish how the group will function.
6. Quality circles should have a leader who directs the group through the work-related, problem-solving activities.
7. Quality circles must have realistic goals and objectives.

The major objectives of quality circles include

1. Nurturing a harmonious supervisor-worker relationship
2. Promoting the job-worker relationship
3. Improving organizational communication
4. Promoting problem-solving confidence
5. Increasing worker commitment and motivation
6. Inspiring effective teamwork

From a supervisory point of view, the above list represents the ultimate outcomes. If, through management and supervisory prac-tices, improved relationships, communication, commitment, con-fidence, motivation, and teamwork result, all elements of a positive supervisory process are active. The culminations of the quality circles process are

1. Reduced errors
2. Improved quality
3. Cost reduction
4. Safety awareness
5. Increased production
6. Problem prevention
7. Better decisions

The implementation of the quality circle concept has both short-term and long-term implications. On a long-term basis, supervisors learn to master the skills needed to improve performance and motivate workers. Job satisfaction is enhanced because workers feel that they are an integral part of the organization, since their views and suggestions are actively sought. In the short term, productivity and quality improvements can be seen immediately.

Like all other systems of management, quality circles also have disadvantages. When implemented properly, it is conceivable that many or all of the disadvantages can be controlled. As a precaution, supervisors must be aware of these potential drawbacks:

1. Not every organization is ready for quality circles. In organizations where many people perform many tasks, they may not be effective.
2. Quality circles require commitment from top management.
3. Management must support and use the quality circle's output. If employees believe that their involvement will not be taken seriously, their interest will diminish.
4. Quality circles are costly, since employees meet during work hours.
5. Quality circles temporarily lead to a drop in production, as employees are removed from their tasks during work hours.
6. Quality circles can become gripe sessions.
7. Failed quality circles cause morale problems.
8. The role of quality circles is frequently misunderstood.
9. Quality circles tend to deal with symptoms rather than problems.
10. Quality circles can be slow and cumbersome in taking action.

With proper preparation, however, quality circles can be introduced with a realistic hope of avoiding the disadvantages and reaping the benefits. Although the concept can represent a radical change in the normal operation of some organizations, supervisors must look beyond the novelty and accept them realistically. Quality circles are most successful when they are introduced as an extension of *what can be*. They are not attention-getting, special activities, but rather effective participative approaches to decision making. Quality circles are not short cuts, but instead are means of introducing techniques with the potential to provide major long-term contributions to an organization. If they are well conceived and properly planned, their benefits will greatly outweigh their disadvantages.

Steps for Success

The following steps should ensure the effective implementation of quality circles.

STEP 1: CREATE A CLIMATE FOR THE PROGRAM

An appropriate climate is created through proper orientation. Effective training and explanation will induce positive involvement. If employees do not understand the program, they will not participate.

STEP 2: SECURE TOP MANAGEMENT SUPPORT AND COMMITMENT

If top management is resistant to the concept, there will be a reluctance to accept and use the ideas emerging from the quality circles. If, on the other hand, top management is primed and committed, quality circles will advance their ideas enthusiastically. This creates momentum.

STEP 3: ESTABLISH OBJECTIVES

To avoid confusion, the organization must effectively communicate clear and realistic program objectives. Additionally, employees must be aware of these goals.

STEP 4: ESTABLISH VOLUNTARY MEMBERSHIP

Employees cannot be forced to participate in quality circles. More appropriately, they should realize the need for and visualize the benefits to be derived from them. Voluntary membership ensures participation from those who want to be involved.

STEP 5: FOLLOW AN AGENDA

Establishing an agenda informs members of the topics to be addressed. A tendency to wander away from the topic is thus eliminated, which permits the group to focus its full concentration on

---

A SAMPLE QUALITY CIRCLE AGENDA

1. Send notice of the time and place of the meeting, with the minutes and agenda of the previous meeting.
2. Start the meeting.
3. Review attendance.
4. Approve minutes of the previous meeting.
5. Discuss pending items.
6. Introduce action items.
7. Discuss new business.
8. Assign tasks and roles for the new action items.
9. Summarize and close the meeting.
10. Establish the time and place of the next meeting.

the problem at hand. This in turn will lead to maximum input and optimal output.

Conclusion: A Final Word on Quality Circles

With proper application, quality circles can bring about excellent results. When management is interested and committed, improved quality, reduced cost, and increased productivity can occur. Quality circles represent a modern decision-making technique that fosters the total involvement of the work force. American organizations owe a debt of gratitude to the Japanese for developing a concept so rich in participatory supervisory principles. It is now up to us to use it effectively.

SUMMARY

One of a supervisor's most important duties is to make decisions. Good decisions help the organization, whereas bad ones hurt it. There is no substitute for good decisions.

A decision is a choice between two or more alternatives. Decisions may be classified according to one of five sets of descriptions:

1. Simple versus complex
2. Short-term versus long-term
3. Individual versus organizational
4. Urgent versus nonurgent
5. Programmed versus nonprogrammed

Decisions are made under one of three conditions: uncertainty, risk, or certainty.

Although age, wisdom, and experience contribute to effective decision making, the process is best approached by following nine steps:

1. Determine the problem.
2. Evaluate the facts.
3. Collect information.
4. Identify the alternatives.
5. Select the best alternative.
6. Implement the choice.
7. Ongoing evaluation.
8. Make the necessary changes.
9. Start again.

Although a supervisor must make a decision, several aids, such as mathematical models, break-even analysis, decision trees, cost-benefit analysis, and operations management, are at the supervisor's disposal.

Two basic approaches are used in making decisions. The humanistic approach considers problems from the human point of view; the environmental approach sees problems in terms of the environment. Their appropriateness depends on the situation, but most people tend to rely more on one than the other.

Personality traits also can influence the way people handle problems. The alternative solutions that are developed reflect the philosophies that are acceptable to the decision maker. Attitudes about taking risks, success, and failure greatly affect the quality of decisions. The ability to be decisive and to seek advice from others contributes to the decision-making process.

Decisions affecting groups are made by either one person or a group, and each method has rewards and drawbacks. Recently, quality circles have found widespread acceptance in all types of organizations.

Jack Baxter's Perplexing Problem

About three and a half weeks ago, Jack Baxter was appointed to the position of production manager. His experience in management and supervision has been somewhat limited, with little or no decision-making experience. The type of jobs Jack has held in the past did not involve typical managerial challenges, and consequently he accepted this new position with a great deal of reluctance.

On Friday afternoon, Mr. Schwartz, the general manager of the plant, approached Jack and asked him for the production figures for next year. He asked him to report the amount of production necessary to be profitable, so all departments could be notified accordingly. Jack was somewhat perplexed by the request and at first was not sure how he could tackle the problem. He returned to his office and began to shuffle through his desk in an attempt to locate data that would help him solve the problem. He discovered a memo that had come down from the accounting department, which stated that fixed costs would be $60,000 next year. He had no idea why the accounting department would send him a report that classifies expenditures for fixed costs.

As he placed the accounting memo back in his drawer, he remembered that he was to attend the staff meeting in the general manager's office. When he arrived at the meeting, Mr. Schwartz was distributing a comprehensive report developed by the marketing department that stated the reasons for a price increase to be instituted. The report indicated that the retail price of the company's product would have to be increased to $10 in order to cover the rising costs. Mr. Schwartz reported that variable costs alone had risen from $3.60 per unit to $4, and that a price increase was the only solution. Ms. Jordon, the sales manager, reported that the sales forecast for next year was $300,000 and that this figure should be achieved, especially since three new sales people had been hired.

The staff unanimously approved the price increase and sales forecast, and, after typical generalities were exchanged, the meeting was adjourned.

Jack returned to his office to deal with his project. He said to himself, "Now I understand the pressures of management—I guess I'll have to estimate what production should be next year. There doesn't seem to be a systematic way of making such a decision."

QUESTIONS

1. Is Jack correct in his assumption, "There doesn't seem to be a systematic way of making such a decision"? Explain.
2. If you were Jack, how would you approach this situation? Be specific.
3. Are any of the analytical aids for decision making applicable in this case? Which ones?
4. Use your answer to the above question to arrive at a decision. Illustrate your answer.
5. How many units need be produced to be profitable? What amount of sales must be generated in order to avoid a loss? What is the total amount of profit that can be expected if the company sells $300,000 worth of merchandise?

CASE STUDY 42

Situations for Decision

The Hargrove Company is a large company and consequently has its share of problems. Its market position is quite secure, but for some reason personality problems run rampant. The following three incidents occurred last week, and each of these situations requires decision making in one way or another.

Situation 1: When Grant Williams entered his department, he saw two employees arguing violently. As he approached the two workers, he discovered that the nature of the argument focused on an open window. One worker indicated that she was cold and desired to have the window closed, whereas the other worker wished to have the window open because he was hot. Continued arguing about the open window nearly led to physical violence. Grant managed to quiet the employees down, but he knew something permanent would have to be done.

QUESTIONS

1. If you were Grant, how would you handle this situation?
2. Do you think this incident is normal?
3. Should Grant separate the workers? Should he get a sweater for the worker who was cold? Would either of these strategies solve the problem?
4. Using the steps of the decision-making process, state the optimal method for dealing with this problem.

Situation 2: Fred McCormick was approached by one of his workers with a problem about office procedure. The worker asked Fred for the best way to submit an order change, since a particular customer had canceled her order. Fred said that these problems rarely occur and that consequently he did not know the best way to handle it. He advised the worker to check with Janet Townsend, since she had handled the last customer change of this type. Fred told the worker that Janet does not know the best way, but that she can get the job done. "If you have any other problems, be sure and keep me posted," he said.

QUESTIONS

1. Evaluate Fred's advice.
2. If you were Fred, how would you handle the situation? Be specific.
3. What are the negative aspects, if any, of Fred's strategy? Elaborate.

Situation 3: Absenteeism records indicate that Alice McCann has missed an exorbitant amount of work during the last three months. Her supervisor, Lee Martin, entered your office and stated, "Something must be done about McCann. She's missing too much time." Since you have the power to hire and fire, you must make a decision.

QUESTIONS

1. What is your decision? How would you arrive at this decision?
2. Use the steps of the decision making process, and discuss your actions as they relate to each step in the process.

CASE STUDY **43**

Quality Circle Answers

You have recently changed jobs and are a supervisor at a mid-sized manufacturing plant. Your previous organization used quality circles as a major form of operation. Your new company is not familiar with the concept, and they ask you the following questions:

QUESTIONS

1. What are quality circles?
2. How can we benefit from them?
3. How and when should quality circles be started?

Terms and Concepts Supervisors Should Know

Alternatives; Break-even analysis; Certainty; Cost-benefit analysis; Decision-making steps; Decision tree; Decisive versus indecisive; Environmental decisions; 50-50 risks; Group decisions; Humanistic decisions; Individual decisions; Mathematical decisions; Murphy's laws; Operations research; Predictability; Risk; Quality circles; Suspended judgment; Type of decisions; Uncertainty.

Questions for Discussion

1. Give examples of programmed and nonprogrammed decisions that are made in your work environment. Provide examples of short-range and long-range decisions. Which type of decisions do you make most often? Why? Discuss the risk involved.
2. Provide an example of a decision that can be aided by a decision tree. Give an example of a decision that can be aided by cost-benefit analysis.
3. Do you favor humanistic or environmental approaches to decision making? What type of approach do you use at home? Is it different from the approach you use at work? Why?
4. What are the five assumptions essential to making an environmental decision? What problem in your community or company might be solved by the environmental approach?
5. Are most of the decisions made at your company based on a group decision or an individual decision? Why do you suppose this is so? Is this the best approach for the company? Is this the best approach for you?
6. Should quality circles be implemented in every organization? Why or why not?

For Further Reading—And More Ideas

Agor, W. H., "How Top Executives Use Their Intuition to Make Important Decisions," *Business Horizons* (January–February 1986).

Bazer, M. H., and H. S. Farber, "Analyzing the Decision-Making Processes of Third Parties," *Sloan Management Review* (Fall 1985).

Bell, D. E., "Disappointments in Decision Making Under Uncertainty," *Operation Research* (January–February 1985).

Brightman, Harvey J., "Constraints to Effective Problem Solving," *Business* (March 1981).

Budd, B., and D. J. Ross, "Affiliation: When Is It the Right Decision? (Hospitals)," *Top Health Care Financing* (Fall 1988).

Deitzer, B. A., and A. G. Krigline, "When Making That Decision," *Management Solutions* (November 1988).

Drucker, P. F., "How to Make People Decisions," *Association Management* (November 1985).

Duchon, D., et al., "Framing the Problem and Making Decisions: The Facts Are Not Enough," *IEEE Transactions on Engineering Management* (February 1989).

Grove, A. S., "Decisions, Decisions," *Modern Office Technologies* (July 1984).

Himes, G., "Solving Problems—Making Decisions," *Supervision* (January 1983).

Horton, T. R., "Deciding About Decisions," *Management Review* (November 1985).

"How to Make Decisions—Intuitively," *Management World* (October 1985).

Johnson, N. P., "A Tough Decision?" *Managerial Planning* (July–August 1984).

Kiechel, W., "Betting Organized (Requires Ability to Make Decisions)," *Fortune* (March 3, 1986).

Kindler, H. S., "Decisions, Decisions: Which Approach to Take," *Personnel* (January 1985).

Kuzela, L., "Communications: Zooming in on Decisions," *Industry Week* (September 2, 1985).

Lindo, D. K., "Delegating Decisions," *Executive Female* (January–February 1986).

Lindo, D. K., "Do You Ever Explain Your Decisions?" *Supervision* (February 1984).

Magnet, M., "How Top Managers Make a Company's Toughest Decision," *Fortune* (March 18, 1985).

Maital, S., "Managing Risk: Were You Framed?" *Across the Board* (January–February 1989).

McCreary, Edward A., "How to Grow a Decision Tree," *Think* (March–April 1967).

Miller, M., "Putting More Power into Managerial Decisions," *Management Review* (September 1984).

Nutt, P. C., "Types of Organizational Decision Processes," *Administrative Science Quarterly* (September 1984).

Rowe, C., "Analysing Management Decision-Making: Further Thoughts After the Bradford Studies (Barrington's and Prize Farms)," *Journal of Management Studies* (January 1989).

Shrivastava, P., and J. H. Grant, "Empirically Derived Models of Strategic Decision-Making Processes," *Strategic Management Journal* (April–June 1985).

Simon, Herbert A., *Administrative Behavior*, New York: Macmillan, 1947.

Wert, P. V., "Guidelines for Decision Making," *Supervision* (December 1984).

White, K. B., "Dynamic Decision Support Teams," *Systems Management* (June 1984).

Whyte, G., "Groupthink Reconsidered," *Academy of Management Review* (January 1989).

Wilson, D. C., and G. K. Kenny, "Managerially Perceived Influence over Intradepartmental Decisions," *Journal of Management Studies* (March 1985).

Supervising Change and Conflict

17

"Why are things different?"

LEARNING OBJECTIVES

When you complete this chapter, you should be able to:
1. Understand the nature and importance of change.
2. Recognize the different types of change.
3. Explain why people resist change.
4. Indicate the guidelines for overcoming the resistance to change.
5. Give a working definition of conflict and organizational conflict.
6. Explain the forms and causes of conflict.
7. Understand how a supervisor can control change.

"If things are going to get better, things will have to change."

This chapter will help you discover your feelings about your work and how they are affected by change and conflict. Consider the following questions by applying the concepts in this chapter along with your personal experiences and opinions:

> What type of change is the most difficult to handle?
>
> Do you and your subordinates resist change?
>
> What are your attitudes about change?
>
> Is all conflict bad? How does conflict become a benefit?
>
> How can a supervisor use change and conflict as a benefit and advantage?

"The disturbing fact is that the vast majority of people, including educated and otherwise sophisticated people, find the idea of change so threatening that they attempt to deny its existence" (Alvin Toffler, *Future Shock*).[1]

WHAT IS CHANGE?

We have been forced to live with the fact that change is a permanent aspect of our lives. Even though previous generations have been affected by change, today's supervisor must acknowledge that we live in an age of rapid change. With high-tech changes occurring on a daily basis, the need to cope with change is absolutely necessary for survival. Change is part of progress, and progress is part of business.

Realistically, the supervisor must be prepared to *accept* change as well as to administer it. In approaching change with this attitude, the supervisor will be able to do more than just *react to* change: he or she will learn to *act with* it.

Change represents one of the most challenging aspects of a supervisor's job. It must be dealt with now! As indicated in John Naisbitt's best-sellers *Megatrends* and *Megatrends 2000*, major transformations are taking place in our society.[2]

---

[1] Alvin Toffler, *Future Shock* (New York: Bantam Books, 1970), p. 20.

[2] John Naisbitt, *Megatrends* (New York: Warner Books, 1982) and *Megatrends 2000* (New York: Warner Books, 1989).

CHANGE AND THE SUPERVISOR'S JOB

Change is a constant challenge

Since change is part of progress, and progress is part of business, change will constantly challenge the supervisor. Because it is inevitable, the supervisor must learn to deal successfully with change. Sometimes it will be sudden, sometimes it will be gradual, but it will always be continual.

Change, in terms of supervision, can be placed in three classes:

1. Internal change
2. External change
3. Technological change

Internal Change

Rules and regulations create change

Internal change includes structural alterations within the organization. Examples of structural change would include merging departments, centralizing the accounting function, or simplifying work methods. Sometimes internal change can result from establishing new policies or rules to include a revision of overtime procedures, a new work schedule, or a new policy about vacations.

External Change

Interest rates and tax laws create change

External change includes those forces in the environment that affect the organization. Government regulations, economic factors, and social demands are representative of external change. These external changes affect the organization in the form of new laws, interest rates, and consumer wants and needs.

Technological Change

Automation and robotics create change

Technological change involves automation, computerization, and robotics. The introduction of these technological aspects has changed our whole method of working. Some people and some jobs have been lost forever, but in the long run the economy will benefit through increased efficiency and profitability.

Technological change has been the trademark of American business. Advances in the past 30 years have been dramatic and progressive; the future promises to be even more so.

Despite the type of change, the supervisor is usually responsible for introducing it successfully. As a result, the supervisor

Subordinates may resist change

must deal with the frustrations and anxieties that usually accompany it, as well as the unanswered questions such as, "Will the change be resisted?," "When should my workers be informed of the change?," and "Am I capable of implementing the change?"

Why People Resist Change

Change may be resisted if introduced improperly

Resistance to change can be used as a yardstick

People resist change for many reasons. Simply because it is resisted does not necessarily mean it will be unaccepted. In many cases, the change may be introduced improperly, and as a result, it may be resisted. Sometimes the change is introduced properly but still may be resisted. The supervisor may use resistance to change as a means of "taking the pulse" of the department. If minor change meets with resistance, this could be an indicator that other problems exist, such as problems of morale, commitment, or trust. It could mean that the supervisor, by implementing drastic change, has created feelings of insecurity in the workers. Perhaps it is a case of not informing the workers about the change until the last minute. Table 17–1 provides a detailed analysis of probable reaction to change as it relates to common management practices.

TABLE 17–1   Probable reactions to change and recommended actions

Activity	Probable Reaction	Reason	Recommended Action
Management implements a sudden change.	Negative	Employees are caught by surprise, with no warning.	Establish better lines of communication and explain the nature of the change prior to implementation.
Management implements a drastic change.	Negative	Employees are uncertain and insecure.	Introduce the change gradually, in increments. Explain the overall reasons for the change prior to implementation.
Change is imposed from above.	Negative	Employees feel left out and that they are not a part of the change process.	Include employees in the change process when possible, and make them feel a part of it.
Management implements a change that is a radical departure from tradition.	Negative	Employees feel criticized and that what they had been doing is no longer valuable.	Obtain input from employees; make them feel a part of the change. Clearly explain the reasons for the change.
Management implements an unpopular change.	Negative	Work group may be against change, and peer pressure forces individuals to resist the change.	Gain approval from group by making them part of the change process from the start. Establish open lines of communication.

Guidelines for Overcoming Resistance

Supervisors must approach change with a careful plan

Sometimes an emergency requires fast actions without warning. When this happens, it is the obligation of the supervisor to move swiftly—make the changes—and offset the reactions to change after the fact. Most of the time, however, the supervisor is not faced with emergencies and has the time to plan an intended change carefully. The following guidelines are designed to overcome resistance to change:

1. Supervisors must work constantly at creating an open climate of trust, honesty, and confidence in the workers.
2. There is no substitute for open lines of communication.
3. Where possible, introduce change on a gradual basis through small increments. It is easier to bring about change a little at a time.
4. When appropriate, encourage employee participation in the change process. In addition to helping overcome the resistance to change, employee participation can generate ideas and suggestions that result in a better plan.
5. Be sure to supply appropriate information. The supervisor should explain *why* the change is being implemented, *how* the employees will be affected, and *what* the change involves.
6. Make sure you have received full approval from your boss to bring about the change.

FOUR STEPS IN BRINGING ABOUT CHANGE

REMEMBER TO C O P E WITH CHANGE

C CHANGE is certain and cannot be avoided. We must always be on the lookout for better methods and better ideas. We do not want to make changes simply for the sake of making them, but rather to improve efficiency, increase profitability, and become more competitive.

O ORGANIZE your thoughts to understand what needs to be changed. Facts must be gathered to simplify the process.

P PARTICIPATIVE management is the way to involve workers in the change process and get them to accept it. Also, employee ideas and suggestions could improve the process.

E EMPHASIZE the benefits of the proposed change and implement it gradually. When implemented, evaluate the results to make sure that the change achieved its objectives. Evaluate the need for future change, but only implement it when it is necessary.

In summary, a supervisor must have a positive attitude about change. Also, sufficient understanding as to why people resist change must exist and, even more importantly, the supervisor must be well versed in the methods to be used to overcome such resistance.

CONFLICT

Conflict is another aspect of the supervisor's job

Conflict can be good

When changes are implemented in an organization, conflict may result. Conflict is another aspect of the supervisor's job. Contrary to early management thought, conflict does not suggest that management has failed. It is *inevitable,* cannot be fully *avoided,* and can actually be *good* for the organization.

Conflict may be defined as a difference of opinion between two or more individuals or groups. *Organizational conflict* results from differences of opinion between employees, work groups, or departments.

Conflict is inevitable because of the personalities involved in all organizations. It cannot be avoided because all workers will not be in total agreement on all issues at all times. For these reasons, conflict will exist. However, it can be good, especially if the supervisor can use the conflict to obtain all the different points of view and harness them in a way that leads to positive change.

Conflict helps to avoid stagnant thinking

Conflict provides the need to question. It provides the opportunity to avoid stagnant thinking and poor decisions. It can be very frustrating for the supervisor who at times plays the role of the person in the middle. Sometimes the supervisor helps the parties to work through the problem successfully, not by making a decision but rather by helping them to see that they both have a vested interest in what happens. In effect, what happens will effect the organization, and they are part of the organization. The problem of conflict must be handled in a delicate manner. The supervisor must be careful to make sure that when the conflict is resolved, it contributes to the common goals of the organization instead of establishing a "winner" and a "loser."

Forms of Conflict

Of the numerous forms of conflict that arise in modern organizations, those listed below are among the most common:

1. *Employee versus employee:* Examples of this type of conflict are the most common: two employees seeking the same promotion or two supervisors striving for a larger share of the organization's budget.

2. *Employee versus group:* This form of conflict results from an employee promoting individual interests at the expense of established group norms. Such an example is an employee seeking to come in late and leave early when the rest of the work group must comply with the rules.
3. *Group versus group:* An organization is made up of many groups, such as production people, sales people, and engineers. Conflict may arise when one group feels that it is being denied privileges being enjoyed by another group.
4. *Employee or group versus organization:* Conflict may result when an employee or group feels threatened by the organization. These conflicts may arise when organizational demands seem to interfere with individual and/or group needs.

Causes of Conflict

Many factors can cause conflict in today's organizations. The following are some of the most common causes:

1. *Resources:* Most organizations do not have unlimited resources, and conflict results from competition for limited promotions and restricted funds.
2. *Goal differences:* All organizations have goals and objectives. However, at times, the marketing department's goal of increasing sales creates the need for different product sizes and colors, which counteracts the production department's goal of reducing costs.
3. *Personality dynamics:* All employees perceive situations from different points of view. Since all employees will never agree on all issues, personality dynamics is the most common cause of conflict.

Outcomes of Conflict

Most people think that conflict is bad because it suggests disagreement, hostility, and an air of uncooperativeness. As a matter of fact, early management thought viewed conflict as a problem to be avoided at all costs.

Under the right circumstances, conflict can be good

Of late, management thought supports the idea that conflict can be a problem, but that under certain circumstances, it can be good. Stephen P. Robbins reports that a general relationship exists between conflict and performance.[3] When no conflict is present, stagnation may result, and performance may suffer. Conditions of limited conflict, however, can trigger motivation, initiative, and creativity. Too much conflict can result in hostility and unhealthy

[3] Stephen P. Robbins, *Managing Organizational Conflict* (Englewood Cliffs, NJ: Prentice Hall, 1974).

conditions. The role of the supervisor is to control the degree of conflict in order to achieve high levels of performance.

Controlling Conflict

Controlling conflict can be geared in three ways:

1. Stopping conflict before it happens
2. Resolving conflict when it happens
3. Encouraging conflict to make it happen

Never ignore conflict

The last thing a supervisor should do about conflict is to *ignore* it, for this causes the conflict to multiply into an even greater problem.

Another ineffective method of limiting conflict is to smooth over the issue by informing your employees that "everything will be all right." Approaching conflict in this manner usually results in the problem getting worse. This method is not recommended.

A popular approach to conflict is *compromise*. This may or may not resolve the conflict, depending on the circumstances. In many instances, compromise results in a winner and a loser, thereby creating more conflict. Sometimes both parties can be appeased by having portions of each of their ideas utilized, in which case the conflict may be resolved.

Confronting conflict can be very effective

Confrontation involves bringing the parties in conflict together to confront the problem. The key individual in this process is the supervisor, who must handle the situation in a very delicate and careful manner. If handled properly, this method can be very effective.

Expanding resources can usually solve conflict

A frequently effective method of handling conflict is *expanding resources*. If scarce resources can be expanded, conflict will usually go away. For example, if two supervisors are both seeking an increase in their operating budget for the coming year, the conflict can be easily resolved by expanding the pool of money to please both parties. The drawback, of course, is that such an approach may not always be possible.

When goals are achieved, everyone wins

The guiding principle to be used by all supervisors when dealing with conflict is *superordinate goals*, which relate to the growth and survival of the organization. Nothing is more important than that. In effect, the supervisor should express all conflict in terms of *superordinate goals*. If an action contributes to the betterment of the organization, everyone wins. Hence individual goals, group goals, and departmental goals are less important than organizational goals. It is within this framework that supervisors must approach conflict. If the supervisor can manage to get each employee, group, and department to think in these terms, conflict can be beneficial.

SUMMARY

Change is a fact of life. Supervisors must be prepared to accept change as well as to administer it.

Change can be placed in three classes: (1) internal change, (2) external change, and (3) technological change. Despite the type of change, the supervisor is responsible for introducing it successfully. If introduced improperly, it will be resisted. Resistance to change may be used as a means of "taking the pulse" of the department.

To overcome resistance to change, the supervisor must work at creating an open climate, maintaining open lines of communication, introducing change on a gradual basis, involving employee participation, providing appropriate information, and having top management's approval of the change.

Change can result in conflict, which is another important aspect of the supervisor's job. Organizational conflict can be defined as a difference of opinion between employees, work groups, or departments. Its forms include employee versus employee, employee versus group, group versus group, and employee or group versus the organization.

The causes of conflict involve resources, goal differences, and personality dynamics. The outcomes of conflict were traditionally considered to be bad. But recent studies suggest that under the right circumstances conflict can be good, since it may trigger motivation, initiative, and creativity. Too much conflict, however, is not healthy.

The major methods for controlling conflict involve stopping it before it happens, resolving it when it happens, and trying to make it happen. Although many techniques exist to deal with conflict, approaching it in terms of superordinate goals is the most effective solution. In effect, employee goals, group goals, and departmental goals are all subordinate to the superordinate goals of organizational growth and survival.

CASE STUDY 44

There Is No Such Thing as a Free Lunch

The ABC Travel Agency was started about three years ago by Charles Adams. Charles operated the entire agency by himself during the first six months of business to keep costs down. He was a one-person show.

As Charles approached the anniversary of his first year in business, sales were going well, so he decided to hire two clerks to help him deal with customer phone calls and visits. At the end of the second year of operation, he added two travel agents to help him handle the significant increase in business. The two clerks and the two travel agents worked well together. The teamwork practices that they employed began to result in increased office efficiency and satisfied customers. Sales began to increase, and Charles was considering adding a new staff member.

The teamwork continued with the clerks and the agents. They became an extremely tightknit group. They did everything together. They took breaks together and always went to lunch together. To maintain the group ties, Charles never interfered. As business began to increase, however, he began to notice an increased amount of customer phone calls and office visits during the lunch hour. Charles felt that staggering the lunch hours was the answer, but he feared that might destroy the teamwork concept. He thought about it and said to himself, "I am the boss. I have the right to make these policy changes. Besides, at lunch time it's getting so busy I'm becoming a one-person show again. That's why I hired the clerks and the agents in the first place."

Charles was not really sure how to handle the problem. He thought about announcing the policy change when his employees returned from lunch. He promised himself that the problem would be solved no later than tomorrow.

QUESTIONS

1. Evaluate Charles's decision to change the lunch hour policy. Do you agree with it?

2. What are the consequences of approaching the change in this manner?

3. Are there better methods to use? Which one? Why? Which is best? Explain.

4. What is the central issue in the case: internal change or technological change?

5. Could conflict result from this change? If so, how can it be avoided? Explain.

CASE STUDY 45

Did We Handle This Change Correctly?

The Sanco Machine Company has always been regarded as a technologically advanced business. Its hallmark of success has always rested on its ability to engage in successful research and development, and to implement the results on a timely and efficient basis.

About six months ago, research and development introduced a new repair device that was capable of assessing assembly-line mechanical breakdowns through computerization.

In the past, Sanco relied on five super-repair technicians. Production records reflect that only minimal production time was lost in the past because these technicians were able to fix the breakdowns quickly and efficiently. Selection and promotion into the technicians' group were a special thing. Only those who demonstrated superior mechanical aptitudes were considered. The pay scale for the super-repair technicians was 35 percent higher than other salaries within the company.

When research and development announced the completion of the new computer repair device, top management hailed the achievement as a technological advance that would serve to keep Sanco out in front of its competition.

It was determined that the computer repair device would reduce the need for super-repair technicians. The company estimated that it would only need three, since the computer would be able to identify breakdowns dramatically faster and much more accurately. It was announced that the new device would be put into operation in three months.

Top management indicated that a training program would be started in about a month. The five super-repair technicians would enter it, and the three with the highest scores would work with the new device and receive a salary increase in the bargain. The other two technicians would be returned to the regular work force with guaranteed positions.

The training program started as scheduled. At the conclusion of the program none of the workers even passed the course. They put little or no effort into it. They indicated they did not have to prove themselves to anybody; they were already the best, and everyone knew it.

It was now getting close to the introduction of the new device, and no one was trained to use it. One executive suggested they open up the training program to the whole plant to find new people with drive and initiative.

QUESTIONS

1. What do you think of top management's suggestion to open the program to the whole plant? Why?

2. Why did the super-repair technicians fail the training course?

3. Is there a better method for handling the situation? Explain in detail.

4. What is the central issue in this case?

Terms and Concepts Supervisors Should Know

Causes of conflict; Compromise; Conflict; Confrontation; Expanding resources; External change; Forms of conflict; Goal differences; Internal change; Organizational conflict; Personality dynamics; Resistance to change; Smooth over conflict; Superordinate goals; Technological change.

Questions for Discussion

1. Discuss change, and how it influences you and others in your company.
2. How do you react to change? Who sets the pace for change in your company? Have there been any problems?
3. Consider the expression, "Unless things change, they will remain the same." React.
4. Who tends to accept change more easily: men or women? younger or older employees? blue-collar or white-collar workers? the supervisor or the subordinates?
5. Discuss superordinate goals in terms of union-management relations.
6. In terms of conflict, is it better to act or react? How does this apply to change?

For Further Reading—And More Ideas

Baker, H. K., and P. I. Morgan, "Building a Professional Image: Handling Conflict," *Supervisory Management* (February 1986).

Berry, W., "Overcoming Resistance to Change," *Supervisory Management* (February 1983).

Black, H. S., "Riding with Change," *Management World* (December 1985).

Caffarella, R. S., "Managing Conflict: An Analytical Tool," *Training and Development Journal* (February 1984).

Caruth, D., "Overcoming Resistance to Change," *Advanced Management Journal* (Summer 1985).

Chasnoff, R., and P. Muniz, "Training to Manage Conflicts," *Training and Development Journal* (January 1985).

Davis, S. M., "Attempting Major Change? Ten Pitfalls to Avoid—and How," *Human Resource Planing* (1984).

Delbecq, A. L., and P. K. Mills, "Managerial Practices That Enhance Innovation," *Organizational Dynamics* (Summer 1985).

Dozier, L., "Crisis Control Is Change Control," *Data Management* (August 1983).

Girifalco, L. A., "The Dynamics of Technological Change," *Wharton Magazine* (Fall 1982).

Grove, A. S., "How to Make Confrontations Work for You," *Fortune* (July 23, 1984).

Kellogg, M. S., "We Must Have a Very Special Climate for Innovation," *Vital Speeches of the Day* (November 15, 1983).

Koepke, J. D., "Responding to Rapid Change Is a Critical Issue," *National Underwriter* (September 3, 1983).

Kotter, John P., and Leonard A. Schlesinger, "Choosing Strategies for Change," *Harvard Business Review* (March–April 1979).

Lawrence, P. R., "How to Deal with Resistance to Change," *Harvard Business Review* (March–April 1986).

Linder, J. C., "Computers, Corporate Culture, and Change," *Personnel Journal* (September 1985).

Lippert, F. G., "Beware the Side Effects of Change!" *Supervision* (March 1985).

Lynn, G., "Seven Keys to Successful Change Management," *Supervisory Management* (November 1984).

Michael, S. R., "Organizational Change Techniques: Their Present, Their Future," *Organizational Dynamics* (Summer 1982).

Muniz, P., and R. Chasnoff, "Assessing the Causes of Conflicts and Confronting the Real Issues," *Supervisory Management* (March 1986).

Naisbitt, John, *Megatrends*, New York: Warner Books, 1982. *Megatrends 2000*, New York: Warner Books, 1989.

Ofner, J. A., "Managing Change," *Personnel Administrator* (September 1986).

Oromaner, D. S., "Winning Employee Cooperation for Change," *Supervisory Management* (August 1985).

Schwartz, J., "Dealing with a Conflict Can Be Sticky for a Manager: Remembering the Feelings of Both Parties Will Aid in Its Resolution," *Office Administration Automation* (July, 1984).

Tichy, N., "Managing Change Strategically: The Technical, Political, and Cultural Keys," *Organizational Dynamics* (Autumn 1982).

Tjosvold, D., "Making Conflict Productive," *Personnel Administration* (June 1984).

Toffler, Alvin, *Future Shock*, New York: Bantam Books, 1970.

Recognizing Special Groups

18

"United we stand, divided we fall."

LEARNING OBJECTIVES

When you complete this chapter, you should be able to:

1. Describe some of the changes that have come about in the work place as a result of the presence of women and minorities.
2. Identify some of the attitudes toward women and minorities.
3. Understand some of the attitudes about hiring, disciplining, and promoting women and minorities.
4. Understand the impact and purpose of the Civil Rights Act.
5. State the doctrine of comparable worth.
6. Explain the Cinderella complex.
7. Understand the difference between prejudice and discrimination.
8. Identify and discuss the ramifications of age in the work place.

"Together . . . we can get the job done!"

This chapter will help you develop questions for class discussion as you formulate an understanding of the impact of women, minorities, and other groups in the work place. Some answers to the questions below may be found in the chapter, whereas others may require personal reflection.

Do you agree with the passage of the Civil Rights Act? Will it solve the discrimination problem? Is reverse discrimination an unfortunate but inevitable outcome of the law, or should it be prevented?

Does the presence of women and minorities on the job affect productivity? If so, are the effects positive or negative? Can women and minorities ever be regarded as truly equal? Explain.

What is prejudice?

What is discrimination?

Does age have any bearing on worker productivity?

A DIVERSE WORK FORCE

Unlike other cultures, the United States uniquely comprises many groups, each distinct in its history and heritage. The "melting pot" concept provides an effective description of our nation. As immigrants landed throughout the centuries, the United States slowly but surely became a composite of cultural diversification.

Over the years, each group made its own contribution to the building of the nation. Their dedication and hard work formed the backbone of America's rise to industrial leadership. As the nation grew, so did organizations. Industrially, a transformation from small entrepreneurship to corporate dominance took place. At the turn of the century, Anglo-Saxons controlled businesses and organizations, and employed the immigrants as their labor force. The offspring of the immigrant work force enjoyed the benefits provided by their parents. Expanded educational opportunities and changing attitudes forced large organizations to view immigrants and minorities in a different manner. Anglo-Saxon dominance has thus been challenged, and past discriminatory practices have been changed through social upheaval, legal decisions, and human concern.

Today's supervisor must realize that times have changed

The complexities and intricacies of organizational life have changed drastically, which today's supervisor must realize. Old attitudes are no longer appropriate; new values and attitudes are necessary. Diverse people and groups have a place in today's organization. Women, minorities, and other special groups are here to stay. It is conceivable that over time others may emerge. To ignore this fact is to ignore reality.

To a large extent, the answer to the problem of dealing with such a diverse work force rests with effective human relations practices. People should be treated as equal, because they *are*. As supervisors learn to approach their workers in this manner, a positive tone for organizational performance will be set. Perhaps organizations can set an example for the nation.

CHANGES IN THE WORK FORCE

The traditional image of a white, male-dominated business world is diminishing. With the passage of the Civil Rights Act of 1964, slowly—but surely—the sex and color of the work force began to change. As women and other minorities continue to make progressive strides, attitudes and values also are changing. As a matter of fact, no area is affected more by these changes than supervision. However, despite the legal and ethical concerns, some people cannot get used to the fact that women and minorities have a place in the business world. With time, many of these attitudes will likely change. Nonetheless, the prevailing viewpoint is less than satisfactory. Transformation cannot occur overnight; it takes time and effort. While the nation is clearly moving in the right direction, each and every member of the work force must play a major role in bringing about the transformation. Proper supervisory attitudes can serve as the catalyst to usher in the change in an orderly and systematic fashion. While knowledge and information are easy to acquire, attitude change does not occur so easily. Beliefs are complex and deeply rooted within the individual. Have you considered your attitudes and values about the issue of women and minorities? Are your beliefs legal and ethical? What about your personal practices? As you consider these general questions, think of how they translate to your on-the-job practices. For example,

- Would it bother you to have a female supervisor?
- What is your attitude about having a black business partner?
- Does working with Orientals, Hispanics, or Jews concern you?
- Do you hire women and minorities because you have to, or because you want to?
- Is the concept of discrimination a legal issue or a humanistic issue?
- Do you promote based on skill and performance, or are color and sex factors that you consider?

Your answers to these questions will largely determine if you are part of the problem—or part of the solution. Will your values and attitudes help bring about the transformation expediently and efficiently? Perhaps you will be the change agent to help solve the problem forever. The sooner—the better!

Four Decades of Change

Sally Ride became the first American woman to fly in space. Sandra Day O'Connor was appointed a Supreme Court justice, and Geraldine Ferraro was the Democratic Party's choice to run for vice-president of the United States in 1984. Lynette Woodard became the first female member of the Harlem Globetrotters. Connie Chung, an Oriental female, achieved success as an NBC News anchor. Many women have been promoted to managerial and executive ranks, while others have opted for entrepreneurship.

During the same time, minorities have made great strides. Jesse Jackson continues to be a positive agent for political and social reform. Many major cities and states are governed by blacks, while others succeed at managerial, executive, and business ownership endeavors. The same can be said for all minorities, as Hispanics, Orientals, and others continue to excel.

While women and minorities have come a long way since the days when the working world was a white, all-male domain, the problem is far from resolved. As a nation, movement is taking place, yet despite the legal guarantees, women and minorities are still less than equal in the job market.

More change is necessary

Current studies show that women and minorities earn less in all fields, and that illegal discriminatory hiring practices still exist. Despite the passage of the Civil Rights Act of 1964 and despite visible minority progress, more change is necessary. The issue is no longer one of legality but of attitude.

WHO ARE MINORITIES?

The purpose of the Civil Rights Act of 1964 is to prohibit discrimination on the basis of national origin, ethnic group, sex, creed, age, religion, or race. From a legal point of view, its goal is to protect the rights of all, especially those groups such as the following, who have experienced discrimination:

- Young
- Ethnic groups (Irish, Italians, Jews, etc.)
- Elderly
- Handicapped
- Hispanics

- American Indians
- Asians
- Blacks
- Disadvantaged
- Drug and alcohol abusers
- Eskimos

- Middle Easterners
- Members of certain religious groups
- Vietnam veterans
- Women

WOMEN

Women form half of today's work force

In 1950, women constituted 20 percent of the work force; today, they are nearly half. Projections by the Bureau of Labor Statistics of the U.S. Department of Labor suggest that more than 60 percent of all women will be active members of the work force by the late 1990s. It is also estimated that 52 to 55 percent of the working population will be female.

Women are an integral part of the work force

Since women are an integral part of the work force at all levels, individuals with biases, stereotyped beliefs, and unfounded opinions about them had best be prepared to change. Unfortunately, women have been the subject of many myths that must be identified and dispelled. To base executive choices on unfounded fact and unrealistic opinion is grossly unfair. A list of some of the myths about women follow:[1]

- Myth 1: The priorities of men and women differ.
- Myth 2: Men have superior mental characteristics and ability.
- Myth 3: Women lack education and experience.
- Myth 4: Women are not good team players.
- Myth 5: Women are unstable, indecisive, and temperamental.
- Myth 6: Women are not career oriented.
- Myth 7: Women lack the motivation and ability to achieve.
- Myth 8: Women can't handle stress and pressure.
- Myth 9: Men work harder than women.
- Myth 10: Women executives will never be viewed positively by men.

Myth 1: The Priorities of Men and Women Differ

Research findings suggest that women's and men's priorities are quite comparable. In fact, according to the results of a major survey by Julia Kagan, "women classify general work success

---

[1] See Julia Kagan, "Who Succeeds, Who Doesn't," *Working Woman*, October 1985, pp. 113–117; "Female Execs' Attitudes Examined," *Delaware State News*, April 8, 1986, p. 12; George El Biles and Holly A. Pryatet, "Myths, Management, and Women," *Personnel Journal*, October 1978, pp. 572–578; "Managing the Woman's Way," *Newsweek*, March 17, 1986, pp. 42–54; U. S. Department of Labor, Employment Standards Administration, Women's Bureau, *Role of Women* (Washington, DC, 1975); "Working Woman Matures," *USA Today*, April 8, 1986; and "More and More, She's the Boss," *Time* 126 (1985), p. 64.

among their main priorities significantly more often than men."
Other similarities also exist. A creative life is an equal concern for
men and women, as is making a contribution to society. Additionally, both genders rate "becoming financially well-off" as
important.[2]

Myth 2: Men Have Superior Mental Characteristics and Ability

According to a California study, women executives have the
same mental characteristics and ability to perform as men. James
Boulgarides of California State University at Los Angeles tested 286
men and 286 women executives, and concluded that men and
women make decisions in the same way, and that both are task
oriented.

Myth 3: Women Lack Education and Experience

On the average, women actually have higher educational levels than men.[3] By and large, women lack experience at managing
and supervising because they have not had the opportunity. When
given the chance, however, women have proved themselves capable. In 1972, 4.6 percent of all executives were women. By 1988,
that figure had more than doubled. As the experience base for
female managers continues to grow, the number of women who
aspire to executive positions will also increase. These factors, when
coupled with the high female educational levels, combine to dispel
the myth.

Myth 4: Women Are Not Good Team Players

Oddly enough, women may have the edge in teamwork despite the widely held belief that men have an advantage in this area
because they grew up playing football and other team sports. Leadership studies at West Point found that male and female cadets
performed equally well in getting the job done. Women were rated
higher when it came to looking out for subordinates' welfare, and
showing interest and human concern.

It has also been suggested that the lessons boys learn on the

---

[2] Kagan,"Who Succeeds," p. 114.

[3] James M. Higgins, *Human Relations Concepts and Skills* (New York: Random House, 1982), p. 274.

playing fields may not always be positive. Male competition generally has someone winning and someone losing. Hostile takeovers and other destructive behavior can result from this competitive instinct. Frequently, such competitive struggle is for personal gain with no regard for the good of the company.

Myth 5: Women Are Unstable, Indecisive, and Temperamental

As the nation shifts from an industrial to a service economy, the need to relate to people on a human basis becomes increasingly important. Some traits considered to be feminine are now recognized as beneficial in the work place. Sympathy and sensitivity are distinct advantages when it comes to getting the best out of people. In some families, females are raised to use their emotions as the basis for decision making. Since business must interact with people who are emotional, women are often more adept and perceptive at interpreting emotional cues.

Myth 6: Women Are Not Career Oriented

A common fallacy about women is that they lack career orientation. This myth suggests that women have been considered poor economic risks because they place family interests over business concerns. It has been said that women will leave work to have children and miss work to take care of children. Actually, statistics do not support this statement. Historically, women did leave the work force to have children, but this trend is clearly changing. Currently, many women who have quit work to have children are now returning to work in record numbers. These women are prepared for the challenges of managing, having learned the arts of compromise, conciliation, and listening through their daily interactions with children. As mothers, they also learned crisis management and have become better organizers.[4]

Myth 7: Women Lack the Motivation and Ability to Achieve

There are no studies to support this myth. As a matter of fact, when given the opportunity, women *are* able to achieve. One noticeable trend has been the increase in entrepreneurial ventures by

---

[4]"Managing the Woman's Way," p. 54.

women. Table 18–1 shows the results of a recent survey that compared the motivations of men versus women in the work place. As shown, little to no difference exists between the work motivations of men and women.

Myth 8: Women Can't Handle Stress and Pressure

Many women have achieved success in typical stress-oriented jobs, such as sales, management, advertising, medical, air traffic control, executive, and supervisory positions.

Myth 9: Men Work Harder Than Women

Recent studies indicate that women work harder than men both at home and on the job. William and Denise Bielby, sociologists at the University of California at Santa Barbara, analyzed data from a national survey conducted by the University of Michigan. Their findings showed that women give more time and attention to their jobs than men, despite the fact that working women spend more than twice as much time on household tasks. More women than men also reported having jobs requiring substantial mental or physical effort.

Myth 10: Women Executives Will Never Be Viewed Positively by Men

According to recent studies, male views about female executives are drastically changing. In a 1965 *Harvard Business Review* survey, 9 percent of the men held favorable attitudes toward women executives. Some 20 years later, 33 percent held this atti-

TABLE 18–1   Work motivations of men versus women

Motivation	Women	Men
To do a good job	91%	85%
To be challenged	81%	71%
To improve myself	81%	82%
To be financially secure	69%	70%
To show others my abilities	62%	46%
To become independent	51%	59%
To help others	51%	57%
To make a mark on the world	22%	26%
To accumulate great wealth	15%	30%

Source: Julia Kagan, "Who Succeeds, Who Doesn't," *Working Woman*, October 1985, pp. 113–117.

tude. In 1965, 51 percent of men felt that women were temperamentally unfit for management, compared to 18 percent 20 years later. Twenty-seven percent of the men surveyed in 1965 felt comfortable being supervised by women, whereas in the mid-1980s almost 50 percent said they would be comfortable working for women.[5]

The Comparable Worth Doctrine

The comparable worth doctrine will have far-reaching effects

The comparable worth doctrine may have implications as far-reaching as civil rights.[6] Over 10 years ago, a union official of the Washington Federation of State Employees requested an examination of wages paid to its members. The study found that jobs that were predominately (70 percent or more) filled by women paid 20 percent less than comparable jobs held by men. The controversy resulted in the U.S. Supreme Court establishing the comparable worth doctrine, which, stated simply, holds that jobs with similar evaluation scores should have comparable pay. Job evaluation is at the heart of the comparable worth doctrine. Although rating systems vary slightly, generally accepted job evaluation factors include

1. Knowledge, experience, and skill
2. Degree of innovativeness or problem solving
3. Risks or accountability for error
4. Interpersonal skills and level interaction
5. Hazard or unpleasantness

The National Committee on Pay Equity released the results of a study in which evaluators rated traditionally male and female jobs by awarding points for skill required, responsibility, and other factors. Table 18–2 reports the findings from three locations.

In 1983, the *Harvard Business Review* surveyed 900 readers for their opinion on the comparable worth doctrine.[7] A summary of the conclusions is as follows:

1. Male and female workers disagree dramatically about the causes of the wage gap. They also disagree about the consequences of establishing a comparable worth policy.
2. Women think the salary gap is caused by biases in organizational hiring and compensation methods. Men, on the other hand, blame

---

[5] "More and More, She's the Boss," p. 64.

[6] For further information on this issue, see George P. Sape, "Coping with Comparable Worth," *Harvard Business Review*, May–June 1985, pp. 145–152; and J. B. Quinn, "Comparable Pay for Women," *Newsweek*, January 16, 1984.

[7] Benson Rosen, Sara Rynes, and Thomas A. Mahoney, "Probing Opinions: Compensation, Jobs, and Gender," *Harvard Business Review*, July–August, 1983, p. 170.

TABLE 18–2   Ratings of traditionally male and female jobs in three locations

Job	Points	Monthly Salary
Minnesota		
Registered Nurse	275	$1,723
Vocational education teacher	275	$2,260
Typing pool supervisor	199	$1,373
Painter	185	$1,707
San Jose, California		
Senior legal secretary	226	$665
Senior carpenter	226	$1,040
Senior librarian	493	$898
Senior chemist	493	$1,119
Washington State		
Licensed practical nurse	173	$1,030
Correctional officer	173	$1,436
Secretary	197	$1,122
Maintenance carpenter	197	$1,707

Source: Benson Rosen, Sara Rynes, and Thomas A. Mahoney, "Probing Opinions: Compensation, Jobs, and Gender." *Harvard Business Review*, July–August 1983, p. 170.

women for choosing low-paying jobs with restricted career opportunities.

Regardless of the reasons for the male-female wage gap and the perceived consequences of the comparable worth doctrine, the problem is real. Most experts agree that it will take time to find a solution, perhaps one or two generations. Experts also suggest that we should begin now by improving the education and career counseling of both men and women. If men continue to pursue occupations that are traditionally male, and women continue to pursue those that are traditionally female, the problem will be prolonged.[8]

The Cinderella Complex

The Cinderella Complex emerges during childhood

Collette Dowling, author of *The Cinderella Complex*, suggests that "many women subconsciously deny their zestful potential on the job, keeping themselves in a psychological limbo waiting for a prince to give them life's meaning."[9] According to the theory, women sabotage their own growth, preferring dependence to independence. The Cinderella complex emerges in childhood, when little girls are influenced by passive mothers and overcontrolling

[8] "Coping with Comparable Worth," pp. 145–152.
[9] Collette Dowling, *The Cinderella Complex* (New York: Summit Books, 1981).

fathers, and develop a submissive outlook on work and life. Dowling quotes psychologist Lois Hoffman, who distinguishes male and female behavior on the job by stating that "driving a point home, winning an argument, beating others in competition, and attending the task at hand without being sidetracked by concern with rapport are all hurdles women have difficulty jumping, no matter how intelligent they are."[10] In effect, the Cinderella complex holds women back and detracts from their self-confidence.

Sexual Harassment

Sexual harassment is a major problem

Unfortunately, sexual harassment on the job is a major problem faced by women. Such harassment may include sexist remarks, verbal profanity, touching, physical abuse, demands for sexual favors, and unwelcomed advances in exchange for preferential treatment. Needless to say, sexual harassment is legally and ethically wrong. Nonetheless, it is common.

Progress must continue

Recent legal actions suggest that women are becoming more aggressive in dealing with this problem, as well they should. It is hoped that this assertive attitude will lead to the ultimate end of the problem. While immediate obliteration is unrealistic, progress must continue. Human beings should not be subjected to this type of treatment on the job.

A Female Action Plan

A sensible approach must be followed

Bias, prejudice, and discrimination are obstacles faced by women in the work force. But instead of sitting back and doing nothing about these problems, a more sensible approach is to follow an action plan for success. Women must develop self-confidence by approaching the challenges of a career realistically. Perhaps the following guidelines, advanced by former San Francisco mayor Dianne Feinstein, can help women attain career success.[11]

GUIDELINE 1: DEVELOP STAYING POWER

Career commitment is not for 3 years but for 30 or more. Be prepared to make the pledge.

---

[10] Ibid.

[11] "Twelve Rules for Getting Ahead," *Working Woman*, January 1986, pp. 84–85.

GUIDELINE 2: NEVER USE YOUR SEX OR FAMILY AS AN EXCUSE

Men do not miss work because of dinner preparation and babysitting problems. Females should not use these excuses either. If you use typical female excuses, the sexual barrier will continue to exist on the job.

GUIDELINE 3: PUT IN MORE TIME THAN ANYBODY ELSE

Be available for extra assignments and volunteer for extra jobs. Get to work early and leave late. These habits lead to promotion and ultimate success.

GUIDELINE 4: NETWORK

Use other women as mentors for counsel and guidance. Seek and share information. Use this network as a source of strength.

GUIDELINE 5: SPECIALIZE

In addition to regular job duties, develop an area of expertise. No matter what your job may be, pursue a special interest. Become an expert. It will increase your value to the organization.

GUIDELINE 6: BE A TEAM PLAYER

Don't be the center of attention. Be willing to support others and work in collective attainment of organizational goals.

GUIDELINE 7: DON'T WEAR YOUR SEX LIKE A BADGE ON YOUR SLEEVE

Do not let feminist activities detract from your performance. Keep your beliefs in perspective. Actions speak louder than words.

GUIDELINE 8: LEARN TO BE A MANAGER

Learn to give and take orders. Be organized. Establish priorities. Practice effective management and human relations principles.

GUIDELINE 9: THANK THOSE WHO HELP YOU

Recognize the contribution of others. Too often we forget to thank those who have done a good job. Don't be afraid to provide a pat on the back when it is deserved.

GUIDELINE 10: USE YOUR APPEARANCE TO CREATE AN IMAGE OF STRENGTH

You will be judged by your appearance. If you want to be a professional, make sure you look like one. Image and appearance are important. Use them to promote strength.

CORPORATE UPDATE

In an attempt to attract and retain females with executive ability, many companies are offering "options." Some of the more popular options include day care support, job sharing, flexible hours, and equal opportunities for advancement. The top four companies offering progressive options and opportunities to women include

1. *Apple Computer (personal computers):* Women hold about 50 percent of the management slots. The company offers flexible working hours and job sharing. Plans for a day care center exist.
2. *Hewlett-Packard (computers and scientific measuring devices):* Women make up 25 percent of the managers and 30 percent of the professional ranks.
3. *Merck (prescription drugs):* Benefits include flexible hours, relocation assistance, adoption aid, financial support for nearby day care centers, and maternity and paternity leave.
4. *Herman Miller (designers of office environments):* Secretaries move into management. The top women can earn $45,000 or more.

GUIDELINE 11: DO NOT CRY

People perceive crying as a weakness. It must be avoided at all costs.

GUIDELINE 12: BE LOYAL

Be loyal to your boss and your company. Loyalty is a major trait that is respected and admired. It is also a leading consideration in the promotional process.

BLACKS AND OTHER MINORITIES

If organizations and supervisors expect to maximize their human resource contributions, they must work to improve their relations with people of different races, colors, creeds, and national origins. Blacks, Spanish-speaking Americans, Asian-Americans, and American Indians are the largest ethnic-racial minority groups in the United States. Additionally, European immigrants comprise a significant portion of the working population.

The Civil Rights Act was just the beginning   While the Civil Rights Act of 1964 provided legal support for blacks and other minorities in the work force, little attention has been given to the influence of race and minority culture on worker interests, issues, concerns, and behavior. It is widely recognized that cultural differences about job attitudes exist among the various groups. Further, because of their cultural differences, many minorities, especially blacks, have suffered inequities in the work place such as elimination or rejection from jobs, lack of upward mobility, and other discriminatory personnel actions. In many cases, skin color influenced hiring and promotional policies. While the current situation is far better than the past, there is ample room for improvement. Instances of unjust job opportunities remain. Progress must continue. The elimination of prejudice and discrimination is everyone's responsibility. While quick solutions are not possible, our collective efforts can expedite the process.

Positive change must continue

PREJUDICE AND DISCRIMINATION

Discrimination is a persistent problem for organizations, management, and workers. All forms of discrimination prevent the organization from reaching its maximum potential. While most people are familiar with certain types of discrimination, the less recognizable forms also deserve serious attention.

What Is Prejudice?

Prejudice is an attitude, not an act

Prejudice is an attitude, not an act. It is a mental habit based on an unfounded opinion with no rational basis. It gives rise to stereotyping and the improper categorizing of all people into groups, without consideration of individual differences. For the most part, prejudice is based on ignorance. For example, individuals who believe that all members of a particular minority group are lazy, unproductive, and irresponsible display their ignorance in subscribing to such illogical, stereotyped thinking.

What Is Discrimination?

Discrimination can occur on the job

By definition, discrimination is the act of demonstrating prejudices. It occurs on the job when actions favor one individual or group over another individual or group because of factors unrelated to personal qualifications or job performance.

Implications

As blacks and other minorities continue to play major roles in corporate America, it is important that organizations and supervisors recognize the cultural implications of this development. The type and quality of human interactions have changed and will continue to change as minorities keep striving for career success in organizational settings. The implications of this phenomenon are three-fold:

1. Organizations must continue to develop policies and practices that guard against discriminatory actions. Additionally, boards of directors and chief executive officers must state unilaterally that the elimination of discriminatory policies is a major, daily priority
2. Managers and supervisors must learn to identify and overcome personal prejudices to prevent them from resulting in job discrimination
3. Blacks and other minorities must
   a. Continue to seek and take advantage of educational opportunities in preparation for organizational challenges
   b. Understand that change does not occur as quickly as anticipated and patiently move forward in a systematic and logical fashion
   c. Be prepared to perform and not expect preferential treatment, recognizing that promotions must be earned

AGE DISCRIMINATION

Age discrimination is unfair and damaging to an organization

Discrimination based on age is an issue concerning every member of the work force. Regardless of race, color, creed, sex, or national origin, age is the one variable experienced by everyone. Everyone at one time is young and, God willing, will grow old. Unfortunately, the upper and lower age brackets of the working population have been subject to discrimination. Many discriminatory practices have emerged from stereotyping and unfounded opinions.

Assumptions based on age are unfair and grossly inaccurate. The world is comprised of older individuals who act young, and younger individuals who act old. From an organizational point of view, productivity is what counts.

By and large, age discrimination is based on incorrect generalizations that are not based on factual information, including the following:

Myths About Younger Employees

- Myth 1: Young workers are immature, disruptive, and rebellious.
- Myth 2: Young workers resent authority and fail to give proper respect.
- Myth 3: Young workers seek immediate rewards for self-gratification instead of organizational contribution.

- Myth 4: Young workers do not understand their role and place in the organization.
- Myth 5: Young workers will change jobs and organizations frequently.

Myths About Older Employees

- Myth 1: Older workers are a health risk.
- Myth 2: Older workers are subject to declining mental capabilities and are thus less productive.
- Myth 3: Older workers are subject to declining physical capabilities and are thus less productive.
- Myth 4: Older workers are set in their habits and less likely to accept change.
- Myth 5: Older workers block the promotion of younger workers.

For the sake of organizational growth and stability, these myths must be dispelled. The only variable that counts is performance. People must judge and be judged only in terms of their ability to produce.

OTHER GROUPS

Job classifications define other groups within the organizational setting. Organizations and supervisors must recognize and understand these groups and the differences among them. Job classification groups include

1. Blue-collar workers
2. Creative workers
3. Hourly workers
4. Knowledge workers
5. Line workers
6. Part-time workers
7. Professional workers
8. Staff workers
9. Technical workers
10. White-collar workers

Organizations and supervisors must refrain from treating members of different groups in the same fashion. Each group possesses individual characteristics, largely determined by the nature of the job. Supervisors must approach each individual and each group with a style unique for that classification. Supervisors must invest time and energy in the study of each job to differentiate the various personalities involved. Each group must be given the free-

---

WHAT DOES AGE REALLY MEAN?

At age 14, Nadia Comaneci was the first gymnast to score a perfect 10 in the Olympics. At age 42, Ted Williams hit a home run in his last official time at bat. Nolan Ryan, at age 43, pitched his sixth major league no-hitter.

Golda Meir was 71 when she became prime minister of Israel. When Ronald Reagan assumed his second presidential term, he was weeks away from his 74th birthday. William Pitt II was 24 when he became prime minister of Great Britain.

George Bernard Shaw was 94 when his first play was produced. Clara Peller, of "Where's the beef?" fame, was 82 when she started her television career.

Mozart was 7 when his first composition was published. At age 16, Benjamin Franklin was a newspaper columnist. At age 81, he was a framer of the U.S. Constitution.

At age 100, Eubie Blake was still writing songs and performing.

What does age really mean?

---

dom to do its prescribed job. This requires the creation of an appropriate climate and supervisory style designed to maximize the contribution of each member and each group.

SUMMARY

The United States uniquely comprises many groups, each distinct in its history and heritage. The "melting pot" concept serves to describe the nation as well as the organizations functioning within its economic system. The cultural diversity creates complexities and intricacies in organizational life. The traditional image of a white, male-dominated business world diminished with the passage of the Civil Rights Act of 1964, which outlaws discriminatory practices and requires organizations to function as equal opportunity employers.

Currently, approximately 50 percent of the work force is female, and organizations must adjust to the influx of women into supervisory, managerial, and executive roles. This requires a change of attitude and the dispelling of unfounded myths about women.

Blacks and other minorities also have been subject to similar prejudicial and discriminatory practices. While recognizable advancements have taken place, improvement is still required.

Age serves as a barrier in some organizations. Age stereotypes, like others, must be recognized as unfounded and dismissed. Additionally, myths about the young and the old must be discarded with haste.

Job classification describes other groups within the organization, including blue-collar workers, creative workers, hourly workers, knowledge workers, line workers, part-time workers, professional workers, staff workers, technical workers, and white-collar workers. Supervisors must treat each group according to the personality differences as determined by the nature of the job.

CASE STUDY 46

Discrimination Against a Woman Stockbroker

Diane Patterson is employed as a broker by Johnson and Hunt, a large metropolitan brokerage firm. Diane was promoted to this position five months ago, when the company lost a few of its brokers to a competing firm. She had previously worked for a number of years as a secretary to Scott Pitts, one of the brokers in the firm, and he recommended her for a promotion when a vacancy occurred.

Although Diane started her duties with enthusiasm, Cliff Stevenson, the office manager, soon felt it necessary to question her on her deteriorating performance. When Diane assumed her duties as broker, Cliff had heard some of the men speak against her resentfully. He also knew that Diane was losing customers for no apparent reason other than the fact that she was female.

When Cliff questioned Diane on this, she replied, "I don't like being the only female in the department. I feel as if everyone is against me here." And she added, "Many of my male clients seem to think that because I'm a woman, I'm not qualified to be a broker." Diane also suggested that perhaps a new start in another department would enable her to carry out her duties as a broker more effectively.

Cliff knows that Diane is capable of per-forming her duties, and with the shortage of brokers in his department he does not want to lose her. Cliff decides to ask Scott's opinion on the problem.

"The men feel threatened by Diane," Scott replied. "They feel that being a broker is a demanding job, and should belong to men only. One of the men said that she has no right to fill a position that may be needed by a man to support his family."

"I find that a bit hard to believe," replied Cliff.

"Believe it, Cliff. Even Harry Morgan mentioned something about not having to worry only about younger men taking over his job, but now he'd have to worry about his secretary."

Having gained an understanding of the problem, Cliff must decide what course of action to take. If you were Cliff, what would you do?

QUESTIONS

1. Would you let Diane go?
2. Would you discuss the problem with the men only, or with Diane present?
3. How could you, as a manager, enhance Diane's status?

CASE STUDY 47

Policy Development

Recently your superior attended a seminar on discrimination and equal employment opportunities. At the weekly supervisory meeting, it was mentioned that your company does not have a policy on this important issue. You have been appointed the chairperson of a committee charged with the development of a policy and a system designed to eliminate discrimination on the basis of race, color, sex, creed, and national origin.

QUESTIONS

1. Describe the policy you would develop.
2. Describe the system you would develop.

CASE STUDY 48

Help Wanted: One Forklift Driver

You are the supervisor of the warehouse in a large paper container manufacturing company, and you have a position open for a forklift operator in your department. This morning the personnel office informed you that three job applicants had completed the initial interviews for the opening in your department.

Your first applicant, Pat Mohan, is a woman 25 years old. You are a bit surprised that Personnel didn't tell you the applicant was female, and you begin to consider how well this young woman would be able to drive and operate the forklift. Although Ms. Mohan might be able to drive the truck, you wonder what effect she will have on the rest of the crew, who are known for their rough habits and language. As these thoughts run through your head, you introduce yourself and ask Ms. Mohan to sit down.

How would you interview her? Role play the situation, beginning with the introduction.

QUESTIONS

1. Would you thank her for coming, but tell her she just wouldn't work out?
2. Would you ask if she can tolerate dirty language?
3. Would you use rough language to see how she reacts?
4. Would you hire Ms. Mohan if she is qualified?

CASE STUDY 49

Sorry, Being First Isn't Good Enough!

Bill Tyson has been employed at a nearby university for three years as a custodian. He recently applied for a position as a gatekeeper, which paid about the same as he was presently earning but had varied hours and offered more people contact, which Bill felt were definite advantages over his present situation.

He handed in a résumé and completed what he felt to be a very successful interview. His supervisor assured him that with his excellent work record and experience, his chances of getting the new position were definitely favorable.

In time the gatekeeper was chosen. It turned out to be a man who was less qualified than Bill and whose previous work record was only passable. The explanation given to Bill was that the university had an affirmative action program and that in or-der to keep the employee scales balanced, they had to give the job to someone from a minority group. When Bill attempted to defend his case, his supervisor told him: "We do have rules and regulations we must follow," making it very clear that the other person's race had been the deciding factor.

Bill did continue to work as a custodian, but he felt resentful and suspicious toward his superiors.

QUESTIONS

1. What are your feelings toward the supervisor's handling of this case?
2. What could or should the supervisor have done to avoid having Bill develop hostile feelings toward the university?
3. How can affirmative action programs benefit organizations?

CASE STUDY 50

A Hiring Dilemma

A recent survey indicates that no women fill supervisory, managerial, or executive positions at your company. Although this circumstance was not deliberate, the company is concerned and believes that immediate action is necessary to correct the problem. The human resource manager has a meet-ing in your department, and asks you for ideas and suggestions on how to remedy the dilemma.

QUESTION

1. What do you suggest?

Terms and Concepts Supervisors Should Know

Age myths; Cinderella complex; Civil Rights Act; Comparable
worth doctrine; Discrimination; Female myths; Minority groups;
Prejudice; Sexual harassment; Stereotyping.

Questions for Discussion

1. What are the implications of the Cinderella complex?
2. Does the doctrine of comparable worth prove that wage discriminatory
   practices exist? Explain.
3. Differentiate between prejudice and discrimination. Discuss their implications in terms of black and other minority groups.
4. Explain job classification discrimination.
5. Does your company have an affirmative action officer in the human
   resource department? Why or why not?
6. What are the guidelines in your company for hiring minorities?

For Further Reading—And More Ideas

"Arguing over Minority Preferences," *Broad-casting* (November 28, 1988).

Boggs, Jerry A., "Comparable Worth as Mis-guided Effort," *The Humanist* (May–June 1986).

Braham, J., "Women at the Top," *Industry Week* (March 4, 1985).

Brimmer, A. F., "The Prospects for Black Busi-ness," *Black Enterprise* (April 1985).

Brophy, B., "The Truth About Women Manag-ers (Interview with F. N. Schwartz)," *U.S. News & World Report* (March 13, 1989).

Colosi, M. L., et al., "Early Retirement Pro-grams: Golden Handshakes or Gilded Shoves," *Labor Law Journal* (December 1988).

"Corporate Women: Just How Far Have We Come?" *Working Woman* (March 1984).

Denton, D. K., "Supervising the Younger Em-ployee," *Supervisory Management* (March 1984).

Distelheim, Rochelle, "The New Shoot-Out at Generation Gap," *Working Woman* (March 1986).

Dowling, Collette, *The Cinderella Complex*, New York: Summit Books, 1981.

Dubno, P., "Attitudes Toward Women Execu-tives: A Longitudinal Approach," *Academy of Management Journal* (March 1985).

"The Effects of Aging on Job Performance and Appraisals," *Personnel* (May–June 1983).

Fraker, Susan, "Why Women Aren't Making It to the Top," *The Humanist* (October 1984).

Gold, Michael Evan, "The Case for Comparable Worth," *The Humanist* (May–June 1986).

Grant, C. T., "Blacks Hit Racial Roadblocks Climbing up the Corporate Ladder," *Business Social Review* (Winter 1985).

Half, R., "I Lost My Job at 54," *Management Accounting* (March 1989).

Henderson, E., "Blacks in Corporate America: Is There a Future?" *Personnel Journal* (January 1986).

Herz, D. E., and P. L. Rones., "Institutional Barriers to Employment of Older Workers," *Monthly Labor Review* (April 1989).

Hutchens, R. M., "Do Job Opportunities De-cline with Age?" *International Labour Review* (October 1988).

"In Good Company: 25 Best Places for Blacks to Work," *Black Enterprise* (February 1986).

Jones, Edward W., Jr., "Black Managers: A Dream Deferred," *Harvard Business Review* (May–June 1986).

Jones, R. T., et al., "How Do You Manage a Diverse Workforce?" *Training and Develop-ment Journal* (February 1989).

Kagan, Julia, "Who Succeeds, Who Doesn't," *Working Woman* (October 1985).

Kovach, Kenneth A., "Subconscious Stereotyping in Personnel Decisions," *Business Horizons* (October 1982).

"Minorities' Training Inadequate," *Personnel Management* (February 1989).

Naisbitt, John, "Women in the Workplace," *Success* (October 1985).

"New Program Matches Experienced Minorities with Employers," *Broadcasting* (February 13, 1989).

Powell, Gary N., Barry Z. Posner, and Warren H. Schmidt, "Women: The More Committed Managers?" *Management Review* (June 1985).

Schlafly, Phyllis, "Comparable Worth: Unfair to Men and Women," *The Humanist* (May–June 1986).

Seligman, D., "Pay Equity Is a Bad Idea," *Fortune* (May 14, 1984).

Stevens, G. E., "Attitudes Toward Blacks in Management Are Changing," *Personnel Administration* (June 1984).

"Why Do Women Earn Less Than Men?" *Changing Times* (April 1984).

"Women of Excellence," *MS* (January 1986).

Working with a Union

19

"How will this change my job?"

LEARNING OBJECTIVES

When you complete this chapter, you should be able to:
1. Understand the nature of labor unions.
2. Briefly explain the history of the labor movement.
3. Explain the importance of good supervisory practices and how they relate to union prevention.
4. Understand why workers join unions.
5. Identify some of the issues that are part of collective bargaining.
6. Understand the nature of complaints and recall the guidelines for handling them.
7. Understand the steps used in grievance procedures.
8. Identify some of the ways to prevent grievances.

"In a successful union-management relationship, everybody wins!"

The topic of unions makes some supervisors uneasy. In fact, many supervisors fear the prospect of unionization. Here are questions that can help you focus on some of the concerns about unions, collective bargaining, grievances, and the shop steward as they relate to supervisors.

What is a union?

Why do unions form?

What makes workers want to join unions?

Is there anything a supervisor can do to prevent unions?

If the company becomes unionized, does my job as a supervisor change? If so, how?

What is collective bargaining? What issues are negotiated?

What are union security arrangements? Do they affect hiring? If so, how?

Who is the shop steward? What does the shop steward do? How do I, as a supervisor, relate to the steward?

Does a union help or hinder my resolution of an employee's complaint? Can I take a stand on this issue?

What are the stages or steps of a grievance procedure? Can I prevent grievances? If so, how?

About one-fifth of the work force in the United States is represented by labor unions. By and large, most unions represent the so-called blue-collar worker, although in recent years, unions have made great strides in other sectors of the work force and now include teachers, office workers, nurses, and engineers. Govenment workers (federal, state, and local) are also joining unions and employee associations at increasing rates. In fact, the public sector represents one of the fastest-growing segments of the current labor movement. Government employees, although limited in their bargaining rights and generally lacking the legal right to strike, have achieved through legislation the right to form and join labor organizations.

In short, unions are accepted socially and legally and are present in virtually all industries of the nation's work force. Since unions are an integral part of our management system, it is important that supervisors recognize, understand, and learn to work with them effectively.

WHAT IS A UNION?

What do they do?

A union is a legal organization that attempts to improve the economic, social, and political standing of its members through a process known as *collective bargaining*. Collective bargaining takes the form of negotiations, and through this process, the union seeks to obtain better wages, fringe benefits, and working conditions for its members. Unions also attempt to help satisfy workers' social, self-esteem, and developmental needs. In short, unions seek to satisfy those needs that are basically unmet via the existing practice of management.

Unions seek to satisfy worker needs

HOW DO UNIONS DEVELOP?

The history of labor unions goes back as far as the 1790s, when carpenter and printer craft unions were formed to oppose wage reductions. For the most part, early labor unions were almost exclusively limited to the northern states. During this period, the courts banned unions as illegal conspiracies in restraint of trade. In case after case, the courts ruled that unions were interfering with an employer's right to run the business. Many employees were hired on the condition that they would not join unions. If the employees did join unions, they were fired. Their names were also placed on a *blacklist*, which was circulated to other employers. Despite these conditions, by 1920 more than five million workers were represented by unions. The great depression created a tremendous setback in union growth. The passage of the Norris–La Guardia Act (1932) and the National Industrial Recovery Act (1933) gave legal assistance to unions, which resulted in their rapid growth. In 1935 the National Labor Relations Act (the so-called Wagner Act) guaranteed the unions' right to exist. It also provided the individual worker with the right to join a union without fear of reprisal or prosecution by the employer. In summary, the Wagner Act stated that employers will be guilty of an unfair labor practice if they

Early labor unions were limited to the northern states

By 1920, there were more than five million union members

The Wagner Act guaranteed the unions' right to exist

1. Interfere with an employee's right to join a union
2. Interfere with union operations
3. Discriminate against an employee because of union membership
4. Penalize union members for reporting management violations of the act
5. Refuse to bargain in good faith with a properly recognized union of their employees.

In 1955, the American Federation of Labor (AFL) and the Congress of Industrial Organizations (CIO) merged, with approximately 35 percent of the nation's work force being unionized. Although that percentage is currently lower (17–20 percent), union membership in total numbers is much larger today, since the size of the work force is larger than ever.

WHY WORKERS JOIN UNIONS

Many workers feel intimidated by management and think they have little chance of being heard as individuals. This is especially true in large organizations. The employees feel that greater bargaining power can be achieved by joining unions. Employees also feel that their basic needs are not being met and that their personal circumstances can be improved through unionization.

Effective supervision can reduce the need for employees to unionize

Sound supervisory and management practices such as the following can create a climate that reduces the need for employees to unionize:

1. Fair wages and fringe benefits as compared to those offered by other companies
2. Satisfactory and safe working conditions
3. Open lines of communication with employees
4. Effective training and orientation programs
5. Participative practices that allow employees a voice in the system
6. Fair and dignified treatment of employees
7. Balanced patterns of employment, void of frequent and drastic layoffs
8. An effective grievance procedure

In review of this list, it must be noted that the supervisor has little control over wages and fringe benefits, since top management usually decides these issues. However, the supervisor does play a major role in most of the other practices and is therefore a central figure in the causes that may lead to unionization.

The organization and the union must work together

Unfortunately, the effective practice of these factors provides no guarantees. A union can still materialize. Should that happen, it is not the end of the world. The supervisor's job becomes tougher but not impossible. The organization and the union must work at establishing a positive relationship built on mutual respect and cooperation. The supervisor is the most important link in this process.

A SUPERVISOR'S ROLE DURING A UNION DRIVE

When a union comes in and attempts to organize the workers in a company, a supervisor must be aware of what can and cannot be done. If a supervisor does something that is illegal, it is regarded as an *unfair labor practice*. Examples of some of the more obvious unfair labor practices are

1. Giving a wage increase only for the purpose of discouraging union efforts
2. Questioning employees about union affairs or about how they plan to vote in the union election
3. Dismissing employees for union activity
4. Promoting workers only because they are union activists
5. Using physical force or threats to discourage union activity

Supervisors can insist that unions carry on their union drive outside the company work area and during nonworking hours. However, workers may talk to their fellow workers about joining the union on company property and during work hours, provided their actions do not interfere with their jobs.

As a supervisor, what should I do during a union drive?

A supervisor can talk to the employees about the union drive but must choose the words carefully. The supervisor can discuss the usual seniority clause in typical contracts and how it may injure the promotion possibilities of young, ambitious workers with little seniority. However, the supervisor must be extremely careful not to say or imply that if workers do not join a union, they will be promoted, given a raise in pay, or offered some other type of reward. A supervisor cannot ask a worker to name other employees who favor the union or who are participating in union activities. The supervisor may listen to this type of information if it is given on a voluntary basis. The supervisor cannot discriminate in any way against employees who are favoring unionization. It is also illegal to give all the easiest jobs to those who do not favor unionization.

The workers make the final choice

In the final analysis, the supervisor should point out to the workers that it is their choice whether they vote for or against the union. It should be emphasized that no matter which way they vote, it will not affect their employment status.

HOW IS THE SUPERVISOR AFFECTED?

Does my job change?

The supervisor's job is drastically changed when the union comes in. Issues about pay, hours of work, working conditions, and overtime must be handled in a different manner. They are covered in the union contract, which must accordingly be followed. The supervisor also loses direct contact with employees over such matters, since the shop steward is the one who speaks for the employees. In effect, management and supervisory practices shift from being one-sided to becoming two-sided.

Does the supervisor negotiate?

Although the supervisor must follow the union contract to the letter, very few companies invite the supervisors to participate in the negotiations. Usually, top management appoints a carefully selected team to represent them in the negotiation. Unions, of course, do the same thing.

COLLECTIVE BARGAINING

What is negotiated?

It would be impossible to list all the issues that are included in collective bargaining practices. The obvious issues include wages, fringe benefits, working conditions, and hours of work. Other major topics are pension plans, seniority systems, grievance procedures, and causes for dismissal.

Supervisor's role

In many ways, the day-to-day practices of the supervisor greatly influence the nature of collective bargaining. If the supervisor treats workers unfairly, ignores grievances, and assigns overtime unjustly, collective bargaining will be very negatively influenced. A supervisor should make fair and reasonable daily decisions according to the contract so that contract negotiations will not be influenced by poor practices at the supervisory level.

**COMMON ISSUES NEGOTIATED IN THE
COLLECTIVE BARGAINING PROCESS**

- Pay
- Overtime and premium pay
- Shift differential
- Holiday schedule
- Vacations
- Rest periods
- Lunch periods
- Seniority
- Layoff and recall procedures
- Leaves of absence
- Equal opportunity
- Fringe benefits (hospitalization, insurance, pension)
- Grievance and arbitration procedures
- Dues check-off
- Employee obligations under the contract
- Management obligations under the contract
- Union security arrangements
- Criteria for transfers
- Procedures for discipline and discharge
- Management's decison-making rights
- Allowable union activities on company time
- Agreements concerning strikes and lockouts
- Probationary periods
- Work hours
- Procedures for absenteeism

UNION SECURITY ARRANGEMENTS

One of the most controversial issues surrounding the development of the labor movement deals with union security, which in labor terms refers to systems of compulsory union membership as a condition for continued employment.

There are several basic forms of union security arrangements, with the following representing the major forms included in contract agreements.

Closed shop

- *Closed shop:* An employer can hire only those people who already are or will be union members before applying for a job. The closed shop was outlawed by the Taft-Hartley Act (1947), but it still exists to some extent in the longshore, lumber, and construction industries.

Union shop

- *Union shop:* An employee is required to become a member of the union within a specified time (usually 30 days) after being hired. Also, the employee must remain a member of the union as a condition for continued employment. The union shop is outlawed in those states that have passed the "right to work" law.

Agency shop

- *Agency shop:* All employees in the bargaining unit who do not join the union must pay a fixed monthly amount to the union as a condition of employment. This amount is usually the same as the standard union dues and is used to defray the union's expenses for acting as the bargaining agent. This arrangement was developed in response to the argument that if workers receive the benefit of union bargaining, they should pay for it.

Maintenance of membership

- *Maintenance of membership:* Employees who are union members at the time the contract is negotiated must maintain their membership as a condition of employment for the duration of the contract. When the contract expires, employees may exercise an escape clause to withdraw from the union. This arrangement was established in the 1940s as a compromise over union membership requirements as a condition for continued employment.

Sole bargaining

- *Sole bargaining:* The union is recognized as the exclusive bargaining agent for all workers, union or nonunion. Union membership is not required as a condition of employment.

Dues check-off

- *Dues check-off:* Management agrees to deduct the amount of union dues from the employee's paycheck and forwards it to the union treasury. Federal law requires that written employee permission be received by the employer to continue this practice.

THE UNION SHOP STEWARD

Role

The job of the union shop steward is to protect the rights of the union members and to make sure that the labor agreement (contract) is being carried out according to expectations. In reality, the

Relationship

shop steward is to the union members what the supervisor is to the company. At times some supervisors get the impression that stewards are attempting to supervise the supervisors. Stewards have no authority to do so. The major responsibility of the steward is to advise the supervisor or an employee about the provisions of the union contract. Being a shop steward is a difficult role to assume, since two masters must be served: As an employee, the shop steward is expected to do the job for the employer according to expectation. As a union representative, the shop steward has commitments to the other employees and to the union. The supervisor must remember this dual role and take it into consideration when dealing with the steward.

Just like other people, some stewards are good, and some are bad. Some are helpful, and some are militant. Some will take advantage of their positions and do as little as possible, whereas others set excellent examples.

The supervisor must work in cooperation with the union steward

When dealing with the shop steward, the supervisor should always be cordial, courteous, and friendly. Do not be either prounion or antiunion. Do not forget that you are a supervisor and in control of your department. Do not lose sight of your departmental goals and get caught up in the details of small, petty labor issues at the expense of company objectives. Try to work cooperatively with the steward. Keep him or her informed of what is being done. Unions are here to stay. If your company has an agreement with the union, work hard at making the contract work. Do not waste valuable time trying to outsmart the steward to take advantage of the union. Instead, use the time to direct your energies toward finding ways to work together and advance the interests of the organizations.

THE GRIEVANCE PROCEDURE

Where unions exist, a formal procedure for the processing of grievances will be spelled out in the union contract. A typical procedure is detailed below and identified in Figure 19–1.

Step 1

If the supervisor cannot solve the complaint, it then becomes a grievance. The employee files a written grievance, and the supervisor meets with the steward or grievance committee (see Figure 19–2). If the problem cannot be resolved at this level, it moves to the second step.

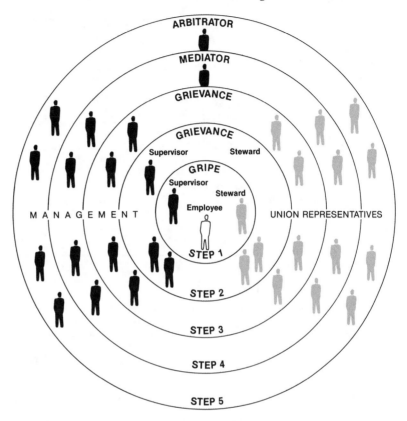

FIGURE 19–1   The five steps through which a complaint involving union and mangement can pass

Step 2

The supervisor's immediate superior and a representative from the labor relations department meet with the union grievance committee. At this point the problem usually involves more than one person and may relate to the individual rights of many. For example, a safety practice in the plant may have serious implications for all who work in the area. If the problem cannot be solved at this level, it moves to top management.

Step 3

Top management from both the company and the local union are now involved. The labor relations director and the plant or division manager meet with the union grievance committee. A representative from the local union may now represent the union's own grievance committee. The costs in terms of time and money

```
┌─────────────────────────────────────────────────────┐
│                   GRIEVANCE FORM                      │
│                                                       │
│   Employee    _____     │
│                                                       │
│   Department _____     │
│                                                       │
│   Job Title   _____     │
│                                                       │
│   Supervisor  _____     │
│                                                       │
│                                                       │
│   Grievance:                                          │
│                                                       │
│   _____    │
│                                                       │
│   _____    │
│                                                       │
│   _____    │
│                                                       │
│   _____    │
│                                                       │
│   _____    │
│                                                       │
│   _____    │
│                                                       │
│   _____    │
│                                                       │
│                                                       │
│   Employee    _____       │
│                                                       │
│   Steward     _____       │
│                                                       │
│                                                       │
│   Received by _____       │
│                                                       │
│   Time        _____       │
│                                                       │
│   Date        _____       │
│                                                       │
└─────────────────────────────────────────────────────┘
```

FIGURE 19–2   A sample grievance form

begin to mount, and both sides usually want to solve the issue as quickly as possible.

Step 4

Members of top management discuss the issues with a group from the national union. If the local union has no national affiliation, an attorney or business agent meets with management representatives.

At this point, both parties could select a mediator, a neutral third party who is called to review the two sides of the issue. The mediator is often someone, such as an attorney or college professor, who is respected by both sides. After hearing both points of view, the mediator recommends a solution. However, his or her decision is not binding on either party.

Step 5

At this stage an arbitrator is usually called in on the dispute. The arbitrator, like the mediator, is a neutral third party. He or she is usually a professional arbitrator recommended by the American Arbitration Association, the Federal Mediation and Conciliation Service, or one of the various state agencies. At this level both sides have usually become polarized, and the arbitrator often spends most of his or her time working separately with the disputing parties.

The arbitrator's decision is binding on management and union

The arbitrator will conduct hearings that are similar to legal proceedings. Witnesses are called, and testimony is recorded. The hearing may be quite informal, however, depending upon the arbitrator's style. The important difference between a mediator and arbitrator is that the arbitrator's decision is *binding* on both the company and the union.

HOW TO PREVENT GRIEVANCES

The only sound way to prevent grievances is to study the reasons behind complaints. Discontent among employees is often created by an accumulation of small, unresolved problems. Remember, supervisors get results through people. The folowing approaches may help supervisors avoid problems:

1. Let each employee know how he or she is doing. Be honest and let workers know what you expect. Help by pointing out how an employee can improve.
2. Give credit when credit is due. Look for the employee's extra performance and verbally reward the person during or shortly after the job.
3. If you think a policy is unfair, express that opinion to your supervisor, not to your subordinates, and suggest changes to improve the policy.
4. Tell employees in advance about policy changes that will affect them, and explain the reasons for each change. If possible get employees to participate in the change.
5. Make the best possible use of each person's ability Instead of stand-

ing in a person's way, give him or her the opportunity for more responsibility and growth.

6. Solicit ideas from your employees. Employees often have great suggestions, which they should be encouraged to develop for jobs or products. Ask what can be done to eliminate bottlenecks and friction.

IF A UNION IS NOT PRESENT

The absence of a union suggests, for the most part, that the workers' needs are being satisfied. However, it is dangerous to become complacent. Organizations must instead consciously assess worker needs, and continue to establish programs and practices designed to meet them. As a priority, organizations must conduct wage and salary surveys to determine fair rates of pay. Within the limits of financial ability, attempts should be made to meet fair pay requirements. Organizations must adhere to OSHA and related federal requirements designed to ensure a safe working environment. Additionally, and perhaps most importantly, organizations must offer supervisory and human relations training to ensure fair and equitable treatment. Finally, a grievance procedure should be established to provide employees with a mechanism to air complaints that is comprehensive, systematic, and free of bias and subjectivity. When these practices are followed on a continuous basis, the foundation for improved and enriched human relationships is established.

A three-fold set of supervisory expectations are suggested in a nonunion environment:

1. The organization must develop and prepare a handbook that clearly outlines all employment policies and procedures. The existence of such a policy manual removes the fear of arbitrary treatment and gives employees a concrete understanding of expectations. Organizations must constantly review and update the manual to reflect social, community, and employee changes.
2. Managers and supervisors must consistently adhere to the fair and equitable practices outlined in the manual. When necessary, they must be prepared to interpret and explain the logic of existing policies, and accept suggestions with an open mind and positive spirit.
3. Employees must accept the policy manual as a contract dictating the boundaries of behavior. They must feel obligated to improvements to policies and practices, thereby enriching the quality of the working environment. When the working environment is enriched, the organization reaches new heights and maximizes profits through dynamics of employee involvement.

SUMMARY

As individuals, we seek fair treatment and attempt to satisfy those needs that are primary to us. If employees receive unfair treatment, low wages, and little job security, they may turn to a union for assistance. However, effective management practices, fair wages, satisfactory work conditions, job security, and open lines of communication will probably discourage the need for unionization.

Approximately one-fifth of the nation's work force belongs to a union. Although some shifts appear to be happening within the labor movement, unions are socially and legally accepted and appear to be here to stay.

The history of the development of unions was long and cumbersome. The court system failed to provide any support for the union movement until the passage of the Norris–La Guardia Act (1932), the National Industrial Recovery Act (1933), and the National Labor Relations Act (1935). With these acts, union efforts began to grow rapidly. By 1955, with the merging of the American Federation of Labor (AFL) and the Congress of Industrial Organizations (CIO), union membership had increased to approximately 17 million workers, representing about one-fourth of the work force. As a result, the supervisor's job has changed drastically. Issues about pay, hours of work, working conditions, and overtime must be handled differently, since they are covered in the union contract. The supervisor, to some degree, loses direct contact with employees over such matters and must work with the shop steward.

Although the supervisor in most cases does not get involved directly with negotiating the contract, the supervisor's activities on a daily basis greatly influence that process. A supervisor must be aware of union security arrangements, since they affect the hiring practices of the organization. Whether or not a company is unionized, employee complaints will arise over such issues as physical conditions, sensory problems, or psychological problems. Some complaints are imaginary, but they should be treated seriously, since the subordinate feels they have merit. The union contract provides guidelines for handling grievances, and such provisions must be followed. Usually the grievance procedure is a five-step process that may lead to the resolution of the dispute by an arbitrator. In companies where no union exists, there should also be a grievance process. Employees want to make sure that their complaints are handled fairly. When dealing with complaints, the supervisor should be calm, listen to the problem, and get all the facts. Asking the employee how he or she would solve the problem may quickly resolve the complaint. When the supervisor has decided what to do about a complaint, reasons for the decision should be explained. If the employee is not satisfied, the available appeal process should also be explained. The supervisor should always follow up to see what the employee intends to do.

CASE STUDY 51

Threats by Angry Billie

Billie Farrari was seated during a coffee break at the textile mill when 265-pound "Monster" Hatfield walked up behind and grabbed him in a bear hug. "Monster" rocked little Billie back and forth, then moved to the other end of the table.

Billie pulled out a pocket knife, made a slicing motion toward Hatfield, and declared furiously: "You S.O.B., don't you ever do that again, or I'll cut your guts out." Hatfield said he would never do it again.

Shortly after the incident Billie was fired for threatening a man's life. He filed a grievance, demanding that the discharge be withdrawn.

Background study on the two men revealed the following information: Billie had a near-perfect disciplinary record during his 20 years at the mill. Before the incident, Billie had been kidding Hatfield, another long-time employee, about the trouble Hatfield was having with his machine. Other workers stated that Farrari had been agitating Hatfield all morning and that they had exchanged angry words. Many employees stated that Billie was prone to verbally abusing other employees. Many employees wondered why the police had not been called in, since a threat with a knife is serious.

When management failed to reinstate Billie, a grievance case was filed by the union. During the hearing Billie testified that horseplay was common in the plant and that even foremen engaged in it. Management denied this. Billie admitted he had threatened Hatfield but asserted his knife could not have possibly reached "Monster" because he was more than a table-length away.

The arbitrator who heard the case noted that Billie gave the impression that he was a rather simple, untutored man. He certainly did not seem to have contemplated the results of such an impulsive act. Billie was reinstated to his job. It was Billie's long record that most influenced the arbitrator. The arbitrator pleaded to Billie that he grow up and cut out the foolishness of verbally jumping on fellow employees. Certainly at 52 years of age Billie could readopt his earlier good behavior patterns.

QUESTION

1. Do you agree with the decision?

CASE STUDY **52**

Dismissal Based on Absenteeism

After 15 years as a good metal plant employee, Joyce Levining began missing work, mostly for illness. In a 3-year period she was absent for 25 weeks, consisting of 3 separate sick leaves and 19 additional days for which she did not have advance permission. For each of the 1-day absences, the supervisor did not question Joyce about her illness. However, after her third sick leave, which lasted more than 4 months, the supervisor terminated her for habitual absenteeism under a plant rule of "habitual absences without reasonable cause." Joyce then filed a grievance.

The company produced evidence of Joyce's numerous absences, but conceded that only one written warning had been issued to her during the 33-month period. This warning had been withdrawn when it was confirmed that Joyce had been hospitalized at the time. The supervisor testified that all absences had occurred for valid reasons.

Joyce's absenteeism had been higher than that of most workers in the plant, but it had not been treated seriously by the company. The union contended that this demonstrated that Joyce was the victim of discriminatory treatment. It claimed she had demonstrated fitness to work at another job after her discharge. Both parties agreed she had been a good worker.

QUESTION

1. Did the company have proper cause to discharge Joyce? (The court's decision is reported at the end of the chapter.)

CASE STUDY **53**

Can Sarah Discuss Her Salary with Others?

"I'm getting a measly monthly salary," Sarah Holland complained to a co-worker. "Mrs. Conford, the personnel director, promised me a raise as soon as I proved my worth. I'm still waiting." Sarah also talked about her salary to another employee, who agreed they were underpaid.

Sarah became so unhappy that she reminded Mrs. Conford about her "promise." The personnel director denied having made such a statement. Later that day, Sarah's friend asked for a raise and was turned down.

When Mrs. Conford learned that Sarah was discussing her salary dissatisfaction with others, she reminded her that the company forbade employees to discuss their salaries with one another. Then she fired Sarah on the spot for violating this rule.

Sarah went before the National Labor Relations Board (NLRB) with charges of unfair labor practices. The company insisted that

1. Sarah had violated its rule that employees keep their salaries confidential.

2. The ban helped the company prevent resentment by employees who earn less.

3. The company hadn't violated the National Labor Relations Act by interfering with employee efforts to organize a union or bargain collectively.

Sarah replied stoutly: "We need not organize a union to get NLRB protection. It's enough if a few employees act together to improve conditions."

QUESTIONS

1. Was Sarah morally wrong for discussing her salary with others?

2. Was Mrs. Conford acting within her rights in firing Sarah?

3. Could Mrs. Conford have handled the problem better? If so, how?

4. What action do you think the NLRB will take? (The answer is given at the end of the chapter.)

CASE STUDY **54**

Does Earl Have Supervisory Potential?

Earl Morris has been with the company for almost 15 years. A union drive was taking place, and Earl appeared to be right in the thick of things. He could be very persuasive, and the workers looked up to him.

Advances by the union appeared to be gaining momentum. Pat Simmons, the plant superintendent, was curious about the current status of the union effort, and she called a meeting of all the supervisors to discuss strategy. She asked the supervisors to indicate who the major activists for the union were. Unanimously, the supervisors suggested Earl.

Pat figured that if Earl could be sidetracked, the union efforts could be defeated. Pat arranged a meeting with Earl. After exchanging the normal greetings, Pat said, "Earl, you have the personality and ability

to be a good supervisor. Since a supervisory opening will be available in the shipping department in about two months, I guarantee you that position if you help the company stave off the union effort. What the heck, Earl, if you're going to be a supervisor, you might as well start acting like one now. Right?"

Earl claimed he would think about it. Pat figured she had solved the union problem.

QUESTIONS

1. Was Pat ethically correct in offering the promotion to Earl?
2. If you were Pat, what would you have done?
3. How do you think the NLRB would rule if they knew of this action?

CASE STUDY **55**

Let's Set Up a Grievance Procedure

Assume you are a supervisor in a nonunionized company. Currently, the company has no procedure for handling complaints or grievances. Top management has stated that each supervisor should handle his or her complaints on an individual basis.

Recently, some inconsistencies have occurred with similar complaints in different departments, resulting in varying outcomes. Top management suggests that these inconsistencies must come to an end.

You are appointed as the chairperson of a

committee designed to establish a grievance procedure.

QUESTIONS

1. Outline the type of procedure that you would like to adopt.
2. Who would participate in the procedure?
3. What happens if, after your system is implemented, grievances are still unresolved?

CASE STUDY **56**

Why Do You Need a Union?

After 18 years of hard work, Ike Peters was promoted to supervisor. Management figured that since Ike has done the work of two people, perhaps he could convey some of his enthusiasm to the workers, especially since quotas in the department have been down lately.

On his first day as supervisor, Ike decided he would set the tone for the department. He announced that quotas were down, but that by the end of the month they would be back on target "or else." He stated that pay was 50 percent higher than in most other companies in the area, and that with the incentive pay system, workers could make double the salary. Therefore, there was no excuse for declining productivity!

After three months, Ike's department failed to make its quota. He accused his workers of being lazy and indicated that if things didn't change, some personnel replacements would take place.

Friction continued to build between Ike and his workers. All of a sudden, the workers began to mention the need for a union. Ike said, "Why do you need a union? Wages are higher than the average, with an excellent incentive system. Benefits are excellent! What's the problem?"

QUESTIONS

1. If you were Ike, what would you say to the workers?
2. What are the workers trying to tell Ike?
3. How could the problem have been avoided?

Terms and Concepts Supervisors Should Know

Agency shop; Arbitrator; Closed shop; Collective bargaining issues; Dues check-off; Grievance procedure; Grievances versus gripes; Maintenance of membership; Mediator; Oral warning; Shop steward; Taft-Hartley Act; Unfair labor practice; Union; Union security agreements; Union shop; Wagner Act; Written warning.

Questions for Discussion

1. List some of the practices that a supervisor should employ to prevent unionization.
2. Outline a grievance procedure for a nonunionized company. Describe each step, and indicate who would be involved.
3. Have unions outlived their usefulness? Why or why not?
4. Prepare an evaluation list that would help to determine if good relations exist between management and the union.

Answer to Case Study 52: "Dismissal Based on Absenteeism"

The National Labor Relations Board heard the case, and Joyce Levining was reinstated with full seniority but without back pay. This decision is without prejudice to the company's future right to suspend or discharge Joyce on evidence that her irregular attendance destroys her value as an employee.

Joyce's long service and admitted competence were taken into consideration. However, she was obligated to be more careful of attendance than others with a better attendance history.

There was a hard choice to make between compassion combined with consideration of long, efficient service, and the reality that the company had been unable to count on Joyce to be available for work at any given time.

Answer to Case Study 53: "Can Sarah Discuss Her Salary with Others?"

Sarah was reinstated with back pay.

For Further Reading—And More Ideas

Anderson, H., "The Rise and Fall of Big Labor," *Newsweek* (September 5, 1983).

Boyd, Bradford B., *Management-Minded Supervision*, 3rd ed., New York: McGraw-Hill, 1984.

Christenson, Christina, Thomas W. Johnson, and Joan E. Stinson, *Supervising*, Reading, MA: Addison-Wesley, 1982.

Craver, C. B., "The Future of the American Labor Movement," *The Futurist* (October 1983).

Dilts, David A., and Clarence R. Deitsch, *Labor Relations*, New York: Macmillan, 1983.

English, C. W., "Companies Learn to Live with Unions in Board Rooms," *U.S. News & World Report* (January 30, 1984).

Fiorito, Jack, and Charles Greer, "Determinants of U.S. Unionism: Past Research and Future Needs," *Industrial Relations* (Winter 1982).

Foulkes, Fred K., *Personnel Policies in Large Nonunion Companies*, Englewood Cliffs, NJ: Prentice Hall, 1980.

Hagsburg, Eugene C., and Marvin L. Levine, *Labor Relations: An Integrated Perspective*, St. Paul, MN: West, 1978.

Haimann, Theo, and Raymond L. Hilgert, *Supervision: Concepts and Practices of Management*, Cincinnati: South-Western, 1982.

Hilgert, Raymond L., "Union/Management Relations: Era of Mutual Interdependence," *The Collegiate Forum* (Spring 1983).

Hoerr, John, "Collective Bargaining Is in Danger Without Labor Law Reform," *Business Week* (July 16, 1984).

Holley, William H., and Kenneth M. Jennings, *The Labor Relations Process*, Hindsdale, IL: The Dryden Press, 1984.

Lloyd, J. L., "Unions at a Turning Point," *World Press Review* (May 1983).

MacCoby, M., "Helping Labor and Management Set up a Quality-of-Worklife Program," *Monthly Labor Review* (March 1984).

Moore, R., and E. Marsis, "Will Unions Work for Women?" *Progressive* (August 1983).

National Labor Relations Board, Philadelphia, PA, *A Guide to Basic Law and Procedures Under the National Labor Relations Act*, Washington, D.C.: Government Printing Office, 1989.

Reisman, Barbara, and Lance Compa, "The Case for Adversarial Unions," *Harvard Business Review* (May–June, 1985).

Ross, I., "Straight Talk from a Union Leader (Interview with Douglas Frazer)," *Reader's Digest* (March 1984).

Seligman, Daniel, "Who Needs Unions?" *Fortune* (July 12, 1982).

Sloane, Arthur A., and Fred Witney, *Labor Relations*, 4th ed., Englewood Cliffs, NJ: Prentice Hall, 1981.

Sullivan, F. L., "Union Organizing in the 1980's: The Campaign for Employee Loyalty," *Supervisory Management* (July 1982).

Sullivan, F. L., "Union Organizing in the 1980's: The Strike," *Supervisory Management* (November 1982).

Tidwell, G. L, "The Supervisor's Role in a Union Election," *Personnel Journal* (August 1983).

Tomkeiwicz, J., and O. C. Brenner, "Supervisor vs. Union Reps: When Fair Is Foul," *Supervisory Management* (January 1984).

"Unions in Retreat," *World Press Review* (January 1984).

Verespej, M. A., "Striking out (Supreme Court Ruling Diminishes Power of Strikes)," *Industry Week* (March 20, 1989).

Watts, G. E., "The Future of Unionism and Work," *USA Today* (November 1983).

"Why Clerical Workers Resist Unions," *Business Week* (May 2, 1983).

Wood, Robert C., "Decline and Fall of a Union," *Inc.* (October 1982).

Individual Concerns: Stress, Burnout, and Time Management

20

"Time is not the problem. It's how we use it that counts." (Peter Drucker)

LEARNING OBJECTIVES

When you complete this chapter, you should be able to:

1. Define and explain the concept of stress.
2. Discuss the individual, managerial, and organizational consequences of stress.
3. Understand the differences between Type A and Type B behavior, and their implications in terms of stress.
4. Define and explain the concept of burnout.
5. Understand and identify the five indicators of burnout.
6. Explain the importance of time management.
7. Identify time-saving techniques.

"Everyone has 24 hours a day, but some people use them better than others."

This chapter will help you develop questions for class discussion as you formulate an understanding of the major concerns facing individuals in a work setting. Some answers to the questions below may be found in the chapter, whereas others may require personal reflection.

Why are some people likely to experience stress?

Can stress have positive outcomes? If so, how?

Is there such a thing as burnout? How does it develop? How can it be cured?

Do supervisors, managers, and organizations have anything to do with causing stress? Burnout? If so, how?

Can effective time-management techniques make an individual more productive? If so, how?

Which is a better motto to follow: "Work harder" or "Work smarter"?

COPING WITH INDIVIDUAL CONCERNS

The information age and its rapid technological advancements have contributed greatly to a constantly changing work place. As Alvin Toffler indicates in *Future Shock,* "Change is occurring so quickly that people will have a difficult time trying to adapt."[1]

Employees must learn to cope and adjust to changing job environments

Unfortunately, as employees attempt to adjust to a constantly changing work environment, the results can be devastating. While some employees are able to cope and adjust, others are not. According to the National Council on Compensation Insurance,[2] more than one out of ten claims for workmen's compensation are stress related. Job stress is becoming a much more serious problem for employers and employees. In a broader sense, the problem is not limited to the individual. When an employee is negatively affected by the pressure of change, the work group, the supervisor, and the organization may also be influenced in various ways, by the following:

An Employee Is Likely to

- Experience extreme frustration
- Fear failure
- Display erratic behavior
- Experience health problems

---

[1] Alvin Toffler, *Future Shock* (New York: Bantam Books, 1970).

[2] "Stress on the Job," *Delaware State News,* Monday, July 8, 1985, p. 1.

A Work Group Is Likely to

- Encounter negative teamwork
- Experience a change in the quality of relationships
- Recognize a change in the immediate work environment
- Experience altered inter and intra departmental relationships

A Supervisor Is Likely to

- Encounter strained relationships with peers and subordinates
- Attempt to manage employees who become unmanageable
- Experience an increased need for counseling among subordinates
- Be subjected to increased absenteeism and turnover

An Organization Is Likely to

- Experience reduced productivity
- Recognize decreased profitability
- Encounter downward trends in quality
- Experience morale problems

The purpose of this chapter is to explore why individuals frequently react negatively to change and pressure. Stress and burnout will be highlighted, with suggested techniques designed for their control. Time management concepts play a major role in reducing the pressure and frustration normally associated with job demands. The chapter concludes with a set of prescriptions to prevent stress and burnout from becoming a problem.

WHAT IS STRESS?

Stress is a normal reaction to life

Stress is a psychological or biological reaction to the demands of life. In job-related terms, stress is usually the result of pressure from increased responsibilities, heavy workloads, and deadlines. When a worker is "called on the carpet" by an angry boss, both the worker and the boss experience a degree of stress. The worker may feel a lump in the throat, dry digestion, sweaty palms, tense muscles, and heart palpitations. Many workers manage to conceal such reactions. However, all of this internal energy and frustration must be released. The angry boss vents the frustration by ranting and raving, while the worker lets it remain inside.

Hans Selye[3] explains stress in engineering terms: When a bridge is built, it must be able to withstand a prescribed amount of pressure and strain. However, too much weight causes the bridge

---

[3] Hans Seyle, "Stress," *The Rotarian* (March 1978); "On the Real Benefits of Eustress," *Psychology Today* (March, 1978), and *Stress in Health and Disease* (London: Butterworths, 1976).

to collapse. On the other hand, if some of the weight is removed, the bridge would be able to withstand the pressure and strain. Individuals are the same. An uncertain, poorly trained, and unqualified worker reacts in the same way as the overburdened bridge. However, a secure, properly trained, and capable worker will be more apt to withstand the strain and pressure of day-to-day job demands.

Individual Reactions to Stress

People react differently to stress

People react differently to stress. Some workers find it stimulating, and tend to respond with higher productivity and better performance. Others react negatively, and often display reduced performance and productivity.

Eustress is pleasant or positive stress. Some workers perform best under pressure. Frequently, deadlines and critical situations serve as a challenge, providing excitement and accelerated performance. Many athletes perform best under pressure. Their adrenaline flows, and they rise to the occasion. Reggie Jackson is often referred to as "Mr. October" because of his ability to display optimal performance under the stressful conditions of the World Series.

Some highly productive individuals experience the positive benefits of stress, including the following:

1. *Increased motivation:* Frequently, pressure produces increased motivation and maximum performance. Some students can't study until the night before an exam, some workers wait until the last minute to prepare an important report, and some athletes thrive on the last few minutes of a close game. Some people purposely keep pressure on themselves in order to accomplish personal goals and objectives.
2. *Increased strength and coordination:* Under stress, some individuals experience a special emotional high that results in increased strength and coordination. Some major league pitchers are able to pitch faster and some quarterbacks can throw farther in the last minutes of a game. Many workers respond the same way under pressure-packed work circumstances.
3. *Increased psychological control:* As deadlines quickly approach, many individuals are able to tune out distractions and channel all of their mental energies to the problem at hand. Such total and complete concentration promotes efficiency and increased productivity.
4. *Increased problem-solving abilities:* Sometimes, when excessive time luxuries exist, we cannot arrive at a decision. Deadlines tend to force us to think out the problem. Many individuals make excellent decisions when time is of the essence.
5. *Better use of time:* When our time and efforts are focused on a given

problem, the results can be extremely efficient and highly productive.

6. *Better use of resources:* Under pressure, we are frequently able to make the maximum use of the resources at our disposal at the last minute. At such times, a shoe becomes a hammer, and a dime becomes a screwdriver.

7. *Enhanced creativity:* Original ideas often emerge under pressure. When we are pressed into action just prior to a deadline, our creativity may be at its peak. In fact, many people need such pressure to respond creatively.

8. *Increased seriousness:* As deadlines approach, there is a tendency to take the problem more seriously. Although some nervousness may emerge, it presents a humbling effect that promotes logical and rational actions. As progress is made, confidence is built, further increasing the chances of high output.

These and other positive outcomes of stress have merit. However, it is not a good idea to procrastinate, counting on possible eustress benefits. Continual exposure to stress can be dangerous. Also, everyone does not experience positive stress outcomes. Rather than depending on eustress, individuals can better prepare themselves to meet their deadlines by planning and scheduling their time. As we learn to manage ourselves, we learn to be more productive. It is far wiser to rely on eustress only when we must.

Individuals should learn to manage their time

Distress is negative stress, which can lead to physical and psychological problems. The on-the-job result of distress is decreased productivity. Off the job, stress can create family and social problems. Individuals experiencing distress become moody, and it is difficult to work or to be with them.

TYPICAL SYMPTOMS OF STRESS

- Insomnia
- Muscle tension
- Erratic behavior
- Increased use of alcohol
- Increased use of tobacco
- Changes in appetite and eating habits
- Feelings of anxiety
- Throat and mouth dryness
- Increased dependency on drugs
- Frequent or constant fatigue
- Fear and nervousness
- Increased accidents
- Feelings of unhappiness
- Concentration problems
- Extreme emotional reactions

The symptoms of stress must be recognized

While there is no easy way to determine how much stress an individual can withstand, it is most important for an individual to learn to recognize the symptoms of stress. When an individual is experiencing distress, the outward signs are obvious. The individual appears upset, looks pale and drawn, acts dull and listless, seems nervous, and shows signs of depression.

Causes of On-the-Job Stress

Job conditions cause stress

In many cases, job conditions can cause stress. Complex changes in organizational structure and problems with other people can promote tension, which results in stress. Supervisors should attempt to limit the amount of pressure they place on their subordinates, although emergency circumstances frequently makes this impossible. Typical work-related stress occurs from the following causes:

1. *Technological change:* While technological advancements improve modern life and increase the chances for organizational survival, they also create enormous amounts of individual job stress. Change creates uncertainty, which leads to stress. When individuals attempt to cope with change, they fear failure. Workers no sooner master the job, when technological advancements modify it. The worker becomes frustrated and begins to feel pressured.
2. *Heavy work load:* An excessive work load creates job stress and pressure, because the individual attempts to keep up yet fails. The worker loses confidence, and an uncomfortable, stressful feeling is created.
3. *Role conflict or ambiguity:* Stress can result when a person does not agree with job expectations (role conflict) or does not understand job expectations (role ambiguity). In either case, frustration results. It is very difficult to feel comfortable on the job if you are not sure what to do. The philosophical conflict that results from not agreeing with job expectations can be equally dangerous.
4. *Underuse:* A stress factor facing many individuals is that of being underused. Although this is more likely to occur during early career stages, it can happen at any time. Feelings of underuse occur when an individual is assigned tasks that are below capability levels. When an individual is overqualified and overeducated for a job, the element of challenge is missing, with stress and fatigue the likely results.
5. *Job insecurity and unemployment:* All employees worry about losing their jobs, some more than others. The threat of job loss, when coupled with family financial dependence, can create pressure. The fear of technological change also poses serious concerns. Although unemployment promotes more stress than the threat of job insecurity, both can lead to self-esteem and self-identity problems.

6. *Inadequate training:* Individuals who are poorly trained lack confidence in their ability to do the job. They become frustrated and filled with anxiety. Eventually, the frustration leads to stress, causing a diminished sense of commitment and reduced productivity.

7. *Inherent job stress:* Certain jobs, by their very nature, are a natural source of job stress. The position of air traffic controller fits this category. This pressure-packed occupation possesses more stressful elements than most other jobs. High turnover, ulcers, and blood pressure problems are common among air traffic controllers.

8. *Inadequate orientation:* If an individual fails to develop a feeling of belonging to an organization, pressure and stress may emerge. The purpose of orientation is to give new employees information designed to ease their adjustment to the job. Research indicates that employees fail to make maximum contributions until they feel a sense of belonging.

9. *Inadequate authority:* Supervisors must have the proper amount of authority to accomplish job goals. Inadequate authority serves as a major source of stress. Can you imagine being held responsible for the performance of subordinates, yet not having the authority to evaluate and correct their mistakes?

Results of Distress

The effects of distress fall into five categories

The potential effects of distress fall into five categories:

1. Personal effects
2. Action effects
3. Conscious effects
4. Physiological effects
5. Organizational effects

Some of the effects in each category follow:

Personal Effects

- Anxiety
- Apathy
- Boredom
- Depression
- Fatigue
- Frustration
- Tension

Action Effects

- Accident proneness
- Increased drinking
- Increased smoking
- Emotional outbursts

STRESSORS

The following lists both on-the-job and off-the-job factors that contribute to stress. Depending on their frequency and their amount, these 25 events can have varying effects.

- Death of a family member
- Serious injury or illness
- Legal encounters
- Marital reconciliation
- Recent job layoff
- Family health changes
- Change in marital status
- Family disappointments
- Business setback
- Personal disaster
- Loss of a loved one
- Change of residence
- Financial loss
- Problems with in-laws
- Death of a spouse
- Problems with son/daughter
- Being fired
- Denial of promotion
- Problems with the boss
- Technological job changes
- Problems with peers
- Upcoming retirement
- Change in work responsibilities
- Personal failures
- Mortgage/loan foreclosure

- Impulsive behavior
- Loss of appetite
- Restlessness

Conscious Effects

- Indecisiveness
- Lack of concentration
- Forgetfulness
- Nonacceptance of criticism
- Denial

Physiological Effects

- Blood pressure problems
- Throat and mouth dryness
- Indigestion
- Breathing problems
- Sweating

Organizational Effects

- Absenteeism
- High turnover
- Accidents
- Drop in productivity
- Quality problems
- Job dissatisfaction

The Need for Balance

Each person has a different stress level

How much stress is too much? How much stress is just enough? These are difficult questions to answer. Each person is different and hence able to withstand differing amounts of stress and pressure.

As discussed, the highest productivity is achieved when there is some stress—but not too much. Appropriate amounts of stress tend to stimulate thinking, induce motivation, and improve concentration (see Figure 20–1). Excessive stress results in frustration, anxiety, and decreased job performance. Ideally, an individual should seek to stimulate appropriate measures of stress while avoiding excessive conditions that tend to be dysfunctional and personally dangerous.

Personality Factors

Some people are more likely to be affected by stress

Some people, by their very nature, have personalities that are more prone to the negative effects of pressure and stress. By the same token, others have personalities that tend to be more resistant to such negative effects. The two forms of behavior, labeled Type A and Type B, respectively,[4] are generally distinguished by the following characteristics:

Type A Behavior

1. Tend to be impatient, nervous, demanding, and uptight. Appear to be in a hurry. Become frustrated while waiting in line, caught in a traffic jam, or anticipating an event.
2. Take on excessive duties and responsibilities. Involved in many projects and generally are spread too thin. Constantly subjected to deadlines. Take delight in being buried with work. Receive pleasure from being overly busy.
3. Tend to be "workaholics." Appear to be so addicted to work that other aspects of life are neglected.

---

[4]Meyer Freedman and Ray H. Rosenman, *Type A Behavior and Your Heart* (New York: Fawcett Crest Books, 1974).

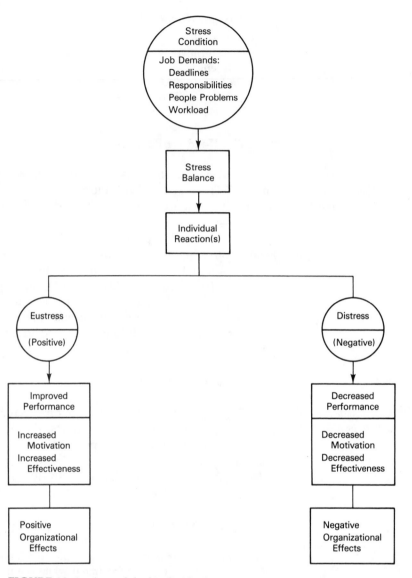

FIGURE 20–1   A model of individual reaction to and outcome of stress

4. Possess erratic behavior. Are explosive, angry, frustrated, and hostile. Tend to speak fast. Tend to channel their anger and hostility into work.

Type B Behavior

1. Tend to display characteristics that are opposite to those of Type A. Are somewhat relaxed, patient, and in *control of themselves*.
2. Have learned when and how to say *no*. Tend to have a realistic schedule.

3. Tend to have a full and complete life style filled with work, fun, and relaxation. Instead of being addicted to work, are addicted to life. Life extends beyond the job.
4. Hostility, anger, and frustration are controlled. Tend to be able to put things in perspective.

Type A personalities play to win; Type B personalities are more relaxed

Examine the characteristics of Type A and Type B behavior. If you are competitive, are achievement oriented, and always play to win, you are Type A. Excessive Type A behavior is more likely to bring about a heart attack.[5] Type B behavior does not suggest a failure to achieve and accomplish, but rather a tendency to operate under a slower and more controlled pace. Test yourself to determine which type best characterizes your behavior.

How to Control On-the-Job Stress

Work-related stress can take four forms:

1. Organization-imposed stress
2. System-imposed stress
3. Boss-imposed stress
4. Self-imposed stress

ORGANIZATION-IMPOSED STRESS

Some organizations tend to be stress oriented. High risk-oriented organizations with liberal goals and objectives tend to impose more stress than those with the opposite characteristics. Examples of organizations imposing stress may include some financial investment institutions, real estate firms, and advertising agencies.

SYSTEM-IMPOSED STRESS

Some jobs are more stress oriented than others. In some cases, sales jobs with excessive quotas may fit in this category. Others may include piecework and assembly-line jobs.

BOSS-IMPOSED STRESS

Some bosses, especially those with Type A behavior, tend to impose stress on those around them, especially those who report to them. At times, stress can be contagious. Demanding bosses may create pressure and stress by forcing or expecting subordinates to meet unrealistic quotas or goals.

---

[5] Ibid.

TEST YOURSELF

Are You Type A or Type B?

Read the following pairs of statements carefully, and in each case place a check next to the one best describing your behavior.

1. _____ a. Regardless of the event (work, games, etc.), I always play to win—at all costs.
   _____ b. At work or sports, I derive great satisfaction from social interaction, participation, and activity.

2. _____ a. All objectives of life can be achieved through work. Work is the road to success.
   _____ b. Work represents an important aspect of life. Family and leisure are also important.

3. _____ a. I frequently feel tense, nervous, and on-the-spot.
   _____ b. I am usually relaxed and generally feel in control of my life.

4. _____ a. I generally cannot sit down to read a book without tapping my foot, moving around, or feeling edgy.
   _____ b. When I read a book, I generally get totally involved.

5. _____ a. In a traffic jam, I generally feel angry, frustrated, and annoyed.
   _____ b. If I get caught in a traffic jam, I usually listen to the car radio or become engrossed in thinking about upcoming social activities.

6. _____ a. I always seem to be in a rush to get things done.
   _____ b. I rarely rush; I simply make every effort to do my best, and if I'm late, I'm late!

7. _____ a. Having to wait for people drives me crazy.
   _____ b. If I have to wait, I take advantage of the time by reading or just relaxing!

8. _____ a. Life is a series of goals. Any interruption that interferes with goal accomplishment must be avoided.
   _____ b. I do the best I can! If I make a mistake, I use it as a learning experience.

9. _____ a. I find myself doing more and more in less and less time.
   _____ b. If I plan and schedule properly, I can be more productive in less time, allowing for some leisure and relaxation.

10. _____ a. Each day, I establish a list of things to do, and feel extremely frustrated and angry if I do not accomplish all of them.
    _____ b. I try to be flexible. I follow a schedule, but the situation will frequently determine a new course of action.

Scoring: Review your answers. For each *a* response, give yourself 5 points. For each *b* response, give yourself 0 points. Total your score and compare it to the following chart:

40 – 50 points: You identify with strong Type A behavior.

30 – 39 points: You identify with above average Type A behavior.

20 – 29 points: You identify with moderate Type A or B behavior.

10 – 19 points: You identify with above average Type B behavior.

0 – 9 points: You identify with strong Type B behavior.

SELF-IMPOSED STRESS

Type A workers impose excessive pressure and stress upon themselves. They set unrealistic goals and are extremely competitive. They neglect all other aspects of life except work. Additionally, they translate job goals into life-and-death situations, while trying to accomplish more and more in less and less time.

CONTROLLING STRESS INDIVIDUALLY AND ORGANIZATIONALLY

Any single source is capable of producing enough stress to frustrate and anger any individual. A combination of two or more sources at the same time is likely to create even more pressure and stress. Although the breaking point differs from person to person, the four sources must be constantly reviewed and monitored. The following individual and organizational guidelines should be followed to help control stress:

Individual Guidelines	*Organizational Guidelines*
1. Establish priorities, and try your best. Don't get frustrated; if all priorities are not achieved, keep the faith!	1. Prepare job descriptions with realistic expectations.
2. Establish realistic goals.	2. Evaluate fairly.
3. Establish realistic deadlines.	3. Establish effective training programs.
4. Don't accept more than you can handle.	4. Establish effective orientation programs.
5. Learn to delegate whenever possible.	5. Establish realistic goals.

Individual Guidelines	*Organizational Guidelines*
6. Learn to relax.	6. Manage through development rather than deadlines.
7. Exercise regularly.	7. Create a stimulating work environment.
8. Maintain a healthy diet.	8. Exhibit a people orientation.
9. Allow for leisure time.	9. Practice effective planning and scheduling.
10. Clarify your values.	10. Control conflict instead of causing conflict.

BURNOUT

Burnout can affect the quality of work

Recently, a phenomenon known as *burnout* has commanded much attention in the daily lives of workers, supervisors, and managers. It has affected the quality of work in organizations and continues to be a concern plaguing society.

When you wake in the morning, do you dread having to go to work? Have you lost your vigor and enthusiasm? Do you always feel tired? Do co-workers refer to you as cranky and irritable? If so, perhaps the symptoms of burnout are present.

Overachievers are more likely to experience burnout

Although everyone is a potential candidate for burnout, overachievers are the most likely to experience this serious problem. Herbert J. Freudenberger has defined burnout as *"a state of fatigue or frustration brought about by devotion to a cause, way of life, or relationship that failed to produce the expected reward."*[6] It is characterized by chronic emotional exhaustion and anger toward the job that frequently develop from intense work stress. Research indicates that burnout often results when a worker feels prevented from making progress toward personal goals. Freudenberger presented the following self-test to help diagnose burnout:

- Are you working more and enjoying it less?
- Do you find it more difficult to confide in others?
- Must you force yourself to perform routine tasks?
- Are you listless, bored, and constantly seeking excitement?
- Would you rather be somewhere else?
- Have you lost the joy of sex?
- Do you drink more than you used to?
- Do you need a tranquilizer to face the day? a sleeping pill to get through the night?
- Are you resigned about your future?

---

[6]Herbert J. Freudenberger, *Burnout* (New York: Bantam Books, 1980), p. 13.

Helping occupations were once thought to be particular targets for burnout. Such workers as nurses, social workers, teachers, and supervisors tend to possess idealistic goals that unrealistically affect those who depend upon them. The inability to achieve goals causes frustration and possible burnout. Supervisors who attempt to be all things to all people and teachers who believe they will reach every student are likely to experience burnout. However, recent research suggests that burnout is not limited to individuals in helping occupations. In today's large, complex organizations, many workers feel they are getting lost in the bureaucratic shuffle. Hence, their efforts tend to be unrecognized, which represents a caution sign that may lead to burnout.

Frustration results from the inability to achieve goals

There are five major indicators of burnout that appear in the following sequence:

Stage 1: *Confusion and Frustration*

Employees with burnout appear puzzled and angry. They are disenchanted with the job and their station in life. They are cranky and extremely difficult to work with.

Stage 2: *Emotional Emptiness*

Employees with burnout appear empty of emotion and physically drained. They dread the prospect of having to go to work. They display no enthusiasm and are negative about things in general. They have little desire to accomplish goals. They tend to be cynical, sarcastic, and pessimistic.

Stage 3: *Erosion of Relationships*

Burnout victims tend to camouflage their problem by displaying detached relationships. They are somewhat elusive and aloof. They appear unsympathetic toward others and uncaring about the organization. At this stage, feelings of burnout are likely to be contagious.

Stage 4: *Decreased Levels of Achievement*

Burnout employees, while once idealistic in terms of goal achievement, tend to sink in terms of output and productivity. Feelings of low personal accomplishment cause the victims to believe that too many obstacles are in the way of success. They ask, "What difference does it make?" "Why should I?" "Does it really matter?"

Stage 5: *Apathy, Withdrawal, and Despair*

During the final stage, burnout victims physically and emotionally remove themselves from reality. Outward signs of not caring become obvious. Employees are negative about the job, the goals, and the organization. Statements such as "things will never improve" and "who cares" are likely to occur at this point.

The Relationship of Stress and Burnout

Burnout is the result of continuous and intense stress

Many theorists contend that burnout is the result of continuous and intense stress. It may begin as employees are deprived of rewards and goals, and become disenchanted with work demands and responsibilities. With greater disparity between expectations and reality, added feelings of anger and frustration result. Slowly but vividly these feelings transform into apathy and withdrawal, causing diminished personal output. Eventually, the organization will suffer. Ongoing efforts to avoid this consequence must be implemented.

Where Does Responsibility Rest?

Burnout prevention involves three parties

While the cause and consequences of burnout tend to be individual and job related, the responsibility for prevention should not be limited to the person. A complete program for prevention and cure involves dividing responsibility among three parties:

1. The individual
2. The supervisor
3. The organization

INDIVIDUAL RESPONSIBILITY

Self-awareness is the foundation of stress avoidance

The first thing an individual must do is understand that burnout exists. Next, efforts must be made to explore one's self-awareness, which is the foundation for avoiding and preventing burnout. An individual must employ constant self-monitoring of personal behavior patterns. Only *you* know the extent of your abilities! Only *you* can adjust your goals to make sure that they are practical and realistic. You are the best judge of the disparity between expectations and reality. If you recognize that you are suffering from the symptoms of burnout, the following actions are suggested to combat the problem:

1. Consider seeking professional help.
2. Take charge of yourself.
3. Realize you cannot change everything.
4. Reevaluate your goals to make sure they are realistic.

If you want to prevent and avoid burnout, the following steps are recommended:

1. Learn how to relax.
2. Put things in perspective.
3. Do not take yourself too seriously.
4. Accept pressure and take responsibility in stride.
5. Clarify your goals and make sure they are realistic.
6. Do not think of failure as an end; think of it in terms of an opportunity. Use it as a learning tool on the way to success.

SUPERVISORY RESPONSIBILITY

Supervisors play a major role in the cause and prevention of burnout. In effect, the supervisor may assume two-fold responsibility in the process:

- *Part 1:* The supervisor may be a victim of burnout. If so, the negative consequences can become contagious, and affect the performance of subordinates and co-workers. Eventually, the organization will suffer.
- *Part 2:* The supervisor may be the reason for the burnout, especially among subordinates. If the supervisor places unrealistic job demands upon subordinates, the pressure and stress, if intensified, are likely to result in burnout.

To avoid developing burnout, the supervisor is advised to practice the individual actions listed above. To avoid causing burnout among subordinates, the following actions are appropriate:

1. Develop realistic goals and objectives for each subordinate.
2. Explain employee expectations very clearly.
3. Employ fair and objective evaluation methods.
4. Recognize employee achievements. Praise a job well done.
5. Be understanding of an employee's mistake. Take corrective action that develops the employee's confidence.
6. Practice effective human relations techniques.

WARNING SIGNS OF BURNOUT

Recently, as you entered the office of one of your subordinates, you noticed two ashtrays filled with cigarette butts. Your initial statement to the subordinate was, "When did you take up smoking?" Your subordinate responded, "A few days ago!"

Your purpose for visiting the subordinate was to discuss a recent drop in productivity. Your subordinate indicated that all of the recent changes in the organization have been frustrating. "I don't know if I'm coming or going. I can't keep up. One of these days, I'm going to call in sick—permanently."

ORGANIZATIONAL RESPONSIBILITY

An organization can cause stress and burnout

The organization can also cause stress and burnout. Haphazard planning and unrealistic goals are likely contributors. An organization can prevent burnout by implementing the following practices:

1. Prepare realistic and accurate job descriptions.
2. Modify and change job descriptions as necessary. Upgrade and monitor activities continuously.
3. Develop, implement, and administer an effective evaluation program.
4. Provide counseling services for all employees.
5. Develop and implement effective programs for training and orientation.
6. Provide preventive medical insurance benefits.
7. Develop a system of rewards that recognizes employee accomplishments and achievements.
8. Emphasize and create a positive atmosphere for human relations.

Burnout must be prevented and controlled

In the final analysis, burnout must be prevented and controlled. Responsibility rests with the individual, the supervisor/manager, and the organization. Frequently, individuals attempt to accomplish too much and experience burnout. At times, supervisors/managers become too demanding—of themselves and their subordinates—thus causing stress and burnout. Organizations, in their quest to achieve goals and accomplish objectives, make demands that are so overwhelming that employees become confused and frustrated.

Organizations should not expect workers to be Superman and Wonder Woman. Supervisors/managers must be realistic in terms of their expectations. Additionally, they must be careful to explain job expectations in clear and understandable terms. Individuals should not be devoured by work. It is part of life; it is not life itself. Learn to "work to live" rather than to "live to work." A well-rounded life style provides protection against burnout. As Kin Hubbard, the American humorist, suggests, "Do not take life too seriously; you will never get out of it alive."

TIME MANAGEMENT

Time utilization is an important element of success

Success, in many cases, is a direct result of the way a person uses time. Many workers never overcome the frustrating thought that they do not have enough time to do their work. By contrast, others keep ahead of their jobs and are not oppressed by their responsibilities. Since everyone—president, manager, supervisor, and worker—has the same 24 hours each day, the difference in these points of view must be the result of time management. Successful people have learned how to manage their time. Others, too, can learn.

Stress and burnout result when a worker attempts to do too much. Feelings of frustration surface because the worker is unable to complete the tasks at hand, leading to a disparity between expectations and reality. Time-management techniques help solve some of the problems associated with this issue. While time management cannot solve or eliminate all stress and burnout problems, it can help workers to manage their time effectively. Some workers, especially those who are disorganized and fail to plan, are unable to maximize their personal performance. They move from task to task, fail to establish priorities, and are unable to use their time wisely. The effective use of time-management techniques can eliminate this problem. Additionally, and perhaps more importantly, it can lead to increases in individual, supervisory, and organizational productivity. In reality, the trick to success is not to work *harder* but rather to work *"smarter."*

Those who achieve success in and out of work are able to get the most out of their day by adhering to rules such as the following:

1. Determine what you want from your time.
2. Determine how you currently use time.
3. Set priorities.
4. Establish realistic deadlines.
5. Use time efficiently.
6. Learn to delegate.
7. Do one thing at a time.
8. Employ time-saving techniques.
9. Avoid procrastination.
10. Learn to work "smarter," not harder!

Determine What You Want from Your Time

Victor Hugo wrote that "when the disposal of time is surrendered to the chance of incidents, chaos will reign." Unfortunately, many workers permit chance to dictate a succession of unscheduled visitors, unplanned activities, unexpected telephone calls, and assorted other interruptions.

Time is too valuable to waste

Time is too valuable to waste. All workers, regardless of position, must plan for each working day. Failure to plan causes the random allocation of time. To promote efficiency and maximize output, all workers *must determine what they desire from their personal time.* What do you want to accomplish? What is a reasonable expectation for today? How can the typical eight-hour day best be used?

The first step in practicing effective time-management techniques is to spend 15 minutes before each work day determining what you expect to achieve. Each day, a course of action must be established so that random activities will not monopolize valuable time. The 15-minute daily investment of time will yield immeasurable returns.

Determine How You Currently Use Time

Is your time currently being used effectively? Is eight hours of work being done during an eight-hour workday? If not, why not? If questions of this type sound all too familiar, perhaps your time is not being used as effectively and efficiently as possible.

Before a worker can determine how time is being used, a time inventory chart must be prepared on a daily and weekly basis (see Figure 20–2). Upon analysis, the following questions can be answered:

- How is the majority of time being spent?
- Is the entire workday productive?
- Are some portions of the workday more productive than others?
- Is time used effectively?

Once these facts have been gathered, it is possible to see how time currently is being spent. At this point, you should decide amounts of time to be spent on the duties listed under each category. From this analysis, daily and weekly goals can be set. Each day, start with the most important task. Model-Netics[7] is a man-

---

[7]Model-Netics is a copyrighted management training program developed by Main Event Management Corporation.

GOALS FOR THE DAY	TIME ESTIMATED (HOURS, MINUTES)	PERCENTAGE	DEADLINE(S)
MUST BE DONE			
SHOULD BE DONE			
NICE TO DO			

ACTUAL USE OF TIME	MUST	SHOULD	NICE	SPECIAL PROJECTS (CREATIVE WORK)
	RECORD TIME SPENT			
8:00 - 9:00				
9:00 - 10:00				
10:00 - 11:00				
11:00 - 12:00				
12:00 - 1:00				
1:00 - 2:00				
2:00 - 3:00				
3:00 - 4:00				
4:00 - 5:00				
TOTAL				
PERCENTAGE				
SUMMARY EVALUATION-				

FIGURE 20–2   Time inventory charts

agement training program based on the theory that learning the difference between "must do's," "should do's," and "nice to do's" will have a great impact on how well time is used. The priority of task activities (see Figure 20–3) illustrates this aspect. It would be extremely dysfunctional to spend valuable segments of the workday doing "nice to do" tasks while failing to accomplish the "must do's." This frequently happens when the morning is spent on "nice to do's" or "should do's" with the expectation of spending the afternoon on "must do's." However, emergencies crop up in

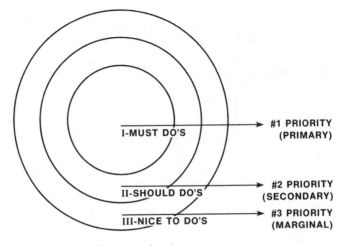

FIGURE 20–3   Priority of task activities

the afternoon, and the "must do's" are not finished. Frequently, the worker takes the "must do" work home, thereby extending the workday. Such an example illustrates the nonoptimal use of time. Wouldn't it have been wiser to complete the "must do's" in the morning? It may have caused less anxiety and frustration!

Set Priorities

Frequently, as the workday is planned, a series of "must do's" are identified. When this situation occurs, it is necessary to review the "must do's" and establish a priority system. Which of the "must do's" is the most important? Which is the second most important? While it is inefficient to complete "nice to do's" prior to "must do's," it is also inefficient to neglect more important tasks in favor of less important tasks. Once priorities are established, it is suggested that they be entered on a daily list to avoid confusion (see Figure 20–4). To advance effective time-management practices further, it is recommended that daily, weekly, and monthly calendars also be kept (see Figures 20–5 to 20–7), with each prioritized item recorded accordingly.

Establish Realistic Deadlines

Realistic deadlines must be established   A realistic deadline must be established for each priority. Caution must be exercised at this point to assure that adequate time is allocated for each task. If deadlines are not realistic, a worker runs the risk of experiencing

THINGS TO DO TODAY

DAY_____

Appointments and Telephone Calls:

_____   _____

_____   _____

_____   _____

                                                    Done
                                                     ✓

1. _____ ☐
2. _____ ☐
3. _____ ☐
4. _____ ☐
5. _____ ☐
6. _____ ☐
7. _____ ☐
8. _____ ☐
9. _____ ☐
10. _____ ☐
11. _____ ☐
12. _____ ☐
13. _____ ☐
14. _____ ☐
15. _____ ☐

Selectform, Inc., Box 3048, Freeport, NY 11520   Form 87 — Printed in U.S.A.

FIGURE 20–4   A sample form for listing daily tasks

1. Frustration
2. Anxiety
3. Feelings of failure
4. Stress and burnout

Attempts to do too much work in too little time result in despair. To keep this from happening, set realistic deadlines.

THURSDAY

14

JUNE

	MAY					
S	M	T	W	T	F	S
		1	2	3	4	5
6	7	8	9	10	11	12
13	14	15	16	17	18	19
20	21	22	23	24	25	26
27	28	29	30	31		

	JULY					
S	M	T	W	T	F	S
1	2	3	4	5	6	7
8	9	10	11	12	13	14
15	16	17	18	19	20	21
22	23	24	25	26	27	28
29	30	31				

7:00
7:30
8:00
8:30
9:00
9:30
10:00
10:30
11:00
11:30
12:00
1:00
1:30
2:00
2:30
3:00
3:30
4:00
4:30
5:00

FIGURE 20–5   A sample daily calendar

Use Time Efficiently

Employees should make the best use of their time

Sometimes, even when priorities are being addressed, a worker is still likely to waste time, or not to make the best use of time. The so-called perfectionist syndrome demonstrates this point. Some workers try to be perfectionists and in doing so run the risk of poor time management. Suppose a subordinate prepares a report for your signature. Before you make any changes in the report, ask yourself if the time spent improving the report

FIGURE 20–6   A sample weekly calendar

justifies the time involved in making the changes. Think of the other priority work you could do instead! Make sure you use time where it counts *the most*.

Learn to Delegate

Delegation reduces stress and enriches employee growth

It is not possible for any one person to do everything. Attempting to do so is almost sure to end in failure. As a matter of practice, all individuals, especially supervisors and managers,

						June
SUN	MON	TUE	WED	THU	FRI	SAT
					1	*2*
3	*4*	*5*	*6*	*7*	*8*	*9*
10	*11*	*12*	*13*	*14*	*15*	*16*
17	*18*	*19*	*20*	*21*	*22*	*23*
24	*25*	*26*	*27*	*28*	*29*	*30*

FIGURE 20–7 A sample monthly calendar

must learn to delegate. Workers who try to do everything run the risk of stress and burnout. Delegating is a sensible technique for developing employees and accomplishing goals. Employees with heavy workloads can reduce the possibility of burnout and increase the likelihood of success through effective delegation.

Do One Thing at a Time

Have you ever tried doing several things at the same time? Usually frustration results. Even worse, chances are that none of the jobs are done properly. Individual productivity can increase by concentrating on one thing at a time. Additionally, the completion of tasks in a timely and efficient manner will help build self-confidence, which in turn creates a positive attitude and improves the approach to work. When you come to work each day with a positive attitude, it's amazing what you can accomplish. A positive attitude can also be contagious.

Employ Time-Saving Techniques

Time-saving techniques can help increase productivity. Two of the suggested techniques are clutter control and the tomorrow test.

CLUTTER CONTROL

Some desks look like disaster areas, with piles of paper scattered in every direction. When this condition exists, a worker is likely to feel buried under the clutter. Frequently, the clutter hinders the ability to concentrate while also creating tension and frustration. Enormous amounts of time are wasted looking for things that are invariably at the bottom of the pile. In addition to looking bad, the clutter contributes to a defeatist attitude.

When piles of clutter arise on the desk, sift through the papers and sort items into the following categories:

1. Immediate action
2. Low priority
3. Action pending
4. Reading material

Immediate action items should remain on the desk, while everything else is placed out of sight. Attack this pile first. Concentrating on one pile at a time increases productivity. As the pile decreases in size, a sense of confidence is established, which spurs motivation and a positive attitude. Continue until the immediate action pile is depleted, at which time the low priority and action pending piles should be respectively addressed. Each day, spend 30 minutes with the reading material. In addition to serving as a relaxation device, this time also promotes individual growth and development. Also make sure that mail is dealt with immediately.

It is so easy to sit back and let the piles grow. When mail is merely reviewed and put in a pile, it must be handled again later, thus doubling the necessary response time. Make it a practice to handle mail at once! The time savings will add to productive work time. Also, a clear desk will contribute to a positive attitude.

THE TOMORROW TEST

When demands are placed on personal time, subject the requests to the "tomorrow test." For example, many times we are invited to a business luncheon or other activity several weeks in advance. When we review our calendars, we notice that the time is open. However, by the time the appointment day approaches, our calendar is jammed! Before accepting any appointments, apply the tomorrow test. Consider the request by looking at tomorrow's schedule and asking, "Is this activity important enough that I would squeeze it into my schedule tomorrow?" If not, reject the offer. Learn to say no! The last thing we would want to do is to make a "nice-to-do" appointment and then, when the time comes, have to put aside "must do's" to keep it!

Avoid Procrastination

Procrastination is deep-rooted

Very few people can honestly say that they are not procrastinators. Procrastination is usually a deep-rooted habit that can be very costly to the individual as well as the organization. It is, as the old saying suggests, the thief of time.

The noted self-help expert Wayne W. Dyer defines procrastination as "the art of keeping up with yesterday by avoiding today."[8] We put things off for many reasons. Most of us would prefer to spend our time doing things that interest us. It would not be unproductive to avoid a "must do" in favor of an interesting "nice to do." Such practices, however, can be costly to both the worker and the organization. As Dyer further explains, other causes for procrastination exist, including the following:

- We can escape unpleasant activities.
- Change can be delayed and risk can be avoided.
- Failure can be avoided.
- Self-doubt can be avoided.
- We can wait for things to change.

Time-wasting activities are like tumors

Time-wasting activities are like tumors; they drain vitality and have a tendency to grow. The only cure is to remove them. Mea-

---

[8] Wayne W. Dyer, *Your Erroneous Zones* (New York: Harper and Row, 1976).

sures must be taken to correct the situation. Unless *you* change, things will remain the same. The following are suggested techniques for stopping procrastination:

- Prepare a list of things you have been avoiding. Prioritize them and establish realistic deadlines for their completion.
- Begin by tackling the most important project.
- Don't be afraid to fail. More importantly, give yourself the opportunity to succeed.
- Eliminate statements such as "I can't" and start thinking in terms of "I will."
- Things can always be better. Learn to be your own change agent.

Learn to Work "Smarter," Not Harder

Attempting to work faster or harder is not the answer. Trying to do more will not solve the problem, but learning to work *"smarter"* will. Learn to practice effective time management to maximize personal productivity, eliminate frustration, and ward off the dangers of stress and burnout.

SUMMARY

Stress continues to be a major individual, organizational, and social concern. When stress strikes, it affects the individual, other employees, the work group, the supervisor, and the organization.

Stress is a psychological or biological reaction to the demands of life. Individuals react to stress in different ways. Eustress is a positive reaction to stress, while distress is a negative reaction. On-the-job stress can be caused by such factors as technological change, heavy work load, and inadequate training. Off-the-job causes include change in marital status, financial setbacks, family illness, and legal encounters. Type A and Type B are the terms generally used to distinguish the two major personality forms. Type A behavior is characterized by impatient, busy, workaholic, explosive, and erratic tendencies, whereas Type B behavior is characterized by relaxed, patient, and controlled tendencies. Type A behavior is more likely to cause stress.

The work setting must be analyzed to determine the four sources of stress: the organization, the system, the boss, and the self. While individual stress tolerance varies, individual and organizational guidelines must be followed to create a safe stress range.

Burnout, a phenomenon that has recently attracted a good deal of attention, is a state of fatigue or frustration brought about by a devotion to a cause, way of life, or relationship that failed to produce the expected result. Burnout follows sequential stages. Theorists contend that it is the result of continuous and intense stress. Responsibility for the cause and prevention of burnout rests with the individual, the supervisor and manager, and the organization.

Time management, in addition to being a method to maximize personal output, is also a way of controlling stress and burnout. If effectively practiced, time management can lead to personal success.

CASE STUDY **57**

What Do You Think?

Discuss the following occupations in terms of the amount of stress they involve:

a. Accountant
b. Top executive
c. Teacher
d. Police officer
e. Assembly-line worker
f. Athlete
g. Supervisor
h. Secretary
i. Naval officer
j. Salesperson
k. Advertising executive
l. Artist

CASE STUDY **58**

Worker Burnout

You and your superior recently attended a seminar on burnout. Your superior indicated that burnout could be a problem in your organization and that steps should be taken for its prevention. Your superior directs you to prepare a 30-minute presentation for all supervisors that explains and defines burnout, illustrates its causes, and indicates its cures. Prepare your lesson plan.

CASE STUDY **59**

Time Study for Kinna Ceramics

Elaine Smith is an industrial engineer employed by a private consultation firm. Recently she had to make an efficiency evaluation of operational procedures at Kinna Ceramics.

The Kinna factory has a large storage capacity and a production unit consisting of two tunnels. The tunnels are brick ovens, 250 feet long, through which a conveyer belt keeps the ceramics moving at a uniform rate.

Both management and labor believe that a worker is needed to operate each tunnel. A third worker is needed to do initial sanding of the ceramics as he or she unloads them from the conveyer belts. Since the tunnels are run around the clock, nine workers are needed, three on each eight-hour shift.

Elaine noticed a major flaw in the present system: The worker unloading ceramics and doing the initial sanding was idled four hours of every eight while the two tunnel workers both did preparatory work. That is, sixteen hours of tunnel work could be unloaded, initially sanded, and stacked in four hours.

Of the following suggested remedies, which seems best?

QUESTIONS

1. Should Elaine recommend staggered shifts for the tunnel workers to keep the end-of-the-line production flow constant?

2. Should Elaine recommend cutting the working hours of the end-of-the-line worker?

3. Should Elaine recommend running two ten-hour shifts of two tunnel workers each, with four hours devoted to end-of-the-line?

CASE STUDY 60

They Improved John's Work Area, but . . .

John Nicholson has been employed at Cars' Unlimited, Inc., for the past three years as assistant to the supervisor. John's work area used to be located on the factory floor, and he directed line operations from a tiny desk placed between the large and noisy machines. He maintained a good relationship with his subordinates over the years, both on and off the job. Many felt that his cheerful outlook and willingness to get involved in any task made him an extraordinary supervisor.

Recently, the installation of new equipment required that John's desk be relocated. The company built a small, glassed-in office at one end of the factory, and they provided John with a telephone system that put him in touch with the various work areas on the floor.

Lately John hasn't seemed to be as interested in his work as he once was. He has even talked about changing jobs, despite his improved working conditions.

QUESTIONS

1. What do you think is wrong?
2. What could have been done to avoid it?
3. What can be done now to improve John's attitude and situation?

CASE STUDY 61

Can I Catch Up?

You feel you are behind in your work. You ask yourself, "Am I given too much work, or am I too slow to handle it?" What should you do?

QUESTIONS

1. How could you change your situation? Explain.
2. How could you change your attitude? Explain.
3. How could you change your time-management habits. Explain.
4. What else can you do?

Terms and Concepts Supervisors Should Know

Boss-imposed stress; Burnout; Clutter control; Distress; Eustress; "Must do's"; "Nice to do's"; Organization-imposed stress; Perfectionist syndrome; Procrastination; Self-imposed stress;

"Should do's"; Stress; Stressors; System-imposed stress; Time management; Time-management techniques; Tomorrow test; Type A behavior; Type B behavior.

Questions for Discussion

1. Compare and contrast eustress and distress.
2. Think of a typical work setting, and cite three examples for each of the following:
   a. Organization-imposed stress
   b. System-imposed stress
   c. Boss-imposed stress
   d. Self-imposed stress
3. Interview three working adults. Determine what they believe to be the leading causes of burnout.
4. Discuss five things a supervisor can do to escape burnout. Discuss three things a supervisor can do to eliminate causing burnout among subordinates.
5. Which of the ten time-management prescriptions is the most important? Explain.

For Further Reading—And More Ideas

Ashkenas, R. N., and R. H. Schaeffer, "Managers Can Avoid Wasting It," *Working Woman* (January 1984).

Blanchard, Kenneth, "Finding the Comfort Zone (Some Stress Contributes to Peak Performance)," *Business Credit* (November 1988).

Blanchard, Kenneth, and Spencer Johnson, *The One-Minute Manager*, New York: William Morrow, 1981.

"Coping with Stress (Special Report)," *Business Credit* (November 1988).

Dunn, D. H., "Putting Your Time to Work Before You Reach the Office," *Business Week* (April 1, 1983).

Elsass, P. M., and D. A. Ralston, "Individual Responses to the Stress of Career Plateauing," *Journal of Management* (March 1989).

English, G., "Beating the Clock: Time to Review Time-Management Training," *Training and Development Journal* (January 1989).

Gountlett, S., "Stress Reduction Tips to Use in and out of the Workplace," *Management Solutions* (December 1988).

Hollingsworth, A. T., and J. Mosca, "Managing Your Time," *Management Solutions* (December 1988).

Joure, S. A., et al., "The Pressure Cooker of Work: How to Deal with Stress in the Workplace," *Personnel Administrator* (March 1989).

Katz, L. G., "Coping with Stress," *Parents* (February 1989).

McKinley, A., "Managing Stress," *Senior Scholastic* (November 12, 1982).

Modic, S. J., "Surviving Burnout: The Malady of Our Age," *Industry Week* (February 20, 1989).

Quirk, T. J., "The Art of Time Management," *Training* (January 1989).

"Rate Your Job Stress," *Prevention* (January 1984).

Ray, J. S., "Having Problems with Worker Performance? Try an EAP," *Administrative Management* (May 1982).

Rosch, P. J., "Coping with Stress on the Job," *Nation's Business* (February 1984).

Saifullah, E., and B. H. Kleiner, "Effective Time Management," *Management Decision* (April 1988).

Scott, Dru, *How to Put More Time in Your Life*, New York: Signet Press, 1980.

Stein, B., "Stress Busters! (Home-Based Working)," *Home Office Computing* (February 1989).

"Stress Aims at Women," *Prevention* (April 1984).

"Stress Stoppers," *Executive Female* (November–December 1988).

Symonds, W. C., "No, They Can't Stop Time, but They Can Help You Manage It." *Business Week* (May 22, 1989).

Thompson, R., "Take Charge of Your Job (Views of P. Nickerson)," *Nation's Business* (April 1989).

"Workaholics," *Current Health* (October 1981).

Name Index

Subject Index